"This welcome text offers many insights into recent changes in work and employment. Its approach is global and local, using case studies to great effect to illustrate key arguments. Its focus on developments that have so far received little attention will be invaluable for both students and specialists."

Miriam Glucksmann, *Emeritus Professor of Sociology,*
Essex University, UK and Visiting Professor of Sociology,
London School of Economics and Political Science, UK

"An ambitious new collection, exploring core concepts in the sociology of work with a critical eye and lively, contemporary examples. Wide-reaching, thought-provoking, and accessible, with clear summaries and practice questions for students. This book will become core reading for all those interested in the changing world of work."

Susan Halford, *Professor of Sociology and Co-Director of*
ESRC Centre for Sociodigital Futures,
University of Bristol, UK

"This book is essential reading for all those interested in the sociology of work. Taking an international perspective, it provides fascinating case studies from across the globe that offer new, rich insights on work and organisations in the 21st century."

Diane Reay, *Professor of Education,*
University of Cambridge, UK

T0292963

Sociology, Work, and Organisations

This accessible edited collection provides global context for undergraduate and postgraduate students studying the sociology of work and organisations. Composed of short, example-led chapters, this book covers a wide range of contemporary topics, including the COVID-19 pandemic, the digitalisation of work, the gig economy, and the shifting roles of women and other marginalised groups.

The book's innovative approach uses case studies as diverse as work–life balance in China, gender pay inequity in Britain and Germany, and the exploitation of workers on the Mexico–US border, to incorporate perspectives from both the Global North and South and provide students with the tools to analyse new developments in the rapidly changing world of work. The book is particularly concerned with inequalities and marginalisation in the workplace, discussing discrimination against women, ethnic minorities, migrants, and older workers. The book also explores how increasing digitalisation, the rise of the gig economy, and the COVID-19 pandemic have impacted working practices and how this relates to precarious employment. Other chapters are dedicated to issues of workplace organisation, including female leadership, work–life balance, and well-being. The book goes on to explore how climate change and policies such as Universal Basic Income may shape the future of work in the near future.

Each chapter also includes useful pedagogical resources, including practice exam questions, key concepts and definitions, and further reading. Therefore, the book will be essential reading for undergraduate and postgraduate students studying the sociology of work, business management, and organisation.

Brian McDonough is Course Leader of Sociology at Solent University, UK. His research specialises in work and the body, human expertise, and the use of information and communication technologies in the workplace. He is author of *Flying Aeroplanes and Other Sociological Tales: An Introduction to Sociology and Research Methods* (Routledge, 2021), co-author of *Universal Basic Income* (Routledge, 2020), and co-author of *Social Problems in the UK* (Routledge,

2015). He has also published on commercial pilot expertise in journals such as *Qualitative Research*, using Heideggerian and Merleau-Pontian philosophy to understand the role of the working body, and how AI and other technologies impact workers in aviation settings.

Jane Parry is an Associate Professor of Work and Employment at the University of Southampton, UK. Her research looks at changes in employment, working practices, and disadvantage in labour markets. She is co-editor of *A New Sociology of Work?* (2005) and has published in journals such as *Work, Employment and Society, Gender, Work & Organization*, and *New Technology, Work and Employment*. A former parliamentary academic fellow, she led the ESRC-funded Work After Lockdown project on organisational learning around pandemic-driven working from home, and has contributed to Radio 4's *Today* programme, various BBC programmes, and written for *The Guardian* on debates on the future of work.

Sociology, Work, and Organisations

A Global Context

Edited by Brian McDonough and Jane Parry

Routledge
Taylor & Francis Group

LONDON AND NEW YORK

Cover image: iStock

First published 2025
by Routledge
4 Park Square, Milton Park, Abingdon, Oxon OX14 4RN

and by Routledge
605 Third Avenue, New York, NY 10158

Routledge is an imprint of the Taylor & Francis Group, an informa business

British Library Cataloguing-in-Publication Data
A catalogue record for this book is available from the British Library

ISBN: 978-1-032-32384-8 (hbk)
ISBN: 978-1-032-32386-2 (pbk)
ISBN: 978-1-003-31476-9 (ebk)

DOI: 10.4324/9781003314769

Typeset in Sabon
by codeMantra

This book is dedicated to Blake, Huxley, Charlotte, Harry, Katie, and all future workers

Contents

Illustrations

Figure

Tables

Contributors

Garfield Benjamin is a Senior Lecturer in Sociology at Solent University, UK. Their research and teaching focuses on societal issues with technology. In particular, Garfield is interested in how power, identity, and inequality function around technologies. They have published in *Surveillance & Society*, *AI & Society*, and *Internet Policy Review*, and recently released the book *Mistrust Issues: How Technology Discourses Quantify, Extract and Legitimise Inequalities* with Bristol University Press.

Helen Blakely is a Research Associate at Cardiff University, and began working as a researcher with the Wales Institute of Social Economic Research Data and Methods (WISERD) in 2015. Her research interests include the sociology of work and employment, with a focus on the quality of work, unpaid care, and the welfare state, with which she engages through ethnographic and interview research methods.

Jessie Bustillos Morales is a Senior Lecturer in the Education Division at London South Bank University (LSBU). She has worked in academia for over 13 years across several institutions in the UK. With an interdisciplinary background including sociology, philosophy, and education, she is interested in exploring educational and social inequalities through innovative theoretical frameworks and creative methodologies, relevant to everyday educational practice. Her scholarship operates in the intersections of youth studies, methodology, philosophy, and critical theory/pedagogy. She has co-authored and co-edited several books published by Routledge.

Dina de Sousa e Santos teaches Criminology and Criminal Justice at Portsmouth University, where she is also the course leader for the MSc in International Criminal Justice and Intelligence, and she is an Associate Lecturer at Solent University. Dina has taught sociology for over 20 years in FE and HE and was the Equality and Diversity Coordinator at Barton Peveril College for seven years, as well as staff governor at the College. Dina has been a member of the Cuba Research Forum for almost 20 years and her research focuses on women and ethnic minority groups in the margins of society.

Helen Devereux is Senior Lecturer at Warsash Maritime School, Solent University, and is interested in the sociology of work – in particular, the diverse ways in which work and employment are organised. Her research explores how the organisation of work and employment at sea impact on the occupational health, safety, and well-being of seafarers. Prior to her academic career, Helen worked as an Officer of the Watch on board chemical tankers.

Amy Duvenage is a Lecturer in Criminology at Solent University, Southampton. Her research interests are in decolonial and postcolonial studies, gender and sexuality, southern African literature, and ubuntu as an African model of justice. She has published articles on ubuntu as a tool for social cohesion in South Africa and on post-apartheid literary representations of queer desire and tradition. Her most recent publication is *Roads to Decolonisation: An Introduction to Thought from the Global South* (2024).

Alan Felstead is a Research Professor and a Co-Director at the Wales Institute of Social and Economic Research and Data. His research focuses on: the quality of work; training, skills and learning; non-standard employment; and the spaces and places of work. His output includes eight books and over 250 journal articles, book chapters, research reports and discussion papers. His latest book, *Remote Working: A Research Overview*, was published in 2022 by Routledge. According to one reviewer, it is 'a must read for anyone interested in how the changing location of work affects our lives'.

Mark Green is co-founder of Work Progressive, the UK Licensed Country Partner for Semco Style. He is passionate about co-creating more progressive ways to organise work and developing practices that enhance people's experiences, enabling them to thrive. He is values-driven, with 20 years' experience in working with a broad range of people to make a positive impact through defining solutions in creative, innovative, and pragmatic ways. With a background in healthcare and consulting, he set up his own business in 2020 with the aim of creating more people-centric, participative, and engaged workplaces. He felt strong alignment with the mission of Semco Style and found them to be the ideal partner to 'shape the future of work'!

Julia Hansch is a Professor of Business Administration. Having studied in both Mannheim and Dartmouth, MA, she went on to work for Bosch Rexroth in Germany and the US. She then went back to the University of Mannheim to pursue a PhD in Business, focusing on corporate governance. Since 2013 she has been a professor in the Faculty of Business at DHBW Mannheim, heading the department for logistics for several years, as well as the equal opportunities commissioner for the faculty. Her research focuses on corporate governance, especially diversity and the impact of legislation on corporations.

Brian J. Hracs is Associate Professor of Human Geography in the School of Geography and Environmental Science at the University of Southampton. He is interested in how digital technologies and global competition are reshaping the marketplace for cultural products and the working lives and spatial dynamics of entrepreneurs and intermediaries in the creative economy. Brian has published articles about the music and fashion industries, value creation and the mobilities of 'talent'. He is currently researching the processes and spatial dynamics of curation, the trans-local nature of cultural scenes and creative economies in Africa.

Maria Hudson is a Senior Lecturer in Human Resource Management and Director of Equality, Diversity, and Inclusion based at Essex Business School, University of Essex. Her research interests are largely connected to the study of inequalities in work, labour markets, and wider society and she has undertaken a wide range of related research projects. Since joining Essex Business School, her research activities have focused on mental health at work and racial discrimination, contributing to understanding the persistence of inequalities and how inequitable employment outcomes might be challenged and eroded.

Natalie Janning-Backfisch is a Professor of Business Administration at DHBW Mannheim. She studied business at the University of Mannheim, specialising in logistics, human resource management and business education. She worked in different positions in logistics and IT consulting, with a focus on human resource management. She became a Professor in the Faculty of Business at DHBW Mannheim, heading the department of International Business in 2022. Her research focuses on competencies and qualifications.

María Encarnación López is Professor of Sociology in the School of Social Sciences and Professions and Deputy Director of the Global Diversities and Inequalities Research Centre at London Metropolitan University. Her research focuses on the violence affecting gendered, sexualised, and racialised communities in hostile global environments, such as the LGBTQ+ community in Cuba, migrant women in transit through Mexico, and Afghan and Syrian refugees in the UK. She has published widely in this area, including the monographs *Homosexuality and Invisibility in Revolutionary Cuba* (Tamesis, 2015) and *Gender Violence in Twenty-First-Century Latin American Women's Writing* (Tamesis, 2022) with Stephen M. Hart.

Clare Kelliher is Professor of Work and Organisation at Cranfield School of Management. Her research examines the organisation of work and the management of the employment relationship. She has focused on flexible working arrangements, and has published her research findings in articles, books, blogs, and through media commentary. Her research has been used in policy development by governments, NGOs, and think-tanks and she has worked with employers to shape their working practices. Her recent ESRC-funded research examined how the government's 'flexible furlough scheme' encouraged employers to experiment with part-time working, often challenging their assumptions about its feasibility and making them more amenable to offering part-time working in the future.

Brian McDonough is Course Leader of Sociology at Solent University. His research specialises in work and the body, human expertise, and the use of information and communication technologies in the workplace. He has published about commercial pilot expertise in journals such as *Qualitative Research* and *New Media and Society* using Heideggerian and Merleau-Pontian philosophy to understand how AI and other technologies impact workers in aviation settings. He has published numerous texts, including: co-author of *Social Problems in the UK* (Routledge, 2015), co-author of *Universal Basic Income* (Routledge, 2020), and sole author of *Flying Aeroplanes and Other Sociological Tales: An Introduction to Sociology and Research Methods* (Routledge, 2021).

Barry McNeill is co-founder of Work Progressive, the UK Licensed Country Partner for Semco Style. He cares deeply about how people experience the world of work and has over 25 years' experience working with leaders, teams, and organisations to create vibrant workplaces where people can thrive. He loves to question the status quo and explore alternative paths and non-conventional approaches. He has an MSc in Human Resource Management and an Executive MBA from London Business School. He is a Fellow of the RSA and an active advocate for reframing the future of work to enable more inclusive, participative work environments for all.

Anna Paraskevopoulou is an Associate Professor of Management and EDI Lead in the Faculty of Business and Law, Anglia Ruskin University, and a Fellow in Global Labor Organization. Anna's primary research into work and inequalities focuses on employment experiences in the contemporary neoliberal economy. Within this theme, she has published extensively on equality and diversity, disadvantaged groups and their labour market outcomes, workplace relations, migration, and the rise of precarious work. She co-authored *Workplace Equality in Europe – the Role of Trade Unions* (2015) and *Undocumented Workers' Transitions: Legal Status, Migration, and Work in Europe* (2011), both published by Routledge.

Jane Parry is an Associate Professor of Work and Employment at the University of Southampton. Her research looks at changes in employment, working practices, and disadvantage in labour markets. Jane was co-editor of *A New Sociology of Work?*, with Pettinger, Glucksmann, and Taylor, and has published in journals such as *Work, Employment and Society*, *Gender, Work & Organization*, and *New Technology, Work and Employment*. A former parliamentary academic fellow, she led the ESRC-funded Work After Lockdown, following organisational learning around pandemic-driven working from home, and has contributed to Radio 4's *Today* programme, various BBC programmes, and written for the *Guardian* on the future of work debates.

Chloë Pearson is a lecturer in Sociology at Barton Peveril College. She recently undertook a qualitative research role at Solent University, funded by the Research Innovation and Knowledge Exchange (RIKE), using ethnographic interview methods to understand workplace inequalities and the precariousness of taxi drivers in Britain. Chloë has also researched the work of actors and professional dancers in the UK, investigating how precariousness affects people working in the arts, a research theme she wishes to pursue in the future.

Naveena Prakasam is a lecturer in Human Resource Management (HRM) and Organisational Behaviour (OB) at the Department of HRM and OB at Southampton Business School, University of Southampton, and Departmental Head of Research. Naveena's primary area of research interest is in leadership studies, with a focus on authentic leadership, as well as critical and diverse approaches to leadership. Naveena's research focus also includes inequalities in organisations.

Helen M. Rand is a senior lecturer in criminology at the University of Greenwich. Her research interests include the construction of deviancy in relation to genders and sexualities with a particular focus on digital sex markets. Her doctoral research looked at the influence of the internet on the organization of sex work, exploring its implications for the lived experiences of both workers and consumers of sex markets. Her research has been published in several peer-reviewed journals including *Feminist Review and Gender, Work & Organization*. Recent research has focussed on student sex workers and HE policy responses. Follow @HelenRand1 on X.

Melahat Sahin-Dikmen is a Senior Lecturer in Sociology at the University of Westminster. Her recent research examines the implications of climate change for the world of work, with reference to building design and construction occupations. She is interested in representations of gender in climate policy and action and the extent to which sustainability practices can be constructed as spaces for achieving equality and social justice. Her recent publications include: *Climate Change, Inequality and Work in the Construction Industry* (2024) and *Workers and Labour Movements in the Fight Against Climate Change* (2024).

Rebecca Taylor is a sociologist of work and organisations at the University of Southampton and co-director of the Work Futures Research Centre. Her broad research interests are in conceptualising paid and unpaid work, digital labour within and beyond the platform economy, organisational change and innovation, and the delivery of public services by the public, private, and non-profit sectors. Recent research has focused on open-source labour and inequalities in unpaid work.

Philippa Velija is Deputy Dean (PG Student Experience and Research Environment) in the School of Arts, Humanities, and Social Sciences at the University of Roehampton. Philippa's research provides a critical sociological analysis of inequality and power in sport and leisure settings, particularly focusing on gender relations in sport. More recently, Philippa has explored the relationship between misogyny, gender, and power in curriculum and HE settings, leading on the implementation of bystander workshops and evaluating school-based interventions on violence against women and girls. Philippa has published several peer-review articles and is author of *Women's Cricket and Global Process* (Macmillan, 2015), and co-editor of *Gender Equity in UK Sport Leadership and Governance* (Emerald Publishing, 2022) and *Figurational Research in Sport, Leisure and Health* (Routledge, 2019).

Mengyi Xu is an Assistant Professor in Human Resource Management (HRM) at the University of Birmingham. Her research focuses on work–life balance and inclusion, new ways of working (e.g. hybrid working, four-day work week), and the future of work. Her research is funded by the British Academy of Management (BAM), Forces in Mind Trust, and Brazil's Civil Service, and published in high-impact journals, international conferences, and HR professional magazine. She has been awarded an Early Career Fellowship (2024–2026) from the Work-Family Research Network and a Research Accelerator Fellowship (2023) from Cranfield University. Externally, she is a Council member of the BAM, a committee member of HRM SIG, and an academic member of the Charted Institute of Personnel Development. She also serves as an external examiner on MSc and BSc HRM programmes at universities in the UK and Malaysia.

Abbreviations

Acas	Advisory, Conciliation and Arbitration Service
AI	artificial intelligence
BAME	Black, Asian and minority ethnic
BBC	British Broadcasting Corporation
BIP	Border Industrialisation Program
CEO	chief executive officer
CFO	chief financial officer
CIPD	Chartered Institute of Personnel and Development
COP	Conference of the Parties
CRT	critical race theory
CV	curriculum vitae (Latin for 'course of life', a summary of work experience)
EAP	employee assistance programme
EC	European Commission
ECR	early career researcher
EDI	equality, diversity, and inclusion
EHRC	Equality and Human Rights Commission
ESG	environmental, social, and corporate governance
ESRC	Economic and Social Research Council
ET	employment tribunal
EU	European Union
FOC	flag of convenience
FTSE	Financial Times Stock Exchange
GNSWP	Global Network of Sex Work Projects
GPG	gender pay gap
HE	higher education

HESA	Higher Education Statistics Agency
HRM	human resource management
ILO	International Labour Organization
IMO	International Maritime Organization
IPCC	International Panel on Climate Change
ITF	International Transport (Workers') Federation
LGBTQ+	lesbian, gay, bisexual, transgender, queer, and other genders or sexualities
MPUCT	Madhya Pradesh Unconditional Cash Transfer
NAFTA	North American Free Trade Agreement
NATO	North Atlantic Treaty Organization
NCDS	National Child Development Study
NGOs	Non-governmental organisations
NHBF	National Hair and Beauty Foundation
NHS	National Health Service (UK)
NRM	National Referral Mechanism
NUM	National Ugly Mugs
OECD	Organisation for Economic Co-operation and Development
ONS	Office for National Statistics
PAR	participatory action research
PBS	Points-Based [immigration] System
PICUM	Platform for International Cooperation on Undocumented Migrants
PPE	Personal Protective Equipment
PSC	Port State Control
SDG	Sustainable Development Goal [UN]
SEWA	Self Employed Women's Association
SWARM	Sex Worker Advocacy and Resistance Movement
TUC	Trades Union Congress
TVUCT	Tribal Village Unconditional Cas Transfer
UBI	universal basic income
UK	United Kingdom
UN	United Nations
UNFCCC	United Nations Framework Convention on Climate Change
UNICEF	United Nations International Children's Emergency Fund
US	United States [of America]
USMCA	US–Mexico–Canada Agreement
WHO	World Health Organization

Acknowledgements

We would like to thank the contributing authors for the time taken to write the chapters and bring cutting-edge research to this textbook. We have been in awe of your wisdom and generosity. We are also extremely grateful to the book's endorsers, the intellectual giants Professors Miriam Glucksmann, Susan Halford, and Diane Reay, who took the time to engage with the text. And we are grateful to our future readers who we encourage to get in touch with us and share their work stories.

Brian would like to acknowledge Jessie's support, and teatimes spent in the kitchen with a laptop, and Santa Teresa Mojito, talking about work and all things more lovely. And his 'little ones', Huxley and Blake, who are a pure joy to be around. He would like to thank Jane as an inspirational scholar and brilliant co-editor, who has turned this textbook into a formidable resource for students. Thanks also to Mark Carlisle and Karen King, for access to the worlds of acting and professional dancing, from which many thoughts are drawn on working lives.

Jane would like to thank Charlie, who has heard more about this book than is probably reasonable in any lifetime, and her mum Liz Parry, for her patience and constant encouragement. Thanks also to The Wolfpack for providing the humour and cynicism needed to negotiate an academic career in the neoliberal marketplace! And to Brian for his vision on this book, and endless ability to see things differently. She would like to acknowledge the funding of UKRI/ESRC under the COVID-19 Rapid Response initiative (Ref.: ES/V009648/1), for funding the research that is drawn upon in Chapter 1.

part 1

Introduction to Work in a Global Context

Reimagining the Organisation of Work Post-Pandemic

Jane Parry

Introduction

The COVID-19 pandemic of 2020–2022 and its dramatic impact on the organisation of work, with whole sectors shut down, transformed, or displaced out of workplaces, has been variously interpreted as a crisis and as an opportunity for accelerated learning. This unique period in global labour relations is interesting to sociological theorists who are looking at how its shifting set of realities might be challenging the certainties that have been assumed for so long around work. Some theorists have presented the pandemic as a crisis for organisations that will have far-reaching impacts on economic and social life: 'perhaps the closest empirical example of a doomsday scenario of relevance to management scholarship' (Brammer et al., 2020: 503). Others have framed it as a time of fast-tracked change around organisation and digitised working, the longer-term effects of which are still evolving. One of the challenges for this edited volume is weighing up the lasting consequences of these mixed effects for organisations and for the future of work.

Theorists such as Rudolph and Zacher have conceptualised the COVID-19 pandemic as a **period effect**, that is, a historical event that affects the entire (global) population rather than a specific group or cohort: 'COVID-19 is about as close to a homogenous and constant period effect as we could ever observe' (2020: 142). Other examples of period effects are the 9/11 attacks, wars, and famines. A caveat here is that a period effect may involve varied effects upon different population groups, at the same time as impacting upon an entire population. The pandemic has been a rare period effect that has affected workplaces around the world

DOI: 10.4324/9781003314769-2

simultaneously and may, indeed, be unique in its consequences. This chapter, then, looks at the period effect of the pandemic upon paid work; in particular, on the organisation of work. Broader impacts for the sociology of work, including the pandemic's effects upon work motivation and careers, are issues that researchers will be exploring for years to come.

This introductory chapter also reflects on how the key concepts that we have come to rely upon in understanding work and organisation might be lacking as sensemaking tools around radically changed environments. It looks more closely at some of the workplace changes of the past two years that were triggered by the pandemic, considering their consequences and legacy, and focusing on remote and hybrid working. The ESRC-funded research Work After Lockdown, which followed organisations during the UK's lockdowns, is used as a case study. Its longitudinal approach, taking repeated observations over time, provides insight into how organisations' work practices evolved during a time of crisis, and how employers anticipated work would look after the restrictions of the pandemic had eased and they were able to establish greater agency over how work was organised (Parry et al., 2021, 2022).

Conceptualising Work and Persistent Challenges around Modern Work

Since the industrial revolution of the late 18th century, the concept of **industrialised society** has been used to demarcate a period when work became mechanised and moved from the domestic sphere into separate (and public) workspaces, with tasks becoming organised in more routinised ways. In the **Global North**, industrialisation was organised around **gendered divisions of labour** and what became known as a **'breadwinner model'**, with men predominantly working in the **public sphere** providing financial support for the family, and women performing the unpaid **private sphere** servicing work necessary to sustain paid workers' public sphere efforts (Horrell and Humphries, 1997).

Coalmining communities were a marked example of this, where women's unpaid domestic support necessitated long hours of manual work. This included the cooking, intensive cleaning, and care of large families, all accomplished without modern white appliances. It was work that was essential to sustain pit-workers' well-being amid the harsh working conditions of the coalmines (Dennis et al., 1956; Williamson, 1982). But, through this maintenance of productive workers, the breadwinner model also shored up capitalist production. Such divisions of labour have been powerfully studied by sociologists in different contexts in order to understand the role of the organisation of work in societal dynamics. Some of the defining ethnographic research on work in the field has drawn attention to the interdependency of paid and unpaid work in labour organisation by looking close-up at the experience of work in different industries. Some key influential texts here have been Ray Pahl's work in the Isle of Sheppey (1984) and Miriam Glucksmann's ethnography in the Lancashire textile industry (2000).

More recently, it has become clear that the breadwinner model, based upon the expectation of nine-to-five contractual employment, poorly represents the UK's increasingly diverse labour market. **The *Taylor review*** (2017) illustrated with detailed evidence the extent of **atypical work** in the UK economy, often described as '**flexible work**', although this is very different from the flexible working arrangements that are more typically driven by employees' diverse needs. Taylor detailed how atypical or non-standardised work had proliferated in the UK since the global financial crisis of 2008–2009. For example, he estimated that there were 1.2 million agency workers, and that 2.8 per cent of the UK workforce were on a **zero-hours contract** (Taylor, 2017). One of the by-products of globalisation has been a rising demand for flexible workers who can help firms adapt to competitive or unpredictable environments. However, these workers often lack employment protection or security, and women, migrant workers, and ethnic minority groups are disproportionately represented in atypical work. Bauman's concept of **liquid modernity** is also relevant here: that modernity and organisational life have become characterised by ongoing uncertainty and continual change (Bauman, 2000). As inequalities show little sign of abating and atypical work masks a complex range of working experiences, many work theorists have shifted the discussion towards job quality and 'decent work'. In this way they have looked at a combination of structural and intrinsic aspects of work, such as meaningfulness, fairness, and autonomy, highlighting that 'bad work' is more likely to be exploitative, provides more limited material and social benefits, and is potentially damaging to workers' health (Kalleberg, 2016; Pettinger, 2019).

Where the terminology around flexible work can be slippery, it is useful to refer to Spreitzer et al.'s (2017) three-fold classification – around scheduling, location, and employment relationships – which has particular relevance for how the organisation of work changed during the COVID-19 pandemic. Flexible work scheduling and the flexibility of work location both proliferated during the pandemic as office-based work was transferred into employees' homes. The conditions of lockdown also forced workers into adaptability around occupational time as their work and non-work responsibilities collided, with schools closed and families often working at home together in spaces that had not been designed to pursue their jobs. The third aspect of Spreitzer et al.'s distinction, flexible employment relationships, was experienced by workers who lacked secure contracts, such as agency or subcontracted workers. Their future in organisations was vulnerable or non-existent during lockdowns as some sectors pared back operations to their most essential functions and workforces. Meanwhile, those on flexible contracts in sectors that faced increased pressure during the pandemic, such as healthcare (in hospitals and care homes) and distribution (e.g. Amazon or Uber Eats), experienced both an intensification of work and greater exposure to risk as an everyday part of their working practices (Beck et al., 2020; Vermeerbergen et al., 2021). Lacking the employment protection associated with regular contracts, atypical workers' choice to engage in such intensified work was arguably limited. Atypical workers were less likely to be able to access the welfare protection of **furlough** when whole sectors contracted or shut down overnight, leaving Spurk and Straub to describe their situation as 'a crisis on top of a crisis' (2020).

Gendered divisions of labour have also produced the dependency and inequalities that characterise **patriarchal societies**; that is, ones whose social systems privilege men (Walby, 1990). The global feminist movement, which started in the 1960s with women campaigning for equal employment rights, challenged these arrangements, as have technological developments that shifted the foundation of the UK economy away from heavy manufacturing and towards the service sector and office-based work, which saw an influx of women into paid employment (Crompton, 1999). A legacy of the breadwinner model is that levels of part-time working in the UK are among the highest in Europe: 22 per cent, compared to an EU average of 15 per cent (OECD, 2022). A common gendered pattern of working in the UK is for women to shift towards a period of part-time working after family formation – an arrangement that Crompton termed a *modified* breadwinner model (1999).

While the UK's Equal Pay Act of 1970 provided important protection for women's progression in the labour market, progress has been slow, with the gender pay gap remaining at 8.3 per cent (ONS, 2022a). This is further discussed by Velija and McDonough in Chapter 3. A less-tracked trend is the 69 per cent increase in female freelancers since 2008 (Yordanova, 2020), which may reflect women's desire to circumvent the barriers faced in employment. Later, in Chapter 9, Hansch and Janning-Backfisch pick up on changes in women and leadership roles during times of crisis. A strong public/private sphere divide has continued to be synonymous with paid/unpaid work in industrialised economies and, until the disruption of the pandemic, the practice of working from home remained a minority experience, associated with particular industries and higher-grade employment.

Changes in the Organisation of Work and the Pandemic: Offices

Industrial organisation changed almost overnight in early 2020, when governments across the globe ordered people to work at home wherever possible, leaving offices – the beacon of **white-collar work** – virtually empty for large parts of the following 18 months. The implicit message in government directives about compulsory working from home was that offices were not economically essential to the functioning of certain types of work. Globally, it has been estimated that 81 per cent of the workforce saw their work affected by different lockdowns (ILO, 2020). Effects were unequal, however, with low-paid workers over-represented in the essential services that remained open (Butterick and Charlwood, 2021), where they were exposed to higher levels of daily risk. Elsewhere, work was displaced into employees' homes and organisations were forced to develop effective ways of managing non-synchronous work (that is, work not co-located and which does not necessarily take place at the same time; see also Chapter 21, by Felstead and Blakely, on changing places of work), as well as virtual communications, although multinational companies had already been developing protocols and practice around these issues for some time. It is this formerly office-based work that saw perhaps the biggest shake-up of the organisation of work during the pandemic, to which this chapter now turns.

Prior to 2020, the majority of paid work had been organised in or around work-place sites, such as offices, factories, and hospitals, a trend consolidated over time since the Industrial Revolution, and discussed in Chapter 8 in Green and McNeill's discussion of power and organisation. Indeed, in January 2020, before the pandemic reached the UK, only 2.7 per cent of employees worked from home all of the time, and 24.9 per cent did so occasionally. This saw a dramatic shift when, in April 2020 (during the first UK lockdown), 31.4 per cent of the workforce were working exclusively from home and 46.1 per cent were doing so at least some-times, with rates in certain industries much higher. For example, by January 2021, in the professional, scientific, and technical sector, 77.3 per cent of employees were working from home some of the time, and 59.3 per cent were doing so all of the time (all data from the Understanding Society COVID-19 Study, University of Essex, 2020–2021). Given that, in the centuries since industrialisation, as-sumptions about the efficient organisation of work taking place in centralised workplaces have remained remarkably persistent, the current period of industrial change, where these norms are being re-examined, is all the more fascinating for work sociologists.

Pre-COVID-19, working from home was more often a privileged practice that those with higher status, such as managers, could adopt in order to earmark some productive quiet time or, conversely, it was seen in the kind of permanent low-paid (and highly gendered) homework associated with the textile industry. However, since 2020, working from home has become a more mainstream part of white-collar work. While mass working from home was normalised by the pandemic, for some time technologies have made working from home possible in a growing proportion of jobs, whether or not this opportunity was implemented in practice. This was witnessed at an individual level outside of standard working hours as employees increasingly checked their emails and remained 'on' at home as well as at work. Melissa Gregg developed the concept of 'presence bleed' to describe the function creep of modern information-based jobs in this way (2011). There are also parallels here with Young's (2018) rich empirical work looking at women re-turners' (from maternity leave) flexible work patterns, in that, as employees inter-act with less standardised working practices, there is a high expectation for them to take responsibility for the self-management of these, including the responsibility of making them a success. This is a frequently unrecognised invisible labour that underpins flexible working.

Given the unusual circumstances of the pandemic, with large parts of the popu-lation under permanent lockdown in their homes, this was not 'normal' working from home, but an extreme situation where the formerly distinctive boundaries between public and private work became fluid. Adding to this blurriness, parents were simultaneously called upon to provide childcare and to support online edu-cation; employees were working alongside their families in makeshift workspaces, or alternatively were working entirely alone for the first time, and the workday stretched to accommodate competing demands upon employees' time, such as feeding families and the emotional work of supporting anxious relatives and children (Parry et al., 2021).

There has been a two-fold unexpected consequence of this period of enforced working from home. First, surveys have consistently reported employees' growing preference to work remotely at least part of the time in the future (Bloom, 2020; Felstead and Reuschke, 2021; Parry et al., 2022), and with that employees' relationships with workplaces have shifted in a way that it is hard to imagine will be reversed. Second, employers have developed insight into the economic efficiencies around performing certain types of work tasks from home, away from the distraction of the workplace, and are increasingly now listening to employees' working preferences and building them into their business planning, analysing them together with estate savings that could be recouped through a revised organisation of work. For example, famously astute at counting the bottom line, the last major law firm moved out of London's peak real-estate district Canary Wharf in late 2022.

As economies around the world have moved out of lockdowns, organisations have been able to experiment more seriously with hybrid working in formerly office-based work, without the constraints of government directives and social distancing guidance. **Hybrid working** – that is, working patterns that blend home and office-based working (Parry et al., 2022) – offers a fundamentally new structure for the organisation of work that was only common in a minority of organisations prior to the pandemic. By late 2022, a year after the UK Government directive asking people to work from home was lifted, 28 per cent of the UK's workforce were working in a hybrid pattern (ONS, 2023). This presents compelling new challenges for managers and leaders at a scale not seen before, balancing curating employees being together in offices in meaningful ways around collaborative activities while retaining the productivity and well-being gains around remote working (Parry, 2022). This is likely to include some reimagining of workspaces in ways that reflect the kinds of work that are identified as best performed centrally and that reinforce social connections.

The Legacy of the Pandemic for the Organisation of Work

Lockdown working from home – that is, an unusually extended and compulsory period of working from home – provided an accidental experiment around remote working, giving organisations unique data about different ways in which work could be configured. Some of this change has been genuinely new and is potentially transformative, but there have also been more regressive trends. One of the challenges for analysts of work and organisation in making sense of these developments is that the pre-pandemic research on **remote working** focused on a rather narrower and more exclusive set of workforce experiences of remote working than the one that we now have evidence around, a point which illustrates the difference between chosen and compulsory working from home, as well as between niche and mainstream working from home. Much of the literature pre-COVID has also used the terminology of 'teleworking' to describe work organised remotely from worksites (Haddon and Brynin, 2005; Harris, 2003), language used much less frequently post-pandemic. We consequently need to assess critically sources in their context in evaluating their application for a new world of work in which the workforce demographic involved was often unprepared for the new working practices that the pandemic forced upon them, and good practice took some time to evolve. One notable exception to the mainly thin empirical evidence based on pre-pandemic remote working is the ongoing research of Nick Bloom at Stanford University in the US. This has provided one of the richest sources of evidence around working from home for contemporary analysts in making sense of the changes to work brought about by the pandemic (Bloom et al., 2015). Felstead and Blakely take up an analysis of this in Chapter 21, drawing attention to how precisely working environments affect productivity.

One of the particularly interesting shifts has been that, as work became located within people's homes, the public/private sphere distinction around productive work became less meaningful. People were performing their jobs in the same space as – and often simultaneously with – providing family care, as evidenced through the windows of Zoom and Teams when children inevitably appeared in meetings during lockdowns. In this context, work–life balance took on new resonance (see Chapter 10 by Xu and Kelliher on balancing work and social life). If hybrid working becomes a permanent modification to the organisation of work, then perhaps in the future industrialisation – with its exclusive location of paid work in the public sphere – might appear as an aberration in the history of the organisation of work. This blurring of organisational boundaries has disrupted the spatial aspect of workplace control that had previously associated presence in a centralised location with productivity and performance. Julia Hobsbawm of Demos has compellingly explored this **liminal** working in her concept of 'the Nowhere Office' (2022), which has generated its own podcast series, and Glucksmann's 'total social organisation of labour' conceptual framework (2000) is as relevant as ever in capturing the transformations that are going on around paid and unpaid work boundaries and the way in which these are gendered.

Second, in many organisations, working from home has been a trigger for the mainstreaming of more heterogenised forms of flexible working (Parry et al., 2022). In other words, over the course of the pandemic, when they had time to reflect on and monitor organisational performance in a different environment, employers have increasingly come to recognise the business benefits of looking *beyond* a nine-to-five, office-based, full-time model of working, which in industrialised societies has been associated with a breadwinner model of the organisation of work. We are coming out of the pandemic, with many organisations experimenting with a whole host of different working arrangements that will help them attract and hold on to staff, supported by broader national policy reform to extend access to flexible working. One manifestation of this has been the global four-day week trials rolled out in 2022, which have recently concluded. In the UK, these saw more than 60 companies participate, with productivity and well-being gains achieved at the same time as a reduction in working hours (de Neve, 2022; Ellerbeck, 2023). This has provided a positive counter to some of the work intensification of the pandemic, with 90 per cent of participating companies committed to continuing with the working pattern. Changes in the UK legislation on flexible working, with the Employment Relations (Flexible Working) Act and supporting secondary legislation coming into force in April 2024, look set to enhance access to flexible working arrangements across workforces further, giving employees the right to request adapted working patterns from the start of contracts.

Given that traditional fixed working patterns exclude particular groups from participating in the ways that they would like, including women, carers, and those with disabilities (Dale, 2021; Norgate and Cooper, 2020), hybrid working that has flexible working overlaid across it can build more inclusive future workforces. The ONS observed that nearly 400,000 older workers dropped out of the labour force during the pandemic (2022b), so policy levers such as flexible work that entice them back into jobs could have strong business benefits. However, a concern remains that a residual (and gendered) flexibility stigma, that is, an organisational bias against employees who work flexibly, might persist in the post-pandemic period. This could give flexible work policy perverse effects, including work intensification and employment discrimination (Chung, 2020; Taylor et al., 2021b).

A novel aspect of this period of work learning is that the importance of employee well-being has come to the fore in understanding productivity, and here there is an opportunity for employee circumstances and preferences to play a stronger role in the future organisation of work (see Chapter 11, 'Well-being and Mental Health at Work'). During the pandemic, regular staff surveys (also known as 'pulse surveys') made strains and stresses more apparent to employers (Hamouche, 2021), and gave them insight into how poor well-being could affect employees' ability to work at full capacity. Correspondingly, more than before, organisations and managers attempted to address and support employee welfare – support here became a key tool for surviving the pandemic. **Diversity management**, previously focused around demographic characteristics, took on a broader and more central role in organisational strategy during the pandemic as the importance of supporting a range of domestic circumstances became a part of managers' routine practice in order to respond to the challenges of compulsory working from home (Parry et al., 2022).

Work practices that evolved during enforced working from home saw a number of changes that offered positive capital for organisations. By necessity, digital learning was accelerated during the pandemic, extending across workforces, which in turn stimulated the development of more diverse forms of collaboration (Gifford, 2022; Parry et al., 2022). Employees became adept at the complex communication techniques necessary to support dispersed teams and that will continue to complement hybrid working, a skillset that was fostered by the experiential learning of pandemic working. Kniffin et al. (2021) have suggested that virtual teamworking during COVID-19 may have increased prosocial behaviour, which could have longer-term workforce benefits, a theory that makes sense in terms of employees going through a shared experience during the pandemic (a period effect). Caligiuri et al. (2020) have pointed to the increased uptake of online training materials as an indication of the enthusiasm for self-directed learning that was observed among workforces removed from workplaces. This learning mindset, which was a key part of reorientating to new ways of working, has also been identified as a key component of sustainable careers (Heslin et al., 2020). For many organisations, extended remote working has stimulated a re-evaluation of leadership qualities around distributed workforces. Outside of offices, the learning from the pandemic was diverse too, as keyworkers adapted their working practices to deliver new and transformed services – for example, healthcare teams working with Personal Protective Equipment (PPE) restrictions to provide rapid intervention around raised demand for acute treatment, often outside of their speciality.

More regressively, pandemic-driven working from home has deepened some work-related inequalities. Gendered inequalities around paid and unpaid work remained persistent despite the greater proximity of both men and women to the domestic sphere. Time series analysis of couples working alongside one another in their homes has highlighted a discrepancy in their input into unpaid work. The Institute of Fiscal Studies found that, during the first lockdown, when schools were closed, 45 per cent of mothers' working hours, compared to 25 per cent of fathers' working hours, were spent looking after children (Andrew et al., 2020). Chung et al.'s (2021) research saw gendered inequalities further replicated in other forms of unpaid work they measured during the pandemic: cooking, cleaning, laundry, and education, for example. The double burden of labour which a modified bread-winner model has imbued upon women has then been further exaggerated by the co-presence of work and domestic spheres of enforced working from home and the lack of temporal distinctions that many countries experienced during the pandemic.

Career theorists have pointed to the longer-term consequences of the dispro-portionate assumption of unpaid work that women took on during the pandemic, combined with their reduced visibility in offices during the advent of hybrid working, on their progression within organisations that continue to associate workplace presence with productivity (Taylor et al., 2021a). Other inequalities that remote working has seen deepen concern young people and those at the start of careers, who reported gaps in their learning where managers had been unable to devote the same time to transmitting daily learning as when they were co-present with staff in workspaces and this was more embedded in their daily practice (Parry et al., 2022). Over the longer term, this threatens to affect younger people's and new starters' professional development, progression, and attachment to organisa-tions, and ultimately could create a skills deficit in organisations.

A further pandemic trend that could have negative consequences if left un-checked is work intensification. Research identified that formerly office-based workers were investing more time in their work during the lockdown – often, for example, donating their previous commuting time to their job and extending the working hours of the day to ensure that tasks were completed (Mutebi and Hobbs, 2022; Parry et al., 2022). While this provided certain productivity gains, well-being surveys were also revealing raised levels of stress and a series of physical health problems associated with this extended work and sedentary lifestyle. For example, the Work after Lockdown pandemic research documented raised levels of musculoskeletal pain, fatigue, and eye strain among the formerly office-based workers who had switched to extended working from home at short notice (Parry et al., 2021). Sick workforces will have detrimental consequences for productivity over the longer term, so there is a strong motivation for organisations to manage good practice around working time. Alongside work intensification, presenteeism has also increased during the pandemic, as employees have worked through illnesses that they might have considered taking sick days for if they had to travel into offices (Shimura et al., 2021). Working through ill-health can be a risky strategy, however, with negative effects for both employees and organisations.

A final area where concern has been raised around the pandemic and hybrid working is around workplace surveillance, in terms of the growing trend for employers to deploy digital tools to monitor work activity (Aloisi and de Stefano, 2021; Vitak and Zimmer, 2023). This is discussed in detail in Chapter 21, 'Changing Places of Work'. While digital surveillance has raised concerns around privacy and organisations transgressing the boundary between work and home, and disrupting spatial power dynamics, this is illustrates where older sociological literature can be valuable in analysing contemporary issues. As Green and McNeill's discussion of Braverman's work (1974) in Chapter 8 illustrates, control of the work process has been a key tool that managers have used to produce compliant workforces and enhance productivity, a concern for organisations amid the uncertainty of the pandemic.

Case Study

Work After Lockdown (Parry et al., 2021, 2022)

This research, funded by the ESRC, followed individual and organisational experiences over the course of 18 months during the pandemic, looking at adaptation around compulsory and extended working from home, what was learned during this period, and how working preferences evolved as organisations moved out of restrictions and started to experiment with hybrid working. It comprised a mixture of secondary analysis of UK national datasets, worker well-being surveys with employees in the professional and public administration sectors (which together represent one in seven of all UK jobs), and case study work and interviews with four organisations (two law firms and two local authorities). Participants in the research shared the unique experience, prior to March 2020, of having office-based jobs, which were then rapidly transformed into being mainly home-based for the course of the 18 months of the research.

The unexpectedly extended nature of working from home caused by the pandemic meant that there was sufficient time for people to become adept at working in a different way, and for good practice to evolve around working from home. The research saw a permanent mindset shift among the UK's formerly office-based workers, with a later survey wave seeing 75 per cent of those surveyed indicating that they wanted to be able to work at home at least some of the time in the future, and a further 13 per cent preferring full-time remote working. By late 2021, then, there was very strong support for hybrid working among employees who had been through pandemic-driven working from home. This group's experiences had seen them observe the personal and organisational inefficiencies of working fixed nine-to-five hours in a single workspace; as one participant commented, 'The grand experiment that nobody wanted has worked.' People were looking to achieve a better balance of office and home-based working in the future than they had seen in their pre-COVID working experiences, one that enabled them to hold on to some of the gains of pandemic working, such as improved workforce trust and better-quality meetings. At the same time, the aspects that they had most missed about offices were opportunities for sociability and collaboration. Office space design will need to get this right if organisations are to harness hybrid workers' motivation to use offices to get together in effective – and non-wasteful – ways.

Surprisingly, for a sudden and unplanned shift into a different way of organis-ing work, workers saw very little negative impact on their productivity, with over two-thirds of those surveyed reporting that they were getting as much done re-motely at home as they did in offices. This finding was borne out repeatedly in the qualitative research with organisations, and summed up by a manager: 'our people were phenomenal, and just kind of dug in and leaned in, and I think everybody felt really proud of that.' Remote working also provided a prompt for organisations to become adept at developing output-based productivity measures, and to shift away from presence-based ones that were inadequate for evaluating more diverse ways of organising work. The managers interviewed, who had observed first-hand their workforces' adaptability to an alternative way of organising work, regarded it as unthinkable that organisations would revert to traditional expectations about work-ing in offices post-pandemic: 'It would be hard to not accept a formal working from home programme. You just couldn't argue against it now, particularly if people's productivity is high. I don't know how you could then try and row back from a very flexible working approach.'

On a personal level, the work–life balance benefits of working from home were strongly recognised by research participants, and many drew attention to how the gains they had amassed around commuting time could be repurposed into both paid work and family life. This affected their well-being, and these gains became particularly notable over time. When well-being was first measured (on the World Health Organization-Five Well-Being Index) early in the research, in the context of rapid movement into an extreme situation, it was low (at 47). A year later, when organisations had got better at supporting remote work and conditions were more normalised, with children returning to school, it had risen to 68 – above the average pre-pandemic level of well-being. A relationship was also observed between well-being and productivity among those surveyed, which provides a strong impetus for organisations to invest in supporting workforce well-being.

The pandemic got organisations talking about the connections between office and home life, because they had little choice but to address this if they wanted to survive the pandemic. But this was an entirely new approach for most organisations, and one that had often fundamentally disrupted their thinking; 'You cannot fake productivity for nearly a year and a half.' An important pandemic learning will be the importance of getting the balance of hybrid working right for both productivity and workforce well-being. A refreshed approach to office space can also be an op-portunity to prioritise environmental concerns in the organisation of work, connect-ing workspaces to public transport and designing more energy-efficient workplaces.

More can be found about the Work After Lockdown research at www.workafterlockdown.uk

Conclusion

This focus on work and organisation in the context of the lockdowns associated with the COVID-19 pandemic offers a number of provocations for the analyses contained in this volume, around a range of work issues. First, in focusing on the work changes associated with mass working from home during the UK's lockdowns, which were replicated in numerous countries, it illustrates that everyday work structures are meaningful and interrelated to global patterns and structures. The implications of a potentially fatal virus that was spread by social contact threw into sharp relief the weaknesses of a system of organising work that required employees to embark upon daily mass travel, on crowded and underinvested-in public transport, to a central location where they were arranged in offices for maximum efficiency, often in open-plan format. Given the pressure of Government directives to reorientate work activities away from the public sphere, employers were forced to reassess rapidly how work could be organised in alternative and more secure formats, constituting a period of unparalleled learning, as well as a disruption of many of the organisation of work assumptions that have been the legacy of industrialised countries. Thus the reverberations of a global health crisis had transformative effects upon workplaces worldwide, a link that drew recognition from the International Labour Organization (ILO, 2020).

This period effect has illustrated the fragility and temporality of some work structures. What had previously appeared to be a stable and logical way of organising work was no longer fit for purpose under a global pandemic, and almost every area of the organisation of work saw change. Office workers made workplaces out of their homes, and the economic distinction between public and private spheres was fundamentally fractured. Essential services rebranded their employees 'keyworkers' and exposed them to levels of risk that had not previously been part of their jobs. For example, workers in social care and bus drivers saw raised and relatively higher death rates from COVID-19 during the pandemic (Butterick and Charlwood, 2021; ONS, 2021); their work now juggled the contradictory expectations of being recognised as economically essential while remaining low-paid. Entire sectors where working from home was not possible were temporarily shut down and employees became inactive (furloughed) with a rapidity that gave them little time to adjust to the insecurity of a new world of work and non-work. Very often it was the underemployed and those in precarious work who were the most vulnerable to labour market shutdown, with little likelihood of finding alternative employment in the formal sector. Everyday occupational inequalities were exacerbated during the pandemic, and embedded in these were gender and ethnic inequalities. For the generation who grew up observing these shifting fortunes around work, it is yet to be established how it will shape their own career ambitions and what they will value most about work.

In the post-pandemic landscape, there is already extensive evidence of workspaces becoming more diverse to accommodate hybrid working patterns, and of environmental considerations being embedded more convincingly into the future of work (see Sahin-Dikmen's account of how climate change is affecting work in Chapter 19). This has included the relocation and reconfiguration of offices, and the incorporation of third spaces of work to provide satellite spaces for employees to convene: where they can collaborate and socialise (Felstead, 2022). This could minimise some of the more deleterious effects of mass commuting that has accompanied industrial organisation. However, as some of the more regressive trends of the pandemic have illustrated, times of change also carry risk, and now is the moment for policy-makers to ensure that the decent work prioritised in the *Taylor review* is placed front stage as workplaces process and apply the learnings of the pandemic.

STUDENT ACTIVITY

Focusing on any two jobs, consider how workers' daily experiences have been changed by working through the pandemic.

- Provide three examples of people forced to work in a different way.
- What was positive and more challenging in their pandemic working experiences?
- How much of this has changed practice, and do you think this will be permanent?

Practice Questions

1. How might remote working affect gender equality?
2. Discuss how hybrid working can benefit employees and organisations.
3. 'The pandemic has exacerbated existing inequalities in the world of work.' Discuss, reflecting on how organisations can address these.

Key Terms

Atypical work
non-standardised work – that is, work that is not full-time, nine-till-five. The *Taylor review* (2017) drew attention to seven key types of atypical work that had become apparent in the UK labour market, including part-time work, agency work, zero-hours contracts, and gig economy work.

Breadwinner model
the organisation of work within households around the expectation that a male partner is engaged in full-time paid work and a female partner in extensive unpaid work to support the functioning of the household and family.

Diversity management
a set of HRM practices that value and support workforce differences to create an environment where all talents are used to their best effect.

Flexible work
variations of paid work around the standardised full-time, workplace-based model, which can include differences around schedule, hours, and location. For example,

part-time hours, job shares, flexitime, remote working, annualised hours, compressed hours, zero-hours contracts, and career breaks can all be considered flexible work.

Furlough
the practice used for the first time on a widespread basis during COVID-19-driven lockdowns, whereby workers whose employment sectors had been temporarily shut down, and whose work was suspended, were subsided 80 per cent of their pay (in the UK).

Gendered divisions of labour
ways that paid or unpaid work is organised in a way that is distinctively gendered. Within organisations, distinctions are often made between vertical segregation (where men and women are concentrated in different occupational ranks) and horizontal segregation (the concentration of men and women in different sectors or types of jobs, such as engineering and education).

Global North
more a concept than a geographical distinction, this term describes countries that are similar in terms of socioeconomic and political characteristics, including North America, Europe, Russia, Australia, and Japan.

Hybrid working
'a blend of home-based and office-based working, which may be fixed or fluid in terms of the proportion of time spent in either location in a typical week' (Parry et al., 2022: 7).

Industrialised society
the organisation of society following the Industrial Revolution in a format where production became heavily mechanised and made intensive use of technology.

Liminal
liminality is the position of being on the boundaries between two states, and is often thought of as a transitionary or transformative status.

Liquid modernity
a theory by Zygmunt Bauman (2000) which purports that societies and organisational life have become characterised by uncertainty and continual change, which contrasts with the assumed concreteness of the past, in particular with modernity.

Patriarchal societies
societies whose social systems privilege men's experiences – for example, through power structures, the organisation of work, and legal frameworks.

Period effect
a historical event that simultaneously affects a population rather than a specific group or cohort, such as the impact of the 2001 terrorist attacks on New York's landmark Twin Towers, or a war.

Public and private spheres
in broad terms, used to denote geographical distinctions regarding where work happens in industrial societies – paid work has taken place in workplaces (the public sphere) and unpaid work occurs within households (private sphere).

Remote working
the performance of paid work in a location outside of the workplace, which can include the home, as well as third spaces such as in hotels, on public transport, or on a university campus.

The Taylor review
a review of modern workplace practices, conducted by Matthew Taylor for the UK Government. It is also known as the *Good Work* report (Taylor, 2017), focusing particularly on atypical forms of work.

White-collar work
work that is performed in an office, the 'white collars' of office workers contrasting with the 'blue collars' of manual labourers. White-collar work can range from administrative roles to managerial ones.

Zero-hours contract
a casual working contract in which the employee is regarded as being 'on call' for an unspecified number of hours each week (which may be zero, as employers are not required to provide a minimum number of hours). Often used in supermarkets, the fast-food industry, casual healthcare work, and hospitality.

References

Aloisi, A., and de Stefano, V. (2021) 'Essential jobs, remote work and digital surveillance: addressing the COVID-19 pandemic panopticon'. *International Labour Review*, 161(2): 289–314.

Andrew, A., Cattan, S., Costa Dias, M., Farquharson, C., Kraftman, L., Krutikova, S., Phimister, A., and Sevilla, A. (2020) *Family Time Use and Home Learning Suring the COVID-19 Lockdown*. Institute for Fiscal Studies, Report R178.

Bauman, Z. (2000) *Liquid Modernity*. Cambridge: Polity Press.

Beck, V., Fuertes, V., Kamerãde, D., Lyonette, C., and Warren, T. (2020) 'Working lives', in M. Parker (ed.), *Life after COVID-19: the other side of the crisis*, Bristol: Bristol University Press, 53–62.

Bloom, N. (2020) *How working from home works out*. Stanford Institute for Economic Policy Research (SIEPR) Policy Brief, June. Stanford: SIEPR.

Bloom, N., Liang, J., Roberts, J., and Ying, Z.J. (2015) 'Does working from home work? Evidence from a Chinese experiment'. *Quarterly Journal of Economics*, 130(1): 165–218.

Brammer, S., Branicki, L. and Linnenluecke, M. (2020) 'COVID-19, societalization and the future of business in society'. *Academy of Management Perspectives*, 34(4): 493–507.

Braverman, H. (1974) *Labour and monopoly capital*. New York: Monthly Review Press.

Butterick, M., and Charlwood, A. (2021) 'HRM and the COVID-19 pandemic: how can we stop making a bad situation worse?' *Human Resource Management Journal*, 31(4): 847–856.

Caligiuri, P., De Cieri, H., Minbaeva, D., Verbeke, A., and Zimmermann, A. (2020) 'International HRM insights for navigating the COVID-19 pandemic: implications for future research and practice'. *Journal of International Business Studies*, 51: 697–713.

Chung, H. (2020) 'Gender, flexibility stigma, and the perceived negative consequences of flexible working in the UK'. *Social Indicators Research*, 151: 521–545.

Chung, H., Birkett, H., and Seo, H. (2021) 'Covid-19, flexible working and implications for gender inequality in the United Kingdom'. *Gender and Society*, 35(2): 218–232.

Crompton, R. (1999) 'The decline of the male breadwinner: explanations and interpretations', in R. Crompton (ed.), *Restructuring gender relations and employment: the decline of the male breadwinner*. Oxford: Oxford University Press.

Dale, G. (2021) *Flexible working: how to implement flexibility in the workplace to improve employee and business performance*. London: Kogan Page.

De Neve, J.-E. (2022) 'Four day week trial confirms working less increases wellbeing and productivity'. *The Conversation*. https://theconversation.com/four-day-week-trial-confirms-working-less-increases-wellbeing-and-productivity-195660

Dennis, N., Henriques, F., and Slaughter, C. (1956) *Coal is our life: an analysis of a Yorkshire mining community*. London: Tavistock.

Ellerbeck, S. (2023) 'The world's biggest trial of the four day work week has come to an end. These are the results'. *World Economic Forum*. www.weforum.org/agenda/2023/03/four-day-work-week-uk-trial/

Felstead, A. (2022) *Remote work: A research overview*. London: Routledge.

Felstead, A., and Reuschke, D. (2021) 'A flash in the pan or a permanent change? The growth of homeworking during the pandemic and its effect on employee productivity in the UK'. *Information Technology and People*. https://doi.org/10.1108/ITP-11-2020-0758.

Gifford, J. (2022) 'Remote working: unprecedented increase and a developing research agenda'. *Human Resource Development International*. 25(2): 105–113.

Glucksmann, M. (2000) *Cottons and casuals: the gendered organisation of labour in time and space*. York: sociologypress.

Gregg, M. (2011) *Work's Intimacy*. Cambridge: Polity Press.

Haddon, L., and Brynin, M. (2005) 'The character of telework and the characteristics of teleworkers'. *New Technology, Work and Employment*, 20(1): 34–46.

Hamouche, S. (2021) 'Human resource management and the COVID-19 crisis: implications, challenges, opportunities, and future organizational directions'. *Journal of Management and Organization*: 1–16. https://doi.org/10.1017/jmo.2021.15

Harris, L. (2003) 'Home-based teleworking and the employment relationship'. *Personnel Review*, 32(4): 422–437.

Heslin, P.A., Keating, L.A., and Ashford, S.J. (2020) 'How being in learning mode may enable a sustainable career across the lifespan'. *Journal of Vocational Behavior,* 117: 103324.

Hobsbawm, J. (2022) *The nowhere office: reinventing work and the workplace of the future.* London: Basic Books.

Horrell, S., and Humphries, J. (1997) 'The origins and expansion of the male breadwinner family'. *International Review of Social History,* 42(5): 25–64.

ILO (2020) *ILO Monitor: COVID-19 and the world of work*, 2nd edition. www.ilo.org/wcmsp5/groups/public/---dgreports/---dcomm/documents/briefingnote/wcms_740877.pdf

Kalleberg, A.L. (2016) 'Good jobs, bad jobs', in S. Edgell, H. Gottfried an E. Granter (eds), *The SAGE handbook of the sociology of work and employment.* London: Sage.

Kniffin, K.M., Narayanan, J., Anseel, F., Antonakis, J., Ashford, S.P., Bakker, A.B., Bamberger, P., Bapuji, H., Bhave, D.P., Choi, V.K., Demerouti, E., Flynn, F.J., Gelfand, M.J., Greer, L.L., Johns, G., Kesebir, S., Klein, P.G., Lee, S.Y, ... Vugt, M.V. (2021) 'COVID-19 and the workplace: implications, issues and insights for future research and action'. *American Psychologist*, 76(1): 63–77.

Mutebi, N., and Hobbs, A. (2022) *The impact of remote and hybrid working on workers and organisations*, POSTbrief 49. https://researchbriefings.files.parliament.uk/documents/POST-PB-0049/POST-PB-0049.pdf

Norgate, S.H., and Cooper, C.L. (eds) (2020) *Flexible work: designing our healthier future lives.* London and New York: Routledge.

OECD (2022) *OECD Employment Outlook 2022: building back more inclusive labour markets.* Paris: OECD Publishing.

ONS (2021) 'Coronavirus related deaths by occupation, England and Wales: deaths registered between 9 March and 28 December 2020'.

ONS (2022a) 'Gender pay gap in the UK: 2022'. www.ons.gov.uk/employmentandlabourmarket/peopleinwork/earningsandworkinghours/bulletins/genderpaygapintheuk/2022

ONS (2022b) 'Reasons for workers aged over 50 years leaving employment since the start of the coronavirus pandemic: wave'. www.ons.gov.uk/employmentand-labourmarket/peopleinwork/employmentandemployeetypes/articles/reasonsfor workersagedover50yearsleavingemploymentsincethestartofthecoronaviruspand emic/wave2

ONS (2023) 'Characteristics of homeworkers, Great Britain: September 2022 to January 2023'. www.ons.gov.uk/employmentandlabourmarket/peopleinwork/employmentandemployeetypes/articles/characteristicsofhomeworkersgreatbritain/september2022tojanuary2023#:~:text=Age%20and%20sex,reporting%20working%20from%20home%20only

Pahl, R.E. (1984) *Divisions of labour.* Oxford: Basil Blackwell.

Parry, J., Young, Z., Bevan, S., Veliziotis, M., Baruch, Y., Beigi, M., Bajorek, Z., Salter, E., and Tochia, C. (2021) *Working from home under COVID-19 lockdown: transitions and tensions.* https://static1.squarespace.com/static/5f5654b537cea057c500f59e/t/60143f05a2117e3eec3c3243/1611939604505/Wal+Bulletin+1.pdf

Parry, J., Young, Z., Bevan, S., Veliziotis, M., Baruch, Y., Beigi, M., Bajorek, Z., Richards, S. and Tochia, C. (2022) *Work after lockdown: no going back – what we have learned working from home through the COVID-19 pandemic.* https://static1.squarespace.com/static/5f5654b537cea057c500f59e/t/623d774d28438102becd9490/1648195411515/Work+After+Lockdown+no+going+back+-report.pdf

Pettinger, L. (2019) *What's wrong with work?* Bristol: Polity Press.

Rudolph, C. and Zacher, H. (2020) '"The COVID-19 generation": a cautionary note'. *Work, Aging and Retirement*, 6(3): 139–145.

Shimura, A., Yokoi, K., Ishibashi, Y., Akatsuka, Y., and Inoue, T. (2021) 'Remote working decreases psychological and physical stress responses, but full-time remote work increases presenteeism'. *Frontiers in Psychology*, 12: 1–10.

Spreitzer, G.M., Cameron, L., and Garrett, L. (2017) 'Alternative work arrangements: two images of the new world of work'. *Annual Review of Organization Psychology and Organizational Behavior*, 4: 473–499.

Spurk, D., and Straub, C. (2020) 'Flexible employment relationship and careers in times of the COVID-19 pandemic'. *Journal of Vocational Behaviour*, 119: 103435.

Taylor, H., Florisson, R., and Hooper, D. (2021a) *Making hybrid inclusive: key priorities for policy makers.* London: Chartered Management Institute/Work Foundation.

Taylor, H., Florisson, R., and Spratt, L. (2021b) *Post-pandemic hybrid working poses new challenges to diversity and inclusion.* London: Chartered Management Institute/Work Foundation.

Taylor, M. (2017) *Good work: the Taylor review of modern working practices.* www.gov.uk/government/publications/good-work-the-taylor-review-of-modern-working-practices

University of Essex, Institute for Social and Economic Research (2021) *Understanding Society: COVID-19 Study, 2020–21* [data collection]. 11th edition. UK Data Service. SN: 8644, https://doi.org/10.5255/UKDA-SN-8644-11

Vermeerbergen, L., Pulignano, V., and Jansens, M. (2021) 'Working hard for the ones you love and care for under Covid-19 physical distancing'. *Work, Employment & Society*, 35(6): 1144–1154.

Vitak, J. and Zimmer, M. (2023) 'Power, stress, and uncertainty: experiences with and attitudes towards workplace surveillance during a pandemic'. *Surveillance and Society*, 21(1), open issue.

Walby, S. (1990) *Theorizing Patriarchy.* Oxford: Blackwell.

Williamson, B. (1982) *Class, culture and community: a biographical study of social change in mining.* London: Routledge and Kegan Paul.

Yordanova, I. (2020) *Women in self-employment.* IPSE report. www.ipse.co.uk/policy/research/women-in-self-employment/women-in-self-employment.html

Young, Z. (2018) *Women's work: how mothers manage flexible working in careers and family life.* Bristol: Bristol University Press.

Chapter Introductions and How to Use this Book

Brian McDonough

Introduction

Chapter 1 laid out some of the fundamental issues facing sociologists of work, including how working lives changed during the COVID-19 pandemic of 2020–2022, as well as how life after lockdown became transformed for certain sectors and groups within the global economy. The chapter gave a way into thinking about work and organisation, by drawing on the current context work is situated (such as COVID, the cost of living crisis, and social inequalities in the workplace), in both the Global North and Global South. Chapter 2 extends this introduction by providing an overview of the topics covered in the book. It also explains the aims of the book, and purpose of each part, and set of chapters.

Sociology, Work, and Organisations: A Global Perspective has been written for undergraduate and postgraduate students. Unlike other sociology of work texts, the approach to this endeavour was two-fold: to showcase cutting-edge research on work issues taking place across the globe; and to include scholars whose research takes place in diverse contexts and places. The diversity of scholarship was important. Contributing authors differ by age, gender, and ethnicity (among other things) and have a foothold in the countries they discuss, either by virtue of their own nationality or via the research time spent investigating topics in those specific places around the world. By drawing on the expertise of researchers whose research is situated in different parts of the globe, this book brings direct and contextualised examples, using fresh and contemporary case studies which have been researched by the authors first-hand.

DOI: 10.4324/9781003314769-3

The textbook is divided into six parts, grouping the chapters into the following overarching themes:

- Part 1: Introduction to Work in a Global Context
- Part 2: Inequalities, Intersectionality, and Discrimination at Work
- Part 3: Organising People and Well-being at Work
- Part 4: Digitalised Work
- Part 5: Workforce Marginalisation
- Part 6: The Future of Work

This chapter will discuss these themes as a way of introducing the key ideas developed throughout the rest of the book, and develops the notion of thinking sociologically, a skill used by social researchers to make sense of the social world.

Global Work and Thinking Sociologically

Perceptions of inequalities and discrimination at work are shaped by what can be thought of as traditionalist, commonsensical, or popularist ideas of work and everyday culture. Bauman and May (2019) lay out the ways in which social scientists think about the everyday world in their book *Thinking sociologically*. They say that,

> whilst deeply immersed in our routines, informed by a practical knowledge oriented in the social settings in which we interact, we may not systematically think about the meaning of what we have gone through or the reasons for its occurrence, nor compare our private experiences with the fate of others; with the exception perhaps, of seeing private responses to public issues paraded for consumption on television and social media.
>
> (Bauman and May, 2019: 6)

In contrast to the routine way of thinking about our everyday experiences, **sociological thinking** takes us into 'a relational understanding – it can see the individual but situates it within a social milieu' (2019: 6).

Thinking sociologically is important for making sense of social issues, problems, and debates within the sociology of work. So much of the topic of work is bound up with **common sense,** and traditional ways of thinking, that it is hard to see work issues and problems when we ourselves are entrenched within them.

Being paid is a good theme on which to begin thinking about the sociology of work. Most of us tend to think about work as 'paid employment', yet sociologists show that most work around the globe goes unpaid. Consider these three examples. First, take the domestic and care work that is involved in managing a household and raising children, where hard labour is carried out with long hours and sometimes little sleep. In a famous British sociological study published in a book called *The sociology of housework* (1974), feminist Anne Oakley described the commitment, dedication, and hard work required by millions of women around the world to do a job that is almost always unpaid. A second example centres on modern slavery – which involves the exploitation and coercion of people – forcing them to carry out some kind of activity (usually) without pay. The International Labour Organization (ILO) estimates that there are 50 million people worldwide in modern slavery. Of these, '28 million are in forced labour and 22 million trapped in forced marriage' (2023: 1). Sexual exploitation accounts for the majority of modern-day slavery cases, with women at the forefront, but many men are also modern slaves, perhaps best exemplified recently in the 2022 Qatar World Cup, where reports of forced labour in the building of football stadiums were widespread.

A third example centres on the labour carried out to harvest fruit. Unlike social scientists, who study the sociology of work, lay people in the Global North visit the supermarket to buy fruit, and may be unaware or have little understanding about the production and work that has gone into getting the fruit from the land to the supermarket shelf. Some of the production can also involve modern-day slavery. One commonsense assumption is that workers who help the fruit reach the supermarket shelf are paid for their labour. However, many workers are not paid a wage, and many will have experienced forms of exclusion, marginalisation, or exploitation within work practices. For example, a report by the ILO on the trade of bananas found that, while workers in Costa Rica and India are largely paid a wage, the banana sectors of Indonesia and Ethiopia rely on smallholder producers, where 'employees are seldom hired and the use of unpaid family members is commonplace' (ILO, 2020: 1). In Indonesia, the issue of pay is exemplified by gender, as men tend to be classified as self-employed while 'the majority of women are classified as unpaid family workers' (ILO, 2020: 9). This issue affects many workers. There are over 90,000 workers in the banana sector of Indonesia, of which one third are women (ILO, 2020: 4).

The issue of pay cuts across many chapters of the textbook. The reader will come across gendered inequalities in terms of pay (Chapter 3); unstable and inconsistent pay in precarious work (Chapter 5); working people who are unpaid (Chapter 15); as well as how technologies permit the outsourcing of work so payments made to workers can be reduced, if paid at all (Chapter 12).

Taken-for-granted World of Work

One of the most difficult skills to learn, as a novice sociologist of work, is to be able to *see* the social inequalities, problems, and impact of global issues from a **social scientific perspective**. Blinded by one's own taken-for-granted assumptions, one can readily overlook or accept the plight of other people's experiences, because their visibility or importance is obscured. In his book *Taken for granted: the remarkable power of the unremarkable*, Zerubavel (2020) draws on the concepts of 'marked' and 'unmarked' to examine the difference between the *special* and the *ordinary* aspects of everyday life. The author highlights how some features of everyday life 'we assume by default' and remain unarticulated, while others are given special attention and are 'explicitly accentuated' (Zerubavel, 2020: 2). He gives the following example:

> the term *working mum* reflects the traditionally marked status of middle-class working mothers, which sharply contrasts with the effectively unmarked status of working fathers. Conventionally assumed by default and thus taken for granted, the latter thereby require no special marking, and a term such as *working dad*, for instance, would actually seem redundant.
>
> (Zerubavel, 2020: 5)

There are other examples of such marked and unmarked status, such as the term 'independent woman', to describe a female who earns her own money and is non-reliant on a husband/partner or father, or 'career woman', but never an independent or 'career man'. Zerubavel (2020: 5) explains that 'men by definition have careers, but women who do so must be marked'. The same goes for 'family man', which gets special status, but never 'family woman'. As things are marked, they become 'abnormalised' while simultaneously normalising what remains unmarked (Zerubavel, 2020). Although marked things are by definition highly noticeable and 'culturally visible', unmarked things escape our attention, slip into the background and into 'cultural invisibility' (Zerubavel, 2020: 6).

Zerubavel's (2020) arguments bear importance for investigating the sociology of work. Normality plays an importance in maintaining social dominance and establishing what is **taken for granted**, accepted, and routine. Everyday people 'make default assumptions without their even realizing they are making them' (Zerubavel, 2020: 6). In workplaces for example, the marking and normalizing of a disabled employee who is a wheelchair user, presumes the normality of able-bodied-ness. In the same way, the marking of femaleness, blackness and homosexuality presumes the normality of maleness, whiteness, and straightness (Zerubavel, 2020). The more dominant a social group, the more likely it is to remain unmarked. The language around work and people reflects cultural prejudices within the societies we live. We talk of manpower and chairmen, but rarely womanpower or chairwoman, and because nurses, for example, are assumed to be female, we must add the word 'male' (as in 'male nurse') to point out it's a man. Mapping out what is marked and unmarked requires a sociologically trained mind. There's a fluidity of the social world that requires us to situate our findings across time and space. This involves viewing issues historically as well as viewing them as they are contextualised in specific countries, cultures, and within language. Throughout this book, authors have exercised their ability to think sociologically, challenge normality, and make visible what is often opaque and taken for granted. The following provides an overview of the themes knitting together the chapters of this textbook.

Inequalities, Intersectionality, and Discrimination at Work

Part 2 of the textbook focuses on the ways in which inequalities and discrimination operate in the workplace. Among many other things, inequalities can range

Brian McDonough

from unequal pay for different groups to the access to certain jobs or positions. Inequalities can be worse for some groups than others, and researchers in this textbook apply the idea of **intersectionality** to show how some inequalities can intersect, such as gender and race, or age and social class. Intersectionality can also apply to discrimination. A young applicant (age) may be turned down for a job application, but a young black applicant (age plus ethnicity) finds that the odds of getting the job are stacked against them. Some believe that racism at work is an exaggeration, but sociological research tells us another story. A group of Oxford University researchers used fictitious names of multi-ethnic groups to apply for 3,000 jobs, keeping the same skills, qualifications, and work experience. They found that, while white British applicants had to apply four times to get a positive response, ethnic minority applicants would have to apply at least seven times (CSI, 2019). The inequalities and discrimination of workers or applicants, and the social factors that intersect, are exactly what Part 2 of the book focuses on.

There are different ways in which discrimination takes place in the workplace. **Direct discrimination** includes prohibiting or banning a person or group of people from work or workplace activities. In the UK armed forces, direct discrimination took place against LGBTQ+ (Lesbian, Gay, Bisexual, Transgender, Queer, and other gender or sexual identities) people for decades. In this example, prejudice towards gay and other LGBTQ+ people was not merely related to some individuals holding homophobic attitudes, but also societal and historical prejudice, often enshrined in law and custom. In July 2023, the British Prime Minister Rishi Sunak gave a state apology for the decades-long ban of LGBTQ+ people working in the UK armed forces. Sunak said that the ban, between 1967 and 2000, was an 'appalling failure of the British state, decades behind the law of this land' (Walker, 2023: 2). A government-commissioned review found that many working in the armed forces had suffered from abuse, violence, homophobic bullying, and harassment.

Using the sociological imagination for understanding the world of work involves a kind of seeing which contextualises workplace activities and prejudices within a historical context. In the UK, for example, it was not until the Sexual Offences Act of (1967) that homosexual acts were legalised, and people were not criminalised for being gay. Elsewhere around the globe, LGBTQ+ rights are not only restricted in the workplace but across society. With more than half of the world's countries having anti-LGBTQ+ laws in place, someone who is openly gay, for example, will not only be shunned and excluded from workplaces and other spheres of society but can find themselves punished with prison sentences. In many countries they can be sentenced to death, such as Iran (Islamic Penal Code, 2013; Article 234), Mauritania (Penal Code, 1984; Article 308), Saudi Arabia (by Islamic Sharia law), Sudan (Penal Code, Act No. 8, 1991; Section 148), and Yemen (see Penal Code, 1994; Article 264), where the death penalty is directly written into law for 'acts of homosexuality', 'sodomy', or 'acts against nature' (as it is described).

Forms of **indirect discrimination** are commonplace across work organisations, too. An office job advertising for someone with more than ten years' experience indirectly discriminates against young people, who will not have been able to gain that many years' experience by virtue of their age, though they may still have all the other necessary skills and qualifications. Indirect discrimination happens when a policy or practice that is applicable to everyone within a workplace puts some individuals or groups at a disadvantage, leaving them worse off than the majority. Another example of indirect discrimination is when employers do not make reasonable adjustments for employees with disabilities. Indirect discrimination can also result from negative stereotyping, where the typical image of the disabled employee, for example, is based on them having lower productivity, more time off work, and a greater dependency on co-workers (Noon et al., 2013). The failure to accommodate people with disabilities is common practice in workplaces around the globe. Breen and Forwell's book *Disability in the workplace: the politics of difference* (2023) shows there are perceived barriers to employing persons with disabilities across work organisations, and changing these perceptions requires, among other things, increased representation of people with disabilities to challenge ableist ideas about how work should be organised. In her book *Disability Harassment at Work*, Buckley (2022) reveals the importance of intersectionality when understanding how disabled women are mistreated in the workplace. While people with disabilities are generally less likely to be employed, women with disabilities are even less likely to be employed than men with disabilities. These inequalities are exacerbated by the fact that disabled people are more likely to be on lower incomes and have precarious contracts and are less likely to protest to management against any mistreatment at work (Buckley, 2022).

In the opening chapter to Part 2 of the book – Chapter 3, 'The Gender Pay Gap' – Velija and McDonough examine why are women paid less (on average) than men. As a prime example, the chapter focuses on UK legalisation on the gender pay gap, including the implementation of gender pay gap reporting. Drawing on various feminist approaches and using a figurational sociological perspective, McDonough and Velija theorise why low wages are explained as 'natural', by showing how the pay gap is facilitated by sexism in the workplace (including other factors such as sexual harassment) that simultaneously disadvantages women in the workplace. The chapter also reveals the typical ways in which many multinational corporations celebrate and even boast about equality and the roles of women within their company, when in fact their own gender pay gap still leaves women behind men in terms of pay. An excellent example of this is illustrated by the 'gender pay bot' (an AI program that automatically reports data on gender pay gaps), which provides comparative evidence on how companies can be challenged in the public domain – shaming work organisations to have a real impact on change. Many people across society, and even within organisations themselves, do not see the gender pay gap. Even when people are made aware of it, they fail to question why it exists, or simply believe it is inevitable. It is for sociologists to identify, question, and challenge such assumptions.

In Chapter 4, 'Racial Discrimination at Work', Prakasam discusses racial prejudice, examining the factors that contribute to racial inequalities in the workplace. Drawing on a case study of the Wellcome Trust, a global charitable foundation, the author shows how racial inequalities are perpetuated, via normalised racist discourses that both people and organisations 'tap into' and which are inherent in everyday work culture and social life. The chapter draws on critical race theory and other theories that help to make sense of racism at work. By doing so, Prakasam reveals how important concepts such as 'intersectionality' and 'inequality regimes' help us to understand and nuance how racial discrimination and prejudice manifest themselves in workplace culture.

In Chapter 5, 'Precarious and Gig Work in the Global Economy', McDonough and Pearson lay out the different types of non-standard work which can be seen in countries all over the world. Seasonal work (employment during specific seasons of the year), fixed-term contracts (non-permanent employment which has a set start and end date), and agency work (not working directly with an organisation, but via a third party) are just some of the types of precarious work discussed in the chapter. Commonsense perceptions of work, the stereotypical conceptions we have of working people, focus on the idea that individuals find a career and have employment for the rest of their lives. Challenging this normative perception of work, McDonough and Pearson argue that most people will hold multiple jobs in their working lives (sometimes simultaneously), and at certain times throughout their lives people will have to take up precarious forms of work whether they want to or not. It is easy to talk with individuals and listen to how they 'get on with it' and even enjoy or take pride in the work they do. But we are missing something crucial if we do not 'think sociologically' (Bauman and May, 2019) and see that what drives these conditions are not individuals themselves, but global economies which are market-driven. A market-driven society benefits from a system in which workers can easily be 'hired and fired'. Precarious work affects all social classes as it cuts across different sectors and socioeconomic categories.

Discrimination by age is taken up in Paraskevopoulou's Chapter 6, 'Age Discrimination in the Workplace'. While the Equalities Act of 2010 offers protection for age discrimination, sociological research nonetheless shows that there are still people being treated differently by work organisations because of their age. Although inequality can affect people of all ages, the author shows how it can significantly impact younger and older people in relation to their conditions of work, including security, pension, pay, or career opportunities. Ageism can also have a detrimental effect on people's lives, their health and well-being, as well as on society as a whole. The chapter examines the different definitions of ageism through a multidisciplinary lens and provides an insight into both scholarly and policy-making approaches. Adopting an intersectional approach, the chapter investigates the degree to which age interacts with other characteristics, such as gender or race and ethnicity, resulting in greater workplace injustices.

Part 2 of the book concludes with Chapter 7, Santos's 'Migrant Sex Work and Survival Sex'. Highlighting the 'cost of living' crisis, the author examines debates around people's agency over whether to work or not and the types of work they do to earn 'good money'. Such is the invisibility of sex work that many campaigners and sociologists claim it is often not recognised as 'work', and this adds to a lack of workers' rights (or lack of rights) in the sex industry. Even prior to the COVID crisis, the reduction of welfare support has impacted on the number of women turning to 'survival sex', by working in the sex industry out of desperation. Amidst this context, Santos draws attention to migrant sex workers, whose circumstances exacerbate the risks, desperation, and exploitation many women in the sex work industry experience.

Organising People and Well-being at Work

Part 3 of this book asks readers to consider the ways in which people are organised at work and how this might impact on mental health and well-being. We are so familiar with hierarchal organisational structures that we rarely dispute or challenge them. This **normalisation** of work practices means, for example, that we know who the various team leaders, supervisors, and managers are within an organisation and know we usually must follow the directives or orders given. Failure to comply with a work organisation's rules and processes can result in sanctions. These can range from being 'out of favour' and sidelined by managers, to being 'spoken to' (an informal reprimand), or having more formal proceedings, like written warnings and disciplinary proceedings. In Chapter 8, 'Managing People and Democratisation of Organisation', Green and McNeill challenge the traditional layered structure of management hierarchy and propose new ways of organising work. They use the term 'democratisation of organisation' to describe a model of organising work whereby power is redistributed, and employees have more autonomy over workplace practices. Employees are rarely motivated by being 'talked down to' or 'bossed about'. Rather, employees want to feel empowered in the work tasks they are involved with in their everyday lives. They provide multiple examples of businesses that are experimenting with alternative models of organisation and reflect on how this affects their employees.

The theme of management and leadership is discussed further in Chapter 9, 'Women Leaders in Male-Dominated Industries'. Authors Hansch and Janning-Backfisch show how perceptions of management have tended to be male perceptions ('Think Manager, Think Male'). This perception, and corresponding attitudes, have contributed to women being underrepresented in executive bodies and management positions. However, in work organisations today, traditional leadership competencies are changing. Drawing on their own research and expertise in this area, Hansch and Janning-Backfisch show how many organisations find that issues in the workplace can be better resolved by turning to women leaders (as opposed to male leaders), who have more desired leadership qualities and competencies to manage a contemporary organisation. Using the example of logistics work, the authors show that traditional masculine qualities can come across as 'harsh' and outdated for a modern workplace. Traits like 'wisdom' and 'compassion', for example, were seen as important for management roles, and both were present more often in female leaders than male leaders in the studies and literature presented by the authors. It is important to remember that the chapter focuses on *perceptions* of women and men in leadership positions – it traces how men and women managers are seen by others in industries such as logistics.

In Chapter 10, 'Work–Life Balance', Xu and Kelliher explore the relationship between an individual's work and non-work life. Drawing on examples from

Brian McDonough

China, the chapter shows how both culture and national policies surrounding work–life balance and flexible working differ from country to country, and can alter employees' experience of the work–life balance. The chapter shows that organisational culture, such as working long hours, can be detrimental to the uptake of work–life balance policies. Xu and Kelliher provide three arguments for implementing work–life balance policies within organisations. There's a business case, which sees workers happier and more productive, helping to look after and retain good staff. There's a legal case, where policy is influencing work organisations to take work–life balance more seriously. And then there's also a social case, where looking after employees' work–life balance is seen as part and parcel of corporate social responsibility. However, while there are many arguments for creating a better work–life balance, the authors show that there are complexities in creating organisational policies that can sometimes exacerbate inequalities rather than resolve them.

Part 3 ends with Chapter 11, 'Well-being and Mental Health at Work', where author Hudson shows why workplaces must continue to improve how mental health, well-being, and provisions for disabilities are managed at work. Drawing on the notion of the 'ideal worker', the chapter reveals how organisations perceive disabled workers as being less productive and therefore less employable than non-disabled workers. With the 'ideal worker' as the yardstick for performance and productivity, disabled workers are often constructed by what they are unable to do. While organisations might improve through better policy and provisions, some disabilities are not visible and may be overlooked and unsupported, and many disabilities and mental health problems are not disclosed to employers, often because of stigma and fear of workplace detriment.

Digitalised Work

Digital technologies are now an important part of work around the globe. Part 4 focuses on how these technologies reconfigure the experiences of workers in what we call digitalised work. In Chapter 12, 'Digitalised Work', author Benjamin outlines the multifaceted ways in which information and communication technologies, digital platforms, and artificial intelligence change and reshape the ways in which people work. While traditional jobs, like manufacturing, may have become digitalised by robots or automatic systems (such as in car manufacturing plants), even service sector and people-facing jobs like university lecturing are also becoming increasingly more digitalised. Consider the courses designed and written up online, or the ways in which students have their work assessed. Even waiting staff working in restaurants use digital platforms to order food and accept payment. However, in this chapter, Benjamin also maps out digital work connecting the Global North and Global South, examining why the digital economy has become a dominating force in global capitalism.

The proliferation in the use of the internet has reorganised the sex work industry and therefore the working lives of sex workers. In Chapter 13, 'Sex Work in the Digital Age', Rand draws on the voices and experiences of sex workers to examine how the internet, and related technologies, has altered commercial sex markets. Unlike Santos's discussion of migrant sex work and survival sex in Chapter 7, Rand turns the attention to the digital platforms themselves, revealing how digitally mediated forms of sex work can provide both opportunities and drawbacks for workers in the industry. The author draws on her own primary research with sex workers to examine fully the changing shape of the industry.

In Chapter 14, 'Blogging and Online Work', Parry and Hracs examine the digitalised solidarities among bloggers and other online workers in response to challenges in a changing labour market that can often separate workers physically from one another. Blogging and online work is big business, drawing on the activities of millions of people from around the globe. Parry and Hracs show how blogging blurs our commonsense ideas about work, such as having specific time allocations (nine-to-five working hours), or set places where work takes place. Since many bloggers see the work as an addition to, or complementary to, their main job, blogging interrupts boundaries between paid and unpaid work, since it is difficult to pinpoint if and in what ways bloggers may have financially benefited from the online work they do. The chapter connects to previous chapters on precarious work, but also paves the way for discussions around unpaid work.

In Chapter 15, 'Unpaid Work', Taylor shows that, at a local level, unpaid work can range from internships of small companies to figureheads of large aid organisations. Unpaid work can be found across the private, public, and non-profit sectors, as well as in community spaces where people often volunteer. Globally, there are workers across every country who are unpaid, though Taylor draws particular attention to how technology permits workers to connect internationally, involved on digital platforms where both paid and unpaid work take place. One example given is open-source labour, where open-source software shares its code in publicly accessible depositories, allowing software developers to build, develop, and bug-fix software but without necessarily being paid for the work. Ultimately, Taylor shows there is nothing intrinsic to a task that means it is not paid. Rather, and importantly, the author shows us that unpaid work must always be understood by the context and the social relations in which it is located.

Workforce Marginalisation

Part 5 of the book focuses on the ways in which different groups of workers, or workforces, can become marginalised. The term 'marginalisation' is most fitting to the chapters in this part of the book, since they discuss workers who have become demeaned, denied access, or socially excluded. This part of the book provides readers with an opportunity to examine detailed examples of workforce marginalisation, and each of its three chapters focuses on particular social groups: migrant workers experiencing xenophobia in South Africa; seafarers experiencing exploitative working conditions in the shipping industry; and workers at the US–Mexico border who, living in turmoil, lack both employment and human rights.

In Chapter 16, 'Xenophobia and the Migrant Labour Force', author Duvenage examines the experiences of migrant workers who have travelled to urban centres

Brian McDonough

to find work. Drawing on a case study from Johannesburg, South Africa, the author examines xenophobia (prejudice of those from other countries) by using the term '*Makwerekwere*', a derogatory and dehumanising term for 'foreigner'. The chapter explores the identity politics of 'insiders' and 'outsiders', which is contextualised historically by apartheid, a system of separateness where groups of people were racially segregated for half a century in South Africa. Exploring tensions around identity and 'unbelonging', the author examines how issues of poor working conditions, low wages, and lack of security are key features of migrant workers seeking work.

In Chapter 17, 'Inequalities of a Global Workforce: The Shipping Industry', Devereux describes the inequalities in the international shipping industry. One major problem identified by the author is that workers on the same ship often have different employment terms and conditions. This means that some workers are paid less for the same amount of labour. Some workers also have to work much longer shifts than others. The issue stems from multinational crewing, where workers of multiple nationalities work on board the same ship, and different employment terms are adhered to by varied nations from around the world. Devereux's chapter perfectly illustrates why we need to understand work from a global context.

In Chapter 18, 'Global Relations and Workers at the Border', López examines the role global markets play in creating places at borders and in border corridors, where people endure precarious and exploitative labour arrangements such as low pay, long hours, and a lack of human rights. López examines how workers at the US–Mexico border experience various forms of discrimination, sexual harassment, sexual violence, and death. These conditions stem from **neoliberalism**, a type of global economics taken up in several chapters within this book. Border corridors are ideal laces to build *maquiladoras*, factories for people who are 'caught up' at border crossings, often unable to move on. Vulnerable and desperate, poor, and undocumented migrants are exploited for their labour. Many of the women at the border are silenced and subjugated by gangs and border authorities, prohibiting any chance of breaking the cycle of violence and inequality. The three chapters in Part 5 describe how workers have been mistreated in both the past and present. In contrast, the following part of the book examines how work may change in the future.

The Future of Work

Part 6 discusses the future of work. This final part of the textbook features three important themes central to how we think about work, and are followed by a conclusion. The opening chapter in this part centres on discussions about climate change and why work must change to accommodate a planet with global warming. Chapter 20 centres on how policy might change people's attitudes towards work – focused on the idea of a universal basic income. Chapter 21 centres on changing places of work and links to a post-COVID era with new technologies that change where we work and how we work. The fourth and final chapter, Chapter 22, concludes the book, discussing new ways of work and reflecting on research methods and methodologies used in this book and elsewhere in the study of work and organisation.

Climate change is perhaps the biggest threat to the planet in which we live. In Chapter 19, 'Climate Change and Work', Sahin-Dikmen examines the inextricable relationship between work and climate change. Work is fundamental to combating climate change, because the production of goods and services drives gas emissions, which pollute the planet. Sahin-Dikmen discusses what a move towards a greener economy might mean for work organisations and working lives, illustrated by a case study on workers within the architecture sector, which must now incorporate climate science, climate policy, and legislation.

In Chapter 20, 'Changing Work and Universal Basic Income', authors McDonough and Bustillos Morales discuss how our relationship to work could change if new policies were put in place to provide a safety net that mitigates against redundancy and unemployment, precarious work and inconsistent levels of pay, and care responsibilities, such as for the young and old. Universal basic income provides a welfare provision that gives every citizen a consistent non-means-tested cash income regardless of whether or not they work (work being a contended concept in this book). McDonough and Bustillos Morales' chapter lays out what it is and how it might change people's relationship with work, and draws on examples from around the world, using a case study based in India.

Felstead and Blakely discuss the ways in which where we work have altered since the COVID-19 pandemic. In Chapter 21, 'Changing Places of Work'. First, many people continue to work from home, despite the end of social distancing measures and other restrictions in place during COVID-19-driven lockdown. However, some workers have switched to a hybrid approach, whereby some work from home while also spending time down at the 'office' or another place of on-site work. But Felstead and Blakely show how remote working has accelerated post-pandemic, enabling work to be carried out almost anywhere and at any time, from libraries to cafés, and even while moving from place to place.

In Chapter 22, 'Conclusion: New Ways of Working', the editors and co-contributors of the textbook lay out how work continues to change by outlining some of the emerging trends in the sociology of work. Within this final chapter, there are also discussions of social movements and protests against low wages, poor working conditions, and a lack of rights. These protests differ from country to country, but they are connected via a neoliberal economic agenda that is worldwide. The chapter provides advice on how future sociologists of work may navigate these issues, and provides a reflection on useful research methods and methodologies, many of which were used by the authors of this textbook.

How to Use This Book

This book has been written with a student audience in mind. The chapters are grouped into parts, but they are also 'stand-alone', so the reader need not go start-to-finish with the entire textbook, but rewind or fast-forward to the chapters most relevant to them. Learning is a messy process and there is no single or right way of using what you read. Each chapter in this textbook has a set of key terms with definitions. These terms will be highlighted the first time they are discussed with a definition at the end of that chapter, but they may also be referred to in chapters further in the text. These are provided to give readers maximum understanding of the main concepts used throughout each chapter. Reading over the key terms may help with revision, but they also help to define difficult terms, some of which may raise controversy. The essay practice questions are also for students and lecturers, to use as they feel fit in their learning and teaching.

Each chapter has a case study, used as food for thought and giving readers examples that can be used to enhance their learning and maximise their understanding. The case studies are taken from examples across the globe. Some of them stem from the authors' own investigations, while others draw on the research carried out by others. Many of the student activities draw directly on the case studies, which can be discussed in university or college classrooms.

STUDENT ACTIVITY

Look over the summaries and choose a chapter from the textbook. Then carry out the following activities:

1. Make some notes about the chapter, and plan a five-minute presentation to your classmate to summarise what you have learned.
2. Note down the things from the chapter that were new to you.

Practice Questions

1. What does thinking sociologically mean, and why might it help researchers understand the world of work?
2. Sociological findings can sometimes contradict commonsense perceptions about work or a work issue. Discuss, and give examples from the textbook.

Key Terms

Commonsense
thoughts, beliefs, and actions which are commonsensical are often shared by large numbers of people (hence the term 'common'), and provide a set of assumptions about the world we live in. Sometimes sociological findings can contradict commonsensical beliefs.

Direct discrimination
refers to explicit rules that prejudice groups of people or individuals. During the 1960s some landlords infamously wrote signs on the door saying, 'No Irish, no blacks, no dogs', purposely to exclude certain groups. Some jobs can directly discriminate, too, by insisting firefighters are of a certain height or that only men may apply, for example.

Indirect discrimination

asking for someone with ten years' experience to apply for a job might indirectly discriminate against young people. Indirect discrimination is common across work organisations.

Intersectionality

the ways in which social aspects of our identity intersect, often to exacerbate social inequalities, such as social class, ethnicity, gender, age, disability, sexuality, religion, and a whole range of other factors.

Neoliberalism

refers to a global economic approach of free market capitalism – with the intention of global wealth spreading prosperity – by allowing markets to 'let rip' and do as they please. The idea is that neoliberalism works best when there is less intervention from governments, who can create tariffs and trade barriers to control prices or protect local industry. Some see neoliberalism as creating economic growth, although others see it as a root source of inequality. (Note: this term appears in many chapters throughout this textbook.)

Normalisation

the process of making situations or practices appear normal, when in fact they may be considered peculiar or strange. A good example is the normalisation of a typical five-day working week, which is rarely questioned.

Social scientific perspective

using the social sciences (scientific research and evidence), as opposed to relying on commonsense or everyday understandings.

Sociological thinking

sociological thinking or thinking sociologically involves drawing on the skills of a sociologist, in being critical, objective, and taking a step back from the world.

Taken for granted

the routine way most laypeople experience the world. Because work culture is so taken for granted, sociologists must make visible what is often 'invisible' (difficult to observe), by drawing on research and gathering data.

References

Bauman, Z., and May, T. (2019) *Thinking sociologically*. London: Wiley-Blackwell.

Booth, R. (2022) 'Job discrimination faced by ethnic minorities convinces public about racism: study finds exposing' inequalities in applications for employment "catches racism red-handed"'. *Guardian*, 15 December. www.theguardian.com/money/2022/dec/15/job-discrimination-faced-by-ethnic-minorities-convinces-public-about-racism

Buckley, L. (2022) *Disability harassment at work*. Bristol: Bristol University Planet.

Breen, J., and Forwell, S. (2023) *Disability in the workplace: the politics of difference*. London: Routledge.

CSI (2019) Centre for Social Investigation Report New CSI report on ethnic minority job discrimination – Nuffield College Oxford University

ILO (2020) *Wages and working conditions in the banana sector: the case of Costa Rica, Ethiopia, India, Indonesia and Viet Nam*, December. https://doi.org/10.13140/RG.2.2.24891.23845

ILO (2023) 'Forced labour, modern slavery and human trafficking'. *ILO*. www.ilo.org/global/topics/forced-labour/lang--en/index.htm

Noon, M., Blyton, P., and Morrell, K. (2013) *The realities of work: experiencing work and employment in contemporary society*. New York: Palgrave Macmillan.

Oakley, A. (1974) *The sociology of housework*. Bristol: Bristol University Press.

Walker, P. (2023) 'Rishi Sunak apologises for past ban on LGBT people serving in military: PM issues apology on behalf of state in line with recommendation of report on decades-long ban'. *Guardian*, 19 July. www.theguardian.com/uk-news/2023/jul/19/rishi-sunak-apologises-for-past-ban-on-lgbt-people-serving-in-military

Zerubavel, E. (2020) *Taken for granted: the remarkable power of the unremarkable*. Princeton: Princeton University Press.

Inequalities, Intersectionality, and Discrimination at Work

chapter 3

The Gender Pay Gap
Philippa Velija and Brian McDonough

Introduction

This chapter provides a sociological analysis of gender pay gap legalisation which was introduced in 2017 in the United Kingdom (UK) as a mandatory reporting tool for all employers with over 250 employees. The **gender pay gap** (GPG) is calculated as the difference in the average hourly wage of all men compared to all women across an organisation (gov.uk, 2024). This is different from **unequal pay**, which refers to paying men and women differently for performing the same jobs and has been legislated against in the UK since the 1970 Equal Pay act (Equality and Human Rights Commission, 2020). The chapter starts by providing definitions of the terms and calculations used in gender pay gap reporting. Later this chapter provides a *sociological* understanding of the gender pay gap as part of long-term social processes, power, and shame. Finally, a case study is provided to consider the ways the gender pay gap is understood.

Defining the Gender Pay Gap: A UK Context

This opening section defines the gender pay gap, using the example of the Gender Pay Gap (GPG) policy in the United Kingdom (UK). From 2017, employers with more than 250 employees must comply with UK regulation on gender pay gap reporting (Abudy et al., 2023). The aim of gender pay gap reporting legalisation was to increase awareness of gender issues in the workplace and to improve pay equality (ONS, 2018). For those organisations with more than 250 employees, the law mandates both public and private employers must publish and report specific figures about their gender pay gap, which includes the mean and median gender pay gap, mean and median bonus gender pay gap, the proportion of men and women in the organisation receiving a bonus payment, and the proportion of men and women in each quartile pay band (gov.uk., 2020). Private and voluntary sector employers must also publish a written statement reflecting on their data and potential actions on their website about their data. Any organisation not complying with the gender pay gap reporting breaches the Equality Act 2010, and therefore penalties for non-reporting include fines for organisations not complying (CIPD, 2020). Despite the threat of fines for non-compliance, many work organisations fail to comply, either by non-reporting or returning inaccurate reports. In 2018, it is reported that 1,456 companies were contacted with enforcement letters, but, to date, there have been no available details regarding how many organisations have been fined or penalised, and little is known about those not reporting (Barr and Perraudin, 2019). Thus, while compliance is high, some organisations do not comply at all.

The terminology adopted in this chapter is drawn directly from the requirements set out in the UK gender pay gap reporting mechanism. To aid readers unfamiliar with the key terms, they are summarised here. The gender pay gap (GPG) is presented as both mean and median data. The mean hourly rate refers to the average hourly wage across the entire organisation, whereas the mean gender pay gap is a measure of the difference between women's and men's mean hourly wage (CIPD, 2020: 5). Median gender pay gap data provide details on the difference between median earning of men and women. An example can be seen in Table 3.1, which demonstrates how the mean and median data may look different for a company (here, UK supermarket Tesco), and why both datasets are presented.

The bonus proportions are calculated from the proportion of relevant employees (male and female) who were given bonus pay during the year, and the bonus pay gap is also calculated as a mean and median, showing how bonuses are paid in an organisation (gov.uk, 2022). Each organisation must also report on quartile pay bands, which are the proportions of full-pay relevant employees (male and female) in lower, lower middle, upper middle and upper quartile pay bands (CIPD, 2020: 5). These are calculated by categorising all employees in an organisation into four even groups according to their level of pay. The purpose of quartile data is to identify the proportion of women in each pay quarter, which is particularly useful to highlight discrepancies in highest and lowest bands of pay, which roles are likely to be paid more significantly in an organisation, and which might be paid the most. Calculations for the pay gap metrics are based on a single pay period around the 'snapshot date' of 5 April (private and voluntary sectors) or 31 March (public sector). In each year, however, bonus gap metrics cover the 12 months up to the relevant date. Some organisations must submit a written statement, and employers should add a supporting narrative and are encouraged to provide an action plan, but these are not mandated (Acas, 2022). Organisations are encouraged to

Table 3.1 Tesco Stores Limited Report

Data	Women's mean hourly pay compared to men's	Women's median hourly pay compared to men's
5 April 2022	10.1% lower	6.7% lower
5 April 2021	8.8% lower	6.3% lower

Philippa Velija and Brian McDonough

publish an action plan outlining how it will tackle the gender pay gap. In the following section, we summarise recent data from the gender pay gap reports before providing a long-term sociological analysis of this.

The most recent report (ONS, 2023) on the gender pay gap (GPG) highlights that, in the UK, more than 10,000 employers reported data. One reason for publishing data on the GPG is to highlight publicly gender pay discrepancies, but there has been very little impact from this policy of reporting, with little change observed in the GPG data. For example, the median gender pay gap increased from 9.5 percent in 2019 to 10.4 per cent in 2020, showing that the gender pay gap is worse, not better. The mean figure has stayed similar, at 13.3 per cent (CIPD, 2021). To put this in context, the analysis of organisations, ranging from private firms to charities and government bodies, shows that on average women were paid 90.2p for every £1 men earned. There are differences across regions of the UK, with England reporting larger gender pay gaps than Wales and Scotland. Only 65 percent of those submitting data in 2021 provided a report, but there is no obligation or requirement to do so. This is noted in a recent comparative report published by Kings College London, who note that companies should be required to provide an analysis and plan, as well as updates on plans to drive forward change (Global Institute for Women's Leadership and Fawcett Society, 2022). This would require companies to engage more fully with the data and reasons for the gender pay gap, as opposed to just being a reporting mechanism. The gap in median hourly pay tended to be slightly smaller for the largest employers: the average pay gap in businesses with at least 20,000 employees was 9.7 per cent, compared to 12.5 percent in employers with 250 to 499 employees (Francis-Devine and Brione, 2022).

A global gender gap is reported by the World Economic Forum (2022). The global gender gap benchmarks 146 countries, providing a cross-country comparison, and does not just cover pay, but also educational attainment, health, and political empowerment. In relation to work, women are globally more likely to be unemployed and data continue to evidence that women are still the main caregivers for children, and costly childcare impacts disproportionately on women than men when it comes to paid work.

Internationally, the impact of gender pay gap reporting varies and is debatable. For example, Baker et al. (2023) note that the disclosure of salaries at Canadian universities reduced the gender pay gap, whereas Gulyas et al. (2021) note that the Austrian Pay Transparency Law has not impacted on the overall gap. Studies of company pay reporting rules have typically found small reductions in the gender wage gap when reporting measures are accompanied by the threat of sanctions and/or relatively high policy visibility, as is the case in Denmark (Bennedsen et al., 2019). Where enforcement mechanisms or wage gap visibility are weaker, these measures seem to have had fewer effects. While the discussion about gender pay gap reporting has focused on outlining its benefits, discussing data and its impact (from a sociological perspective), other questions could be asked. The following section outlines how a sociological analysis can help us explore some of the complexities in understanding legalisation around gender pay data and how it relates to power relations.

Explaining the Gender Pay Gap: Why are Men Paid More than Women?

Different reasons why men are paid more than women are discussed in the sociology of work literature, which we focus on next. A starting point for understanding the gender pay gap is to understand the cultural values attached to men and women's work (sometimes referred to as **cultural feminism**). While men are seen as exhibiting masculine qualities (being rational, assertive, and authoritative), ideal for the more highly paid management and leadership positions, women are perceived, and 'stereotyped' (Nguyen, 2021: 124), as having feminine 'qualities' (being empathetic, caring, and nurturing), which directs them to roles which are less well paid and often more precarious. Secretarial work, for example, has historically been associated with women, in the UK and globally. Being a PA (personal assistant) often involves being deferential, duteous, and servile to a manager (often male) or management (often majority male). When women do occupy better paid positions, it is not without struggling against what is known as the '**glass ceiling**' (see Stone, 2022: 6), a barrier to advancing one's career which usually affects women, as well as those from certain minority groups. Because of the different cultural values placed upon men and women, they are measured against different expectations, in the sense that a man demanding a pay rise is seen as 'progressive' and 'ambitious' but the same demand from a woman is perceived as her being 'difficult' and 'burdensome'. Workplace culture, in this sense, reflects the same **patriarchal** (male-dominated and male-superior) domestic culture many women have for centuries found themselves in: they are subordinate to their male counterparts' power in a society created by men for men. The result of this cultural inheritance of gendered norms and values is that men find themselves in organisations and roles which have been created from the outset for men. Surgeons, barristers, and CEOs are just some of the jobs that men dominate – and also some of the most highly paid employed roles in the UK.

While the cultural position of men and women is a good starting place for understanding the gender pay gap, there are also other ways of making sense of it. One argument for explaining why women should be in better paid and higher status jobs relates to social justice arguments (Velija and Piggott, 2022; Women on Boards, 2016), which stress matters of fairness, human rights, and gender justice (**liberal feminists** have for a long time fought for gender equality in the workplace). The arguments for gender diversity stem from more progressive thinking around equality for women and reflect the moral and societal values of our time. Such morals and values are always socially constructed and differ from one society to another. However, as ideas around what is 'morally right' or 'fair' change over time, they can be mandated through laws such as the Equality Act (2010), and then also through wider changes to behavioural norms and expectations between groups. For the latter, this requires greater mutual identification, and appreciation between men and women in the workplace.

Perhaps a more pertinent perspective for analysing the gender pay gap is to draw upon **figurational sociology**. A figurational approach to understanding

Philippa Velija and Brian McDonough

power relations adopts a long-term approach to understanding the role of inter-dependence in power relations (Dunning and Hughes, 2012). Interdependence, a key concept in figurational sociology, captures the ways people are dependent on each other (Elias, 1978), and sees power as a structural characteristic of all human relationships (Elias, 1978). This approach emphasises that power relations are fluid, and in flux. The related concept of functional democratisation, used by Elias, captures the social transformation of power relations over a long period of time, towards equalisation. This transformation (which is not necessarily linear) occurs through denser webs of interdependence between groups, which result in diminishing contrasts and increasing varieties between people and group (Mennell, 1998).

When considering gender relations, in work or elsewhere, a figurational approach seeks to understand the increase in mutual identification (when groups have to work more closely together) between men and women to understand the ways (groups of) people exert varying degrees of reciprocal influence and control. In applying Elias to understanding gender relations, Brinkgreve (2004) traces how changes in gender relations can be understood as being related to shifts in caring responsibilities and greater access to labour market occurred through denser chains of interdependence between men and women (Dunning, 1999). This reflects greater reciprocal dependency between men and women in the workplace, whereby men and women have to work together more closely and respect each other's views. As with any power relations, these need to be conceptualised as *moving towards equality*, and not *equal*, as it is important to reflect the ongoing inequalities between groups that continue. Functional democratisation occurs when less powerful groups become more important for relatively powerful groups or when the powerful group is not as relied on by the former. This implies that relations of interdependence become less one-sided and more even (Wilterdink, 2021). Functional democratisation is used by Elias (1978) as a sensitising concept to explain the way power changes over time. He explains how power and interdependence are related to either decreasing or increasing inequality. Changes in power relations, especially when moving towards greater equality may be challenged and resisted by groups who do not value change and may continue to have nostalgic views on how things used to be (Dunning, 1999).

Women's access to the workplace has not been linear, or without resistance, and this has been particularly contested in positions of senior leadership (see also Chapter 9, 'Women Leaders in Male-Dominated Industries'). To be accepted as leaders, women have had to draw on a wider range of behavioural norms as a power resource to justify their roles. These include justification of women in the workplace, attending women leadership sessions which coach women to lead in more traditional accepted ways, as well as frequent advice on dress code. In more recent years, Clayton-Hathway (2021) outlined that the arguments for greater equity in senior management positions have included both business and moral justifications, which suggests that women's involvement at board level may increase business performance with an improvement 'bottom line' (Women's Leadership Foundation, 2022). Clayton-Hathway's report goes on to stress how boards containing more than one woman performed better (economically) than all male boards. This is an example of functional democratisation: on the one hand, more women on boards reflects a shift in power balances in the workplace between men and women; and, on the other, the need for a campaign that stresses the business and economic value women bring to boards reflects the ongoing inequity. The fact that such reports outline the benefit of women to boards demonstrates that women are still not accepted on boards for their contribution to work.

Gender Inequality and the History of Behavioural Codes at Work

While women being in the workplace is a common occurrence in Western societies, women's access to the workplace reflects wider gender relations and struggles. Women's move from being confined to the home to the workplace has been a long-term process. In Wouters' (2004) analysis of women, work, and manners, he discusses a quote from Troubright that shows that, by 1926, changes had been made with regards to women's work: 'there was a time not so long ago when women's interests were confined chiefly to the home. For a woman to be actively engaged in some business profession meant one of two things, either she was an old maid or she was queer' (Troubright 1926, cited in Wouters, 2004: 33).

Wouters (2004) adopts a figurational and long-term approach to understanding gender relations. In *Sex and Manners* (2004), Wouters traced these comments through advice books around behavioural codes at work, using empirical data that chart the changing relationships between men and women in America, The Netherlands, England, and Germany. He provides a detailed analysis of changes in courting (dating), work, intimacy, and the balance of social controls between men and women. In the workplace, Wouters (2004) charts how men and women had to learn to relate to one another regardless of gender expectations and how this changed over the last 100 years. In his analysis of the place of work across different countries, he discusses how advice on women at work historically focused on being feminine and attractive to men. In the 1950s, advice shifted and began to focus on women and the need for them to be wary of being seen as a sexual attraction at work, as exemplified here: 'now that class distinctions in speech, dress, and behaviour are disappearing ... it is much more likely today she will catch the bosses' eye' (Edwards and Beyfus, cited in Wouters, 2004: 42). By the 1960s, Wouters (2004) notes this advice had become outdated, but a constant discussion of the tension between formality and distance in working relations between men and women. Remained.

By the 1980s, another shift became evident. Wouters (2004) noted how business codes and social occasions for advice on relations between the sexes were becoming more synonymous: 'good modern manners dictate that courtesies are extended by everyone to anyone who might welcome them' (2004: 23). By the 1990s advice for behaviour at work was more likely to perceive men as part of the problem, and the office party as a potential hazard for unwanted behaviours. This shift of advice for men and women at work sensitises us to changes in access to, and the behaviour of, people in the workplace. Wouters (2004) demonstrates, through using data from books on manners, how power relations have changed in the workplace over time, and how this relates to how both men and women are expected to behave (and how these expectations also change over time). His book also demonstrates, in the documentation of gendered etiquette, how important these behaviours were considered. Some modern examples would be Dignity at Work policies, which likewise outline behavioural expectations of people in the workplace.

While Wouters' (2004) analysis focuses on behavioural codes, the relationship between these and wider social changes, such as legislation, are interlinked. The emergence of new legislation that seeks to equalise power relations also enforces changes to behavioural codes. For example, in the UK, 2010 sexual harassment at work is deemed as unlawful discrimination in the Equality Act. This signals a change in power relations, as it becomes unlawful, and legislation enables a way for women to report issues of harassment that impact on their success at work. Nevertheless, ongoing inequalities remain, as many cases go unreported. In 2020, the Government Equalities Office published a report on sexual harassment. In this report, 30 per cent of women reported sexual harassment in the workplace, and most incidents were reported in social settings with work colleagues. These incidents demonstrate the ongoing inequality in workplace gender relations that female colleagues experience.

Ernst's (2003) work, which draws on Elias as a theoretical framework, explores the relative exclusion of women from management and leadership positions at work, exploring the ways in which stereotypes about women in business reflect ideas about women, motherhood, and their position in society. Furthermore, there are established and pervasive perceptions of, and stereotypes about, women that reinforce the idea of women's unsuitability to leadership. These often centre on being too emotional or draw on fixed ideas about women's capabilities. In a wider business context, Ernst (2003) notes that a process-figurational approach helps to explain that 'Gender seems to be one of the main dividing and conflicting factors in organisational life' (2003: 280). Her research examines how the dominance of men, and masculine characterisations of effective management practices and processes, reinforce the monopolisation of gender power, leaving high degrees of resistance to gender equity. Changes in power relations between groups also require more moderate and greater self-control in more situations, and this may include regulating inappropriate comments in professional settings.

A more recent example of gender equity in the workplace can be seen during COVID-19 and the unprecedented lockdown faced by many across the globe. On 11 March 2020, the World Health Organization (WHO) declared COVID-19 a global pandemic. Due to high transmission rates, many countries enforced public health measures to reduce the spread of the virus. The UK government implemented various national and local tiered lockdowns, which for many people meant their daily routines were altered, as people had to work from home and children did not attend school. This was a monumental shift in routine for families and workers. During this time inequalities and the gendered division of labour became more apparent (Fisher and Ryan, 2021). For example, mothers reported increased domestic and care work, 5 per cent reduced their paid work hours, and they took on more responsibility for the education of children (Fisher and Ryan, 2021). These issues brought to the fore the continuing inequalities faced by women at work (and home), highlighting the ways that women's access to work was often additional to managing the home, children, and family, in ways that are not always expected of men. Such inequity in care responsibilities for men and women reflect ongoing inequality in gender and family relations, impacting women's access to paid full-time work, which in turn influences the gender pay gap.

The Gender Pay Gap Bot

In what ways might the reporting of the gender pay gap (GPG) impact on work organisations and equality? A key element of legislating the GPG reporting was to publicly expose the gendered differences in pay across organisations in the UK. On International Women's Day (IWD) 2022, an X (formerly Twitter) account called 'Gender Pay Gap Bot', launched by Francesca Lawson, provided data on the gender pay gap of organisations who were celebrating International Women's Day. Whenever a company posted about IWD, the Bot automatically posted their median gender pay gap, revealing that the companies posting about successful women in their own companies were blemished by the fact that, on average, women were paid less than men. For example, professional services firm Deloitte UK posted a story about a successful woman in their organisation, only to have the Gender Pay Gap Bot post straight back that 'In this organisation, women's median hourly pay is 13% lower than men's' (Colvin, 2023: 1).

The exposure revealed how organisations declaring support for events like IWD continue to have extensive gender pay gaps. The Gender Pay Gap Bot used publicly held data to publish an organisation's median hourly pay, aiming to challenge the social media sentiment of so-called empowerment and celebration and highlighting the ongoing inequalities around pay (https://genderpaygap.app/).

The Twitter account demonstrates some of the ways organisations juxtapose their image around equity and gender with the reality of the gender pay gap data, which highlight that ongoing patterns of inequality exist. Thus, gender pay gap legalisation can be seen as a way of trying to enforce or speed up more equitable relations in the workplace. As an employer, having to publish your data as an organisation publicly identifies organisations that have high gender pay gaps. The fact that this topic has evoked such a reaction among some people – given that the Bot has 254,000 followers at the time of writing (2023) on Twitter – illustrates its shame-inducing capacity i.e. being labelled as an 'unfair' or essentially 'sexist' organisation. This indicates the broader attitudinal changes that have taken place concerning gender relations.

We can better understand the role of the Gender Pay Gap Bot if we turn back to Elias (Dunning and Hughes, 2012) and figurational sociology. Elias provides a theoretical analysis of how the emotional levers of shame, embarrassment and stigmatisation, can influence external behavioural regulations. In short, he highlights how people respond to shame in ways that encourage them to modify or change

Philippa Velija and Brian McDonough

their behaviour. Elias (Dunning and Hughes, 2012) demonstrated empirically that, within modern societies, shame has become an increasingly dominant agent of social control, due largely to its progressively taboo and invisible nature. In later work, Wouters (2007) identifies how shame and embarrassment are expressed differently in different cultures and time periods, demonstrating the social construction of these emotions and responses. While shame is often conceptualised as an individual emotional response (Scheff, 2000), there is a social dimension to shame, and we are shamed through interactions with others (Goudsblom, 2016). Shame can also occur as a collective phenomenon (Goudsblom, 2016), and can therefore be used as a way of understanding responses to being embarrassed (if not adhering to behaviour codes of our time).

Elias's observations on shame as a form of social control, and the relationship between shame and embarrassment, offer a useful tool for thinking about gender pay gap reporting. Elias sensitises us to the fact it is not solely an individual response, but how evoking shame can be reflective of social expectations and standards of our time. The Gender Pay Gap Bot continues to be active and, on IWD 2023 once again, it played a role in highlighting and challenging those employers who declared their support for IWD. Interestingly, in 2023, the Gender Pay Gap Bot was amended to make it 'less embarrassing for employers', by also adding the percentage point decrease from the previous year (Ford, 2023). Highlighting the way collective shame can impact on organisations provides an analysis that goes beyond policy to consider the ways shame and embarrassment can be strong levellers for evoking a response.

Overall, reflecting on the example of the Gender Pay Gap Bot shows that many large work organisations produce a great deal of rhetoric on equality, which can be challenged by the data on gender pay gaps. The response by organisations to the posts about their organisation was also telling in understanding what Ernst (2022) calls the contradictions between official agreements of solidarity, gender equality and acceptance of women's rights, and the simultaneous fragile gender order of oppression and power. Some organisations deleted the responses from the Bot, and some deleted their original posts, while others responded with the actions and reflections on their pay gap. This highlights how the issue is accepted and addressed differently by organisations.

Case Study

Asda Supermarket Gender Pay and the Gender Pay Dispute

UK supermarket chain Asda has experienced several issues around gender pay that highlight ongoing gender issues in the workplace (Asda, 2023). While the Asda case focuses on equal pay, not the gender pay gap, it underlines how there are still cases of unequal pay that need resolving. Asda shop workers have been fighting for equal pay, challenging the pay disparity between shop-floor workers (who are mainly female) and those who work in the depot (who are predominantly male). The pay difference between the shop floor and depot is between £1.50 and £3 per hour – a significant sum over a 20-hour (a part-time role) or 40-hour (a full-time role) week. In response, Asda argued that the roles were different and so justified the pay difference. The Asda pay dispute (BBC, 2021) focused on whether the shopworker and depot-worker's roles are similar enough for a case to be considered under equal pay legislation. The Supreme Court ruled they could compare the roles, thus enabling employees to take further action. The argument about pay and gender focuses on the idea that men working in a role in the depot is more valuable than women doing a similar role in stores (front-facing or in the backroom).

While the pay dispute has continued, Asda have focused on reducing gender pay gaps, to illustrate and juxtapose their position by highlighting progress. This highlights the ways in which public data can shame organisations into action. For example, in 2022–2023, women's median hourly pay in Asda was 4.7 per cent lower than men's, which has reduced from 8.9 per cent since the data were first published in 2017–2018 (Gender Pay Gap Service, 2017). In a report on their newsroom website, Asda highlighted that, in order to reduce the gender pay gap, they had focused on increasing the number of female colleagues in senior leadership roles, and they held a six-month development programme to increase female representation. With over 300 women taking part, and 96 female colleagues taking the apprenticeship programme, this demonstrates how gender pay gap data can be problematic for organisations and may drive a response that enacts change. Publicity on an organisation's gender pay gap may evoke a response, especially if that impacts on the business.

Overall, this case study shows that gender pay gap reporting has the potential to impact on organisations to act in ways that show they are committed to equity. These actions may not just be outward-facing, but also impact on those working for an organisation, or seeking employment, as organisations work to show how committed (or otherwise) they are to equitable practices.

Conclusion

The introduction of mandatory gender pay gap reporting reflects a specific time in women's acceptance in the workplace. A sociological analysis understands this legalisation as part of an attempt to address the ongoing long-term power imbalances which continue to impact on women's access to, and acceptance in, the workplace. Elias's approach to understanding power alerts sociologists to focus on power relations between interdependent groups and reciprocal dependency, and therefore gender pay reporting does give women a platform to challenge organisations and a reason for organisations to respond. By obliging employers to look at the data and report them, gender pay reporting requires greater levels of understanding *between men and women in* organisations, so there must be an attempt to understand better how the gender pay gap impacts employees. Employers are forced to see the position of low pay and part-time work, as well as barriers to promotion from the standpoint of women, and to attempt to understand and address inequalities.

Philippa Velija and Brian McDonough

Unlike other perspectives on shame, through a figurational sociological lens it cannot be understood as a solely individual feeling or response, but rather as being reflective of social expectations/standards of the time. Gender pay gap reporting therefore reflects an attempt to mandate those not moving towards equality. Legalisation and policy implementation may encourage both employers and employees to act. Of course, not all people adapt at the same time or in the same ways, and there is also likely to be a timelag before new behavioural ideals (Alikhani, 2014), with some people and organisations resisting attempts to reorganise familiar existing patterns. Yet, by making organisations publish these data, there is a process of shaming those organisations with large pay gap data, while it simultaneously offers an opportunity for other organisations to demonstrate their compliance. This indicates that, while a pattern towards equalisation is apparent, there are some differences across the sectors, although there may be a greater requirement towards compliance over time. However, the complexity of power relations means that these data, while public, can also be pushed behind the scenes in an organisation and privately ignored, or that sentiments can be made about equity while not addressing ongoing cultural issues that continue to marginalise women and limit their access to specific valued jobs with organisations. The extension of gender pay gap reporting to more employers may further support people and organisations to engage in measures that support gender equity in the workplace. As sociologists, we must continue to understand the ways such policy and legal mandating can impact on behavioural norms that support equity in workplaces.

STUDENT ACTIVITY

Using the government website (www.gov.uk/find-gender-pay-gap-data), which hosts all the gender pay data, take a look at the gender pay gap reports from two or three employers over four years. Try to look for organisations that are different and give you comparisons – for example, the NHS, a private company, and a smaller specialist industry company – and look at the reports they have produced. Answer the following questions:

- Create a table with the mean and median gender pay gaps, bonus pay gap data, and quartile data across the four years. How have the organisations' data changed?
- How strong is the narrative they have provided on the gender pay gap?
- Are they apologetic or defensive about their data? How do you know? What language do they use?

Practice Questions
- Explain the significance of the gender pay gap to gender relations in the workplace.
- Explain how the gender pay gap can reflect both power advances and ongoing inequalities in the workplace for women.

Key Terms

Cultural feminism
refers to a perspective that is critical of the ways in which women are construed in everyday life (culture). Cultural feminists consider women as being innately different from men and that the weaknesses associated with being female can be reframed as strengths.

Figurational sociology
'figurational sociology' or 'process sociology' are terms which became attached to a research tradition strongly influenced by the work of Norbert Elias (1897–1990). The central concerns of 'figurational studies' are understanding the connections between power, behaviour, emotions, and knowledge through a (to a greater or lesser extent) long-term perspective.

Gender pay gap (GPG)
calculated as the difference in the average hourly wage of all men compared to all women across an organisation (gov.uk, 2024).

Glass ceiling
an 'invisible' barrier to progressing one's career, usually affecting women, but also those from certain minority groups. Sociologists often discuss how best to break the glass ceiling in order to give women advancement in the world of work.

Liberal feminists
refers to a social group that believes in changing society through liberal democracy, by implementing policies around gender equality, and changing laws to counterbalance the disadvantages experienced by women in society.

Patriarchal
a term referring to a system or set of processes dominated and controlled by men. For example, many workplaces are said to be patriarchal.

Unequal pay
refers to paying men and women differently for performing the same jobs; it has been legislated against in the UK since the 1970 Equal Pay Act (Equality and Human Rights Commission, 2020).

References

Abudy, M.M., Aharon, D.Y., and Shust, E. (2023) 'Can gender pay-gap disclosures make a difference?' *Finance Research Letters*, 52: 103583.

Acas (2022) 'Gender pay gap reporting'. www.acas.org.uk/gender-pay-gap-reporting

Alikhani, B. (2014). Towards a process-oriented model of democratisation or de-democratisation. *Human Figurations*, 3(2), June. https://quod.lib.umich.edu/h/humfig/11217607.0003.202/--towards-a-process-oriented-model-of-democratisation-or-de?rgn=main;view=fulltext

Asda (2023) 'Asda reduces gender pay gap'. *Asda.* https://corporate.asda.com/newsroom/2023/01/13/asda-reduces-gender-pay-gap#:~:text=In%20a%20report%20submitted%20to,7.6%25%20(2021%3A%208%25

Baker, M., Halberstam, Y., Kroft, K., Mas, A., and Messacar, D. (2023) 'Pay transparency and the gender gap'. *American Economic Journal: Applied Economics, 15*(2, April): 157–183. www.aeaweb.org/articles?id=10.1257/app.20210141

Barr, C., and Perraudin, F. (2019) 'Lack of sanctions "makes a mockery" of gender pay gap reports'. *Guardian.* www.theguardian.com/society/2019/feb/28/lack-of-sanctions-makes-a-mockery-of-gender-pay-gap-reports

BBC News (2021) 'Asda workers win key appeal in equal pay fight'. *BBC News.* www/bbc.co.uk/news/business-56534988

Bennedsen, M., Simintzi, E., Tsoutsoura, M., and Wolfenzon, D. (2019) *Do firms respond to gender pay gap transparency?* NBER Working Paper Series. Cambridge, MA: National Bureau of Economic Research. www.nber.org/system/files/working_papers/w25435/w25435.pdf

Brinkgreve, C. (2004) 'Elias on gender relations: the changing balance of power between the sexes'. In S. Loyal and S. Quilley (eds), *The sociology of Norbert Elias.* Cambridge: Cambridge University Press.

CIPD (2020) 'Pay fairness and pay reporting'. Retrieved 1 May 2020 from www.cipd.co.uk/knowledge/strategy/reward/pay-fairness-reporting-factsheet#gref

www.ons.gov.uk/employmentandlabourmarket/peopleinwork/earningsand workinghours/bulletins/genderpaygapintheuk/2023

Clayton-Hathway, K. (2022). Governance and leadership in British horseracing: a gender perspective. In P. Vellija and L. Piggott (eds), *Gender equity in UK sport leadership and governance.* Leeds: Emerald Publishing Limited, 163–178.

Colvin, C. (2023) 'How one bot crusade to explore the UK gender pay gap went viral'. Retrieved 27 April 2023 from www.hrdive.com/news/gender-pay-gap-bot-twitter-2023/644402/

Dunning, E. (1999). *Sport matters: sociological studies of sport, violence, and civilization.* Hove: Psychology Press.

Dunning, E. and Hughes, J. (2012) *Norbert Elias and modern sociology: Knowledge, interdependence, power, process.* Bodmin: Bloomsbury Academic.

Elias, N. (1978) *The civilising process, Vol.1, The history of manners.* Oxford: Wiley Blackwell.

Equality and Human Rights Commission (2020) 'Equal pay'.www.equalityhumanrights.com/guidance/equal-pay#:~:text=claimants%20are%20women.-,What%20equal%20pay%20means,and%20employers%20must%20follow%20it

Ernst, S. (2003). From blame gossip to praise gossip? Gender, leadership and organizational change'. *European Journal of Women's Studies, 10*(3), 277–299.

Ernst, S. (2022). Hidden gender orders: socio-historical dynamics of power and inequality between the sexes. In D. McCallum (ed.), *The Palgrave handbook of the history of human sciences.* London: Palgrave Macmillan. https://doi.org/10.1007/978-981-15-4106-3_52-1

Fisher, A.N., and Ryan, M.K. (2021) 'Gender inequalities during COVID-19'. *Group Processes & Intergroup Relations*, 24(2): 237–245.

Ford, L. (2023) 'Viral gender pay gap bot can be "catalyst" to keep pressure on, says co-founder. *Independent*, 8 May. www.independent.co.uk/tech/people-ryanair-manchester-the-new-york-times-university-b2296194.html

Francis-Devine, B. (2022) 'The gender pay gap'. House of Commons Library. Available at https://researchbriefings.files.parliament.uk/documents/SN07068/SN07068.pdf

Francis-Devine, B., and Brione, P. (2020). 'The gender pay gap'. Research briefing, House of Commons Library. Retrieved 1 May 2021 from https://commonslibrary.parliament.uk/research-briefings/sn07068/

Gender Pay Gap Service (2017) 'Asda Stores Limited: gender pay gap report'. https://gender-pay-gap.service.gov.uk/EmployerReport/AV59NcZc/2017

Global Institute for Women's Leadership and Fawcett Society (2022) *Gender pay gap reporting: a comparative analysis*. Kings College Report. www.kcl.ac.uk/giwl/assets/gender-pay-gap-reporting-a-comparative-analysis.pdf

Goudsblom, G. (2016) 'Shame as social pain'. *Human Figurations* 5(1). https://quod.lib.umich.edu/h/humfig/11217607.0005.104?view=text;rgn=main

Government Equality Office (2020) 'Government response to consultation on sexual harassment in the workplace'. www.gov.uk/government/consultations/consultation-on-sexual-harassment-in-the-workplace

Gov.uk (2020) 'Statutory advice: gender pay gap reporting – information for employers'. Retrieved 1 April 2020 from www.gov.uk/guidance/the-gender-pay-gap-information-employers-must-report.

Gov.uk (2022) *Gender Pay Gap Report: 1 April 2020 to 31 March 2021*. Competition and Markets Authority (CMA), 27 January. Available at www.gov.uk/government/publications/gender-pay-gap-report-2020-to-2021/gender-pay-gap-report-1-april-2020-to-31-march-2021

Gov.uk (2024) ‚Statutory guidance: making your calculations'. www.gov.uk/government/publications/gender-pay-gap-reporting-guidance-for-employers/making-your-calculations#:~:text=Take%20the%20mean%20(average)%20hourly,Multiply%20the%20result%20by%20100.

Gulyas, A., Seitz, S., and Sinha, S. (2021) 'Does pay transparency affect the gender wage gap? Evidence from Austria'. *American Economic Journal: Economic Policy*, 15(2): 236–253.

Mennell, S. (1998). *Norbert Elias: an introduction*. Dublin: University College Dublin Press.

Nguyen, T.D. (2021) 'Gender stereotypes: the profiling of women in marketing'. In J. Marques (ed.), *Exploring Gender at Work*. Cham, Switzerland: Palgrave Macmillan. https://doi.org/10.1007/978-3-030-64319-5_7

Office for National Statistics (2018) 'Understanding the gender pay gap in the UK'. www.ons.gov.uk/employmentandlabourmarket/peopleinwork/earningsandworking-hours/articles/understandingthegenderpaygapintheuk/2018-01-17

Office for National Statistics (2023) 'Gender pay gap in the UK'. www.ons.gov.uk/employmentandlabourmarket/peopleinwork/earningsandworkinghours/bulletins/genderpaygapintheuk/2023

Scheff, T.J. (2000) 'Shame and the social bond: a sociological theory.' *Sociological Theory*, 18(1): 84–99.

Stone, K.L. (2022) *Panes of the glass ceiling: the unspoken beliefs behind the law's failure to help women achieve professional parity*. Cambridge: Cambridge University Press.

Vellija and L. Piggott (eds) (2022) *Gender equity in UK sport leadership and governance*. Leeds: Emerald Publishing Limited.

Wilterdink, N. (2021). 'The question of inequality: trends of functional democratisation and de-democratisation'. In F. Delmotte and B. Górnicka (eds), *Norbert Elias in troubled times: figurational approaches to the problems of the twenty-first century*. Cham, Switzerland: Palgrave Macmillan, 19–42.

Women On Boards (2016) '2016: Women on Boards celebrates years of hard work'. www.womenonboards.net/en-au/resources/boardroom-diversity-index/2016-draft#:~:text=The%20percentage%20of%20women%20on,2015%20to%2021%20per%20cent

Women's Leadership Foundation (2022) 'CEOs for women on boards'. *Women's Leadership Foundation*, February 18. www.womensleadershipfoundation.org/news/ceos-for-women-on-boards

World Economic Forum (2022) 'Global gender gap report 2022'. Retrieved 11 May 2023 from
www.weforum.org/reports/global-gender-gap-report-2022/

Wouters, C (2004) *Sex and manners: female emancipation in the west 1890–2000*. London: Sage.

Wouters, C. (2007) *Informalization: manners and emotions since 1890*. London: Sage.

chapter 4

Racial Discrimination at Work

Naveena Prakasam

Introduction

A report by the Trades Union Congress (TUC) found evidence of widespread racism in the UK labour market, the overwhelming impact of which can be seen through poorer mental health and the lack of career progression among people of colour (TUC, 2022). These TUC findings are not unique and are repeated elsewhere. The impact of racism has been noted across the global context, including the United States (Kaltiso et al., 2021) and Japan (Tsuda, 2022), and has been found to be an international phenomenon (Quillian and Midtbøen, 2021). Feeling discriminated against in the workplace can have a devastating impact on one's health, as well as resulting in lower work commitment (Wingfield and Chavez, 2020). Given its pronounced impact, it is important to comprehend fully the nature of racial discrimination at work.

This chapter focuses on racial discrimination at work. The racial inequalities that are prevalent in everyday organisation and organisations are examined. There are several factors that contribute to racial inequalities at work; for instance, both employers and employees tap into racist discourses, sometimes unknowingly and without effort, meaning that racial prejudice and racist decision-making become part and process of working lives, and as a result these practices contribute to racial stratification, thereby highlighting the fundamental role of organisations in perpetuating racial inequalities. A case study is presented based on Wellcome Trust, a global charitable foundation, which exemplifies these issues.

This chapter explores theories such as critical race theory, intersectionality, inequality regimes, a theory of racialised organisations, as well as postcolonial and decolonial theories, which uncover wider and deep-seated societal racial prejudices and the role they play in racial discrimination at work. It addresses responses

DOI: 10.4324/9781003314769-6

to the challenges of overcoming these prejudices through a discourse of employment policies and work practices. Again, the Wellcome Trust case study is drawn upon as an example of the effectiveness of such policies and practices.

The chapter is structured as follows. First, the definitions of racial discrimination, race, racialisation, racism, and the different ways in which racism might manifest in the workplace, are outlined. Next, an overview of critical race theory is provided. Other notable theories, such as intersectionality, inequality regimes, and a theory of racialised organisations, are subsequently discussed. These theories shed light on macro- (wider structural), meso- (organisational), and micro- (individual) level manifestations of racial discrimination. Relevant empirical studies are reviewed in order to obtain a richer understanding of how racism permeates these levels. Racial inequalities across all these levels are evidenced in the case study, which validates the far-reaching impact of racism both in and beyond the workplace. Postcolonial and decolonial theories are discussed to examine the impact of colonialism on prevalent racial inequalities within the global context. Interventions in scholarship and practice are then critically considered. The case study on Wellcome Trust is explored to elucidate how racist practices and policies not only impact individuals at the organisation but can have a global impact, affecting the wider health and science research sector.

Defining Race

Before discussing theories that help us understand racial discrimination at work, it is useful to clarify and define a few important terms in this section. These include racial discrimination, race, racialisation, racism, institutional racism, and structural racism.

Racial discrimination can be understood as treating individuals differently because of their race. The discrimination may occur directly or indirectly. An example of direct discrimination would be if an individual were not hired for a job due to their race. A policy preventing an individual from being recruited for a job would exemplify indirect discrimination. For instance, if working at a hairdresser's required individuals not to cover their hair, this would discriminate against Muslim women and Sikh men (Equality and Human Rights Commission, 2020). When companies ban certain kinds of hairstyles, such as dreadlocks, even though such policies apply to all employees, they would inevitably have a disproportionate impact on Black employees (Wingfield and Chavez, 2020). The latter is an example of organisational-level indirect discrimination taking effect due to organisational policies.

Race can be viewed as a complex and multidimensional construction and can be understood as a relationship between individuals that is constructed through the distribution of 'social, psychological and material resources' (Ray, 2019: 29). Even though the understanding of race as a naturally occurring biological phenomenon has been abandoned (Murji and Solomos, 2015), the quasi-biological application of race continues to prevail (Greedharry et al., 2020). Quasi-biological in this context refers to the implicitly biological application of race, which has continued despite the recognition that it is a social and cultural construction. One reason for this could be that prevailing analyses about race have not specified what exactly about race is socially and culturally constructed, and how they are so (Hacking, 1999), although this is now starting to change, as reviewed later in this chapter. Racialisation is the application of racial meaning to 'resources, cultural objects, emotions, bodies ... organisations' (Ray, 2019: 29), and racism is the justification of racial inequality, whose overt and covert forms can be seen across various levels in society. An example of racialisation occurring at the macro level would be the production of Latino racialisation due to anti-immigrant laws such as the HB 56 bill in Alabama (historically a state known for racial exclusion, as it practised segregation long after the legal end of slavery). This bill was aimed at curtailing illegal immigration and, on the surface, it appears race-neutral. However, this is a racial project, because of its disproportionate effect on Latino populations due to restrictions on their access to resources (Jones and Brown, 2019). For instance, the bill allows police officers to detain individuals of colour based on a suspicion that they may be undocumented immigrants (ACLU, 2023).

At the macro level, which relates to wider societal systems such as the legal system, education system, as well as various institutions, we are confronted with structural and institutional racism. It is therefore useful for us to differentiate between structural and institutional racism. While these terms are interrelated, they do have certain subtle differences. While structural racism refers to the wider social and political disadvantages that people of colour face, whether it is increased poverty, or more deaths due to the COVID-19 pandemic (see Parolin and Lee, 2022), institutional racism refers to institutional processes, attitudes, and behaviours that discriminate against people of colour. For instance, stop and search processes that discriminate against certain groups would be an example of institutional racism (Lander, 2021).

Now that a few important terms have been defined, the following section proceeds to discuss critical race theory.

Critical Race Theory

This section draws on a school of thought known as critical race theory (CRT), which helps further our understanding of racial discrimination in the workplace. CRT focuses on deep-seated and systemic oppression that makes everyday racism seems normal (Gillborn, 2018), and was formed when a group of activists, practitioners, and legal scholars came together to write about the continued existence of racial inequalities despite the legal changes made after the civil rights movement in the United States (Delgado and Stefancic, 2017). While CRT started off within the legal field, by challenging the race-neutral facade of the law, its usefulness extends beyond the legal system. Derrick Bell, through his anti-racist activism, shaped the field by using his lived experience of resisting racism within the legal system. CRT focuses on lived experiences of people of colour and uses storytelling and counter-narratives to capture their voices to challenge racism (Christian et al., 2019). It is fundamentally based on a realist point of view of racism (Bell, 1995), according to which individuals who are confronted with racism had better have no delusions about the persistence of racial inequality.

Several applications of CRT can be seen in contemporary empirical research. For example, a study explored counternarratives of migration experiences of people of colour, examining how migration flows are moulded by patriarchy, white supremacy, and global capitalism (Golash-Boza et al., 2019). Another study investigated Black women's leadership experiences through their narratives by analysing their accounts to uncover that race, class, and gender are markers of power which reinforce forms of oppression and emphasise the importance of using an intersectional lens (Jean-Marie et al., 2009). An important theory that is connected to CRT is known as intersectionality, which considers multiple intersecting dimensions of inequality. This theoretical lens is explored in the following section.

Intersectionality

This section explores intersectionality, which originated as a means to examine the complex inequalities experienced by Black women in the United States due to their race and gender. It also discusses Inequality regimes, further our understanding of intersectionality, particularly in relation to organisational practices.

The term 'intersectionality' originates from Black feminism (Crenshaw, 1991; Hill Collins, 1990; hooks, 1989) – and has contemporarily become a means of examining intersecting identities (Johansson and Sliwa, 2014; Czarniawska and Sevón, 2008). Within organisation studies, intersectionality is employed to examine how systemic power relations intertwine with identities related to gender, race, class, ethnicity, religion, and age (Holvino, 2010; Zanoni et al., 2010; Liu, 2018), which highlight barriers in career progression among women of colour.

To conceptualise intersectionality, Acker (2006) put forward the theory of inequality regimes. Inequality regimes can be defined 'as loosely interrelated practices, processes, actions, and meanings resulting in and maintaining class, gender, and racial inequalities in particular organisations' (2006: 443), and are characterised by power differentials between those high up in the hierarchy, such as managers and leaders, and those at the lower levels of organisational hierarchy, such as production workers. Those with more power have increased access to resources. Acker (2006) argues that all organisations have inequality regimes. Moreover, over time even those organisations with obvious egalitarian goals develop inequality regimes.

Acker (2006) focuses on three bases of inequalities in theorising inequality regimes, including class, gender, and race. Class is defined by the differential access as well as control of resources, and by its very nature is characterised by inequality. If we were to think of organisations, the CEOs of large organisations would be at the top of the hierarchy in global society, demonstrating that there are similarities between hierarchical positions in organisations and class in the wider context of society. Historically, while gender was integrated with class, this is now less likely the case, as witnessed by the increase of women across organisational class structures. However, organisational processes continue to remain gendered, evidenced by the existence of fewer women in top leadership positions. Race is integrated with class and gender, as racialised individuals were left out from most organisations in the United States, and these organisations went on to shape the class structure of wider society, which was both gendered and racialised. If we were to look at the Financial Times Stock Exchange (FTSE) top 100 CEOs, only nine of them are women (McDonagh and Fitzsimons, 2022), and none of them are women of colour.

According to Acker, inequality regimes in turn lead to the reproduction of complex inequalities based on race, gender, and class. Some of these organisational processes and practices include hierarchies, how work is organised, recruitment and hiring processes, wage setting, as well as informal interactions (Acker, 2006). In line with Acker (2006), a subsequent integrative review by Amis et al. (2020) confirmed that organisational practices including hiring, promotion, compensation, role allocation, and structuring led to the reproduction of organisational inequalities. In fact, these organisational practices worked to create a system of institutionalised inequality. Such practices do not work in isolation but have a cumulative effect (Amis et al., 2020).

This section considered how race – when interlocked with other identities – can lead to a complex reproduction of inequalities, which are heightened due to these multiple categories of difference. Based on these arguments, it can be concluded that organisations are both gendered and racialised. Racialised organisations are discussed in the next section.

Racialised Organisations

Nkomo (1992) argued that management and organisational theory has never been race neutral, and that organisations have been constituted by race. She had therefore proposed that race must be studied as an analytical concept within management and organisation studies (MOS). Nearly 30 years later, Nkomo (2021) argues that there is still significant work to be done to 'elevate race to a significant analytical concept in MOS' (Nkomo, 2021: 216).

This section reviews Ray's theory of racialised organisations. This is followed by a discussion of an empirical study by Wingfield and Chavez (2020) that offers support to this theory through a qualitative investigation of racialised experiences of individuals in the healthcare sector in the United States. Ray (2019) put forth a theory of racialised organisations, which argues, akin to Nkomo's (1992) point, that organisations are fundamentally racial structures, and that race is constitutive of organisations. This means that the formation of organisations, and their processes and hierarchies, are fundamentally racialised. Nkomo and Al-Ariss (2014) provide support to this point through their historical examination of industrialisation, which is associated with white supremacy due to the use of slave labour in mills and factories in the industrial south in the US (Foner and Lewis, 1989). White labour was costlier than slave labour, as white workers were paid more, due to being white and free.

Naveena Prakasam

Ray (2019) calls for bridging the gap between race theory and organisational theory and viewing them in conjunction to grasp fully the role of organisations in the institutionalisation of racism. A more pronounced merger between race theory and organisation theory would help reveal the hidden processes and mechanisms within organisations that ultimately lead to the production of racial stratification. Organisations are key to understanding the processes of racialisation, not just at the organisational level, but across the wider institutional, as well as individual, levels. A greater exploration of these hidden processes through the bridging of this gap between these theories would eventually help organisations to come up with more effective interventions in addressing racial inequalities in organisations (Ray, 2019).

It is useful in this instance to understand broadly what organisation theory and race theory posit, and to examine their differences. Organisation theory sees organisations as race-neutral entities. Max Weber, a classical social theorist, introduced the notion of organisations as rational bureaucracies (Weber, 1978). Following Weber, scholars conceptualised organisations as entities coming together to accomplish rational or extra individual goals. Several conceptualisations of organisation ignore the fact that organisations were established by the exclusion of racial others. An example of such an exclusion includes the obliviousness of organisational dependence on cotton produced by slave labour (see Beckert, 2015; Foner and Lewis, 1989). Institutional theorists do move further, by demonstrating the impact of wider external factors such as legislation on organisations. However, they still fail to see race as an organising principle (Greedharry et al., 2020). Race as an organising principle refers to the manner in which an organisation is formed is embedded within race, where race is an institutionalised field.

Race theory, as seen in the preceding section, focuses on the state, and other macro-level systems, and places emphasis on the idea that racial inequality is institutionalised (Bonilla-Silva, 1997; Feagin and Elias, 2013, as cited in Ray, 2019). However, in doing so, race scholarship has given little importance to the role of organisations in institutionalising racial inequalities (Ray, 2019). For example, it is necessary to consider the processes and practices taking place at the level of the organisation that have in turn led to the racism in the legal system. Despite evidence from race scholarship that racial inequality is institutionalised, the role of organisations in institutionalising racism has not been fully theorised. It is therefore important to recognise that organisations have a fundamental role to play in the reproduction of racial inequality. It is vital to problematise the notion that organisations, hierarchies, and processes are race-neutral, and we must therefore question the operationalisation of race as a personal identity. To exemplify this point further, we can return to the example of how policies on banning certain hairstyles such as dreadlocks would have a disproportionate impact on some employees. Another example would be discrimination occurring in the context of university applications in the US, where Castilla (2022) found that white men applicants were more likely to get application endorsements than women and minorities. One reason for limited exploration of the role of organisations in institutionalising racism is because studies of race in organisations are often done in silos and are removed from the consideration of the wider racialised social systems. While this is now changing (see Wingfield and Chavez, 2020), further work remains to be done in bridging this gap.

Ray (2019) offers four tenets. The first is 'racialized organizations enhance or diminish the agency of racial groups' (26). This means that agency is shaped by an individual's position in racialised organisations. For instance, if there were a higher number of people of colour at the lower end of the organisation's hierarchy, then this would have an impact on factors outside the organisation. Examples of such factors include health, job access, political power, and life expectancy. The second tenet is that the unequal distribution of resources is legitimated by racialised organisations. Historically, this was made possible by the exclusion of racial others through segregated organisations. This has happened implicitly through seemingly neutral bureaucratic processes that created a racialised hierarchy through segregation. The result of such segregation would mean that organisations with a larger proportion of people of colour are under-resourced.

The third tenet is that whiteness is a credential. Credentials are statuses created by organisations to demonstrate suitability for employment. Irrespective of legal restrictions on racial discrimination, due to patterns of thoughts that associate people of colour with poor work ethic and attitudes, employers oppose hiring them. Whiteness is hence seen as a credential, or a form of property which affords individuals further access to resources. The fourth tenet that Ray offers is that 'the decoupling of formal rules from organisational practice is often racialized' (Ray, 2019: 26). Decoupling happens when there is a contradiction between regular organisational routines and policies that are adopted to appease external entities. There are several examples of racialised decoupling. For instance, diversity policies are adopted in organisations as a public relations exercise rather than to genuinely change the racial distribution of organisational power. In terms of resolving discrimination cases, even though there are mechanisms in place to protect minorities, what happens in practice is that organisational policies are decoupled from the wider legal enforcement mechanisms. For example, evidence shows that even individuals that come forward with well-supported complaints get banished. This is because the way organisations respond to complaints is worse than the discrimination that occurs, which can be attributed to racialised decoupling (Roscigno, 2007, as cited in Ray, 2019). In Ahmed's (2021) book *Complaint!*, the author argues that racism is dismissed as a complaint, and as a result is diminished, and even when policies are used as evidence to support a complaint the complainant isn't guaranteed success. Through the examination of oral and written testimonies from students, academics, researchers and administrators in higher education, Ahmed (2021) highlights the contradiction between what is supposed to happen when complaints are made, and what actually happens. In doing so, she reveals the complex institutional power dynamics at play by exposing the formal institutional systems and procedures that are complicit in burying complaints.

A significant takeaway from Ray's (2019) theory is that racial inequality at the macro, meso, and individual levels are interrelated. Moreover, organisations are responsible for reinforcing the enactment of racial meanings occurring at the macro level. It is important to see organisations as fundamentally racialised, which gives rise to questions that would dismantle the existing racial order. Ray (2019) argues that the notion that organisational structures, hierarchies, and processes are race-neutral must be abandoned altogether.

Wingfield and Chavez (2020) found empirical evidence to support Ray's (2019) theory of racialised organisations through their study in the healthcare industry. Their research design involved 60 semi-structured interviews with doctors, nurses, and technicians, and involved participant observation. Wingfield and Chavez's (2020) findings revealed that it isn't just being Black in majority white environments, but an individual's position within the organisation that determines whether they perceive racism to be individual, organisational, or structural. For example, instances of individual-level discrimination were more pronounced among Black technicians. These involve white patients refusing to let Black technicians perform basic procedures or expressing doubts about their skills in general. These technicians also experienced individual discrimination from their supervisors within the organisation, such as being asked to wear a business suit during an interview when no one else was wearing one.

Black nurses experienced individual- as well as organisational-level discrimination. Examples of individual-level discrimination include Black nurses being perceived as lazy and being accused of a poor work ethic. In terms of organisational-level racial discrimination, racialised credentialling was identified. This was illustrated by employers' focus on which schools the nurses went to during the hiring process. Credentials of those who went to historically Black universities and colleges were devalued, which resulted in Black nurses being disadvantaged during such organisational processes such as hiring. Black doctors experienced racial discrimination differently to nurses and technicians. For them, individual-level discrimination was rare. The only exception to this was emergency medicine, which suggests that organisational variation determined racial discrimination. This means that there are organisational factors that determine how racial discrimination is experienced. Black doctors highlighted structural racism, examples of which included barriers of getting into medical schools. Organisational-level racism included hiring processes, which included white candidates being preferred over Black candidates due to personal connections. Access to mentoring was also highlighted as an example of organisational-level racial discrimination (Wingfield and Chavez, 2020).

The differences between the experiences of racism between technicians, nurses, and doctors in this study indicate that the positioned status of individuals determine the type of discrimination they experience, and that variations of perceived discrimination are linked to organisational processes. The theory of racialised organisations recognises that there might be variations between different organisations, as opposed to theories of structural discrimination, which indicates that those systems will always perpetuate racial inequalities (Wingfield and Chavez, 2020).

Postcolonial and Decolonial Theory

This section briefly examines the contribution of postcolonial and decolonial theories in furthering our understanding of race within organisations. Postcolonial theory can be defined as a school of thought that came about because of scholarship from South Asia and the Middle East (Bhambra, 2014), which focused on the impact of colonialism around the world.

Nkomo (2021) argues that postcolonial theory has implications for theorising race in organisations. Colonialism cannot just be relegated to the past; the effects of it can be seen today (see Mignolo, 2007; Pierce and Snyder, 2020; Quijano, 2007) reflected in global economic inequalities emerging from colonialism. The impact of this can be seen in the existing divide between the world's wealthiest and poorest countries. Colonialism enabled the racial stratification of people all over the world, and justified the conquest of lands of non-white races, by positioning it as a 'civilizing mission' (Nkomo, 2021: 216).

Nkomo (2021) puts forward four main implications of postcolonial theory for the understanding of race in organisations. First, we need to understand how racialised structures and practices within organisations are colonially produced. For example, this would involve considering the origins of management theory shaped by colonialism and slavery. Second, instead of examining racial identities from the point of view of social identity, postcolonial theory allows us to understand the role of colonialism in constructing racial identities. Third, intersectional understandings of race in organisations, which incorporate postcolonial feminist perspectives, would shed light on the gendered aspects of race in organisations. Fourth, a decolonial approach could be used to put an end to systemic racism.

Decolonial theory challenges Western and Eurocentric dominance of the existing social order. As Mignolo (2011) highlights, this Eurocentric perspective has created a worldview that the Euro-centred social order is superior to the rest, which has created an asymmetrical distribution of power by creating a hierarchy between races, cultures, and identities. Challenging these West-dominant accounts will help organisations gain back their cultural identities. This has been captured by Jimenez-Luque (2021) in the context of leadership, in which decolonial leadership emerged in a Native American organisation to resist the dominant social order. Emancipatory processes were observed among individuals to bring about social change. The Native American organisation offered health services to the local Native American community by adopting an indigenous approach informed by a holistic approach to health. The emancipatory processes included 'creating a safe place for cultural resistance and decolonization … and providing a platform for collective identity and action' (Jimenez-Luque, 2021: 161).

Hence, both postcolonial and decolonial theories offer important insights challenging the Western hegemony seen in work practices and production of knowledges within organisations, which are intertwined with the construction of race in organisations across the global context.

Naveena Prakasam

Considering Interventions in Scholarship and Practice

The preceding paragraphs have discussed theoretical lenses that highlight the role of organisations in the institutionalisation of racism. It is useful to examine critically policy and practice interventions that are aimed at eradicating racism in organisations. Several anti-racist interventions in large organisations form part of the larger umbrella of diversity. As Nkomo (2021) argues, subsuming race under diversity might dilute discussions on race. What the Wellcome Trust has done (see the case study in this chapter) seems to be an exception, with their specific focus on anti-racism interventions. Even though Wellcome failed to achieve its ambition to be leading anti-racist organisation due the policy and practice contradictions, there were still pockets of good practice that could be identified. Recognising institutional racism is an important first step towards addressing the problem. Their policy interventions at the macro level, which involved embedding inclusive funding criteria as well as representative datasets from low- and middle-income countries, have potential to have a wider global impact. Adopting a decolonial lens, such representative datasets are useful in challenging Western hegemony in research, as knowledge is shaped by unequal power relations between the Global North and Global South (Mignolo, 2011).

Many large organisations, such as multinational enterprises, have embedded diversity policies. Noon and Ogbonna (2021) empirically examined the diversity and inclusion initiatives in a UK division of a multinational enterprise, where diversity had been made a strategic priority. However, the creation of organisational practices to align with the new strategic priority of diversity saw many challenges. For example, it was found that managers lower down in the organisational hierarchy half-heartedly engaged with the diversity agenda. Tensions were also observed in the top management's introduction of mandatory diversity training. Noon and Ogbonna (2021) also found that diversity was viewed as a people management burden, revealing a contradiction between organisational practices and the wider strategy. These findings can be viewed through the lens of Ray's (2019) tenet of racialised decoupling, as discussed in the previous section. There is often a contradiction between wider elements such as legislation, policies, and (in this case) a wider strategic objective on diversity and inclusion, and organisational practices. This is due to organisations being racialised (Acker, 2006; Nkomo, 1992, 2021; Ray, 2019) as well as gendered (Acker, 2006).

There are issues with superficial approaches to addressing racism, such as the adoption of image-enhancing diversity-related exercises. For instance, in the academic sector, it is argued that co-optation of people of colour in equality, diversity, and inclusion committees is giving legitimacy to accreditations and charter marks, which do not ensure safety for people of colour (Dar et al., 2021).

In line with Ray's (2019) tenet of whiteness as a credential (discussed earlier), Swan (2017) argues that whiteness is about power and privilege. However, race is only seen as affecting those of colour within most organisational scholarship. Therefore, it is important to recognise the social construction of racialisation that produces white people as much as it does people of colour (Greedharry et al.,

2020). Within the global context, asking for the production of knowledge to be de-
colonised, Banerjee (2021) argues for dialogic and reflexive collaborative practice
while researching phenomena within the Global North and Global South contexts.
While being reflexive is about self-understanding and being aware of one's own
position and privilege considering the power asymmetries, a dialogical approach,
which involves engaging in dialogue with others, would allow for collaborative
investigation of the Global North–South context. Doing so would challenge the
dominance of Eurocentric Western assumptions in the production of knowledge.
Applying this to our case study below – including people with lived experience, as
well as representative datasets from low- and middle-income countries as a funding
criterion – can help start to address systemic issues in knowledge production.

Case Study

Anti-racism Interventions at a Global Charitable Foundation

This case illustrates examples of racism at structural and organisational, as well as individual, levels. Wellcome Trust is a global charitable foundation in the UK that funds
cutting-edge global health and scientific research. To eradicate racism, Wellcome
had publicly introduced an Anti-Racism Programme and a set of Anti-Racism Commitments. Wellcome's goal was to become a leading Anti-Racist organisation within
the health and science research sector, which would have a global impact within the
wider health and science research sector.

An independent evaluation was carried out to assess the progress of the Anti-Racism
Programme. The evaluation revealed that inadequate progress was made at the Trust,
both internally (as an employer), and externally (as a funder). The report, based on
interviews and focus group discussions, uncovered that there were substantial challenges that would constrain progress on anti-racism if left unaddressed. This would not
only impact the organisation internally, but also influence the wider research sector.

While some positive changes were observed in behaviours and attitudes, it came to
light that Wellcome had in fact allowed institutional racism to worsen, in addition to
failing to implement anti-racism practice. More importantly, it was revealed that, due
to 'harmful action and inaction' (The Social Investment Consultancy et al., 2022: 5),
Wellcome has sustained and aggravated systemic racism within the wider research sector. Among staff that identified as Black and people of colour, 25 per cent experienced
discrimination and unfair treatment due to their identity and 50 per cent felt that performance and promotion decisions weren't made fairly. For instance, performance ratings indicated bias, where white staff received higher ratings as compared to others.
The importance of an intersectional approach to understanding institutional racism is
evidenced by the experiences of women of colour, who were disproportionately impacted. This was particularly the case when it came to career progression. For instance,
a limited number of women of colour were hired into lead/management positions.

Organisational level discrimination involved the organisation design processes,
characterised by inconsistencies, which disproportionately affected staff from minority
groups. For instance, loss of people of colour from certain teams was not adequately
acknowledged. At an individual level, staff experienced microaggressions and other

Naveena Prakasam

forms of informal discrimination, and 40 per cent did not trust Wellcome to handle it appropriately. Moreover, the staff experiencing such discrimination were expected to bear the responsibility of creating change, producing an additional burden for them.

Examples of good practice in the adoption of anti-racism principles were seen in the mental health team. Mental health team is one of the four main areas of focus in Wellcome's research. The team embedded funding criteria around equitable research environment, as well as built-in lived experience expertise, into their projects. For example, such lived experience would include experience of race-based discrimination. They are also actively looking at building a more representative and inclusive dataset, which would consider low- and middle-income contexts. This would have a far-reaching impact on the research space globally.

Good practice was also seen in the Data for Science and Health Team. Some of their actions with a wider impact on global context include representation from diverse countries, including low- and middle-income countries, and improving data diversity. Data diversity can be understood as the extent to which the data within a particular dataset would vary across different dimensions of diversity. For instance, having data from all regions would ensure that the data are in fact representative, to enable better insights and interventions.

Conclusion

This chapter explored key theories that further our understanding of racial discrimination at work. The chapter began by defining race, and the key terms that relate to racial discrimination at work. Critical race theory was explored, which helps uncover deep-seated systemic racism, and is built on the belief that individuals should not have delusions about the persistence of racial inequality and that racist systems and processes are disguised as race-neutral.

Several theories were discussed subsequently. For instance, intersectionality examines the importance of considering interlocking forms of oppression such as gender and race in conjunction. Intersectionality emerged from Black feminism to reveal the complex forms of inequalities experienced by Black women. Inequality regimes were also discussed, proposed as an approach to conceptualising intersectionality underscoring the importance of race, gender, and class in organisations and conceptualising organisations as sites containing inequality regimes. By examining racialised organisations, the chapter examined the role of organisations in institutionalising racism. The focus of race as a foundational principle continued, and the four tenets proposed by Ray (2019) were explored. The chapter reviewed an empirical study that lends support to the theory of racialised organisations in the healthcare sector. This study unveils the role of organisational factors in the experiences of racism across individual, organisational, and structural levels.

Postcolonial and decolonial theories were discussed, as race is inextricably linked to colonialism, and these approaches help us gain a better understanding of how the sociohistoric context shapes race due to colonialism. Interventions in scholarship and practice were then critically examined, while drawing connections to the case study. Through the case study of a leading global charitable foundation, racism was observed at structural, organisational, as well as individual levels. The case study also sheds light on the challenges of implementing anti-racist interventions.

STUDENT ACTIVITY

Based on the case study in this chapter, identify instances of individual, organisational, and institutional racism. Based on the discussion of theories within this chapter, consider how the three are interrelated. The link to the report is https://cms.wellcome.org/sites/default/files/2022-08/Evaluation-of-Wellcome-Anti-Racism-Programme-Final-Evaluation-Report-2022.pdf.

Practice Questions

1. Critically analyse why the conceptualisation of organisations as race-neutral entities is problematic.
2. In what ways, and to what extent, do organisations perpetuate institutional racism?
3. Critically evaluate the importance of an intersectional approach to addressing inequalities at work.

Key Terms

Critical Race Theory
refers to a theoretical lens which examines how race dictates the unequal distribution of resources across social, political, and legal systems.

Decolonial theory
a theory that challenges Western and Eurocentric dominance on knowledge production and practices, and was developed by Latin American scholars.

Inequality regimes
a term introduced by Joan Acker, which broadly refers to a set of interrelated processes and practices that contribute towards furthering inequalities in organisations.

Institutional racism
refers to institutional processes, attitudes, and behaviours that discriminate against people of colour.

Institutional theory
a field of study which focuses on the role of macro level systems such as political, legal, and economic systems on the formation and functioning of organisations.

Intersectionality
a term with origins in Black feminism that refers to the recognition of how multiple intersecting identities, such as gender, race, class, etc. create overlapping systems of discrimination and disadvantage.

Organisation theory
a field of study that is broadly focused on the functioning, processes, and design of organisations and the impact of external environment on organisations.

Postcolonial theory
a theory that focuses on the impact of colonialism and imperialism around the world, and is based on the works of scholars primarily in South Asia and Middle East.

Quasi-biological
refers to being like biological, but not actually biological.

Race
a multidimensional construction that can be understood as a relationship between individuals constructed through the distribution of resources.

Racial discrimination
can be understood as individuals being treated differently due to their race.

Racial stratification
the process of differentiation within a population into hierarchical racial groups, creating structured inequalities.

Racism
the justification of racial inequality.

Rational bureaucracy
a concept put forth by Max Weber; a term that refers to an ideal type of organisation in which goals are achieved through formal rules and regulations.

Structural racism
refers to the wider social and political disadvantages face by people of colour.

References

Acker, J. (2006) 'Inequality regimes: gender, class, and race in organizations'. *Gender and Society*, 20(4): 441–464. https://doi.org/10.1177/0891243206289499

ACLU (2023) 'Analysis of HB 56, "Alabama Taxpayer and Citizen Protection Act"'. *ACLU*. Retrieved 3 June from www.aclu.org/other/analysis-hb-56-alabama-taxpayer-and-citizen-protection-act

Ahmed, S. (2021) *Complaint!* Durham, NC: Duke University Press.

Amis, J.M., Mair, J., and Munir, K.A. (2020) 'The organizational reproduction of inequality'. *Academy of Management Annals*, 14(1): 195–230. https://doi.org/10.5465/annals.2017.0033

Banerjee, S.B. (2022) 'Decolonizing management theory: a critical perspective. *Journal of Management Studies*, 59(4): 1074–1087. https://doi.org/10.1111/joms.12756

Beckert, S. (2015). *Empire of cotton: a global history*. New York: Vintage.

Bell, D.A. (1995) 'Who's afraid of critical race theory'. *University of Illinois Law Review*, 4: 893–910.

Bhambra, G.K. (2014) 'Postcolonial and decolonial dialogues'. *Postcolonial Studies*, *17*(2): 115–121. https://doi.org/10.1080/13688790.2014.966414

Bonilla-Silva, E. (1997) 'Rethinking racism: toward a structural interpretation'. *American Sociological Review, 62*(3): 465–80. https://doi.org/10.2307/2657316

Castilla, E. J. (2022) 'Gender, race, and network advantage in organizations'. *Organization Science*, 33(6): 2364–2403. https://doi.org/10.1287/orsc.2021.1534

Christian, M., Seamster, L., and Ray, V. (2019) 'New directions in Critical Race Theory and sociology: racism, white supremacy, and resistance'. *American Behavioral Scientist*, 63(13): 1731–1740. https://doi.org/10.1177/0002764219842623

Crenshaw, K. (1991) 'Mapping the margins: intersectionality, identity politics, and violence against women of color'. *Stanford Law Review*, 43(6): 1241–1299. https://doi.org/10.2307/1229039

Czarniawska, B., and Sevón, G. (2008) 'The thin end of the wedge: foreign women professors as double strangers in academia'. *Gender, Work and Organization, 15*(3): 235–287. https://doi.org/10.1111/j.1468-0432.2008.00392.x

Dar, S., Liu, H., Martinez Dy, A., and Brewis, D.N. (2021) The business school is racist: act up! *Organization*, 28(4): 695–706. https://doi.org/10.1177/1350508420928521

Delgado, R., and Stefancic, J. (2017). 'Introduction'. In *Critical Race Theory*, 3rd edition. New York University Press, pp. 1–18.

Equality and Human Rights Commission (2020) 'Race discrimination', 20 February. Retrieved 7 December from www.equalityhumanrights.com/equality/equality-act-2010/your-rights-under-equality-act-2010/race-discrimination#:~:text=at%20a%20disadvantage.-,Example%20%E2%80%93,a%20position%20as%20a%20stylist

Feagin, J., and Elias, J. (2013) 'Rethinking racial formation theory: a systemic racism critique'. *Ethnic and Racial Studies 36*(6): 931–960. https://10.1080/01419870.2012.669839

Foner, P.S., and Lewis, R.L. (1989) *Black workers: a documentary history from colonial times to the present*. Philadelphia, PA: Temple University Press.

Gillborn, D. (2018) 'Introduction to vol. I'. In A. Dixson, D. Gillborn, G. Ladson-Billings, L. Parker, N. Rollock, and P. Warmington (eds), *Critical Race Theory in education: major themes in education*, vols 1–4. Abingdon: Routledge.

Golash-Boza, T., Duenas, M.D., and Xiong, C. (2019) White supremacy, patriarchy, and global capitalism in migration studies. *American Behavioral Scientist*, 63(13): 1741–1759. https://doi.org/10.1177/0002764219842624

Greedharry, M., Ahonen, P., and Tienari, J. (2020) 'Race and identity in organizations'. In A.D. Brown (ed.), *The Oxford handbook of identities in organizations*. Oxford: Oxford University Press, pp. 654–668.

Hacking, I. (1999) *The social construction of what?* Cambridge, MA: Harvard University Press.

Hill Collins, P. (1990) 'Black feminist thought in the matrix of domination'. *Black feminist thought: knowledge, consciousness, and the politics of empowerment, 138*(1990): 221–238. Available at https://archive.cunyhumanitiesalliance.org/introsocspring20/wp-content/uploads/sites/50/2019/03/Collins.Black-Feminist-Thought.pdf

Holvino, E. (2010) 'Intersections: the simultaneity of race, gender and class in organization studies'. *Gender, Work and Organization, 17*(3): 248–277. https://doi.org/10.1111/j.1468-0432.2008.00400.x

hooks, b. (1989) *Talking back: thinking feminist, thinking Black*, vol. 10. Boston, MA: South End Press.

Jean-Marie, G., Williams, V.A., and Sherman, S.L. (2009) Black women's leadership experiences: examining the intersectionality of race and gender. *Advances in Developing Human Resources, 11*(5): 562–581. https://doi.org/10.1177/1523422309351836

Jimenez-Luque, A. (2021) 'Decolonial leadership for cultural resistance and social change: challenging the social order through the struggle of identity'. *Leadership, 17*(2): 154–172. https://doi.org/10.1177/1742715020952235

Johansson, M., and Śliwa, M. (2014) 'Gender, foreignness and academia: an intersectional analysis of the experiences of foreign women academics in UK business schools'. *Gender, Work & Organization, 21*(1): 18–36. https://doi.org/10.1111/gwao.12009

Jones, J.A., and Brown, H.E. (2019) 'American federalism and racial formation in contemporary immigration policy: a processual analysis of Alabama's HB56'. *Ethnic and Racial Studies, 42*(4): 531–551. https://doi.org/10.1080/01419870.2017.1403033

Kaltiso, S.-A.O., Seitz, R.M., Zdradzinski, M.J., Moran, T.P., Heron, S., Robertson, J., and Lall, M.D. (2021) 'The impact of racism on emergency health care workers'. *Academic Emergency Medicine, 28*(9): 974–981. https://doi.org/10.1111/acem.14347

Lander, V. (2021) 'Structural racism: what it is and how it works'. *The Conversation.* Retrieved 20 November from https://theconversation.com/structural-racism-what-it-is-and-how-it-works-158822

Liu, H. (2018) 'Re-radicalising intersectionality in organisation studies'. *Ephemera: Theory and Politics in Organization, 18*: 81–101.

McDonagh, M., and Fitzsimons, L. (2022) 'Women Count 2022: the role, value, and number of female executives in the FTSE 350'. *The Pipeline.* https://execpipeline.com/women-count/women-count-2022/

Mignolo, W.D. (2007) 'Coloniality of power and de-colonial thinking'. *Cultural Studies, 21*(2–3): 155–167. https://doi.org/10.1080/09502380601162498

Mignolo, W.D. (2011) 'Geopolitics of sensing and knowing: on (de)coloniality, border thinking and epistemic disobedience'. *Postcolonial Studies, 14*(3): 273–283. https://doi.org/10.1080/13688790.2011.613105

Murji, K., and Solomos, J. (2015) *Theories of race and ethnicity.* Cambridge: Cambridge University Press.

Nkomo, S.M. (1992) 'The emperor has no clothes: rewriting "race in organizations"'. *Academy of Management Review, 17*(3): 487–513. https://doi.org/10.5465/amr.1992.4281987

Nkomo, S.M. (2021) 'Reflections on the continuing denial of the centrality of "race" in management and organization studies'. *Equality, Diversity and Inclusion: An International Journal, 40*(2): 212–224. https://doi.org/10.1108/EDI-01-2021-0011

Nkomo, S.M., and Al Ariss, A. (2014) 'The historical origins of ethnic (white) privilege in US organizations'. *Journal of Managerial Psychology*, 29(4): 389–404. https://doi.org/10.1108/JMP-06-2012-0178

Noon, M., and Ogbonna, E. (2021) 'Controlling management to deliver diversity and inclusion: prospects and limits'. *Human Resource Management Journal*, 31(3): 619–638. https://doi.org/10.1111/1748-8583.12332

Parolin, Z., and Lee, E.K. (2022) 'The role of poverty and racial discrimination in exacerbating the health consequences of COVID-19. *The Lancet Regional Health – Americas*, 7: 100178. https://doi.org/10.1016/j.lana.2021.100178

Pierce, L., and Snyder, J.A. (2020) 'Historical origins of firm ownership structure: the persistent effects of the African slave trade'. *Academy of Management Journal*, 63(6): 1687–1713. https://doi.org/10.5465/amj.2018.0597

Quijano, A. (2007) 'Coloniality and modernity/rationality'. *Cultural Studies*, 21(2–3): 168–178. https://doi.org/10.1080/09502380601164353

Quillian, L., and Midtbøen, A.H. (2021) 'Comparative perspectives on racial discrimination in hiring: he rise of field experiments'. *Annual Review of Sociology*, 47(1): 391–415. https://doi.org/10.1146/annurev-soc-090420-035144

Ray, V. (2019) 'A theory of racialized organizations'. *American Sociological Review*, 84(1): 26–53. https://doi.org/10.1177/0003122418822335

Roscigno, V.J. (2007). *The face of discrimination: how race and gender impact work and home lives*. Lanham, MD: Rowman & Littlefield Publishers.

The Social Investment Consultancy, The Better Org., with advisory from Ngozi Cole, Lyn Cole Consultancy. (2022) *Evaluation of Wellcome Anti-Racism Programme final evaluation report – public*. https://cms.wellcome.org/sites/default/files/2022-08/Evaluation-of-Wellcome-Anti-Racism-Programme-Final-Evaluation-Report-2022.pdf

Swan, E. (2017) 'Keep calm and carry on being slinky: postfeminism, resilience coaching and whiteness'. In *Postfeminism and Organization*. Abingdon: Routledge, pp. 57–84.

Tsuda, T. (2022) 'Racism without racial difference? Co-ethnic racism and national hierarchies among Nikkeijin ethnic return migrants in Japan'. *Ethnic and Racial Studies*, 45(4): 595–615. https://doi.org/10.1080/01419870.2021.1993296

TUC (2022) *Building an anti-racist trade union movement*. Available at www.tuc.org.uk/sites/default/files/2022-09/ARTFReport2022.pdf

Weber, M. (1978) *Economy and society: an outline of interpretive sociology*, vol. 2. Berkeley: University of California Press.

Wingfield, A.H., and Chavez, K. (2020) 'Getting in, getting hired, getting sideways looks: organizational hierarchy and perceptions of racial discrimination'. *American Sociological Review*, 85(1): 31–57. https://doi.org/10.1177/0003122419894335

Zanoni, P., Janssens, M., Benschop, Y., and Nkomo, S. (2010) 'Guest editorial: unpacking diversity, grasping inequality: rethinking difference through critical perspectives'. *Organization*, 17(1): 9–29. https://doi.org/10.1177/1350508409350344

chapter 5

Precarious and Gig Work in the Global Economy

Brian McDonough and Chloë Pearson

Definitions and Types of Precarious Work within a Global Context

Precarious work exists all around the globe in different forms – from seasonal and fixed-term work to agency work and freelancing. The Sherpas, a Tibetan ethnic group based in north of Kathmandu, Nepal, are known for their skills in mountaineering. Recognised for their knowledge and ability to climb freezing-cold mountains, with low levels of oxygen, they are typically employed by Western adventure and mountaineering companies, who pay them to navigate and carry equipment up and down the mountain for Western travellers. Every year, however, many Sherpas get injured, and some lose their lives, working for mountaineering firms who provide little compensation to the families of the injured or deceased. Cultural anthropologist Sherry Ortner (2022: 4) said of the Sherpas: 'They are usually silent partners to the international mountaineers, carrying supplies, establishing routes, fixing ropes, cooking, setting up camps, sometimes saving the climbers' lives, and sometimes themselves dying in the process.'

While mountaineering is a livelihood for the Sherpas, it is usually one kind of precarious work called **seasonal work**, meaning that workers go for months on end without regular income to support themselves and their families. They are seasonal workers whose wages are subject to the sport of mountaineering, with tourists (and/or mountaineering fanatics) wanting to explore the mountainous regions of Kathmandu. Like many seasonal and precarious workers around the world, the story of the Sherpas involves a 'history of strikes on expeditions, from the earliest to the present, for better pay and equipment and – always at the same time – for

DOI: 10.4324/9781003314769-7

more respect' (Ortner, 2022: 4). The example of the Sherpas tells us about seasonal work; just one type of precarious work. However, there are many other types of precarious work, as will be discussed in this chapter.

Fixed-term contracts can be considered precarious because the worker is only contracted for a set period of time. Blanpain et al. (2010: 2) say that 'enterprises worldwide have reaped the advantages of hiring employees on a contractual fixed-term basis, thus derogating from their traditional participation in the social protection of workers and insulating themselves from legal liability for unjust dismissal'. There are numerous examples of fixed-term contractual work. Professional dancers may have a fixed-term contract for the length of a theatre production or show and will be out of work again as soon as the show has come to an end. Van Assche's (2017: 1) study of the Brussels contemporary dance scene in Belgium found that dancers were constantly 'performing precarity' in their working lives on short-term contracts and struggled to survive financially as dance artists. In higher education (HE), fixed-term contracts are also commonplace and, although used for covering maternity leave of some employees, they are often used more broadly by universities just because it is less of a financial commitment to offer permanent contracts (Arday, 2022). The HESA (Higher Education Statistics Agency) reported that, among the academic staff of 2021/22, some 77,475 of them (that's 33 per cent) were on fixed-term contracts (HESA, 2023). In these examples the employee must begin looking for work again, sometimes midway through their contract, bringing uncertainty about pay, location of work, and family commitments (such as where to send their children to school, amidst anxiety around having to move home again).

In the hospitality sector, there are many **agency workers** (sometimes known as indirect workers) doing jobs at festivals, music events, and theatre productions or shows who are employed, not by the organisation itself, but a third-party employer. Agency workers can earn less than permanent members of staff because the third-party agency takes a proportion of the money paid by the organisation. There is a lack of official data on the number of agency workers in the UK, but the *Taylor review* (2017: 24) reported varied estimates of between '800,000 to 1.2 million workers'. Agency staff can be sent from job to job, working different hours week to week, with different people and in different places. Many agency workers are young people (though not all) and gain valuable experience of working with others in diverse environments, but they are often placed on fixed-term or low-hour contracts, not knowing how much they may earn from month to month. Uncertainty around hours and wages can make planning for the future difficult, and important financial actions like applying to a bank for a mortgage to buy one's own home can be impossible without a steady source of income and 'proper' contract. Agency work is rife in Britain's NHS, where healthcare companies are brought in to cover staff shortages and employees are subcontracted.

Although the term '**freelancing**' may sound avant-garde and glamorous (e.g. 'She freelanced for the BBC and other television companies'), the truth is that most freelancing is a way for organisations to 'employ' people without the need to provide holiday pay, maternity and paternity pay, national insurance and pension

Brian McDonough and Chloë Pearson

contributions, and other social security payments that traditional employment contracts require by law (certainly in European countries and the US). According to the UK's National Hair and Beauty Federation (NHBF, 2023) 57 per cent of hairdressers in British salons are freelance. This means they are self-employed, rent space from salons to earn a living, and are not guaranteed a regular income. Many of these hairdressers have the freedom to work hours that suit them, but not all. Freelancing can be precarious, because work is insecure and pay can differ from one month to the next.

This section has introduced some of the different kinds of precarious work and helped to make sense of how one can understand the notion of 'precarious work'. As the examples have shown, precarious work can be understood as a type of employment that lacks the security of a regular or standard job. Terms such as 'insecure employment', 'unstable employment', 'casual employment', 'under-employment', 'atypical work', 'dead-end jobs', and 'low wage work' have been used to describe precarious work (see European Commission Research, 2004; also see Taylor, 2017). Not only does precarious employment provide a lack of social identity and sense of work (Kirk and Wall, 2010), but, as the examples discussed show, it also usually links directly to a lack of personal security. The next section of the chapter discusses the reasons why precariousness is such a key feature of work in contemporary society. It emerges from a type of global economics called neoliberalism. (Note: this key concept is discussed in the following section, but also defined in Chapter 18, 'Global Relations and Workers at the Border'.)

Precarious Work and Neoliberal Economics

A popular perspective represented by many politicians, sustained via the media, and mirrored in public perception, is that individuals in precarious work choose the job they do and enjoy it. However, most people do not choose to work, but *must* work, and the work people carry out is not merely the result of choices that made by individuals and families, which are driven by **neoliberal economics**. The term 'neoliberalism' refers to the ways in which free markets operate around the globe. Milton Friedman (1912–2006) was an influential economist and statistician, whose work *Capitalism and freedom* (1962) was based on a principle of economic and individual freedom. Along with economist Friedrich Hayek (1899–1992), author of *Constitution of liberty* (1960), Friedman would become known as a free market thinker whose ideas would describe a 'laissez-faire' ('let it rip') style of economics in which markets could effectively do as they please. Free market thinkers such as Friedman and Hayek illustrated how free market capitalism could rapidly expand markets, creating economic growth, making use of global markets.

A result of free market policies is that governments around the world are less concerned with intervening in markets and instead in deregulating them. Deregulation essentially means cutting red tape such as the removal of tax duties used to import a product into a country. Governments can intervene with the market by putting higher taxes on competing products and services, but the neoliberal agenda encourages fewer taxes and more free flow of the purchasing of goods and services. In a neoliberal world, the labour of workers is a commodity to be bought and sold, so people can be hired one minute and quickly disposed of the next. With the opportunity to source cheap labour by searching around the globe, multinational companies can exploit contractual conditions, looking for and hiring cheap labourers in countries from around the world. Take, for example, British banks, who have outsourced customer service and office teams abroad for many years. Barclays Bank plc, UK, for instance, has outsourced many call centre workers to India, where it employs some 20,000 workers and where labour costs are much lower than paying local British workers (Neville, 2021). It is not individuals or governments that dictate these relations, but global markets.

While allowing the free market to 'rip' can arguably create economic growth, there are several downsides, including the precariousness of working lives. Markets are unpredictable, so a cheap labour supply in one country may soon be replaced by that of another, meaning that workers are recruited, trained up, and disposed of 'if and when' the market dictates. This puts the idea of 'choosing a career' on hold. In fact, we are more likely to choose several careers today than picking out just one. **Thatcherism** in the 1970s and 1980s was largely based upon free market economics (British Prime Minister Margaret Thatcher even met with the economist Friedrich Hayek to consult on the economy). Thatcher and her Conservative government infamously allowed the closure of most of Britain's collieries, resulting in hardship and mass unemployment in large areas of the UK (and becoming one of the most notorious industrial disputes in British history). In their recent book *The shadow of the mine: coal and the end of industrial Britain*, sociologists Beynon and Hudson (2021) detail the deindustrialisation of Britain and reveal how Thatcherism excluded working-class miners from political and social life (by allowing the mining industry to fall), in favour of letting the neoliberal market do as it pleases.

Perhaps more significantly, the Thatcher era, and the neoliberal ethos which has dominated the Western world since the 1980s, has created a labour market which is almost completely controlled by market forces. With lax labour laws, or ones which intentionally promote 'flexibility' for companies to employ workers using poor contractual conditions, organisations get away with maximising profits at the expense of precarious employment for many workers. The Marxist-influenced economist Guy Standing (2015) defined this new class of global workers as **'the precariat'** ('precarious proletariat'), to denote the commonly insecure and unstable employment conditions workers from around the world, and from all kinds of occupations and industries, were experiencing. Standing (2015: 51) explains that even human labour has become commodified, so that work activities can be 'offshored (within firms) or "outsourced" (to partner firms or others)' to other places and countries. **Outsourcing** fragments the labour process – for instance, careers become disrupted when workers never know if their jobs will be replaced by cheaper labour from abroad, and the ability to plan ahead is limited.

Zero Hours, Online Platforms, and the New Gig Economy

One of the most infamous forms of precarious work is zero-hour contracts (as defined in Parry's Chapter 1, 'Introduction: Reimagining Work and Organisations Post-Pandemic'), whereby workers are contracted to a company but have no hours of work per week guaranteed. These are considered some of the most exploitative forms of relationship between employer and employee, a contract which effectively says to the worker, 'I can pay you if and when I want to.' Zero-hour contracts are commonplace across the globe, where workers never know if their livelihood (earnings) could end at short notice. These types of contracts are ones that the European Commission (2004: 47) say have 'instability, lack of protection, insecurity and social or economic vulnerability'. Some governments around the world recognise the problems with precarious work and aim to tackle it. For example, in 2022, the European Commission stated that 'all workers in the EU will have a right to effective measures that prevent abuse of zero-hour contracts' (2022: 1). This includes 'the right to the predictability of work', 'right to compensation when the employer cancels the work assignment', and 'possibility to request a more stable form of employment' (European Commission, 2019). However, enforcing these rights in Europe are difficult, and largely relies on compliance from organisations themselves. Changes in the EU affect workers from all types of job. Indeed, zero-hour contracts are not just typical working-class occupations – like taxi drivers, retail workers, and seasonal workers – but are also applicable to doctors, lawyers, and university lecturers.

The internet and the use of online platforms not only facilitates a world where casual work can be 'picked up' more easily, but also where workers can be got rid of at short notice. This new kind of working environment has given rise to what has become known as the '**gig economy**' – a term used to describe the workforce labour market where 'on-demand' (Smith and Leberstein, 2015) jobs or 'gigs' are offered on an often low-paid, one-off basis (Duggan et al., 2022). Similar to the 'gigs' of musicians and live performers, gig workers turn up for 'one-off' service and payment. In Britain, The Chartered Institute of Personnel and Development (CIPD) estimates 'that there is approximately 1.3 million people (4% of all employment) working in the gig economy in the UK' (Taylor, 2017: 25). Many examples of gig work can be found in modern economies, including 'Upwork, Uber, TaskRabbit, Fiverr, Just Eat, Airtasker, Amazon Mechanical Turk, Deliveroo, and Freelancer' (Duggan et al., 2022: 7). Online platforms act as intermediaries that provide a steady stream of labour supply. In China, gig workers operate the takeaway services (they call it *waimai*, meaning 'takeout'), and gig work is common among online dating and gaming industries, as well as sales and, of course, taxi services (Baker-Brian, 2022). Delivery services like UberEats and Deliveroo provide takeaway food to customers who prefer to dine at home. The couriers in these companies have, arguably, been exploited by the organisations because of their atypical or non-standard forms of employment. Workers are not given proper employment contracts, but are made to be self-employed, or 'independent' workers (Tassinari and Maccarrone, 2020: 2), submitting their own invoices as if they're separate entities from the organisations that they are part of daily, but not employed by. Couriers on these kinds of contracts are often paid by the job instead of by the hour. They have no paid holidays or sick pay, usually no right to minimum wage, and little protection from dismissal (McDonough and Bustillos Morales, 2020).

The gig economy lacks enforced regulation and standards that more traditional work has, partly because enforcing such regulations with work on online plat-forms can be less straightforward (Stewart and Stanford, 2017). For example, gig workers are expected to have general liability insurance, should a customer or organisational space become hurt or damaged because of actions of the gig worker. While the 'gig economy' creates new jobs and services, it also redirects significant risks and responsibilities from businesses to the workers in the 'gig economy' (Woodcock and Graham, 2020). Gig workers are encouraged (often expected) to seek their own insurance for injury at work, as well as paying into their own private pension schemes. This onus of responsibilities which shift to the individual are part and parcel of a neoliberal economy. When workers complain of lack of pay, poor hours, and bad working conditions, the neoliberal response is to place the responsibility back on to the individual. The onus is on the individual to work harder, find better pay, or locate more work.

Case Study

British Uber Drivers Working in the Gig Economy

Bill has been an Uber driver in London for more than ten years. He says that 'the good thing about being an Uber driver is that if you don't want to go to work, then you don't have to'. He continues: 'I like how flexible I can be. The other day it was my birthday, and I didn't have to go to work, mainly because there was no one telling me I had to go to work.' Gig work provides benefits for workers in terms of flexibility, which Bill perceives positively, but he also acknowledges the fact that days off go unpaid: 'You're the only one that loses out; you earn less money. If I took days off all of the time, then I wouldn't have any money.' Bill works at night, normally starting 'between 16:00 and 18:00' and then stays out working until 'about 02:00–03:00 in the morning'. He states that, when working in the daytime, 'you sit in traffic a lot, so it takes a lot longer to get anywhere', whereas at night 'you could have done four jobs' in the same amount of time of doing one in the day. Bill says that 'your earning power is higher on a Friday night because of Uber's "surge pricing"'. When high de-mand outweighs the supply, Uber prices increase, giving the employee more income. However, when the busy weekend is over, supply outweighs demand, prices become cheap, and there is a lack of business for the driver, who either retreats home with little pay or competes in online queues with other Uber cabs wanting custom.

Because of the nature of the gig economy's on-demand earning, for a 'one-off' service, Bill has calculated that if he works at unsociable hours he can earn more. Some gig work has its risks. Bill explains the risk he has when driving in terms of

Brian McDonough and Chloë Pearson

finances: 'When you go over 20 mph, you're putting yourself at risk all the time, but at the same time you want to be as efficient as you can in terms of time so you can earn more, so sometimes I do break the speed limit, only a little.' Another risk of his work is to his health. Bill explains that, in the past, before electric cars became more commonly used by Uber drivers, many breathed in the smoke and pollution. He adds: 'Taxi drivers and bus drivers die younger because of that reason, breathing in pollution, especially in London.' Despite increased use of electric vehicles by both Uber drivers and general vehicle users, this is now less of a concern, but Bill still says there are risks to his health due to his work. He says he is concerned about 'being unfit' due to 'sitting down all day'. In addition, there are risks to his safety. Bill describes a recent incident where the police were called upon because somebody tried 'to attack me and tried to smash the car up' and that he has 'had quite a lot of trouble over the years', advising to 'always keep the door locked'. This illustrates how such gig work can be seen negatively. Bill describes how the COVID-19 pandemic meant that many people who would usually use Uber were no longer going out, due to many services and destinations being shut during national lockdowns. Bill says, 'There was no work, hardly at all because no one was going out ... some days I would only get one job. You were lucky to earn anything at that time.' Bill said that until recently every Uber driver was 'self-employed' and that means that, in terms of things such as taking holidays, 'we had to budget for that in our earnings over the year'. The same applies to 'funding your own private pension'. Bill's work vehicle also requires him to use his own finances to 'maintain and pay for it, and then insure it. It can be really expensive, but you just have to budget for it.' Bill adds that it is easier to work for Uber than for the taxi industry, because there are fewer regulations to pass. For example, to become a London taxi driver, drivers must complete 'the knowledge' – a test they are required to pass, which covers all routes and roads in London and takes around three years to learn. However, to work as an Uber driver, Bill describes that all that is needed is 'an English test, criminal reference check and then you can apply for a private hire licence. It's much easier.'

In February 2021, the Supreme Court decided that Uber exerted such control over their drivers that they could not realistically be regarded as independent contractors. The ruling said that Uber drivers are *workers* and are consequently entitled to the legal entitlements that workers enjoy. Since, Uber have had to provide certain rights to their drivers, including National Living Wage, holiday pay, and access to a pension. However, being a worker includes having the same total flexibility as someone who is self-employed, by being free to choose exactly when and where you work. According to lawyers who represented the Uber drivers in this case, tens of thousands of UK Uber drivers could still be entitled to compensation for when they were paid below the minimum wage and for occasions when they took any unpaid holiday leave.

Conclusion

Precarious work is a global phenomenon that aligns itself with neoliberal economics – global market forces which drive economic change. The onus is put on individuals to find work and security, but the individual's life chances are usually determined, first and foremost, by global markets. As a result of a market- driven economy, people must be flexible to the types and forms of work they take part in. Gone are the days of a single career: most people in contemporary society must work in different careers as well as taking part in precarious forms of employment in one time or another throughout their lives. For many social groups described in this chapter (including Sherpas, dancers, lecturers, and taxi drivers), precarious work is constant, without any prospect of being awarded a permanent post or standard job.

This chapter described many types of precarious work, including 'gig work', that often operate using online platforms as part of the 'gig economy'. The gig economy is not only characterised by rapid market fluctuation, change, and opportunity (Mulcahy, 2016), but also by precarity (McDonough, 2017; Standing, 2015). The gig economy makes working life precarious for many, because the labour involves instability, insecurity, temporary contracting, and unguaranteed hours, including a lack of social rights and protections (Kalleberg and Vallas, 2018; Rubery et al., 2018). Many 'gigs' are often offered via online platforms (Healy et al., 2017; Duggan et al., 2022), such as the delivery services offered by companies like Deliveroo, or taxi services such as Uber (see this chapter's case study).

The case study, on Uber, reveals many of the issues that precarious workers are faced with in everyday work, including lack of holiday pay, pension, and national insurance contributions. But the ruling by the Supreme Court shows that change is possible and that work conditions can be improved through law and social policy. British Labour Party politician Justin Madders promises to bring in employment protection against atypical work should his party win the 2024 election. And so, although precarious work is likely to stay around for a long time (as the case study reveals), this is not an inevitable way of working and living, but something which is being challenged all the time by workers' rights groups, trade unions, and others who believe that changing precarious work is possible.

STUDENT ACTIVITY

Defining types of precarious work: choose a sector of industry where you might find precarious workers and using the key glossary terms in the opening sections of this chapter, identify as what 'type' of precarious work this may be characterised.

Practice Questions

1. To what extent is precarious work a choice made by individuals or driven by neoliberal economics?
2. The new gig economy is good for workers since it provides flexibility and autonomy. Discuss.
3. Drawing on the Uber case study discussed in this chapter, explain what problems gig workers experience and how law or policy change might improve work arrangements.

Brian McDonough and Chloë Pearson

Key Terms

Agency workers

people who are employed by an intermediary (an agency), who act as a go-between for employer and employee. Agencies will usually take a slice of the employee's wage or place an add-on charge for the employer. Music festivals, one-off shows, and temporary administrative work (sometimes known as 'temping') often involve the use of agencies in these kinds of employment.

Fixed-term contract

a written agreement between employer and employee for a set period. For example, fixed-term contracts are common in higher education, particularly for covering maternity leave, but they are also created to fit in with short-term economic plans for the university, so they need not commit long term to paying workers.

Freelancing

a type of work whereby the worker is usually self-employed, invoicing organisation(s) for the work they carry out on behalf of them. Freelancers should be 'free' to work for multiple organisations, charging them a fee for one-off projects or work they are involved with. But many 'freelancing' jobs are more like standard jobs, where the organisation expects the so-called freelancer to commit to regular hours yet avoids paying their national insurance contributions, holidays, pension contributions, and other provisions standard for a regular job.

Gig economy

workforce labour market characterised by on-demand, one-off, or temporary tasks. Within the gig economy, digital platforms are often used for jobs – found by gig workers and customers requesting them – such as Uber and other ride-hailing apps. Other examples of work within the gig economy include one-off childcare, Airbnb, courier delivery, and freelance photography.

Neoliberal economics

an economic model advocating free markets and supporting economic liberalism. The term refers to a competitive market-driven economy. Neoliberalism is driven by the idea that limited government intervention and regulation in the economy is desirable and economically beneficial.

Outsourcing

the business practice of using a third party to complete task(s) for the business that typically would have once been completed by and within the business. The third party may be an individual worker or a different company. For example, both factory and office work in Western countries is often outsourced abroad, where cheap labour can be found.

Precariat

A new type of class outlined by Standing (2011), characterised by those found in temporary work contracts, lacking occupational identity, and conventional-work wage benefits such as pensions. This new social class emerges from a neoliberalist economy and is typified by job insecurity and precarious work.

Precarious work
refers to insecure, low-paid, temporary labour lacking the social rights and protections found in traditional forms of work. Precarious work and working conditions come with risk, as employment conditions are often unstable.

Seasonal work
labour activity during particular seasons of the year. For example, fruit pickers often find work during the months when fruit is ripe for picking, but may be without work for the rest of the year. For this reason, seasonal work is precarious.

Thatcherism
a political ideology of former British Conservative Prime Minister Margaret Thatcher. It favours competition and the free market, believing in freedom for individuals from governmental and other external-authority intervention to the economy. Associated with neoliberalism.

References

Arday, J. (2022) '"More to prove and more to lose": race, racism and precarious employment in higher education'. *British Journal of Sociology of Education*, 43(4): 513–533.

Baker-Brian, A. (2022) 'Getting giggy with it: the rise of China's gig economy'. *Thatsmags*. www.thatsmags.com/beijing/post/34771/china-s-gig-economy-growth

Beynon, H., and Hudson, R. (2021) *The shadow of the mine: coal and the end of industrial Britain*. London: Verso.

Blanpain, R. Nakakubo, H., and Araki, T. (2010) *Regulation of fixed-term employment contracts: a comparative overview*. Bulletin of Comparative Labour Relations, no. 76. Aalphen aan den Rijn, Netherlands: Kluwer Law International.

Duggan, J., et al. (2022) *Work in the gig economy: a research overview*. Abingdon: Routledge.

European Commission Research (2004) *Precarious employment in Europe: a comparative study of labour market related risks in flexible economies*. ESOPE. Available at: https://op.europa.eu/s/zLgJ [Accessed: 23 January 2020].

European Commission (2019) *Towards transparent and predictable working conditions*. https://ec.europa.eu/social/main.jsp?langId=en&catId=1313

European Commission (2022) *Transparent and predictable working conditions*. https://ec.europa.eu/social/main.jsp?langId=en&catId=1313

EU (2022) *The EU in 2022: general report on the activities of the European Union*. https://op.europa.eu/webpub/com/general-report-2022/en/

Friedman, S., and Laurison, D. (2019) *The class ceiling: why it pays to be privileged*. Bristol: Polity Press.

gov.uk (2018) 'Ethnicity facts and figures: unemployment'. Accessed: 23 January 2020 from www.ethnicity-facts-figures.service.gov.uk/work-pay-and-benefits/unemployment-and-economic-inactivity/unemployment/latest

Healy, J., Nicholson, D., and Pekarek, A. (2017). 'Should we take the gig economy seriously?' *Labour & Industry: A Journal of the Social and Economic Relations of Work*, 27(3): 232–248.

Higher Education Statistics Agency (HESA) (2023) 2022/23 collection. *HESA*. www.hesa.ac.uk/innovation/data-futures/202223-collection

Kalleberg, A.L., Vallas, S.P. (2018) 'Probing precarious work: theory, research, and politics'. *Research in the Sociology of Work*, 31(1): 1–30.

Kelly, S. (2011) 'The pros and cons of self-employment in the hairdressing sector'. *The Independent*. 1 July.

Kessler, S. (2018) *Gigged: the gig economy, the end of the job and the future of work*. New York: Macmillan.

Kirk, J., and Wall, C. (2010) *Work and identity: historical and cultural contexts*. Palgrave Macmillan.

McDonough, B (2017) 'Precarious work and unemployment in Europe'. In S. Isaacs (ed.), *European social problems*. London: Routledge, pp. 95–112.

McDonough, B (2020) 'Coronavirus-poverty, precarious work and the need for a universal basic income' *Discover Society*, 26 March. https://discoversociety.org/2020/03/26/coronavirus-poverty-precarious-work-and-the-need-for-a-universal-basic-income/

McDonough, B (2021) 'Precarious work, the new gig economy and unemployment'. In S. Isaacs (ed.), *Social problems in the UK: an introduction*. London: Routledge.

McDonough, B., and Bustillos Morales, J. (2020) *Universal basic income*. London: Routledge.

Merton, R.K. (1938) 'Social structure and anomie'. *American Sociological Review*, 3(5, October): 672–682.

Merton, R. (1957) *Social theory and social structure*. New York: The Free Press.

Mulcahy, D. (2016) *The gig economy: the complete guide to getting better work, taking more time off, and financing the life you want!* New York: HarperCollins.

Mulheirn, I. (2013) 'The myth of the "welfare scrounger"'. *New Statesman*, 15 March. www.newstatesman.com/business/economics/2013/03/myth-welfare-scrounger

National Hair & Beauty Federation Ltd (NHBF) (2023) www.nhbf.co.uk/home

Neville, S. (2021) 'Barclays shifts call centre operations to UK from India due to Covid crisis'. *Evening Standard,* 30 April. www.standard.co.uk/news/uk/india-barclays-jes-staley-new-york-canary-wharf-b932610.html

Ortner, S. (2022) *Sherpa: stories of life and death from the forgotten guardians of Everest*. London: Cassell.

Rubery, J., et al. (2018). 'Challenges and contradictions in the "normalising" of precarious work'. *Work, Employment and Society*, 32(3): 509–527.

Smith, R., and Leberstein, S. (2015). *Rights on demand: ensuring workplace standards and worker security in the on-demand economy*. New York: National Employment Law Project.

Standing, G. (2015) *The precariat: the new dangerous class*. London: Bloomsbury.

Standing, G. (2021) 'Rescuing the concept of precarity'. *Social Europe*, 7 September. www.socialeurope.eu/rescuing-the-concept-of-precarity

Stewart, A., and Stanford, J. (2017) 'Regulating work in the gig economy: what are the options?' *Economic and Labour Relations Review*, 28(3): 420–437.

Tassinari, A., and Maccarrone, V. (2020) 'Riders on the storm: workplace solidarity among gig economy couriers in Italy and the UK'. *Work, Employment and Society, 34*(1). https://doi.org/10.1177/0950017019862954

Taylor, M. (2017) 'Good work: the Taylor review of modern working practices'. *Gov.uk*. www.gov.uk/government/publications/good-work-the-taylor-review-of-modern-working-practices

Van Assche, A. (2017) 'The future of dance and/as work: performing precarity'. *Research in Dance Education* 18(2): 1–15.

Woodcock, J., and Graham, M. (2020) *The gig economy: a critical introduction*. Bristol: Polity Press.

chapter 6

Age Discrimination in the Workplace

Anna Paraskevopoulou

Introduction

Stereotyped beliefs and prejudices about physical appearance can play a role in the way we are being treated in the workplace. Gender, skin colour and ethnic background are potential sources of advantage or disadvantage in employment. **Age** is another, and discrimination on the grounds of a person's age can affect employees at different stages in their working life. In discussing age discrimination, it is important to consider the term '**ageism**', which has been used since the 1960s. Ageism can be directed at all ages and refers to the way we think, feel, or act towards people from different age groups. **Discrimination** based on ageist views, policies, or structures has been illegal in the UK since 2006 following the introduction of Equality Framework Directive 2000/78/EC and was incorporated into the Equality Act of 2010.

This chapter focuses on age discrimination: how it manifests itself in the workplace and its impact on employees. The first part of this chapter looks at the different definitions of ageism and age discrimination, the existing legal protection, and the different types of age discrimination the law covers. Examples are provided to illustrate the main points. The second part looks at how theories and policies have been conceptualised. From a sociological approach, policies and the legal obligations of employers can be described as features of the social discourses around equality and diversity and inclusion in modern workplaces, contributing to our understanding of the complexities and multifaceted aspect of age discrimination. This section therefore examines other discourses that complement the study of ageism by considering the significance of different contexts. The third part of this chapter discusses practical recommendations that constitute good practice for organisations to consider. These will help to enhance the organisational image and

DOI: 10.4324/9781003314769-8

organisational culture and provide protection for both employers and employees. The final section of the chapter provides a case study that illustrates how age discrimination unfolds in workplaces as well as the way it is being internalised by employees. Intersectional elements of the case study are also considered. Some revision activities help the reader to revise the main points raised in the chapter, but they also highlight areas for further investigation for those that have a particular interest in the study of **equality, diversity,** and **inclusion** (EDI). The final section concludes with a glossary of key terms and relevant organisations.

Definitions and Main Concepts of Ageism and Age Discrimination

Ageism, as a term, was arguably first used by Robert Butler (Achenbaum, 2015), who defined it as a 'process of systematic stereotyping or discrimination against people because they are old, just as racism and sexism accomplish with skin colour and gender' (Butler, 1975: 4). Ageism manifests itself at both individual and organisational levels, leading to discrimination against older people in various aspects of life, such as housing, health, and accessing services in general. In terms of employment, age-related discriminatory practices can relate to retirement policies or biases in the hiring process that exclude older people. Current literature focuses on ageism as a discriminatory practice, mostly being described as age discrimination, and defined as actively excluding people from **access to employment, organisational structures,** systems, and processes, or as a prejudice that leads to the formation of attitudes and **stereotypes** (Andersen and Taylor, 2011). The two concepts are often used interchangeably.

Regularly perceived within the context of demographic change, age discrimination is increasingly recognised as an important problem in contemporary society, and consequently policy-makers and international organisations have introduced policies that raise awareness about the causes and effects of age discrimination on individuals, organisations, and across societies. According to the International Labour Organization (ILO), there has been a significant demographic change across the world's population and it is estimated that, by 2030, there will be more people above the age of 60 and most will be living in developed societies (ILO, 2013). In its Centenary Declaration on the Future of Work, the ILO accepted that such demographic changes would shape the future of work in the same way as other factors, like climate change and globalisation. This declaration was adopted by the 108th International Labour Conference in 2019.

However, age biases and stereotypes have been perceived 'as socially and culturally constructed' (Krekula et al., 2018: 37) and can be experienced by any age group, not just older employees. Ageism, therefore, has been conceptualised within a range of contexts, such as the media, workplace, education, and policy, and includes all ages (Snape and Redman, 2003), showing that both old and young people experience discrimination in the workplace and in other areas of life because of their age. In fact, a recent study reported that 26 per cent of British adults experienced some form of age prejudice, and this proportion is higher than prejudice

Anna Paraskevopoulou

based on any other characteristic (Abrams et al., 2018). Despite the high number of people reporting age discrimination, ageism is not yet considered as a serious form of discrimination, nor is it treated seriously. This is reflected in tribunal data in England and Wales where 1,770 decisions were taken between 2017 and early 2023 on age discrimination under the Equality Act 2010, compared to 4,031 decisions for race discrimination and 2,946 decisions for sex discrimination during the same period. Many age-related tribunal claims are withdrawn or not proven. However, these data are not unexpected: age discrimination is a newly recognised characteristic, in comparison to race or nationality, and therefore there is still less awareness about it.

A simple and useful definition is provided by Ayalon and Tesch-Römer (2017: 1), whereby ageism is defined as 'stereotypes, prejudice, or discrimination against (but also in favour of) people because of their chronological age'. Ageist attitudes are developed, shaped, and reproduced in all aspects of everyday life. They are part of the lived experiences of individuals of any age. In the workplace, they can potentially play a pivotal role in decisions around recruitment, promotion, or redundancy, but they also influence appraisals and decisions on rewards, training, and development as well as day-to-day interactions with managers and other employees (Shore and Goldberg, 2004).

Stypińska and Turek (2017) distinguish between 'hard' and 'soft' age discrimination experienced by older people; however, the conceptualisation can be equally applied to younger employees. This categorisation is a useful analytical tool that helps us better understand the effects of age discrimination on individuals and the type of practices developed by employers to tackle age discrimination. 'Hard' age discrimination relates to harmful practices directly related to people's working life; for example, not being hired or promoted, or actively being excluded from processes because of their age. 'Soft' age discrimination refers to stereotypes that tend to be both common and universal, and they can be positive or negative. However, according to Stypińska and Turek, both can have a detrimental effect on individuals and can lead to 'hard' discriminatory practices.

In 2021, the World Health Organization published a report on ageism, highlighting that older and younger workers can be disadvantaged in the workplace because of existing stereotypes. The report (see Table 6.1) lists examples of existing and widespread stereotypes (positive and negative) in relation to employment.

Table 6.1 is representative of most findings on age discrimination research in the UK and worldwide, as well. Such perceptions are often normalised and employed in evaluating each other (Finkelstein and Truxillo, 2013). They can therefore have a positive or negative impact on employees, on how they engage in the workplace (Kulik et al., 2016), how they are being treated and managed, or how policies are designed and implemented in organisations (Bal et al., 2011), and these perceptions have an impact on the way people view themselves. Internalising these stereotypes can pose **barriers** to individuals' career paths and chances to benefit from wider opportunities. They can also disrupt work operations: for example, communication, interactions, and knowledge exchanges between different generations (Fasbender and Gerpott, 2021).

Table 6.1 Age Stereotypes in the Workplace

Stereotypes in the workplace	Young	Old
Positive	• Energetic • Ambitious • Tech-savvy • Hard-working (middle-aged)	• Reliable • Committed • Experienced • Hard-working • Socially skilled • Good mentors and leaders • Able to deal with change
Negative	• Narcissistic • Disloyal • Entitled • Lazy • Unmotivated • Easily distracted	• Incompetent and unproductive • Unmotivated • Resistant to change • Harder to train and unable to learn • Not flexible • Not technologically competent

Source: World Health Organization (2021: 4).

Workplace disparities based on age tend to persist even after qualifications, skills, and competences and other human capital factors are taken into consideration. Age discrimination can relate to other inequalities based on class and social background, health, or housing; therefore, an intersectional approach (looking at other inequalities that intersect) is often adopted in both academic and policy-oriented research. Discriminatory practices at work cannot, therefore, be explained by focusing on simple or single factors, as in most cases discrimination and inequalities are embedded in organisational cultures and structures. For this reason, the study of ageism is both versatile and multidisciplinary, attracting the attention of sociologists looking at the ageing processes and intergenerational patterns as well as social structures, cultures, and agency. Economists tend to focus on the labour market outcomes and evidence of taste-based discrimination or statistical discrimination. Psychologists study ageist behaviours, attitudes, and the effects of stereotypes. Organisational studies look at formal and informal processes and structures, the role of leadership, strategy, human resource management systems, **organisational cultures**, and climates. Finally, employment relations scholars consider power dynamics and the role of trade unions.

Age Discrimination and the Law

Following the European Council Directive 2000/78/EC, 27 November 2000, the UK incorporated age discrimination legislation into the Equality Act 2010. The law provides protection against unfair treatment to both job applicants and employees because of their age. Individuals should not be discriminated against because (EHRC, 2020):

- they are (or are not) a certain age or in a certain age group
- someone thinks they are (or are not) a specific age or age group (discrimination by perception)

Anna Paraskevopoulou

- they are connected to someone of a specific age or age group (discrimination by association).

According to the Equality Act 2010, age groups can be wide – for example, people over 50 or under-18s – or they can be specific – for example, people in their mid-40s (EHRC).

There are four main types of age discrimination.

1. Direct discrimination occurs when people are treated differently at work because of their age. This can include being denied access to promotion because an individual is considered too old, or a job applicant not being offered a job because they are considered too young. However, there are some exceptions to the law (known as 'objective justifications') and an individual may not be hired for a job because of their age when there is proof that health and safety may be at risk.

___

Example

Mark is a manager in a large engineering company and is looking for a new employee to join its IT team. The company has recently purchased a new and complicated software system for its IT operations. Mark instructs the HR manager to exclude older candidates, because it is unlikely that they will understand the new software. Mark's position assumes that only young employees can understand new technologies and it therefore discriminates against older workers. The action is unlawful.

___

2. Indirect discrimination can happen when policies are introduced by an organisation that put people at disadvantage because of their age; for example, training and development being offered to recent graduates only. If an employer can prove the necessity of a particular policy (an objective justification), then indirect discrimination may be permitted. The recognition of indirect discrimination by the law is essential, because it takes into consideration the importance of identifying and protecting against subtle and complex forms of discrimination that can be more harmful than the direct and easily identifiable derogatory behaviours and discriminatory practices.

___

Example

The manager of 'Get Active' gym is advertising for additional staff to provide induction sessions to new members. The advertisement is asking for people with at least five years of experience. Unless the manager can justify the need for five years' experience, the advertisement may indirectly discriminate against young people entering the labour market.

___

3. Harassment is when employees are humiliated, offended, or degraded because of their age or the age of someone they are associated with – for example, a partner. There are no objective justifications for harassment; however, if incidents of harassment occur in the workplace and the employer can prove that adequate measures were taken to prevent such behaviours, then the victim is not able to claim for age discrimination, although it is possible to do so from the harassers.

Example

Mira is a recent graduate who has joined a hospitality organisation. Most employees are over 30 years old, although there is a good number of employees in their early 20s. There is a regular office joke about the 'snowflake generation', their attitudes to work and their expectations. Mira feels uncomfortable, because of comments being made daily by the majority of employees. This is a form of age-related harassment, because the employer is not acting to change the organisational culture.

4. Victimisation is when people are treated differently because they have made a complaint under the Equality Act 2010, or they have actively supported someone who has made a complaint.

Example

John is a member of a small team in a sales organisation. The team works well together and for the last three years outperformed everyone, generating large profits for the organisation. The manager decided to promote members of the team as a reward for their performance. Maya, however, was told that she will not receive a promotion because she is near retirement and there is no point. John finds this unfair and makes a complaint. The manager remembers this, and cancels a training course that John was booked to receive. This is an example of victimisation.

The Equality Act 2010 also makes provisions for when different treatment – because of age – is justifiable. Examples include the advertisement, recruitment, and selection of an individual for a post when a particular age group is essential, such as a young actor to play the role of a young person. Another example is when the employer decides to take positive action to encourage the development of a group of workers underrepresented because of their age. An organisation may also offer a service to customers, targeting a particular age group – for example, a GP surgery offering flu jabs to people over 60 years old.

The **Advisory, Conciliation and Arbitration Service (Acas)** and the **Equality and Human Rights Commission (EHRC)** are two bodies in the UK that offer updated advice to employers, employees, and individuals about the Equalities Act and the workplace (see Key Terms for more details).

Anna Paraskevopoulou

Conceptualising Age Discrimination and Proposing Solutions

Age has been perceived as different from other socially constructed identities such as gender, race, or religion and beliefs, because, despite the extent of research and literature on the topic, ageism has not attracted as much criticism as sexism or racism (Gendron et al., 2018). It is therefore more tolerated and widespread; it remains unchallenged and is 'ingrained in our culture' (Palmore, 2015: 874). It also affects individuals at different stages of their working lives and careers, putting up different types of barriers and affecting employment status and employment conditions.

Theories of employment discrimination and equality and diversity have been widely utilised to explain age discrimination. According to Budd (2011), different conceptualisations of work itself help us to understand, but also to find solutions for, discriminatory practices based on age or other identities. If work is viewed as an 'economic transaction', then the competitive economic landscape leaves no room for discrimination because organisations that refuse to hire, promote, or provide equal pay for marginalised groups will eventually experience stagnation (Budd, 2011). This is also the main concept behind the 'diversity management' approach, which is based on the recognition that age diversity (and diversity in terms of other categories such as gender or race) of staff brings benefits to the business. Diversity management has evolved to develop an inclusive organisational culture in an effort for organisations to use fully the skills, competences, and talents of their employees as a means of gaining competitive advantage (Kirton and Greene, 2021).

The social justice perspective, on the other hand, is sceptical of the business case arguments and of the effects of discrimination on business operations. Scholars have argued that the inequalities in the workplace are unfair and unjust, and therefore policies must be developed to tackle such practices. The emphasis here is on the 'duty of care', or social duty, employers have for their workers (Kirton and Greene, 2021). This perspective is concerned with the ethical and moral dimension of employment relations, and the scope of diversity at work is about achieving a workforce balance. This is considered a key social goal regardless of whether this makes good business sense. Discussions about 'good employers' or 'good practices' (as we shall see later) are part of this perspective.

The human resource management perspective takes a similar approach and views discrimination as the result of misinformation or limited understanding of the value employees bring to an organisation in the form of experience or talent. From this perspective, effective management of age-diverse teams can increase productivity (Li et al., 2011) and promote innovation (Guillén and Kunze, 2019) because of good communication and diversity of experiences and skills. Policies proposed are based on training and development for minoritised groups to advance their skills and provide better value for the organisation. Training and development are offered to management and leadership teams to gain a better understanding of inclusive practices and the techniques in promoting these. The human resource management perspective also includes gathering and monitoring staff data to evaluate and improve performance, engagement and well-being and innovation. Raising awareness on age-inclusive policies form part of Strategic Human Resource Management (SHRM).

Most studies conducted on diversity include a discussion about multiple forms of discrimination; in other words, they adopt an intersectional approach. Age has often been studied in conjunction with other characteristics, such as race or gender (Drydakis et al., 2023). Intersectionality as a concept was first devised by Kimberlé Crenshaw, an American legal scholar and civil rights activist who challenged existing feminist values in the 1980s. The concept introduced class and race as fundamental to the analysis of women's position (especially black women) in society and the workplace, in contrast to unitary approaches focusing on one social category (such as age). Consequently, intersectionality is very useful in exposing the complexities of social inequalities and can better inform the study of labour market discrimination.

Different Contexts and Impact of Age Discrimination

Gold and Smith (2023) summarise the different contexts and levels where discrimination takes place and that are also applicable to age discrimination.

First, age discrimination can have an impact on the individual – in fact, all employees – during their working life, affecting their career choices and paths, promotions, and whether they receive appropriate training, gain more responsibilities, or simply find a job (Paraskevopoulou and McKay, 2015). At an individual level, when workers internalise these norms and stereotypes, these may affect employee health. It may also result in the occurrence of discrimination, but which goes unnoticed (Laczko and Phillipson, 1990).

Second, organisational discrimination refers to the existence of an organisational culture that tolerates and permits discriminatory practices. This is reflected in more subtle forms of discrimination – for example, in the language used or everyday interactions – as well as in organisational processes, policies, and structures (Jones et al., 2017). Individual employees in organisations may have their own stereotyped views of younger or older workers; however, these may not be shared by organisations. For example, a manager may think that older people should retire in their 60s, whereas the organisation might have a policy of encouraging employees to retire at their own pace.

Third, a broader form of discrimination relates to practices at the institutional level that favour dominant groups while systematically excluding others, often from minoritised groups. Example institutions include the police, army, the health system, and the education system of a country; and examples of policies and practices can be found in the language used, general culture, impact of gender or race, type of contracts offered, or wages earned (Sargeant, 2007). The impact of these is differential treatment, the creation of barriers to accessing services and opportunities, and hence the exclusion of people from vital provisions. An example of institutional age discrimination for older people is limiting access to health and social care, as they are often being referred to generic services rather than services tailored to their needs

(CPA, 2009). In the workplace, institutional age discrimination can take place when, for instance, older workers are excluded from training and development classes.

A fourth type of discrimination listed by Gold and Smith (2023) is **unconscious bias,** based on deep-rooted views and **prejudices,** which we form during our socialisation process, but also in later life because of living in an unequal society (de Paula Couto and Rothermund, 2019). Unconscious bias is reflected in our language, attitudes, and behaviour towards people and in our decision-making. Unlike conscious bias, unconscious bias is difficult to detect and eliminate (Noon, 2018). Organisations often include unconscious bias training for employees and management, and they may take other measures, such as not publishing candidates' names or ages during the recruitment process.

Good Practice

Good practice refers to the different strategies, policies, and approaches that private, public, and third-sector organisations adopt to improve services in a consistent way. These qualify as good practice, because research and evaluation outcomes support their value, effectiveness, and efficiency. More recently, there is also an emphasis on sustainability. Some good practice solutions have been offered to organisations to tackle age bias and discrimination.

Organisations such as the Chartered Institute of Personnel and Development (CIPD), Ageing Better, the Advisory, Conciliation and Arbitration Service (Acas), the Equalities and Human Rights Commission (EHRC), and the House of Commons, make good practice recommendations to employers to introduce structures that promote inclusion and diversity. People professionals, line managers, and leaders all play a key role in designing such policies.

Trade unions are also important in encouraging social dialogue between employers, employees, and government bodies. A study by Paraskevopoulou and McKay (2015) showed trade unions across Europe developed several initiatives to raise awareness on age discrimination and promote policies to tackle it in the workplace. These include: negotiating collective agreements to help employees near retirement age; providing advice and guidance to young people newly entered in the labour market; advice on age-friendly policies; and collaboration with NGOs to provide greater support.

Some good practice recommendations are more generic and refer to equality, diversity, and inclusivity (EDI), while others are specific to the development of age-friendly policies. General recommendations include the development and use of written inclusivity and diversity policies communicated to the staff. These guidelines can provide evidence of reasonable steps taken by the employer and can be used in future tribunal cases. They can also show that the organisation takes its legal and social responsibilities seriously and that it is therefore a desirable place of employment. EDI policies can help with employee engagement and happiness too. Promoting flexible working is another general good practice. This can include offering flexible work arrangements for people with care responsibilities or offering part-time/job-share contracts. Good quality flexible work should be an option rather than a mandatory arrangement.

More age-specific good practice recommendations highlight the eligibility and access to training and development for all age groups, including employees close to retirement. Research has found that all employees benefit from learning how to use their skills and talents better. The same argument is extended to promotions as well as rewards: both should be offered to employees, without taking into consideration how old or how young they are. Employers should not make judgements about fitness for work based on an individual's age. Medical advice should involve occupational health and should be free of prejudices on age and ability to work. In recruitment and selection processes, research has revealed that age does often influence hiring decisions. Good practice recommendations have been offered to improve the recruitment system of organisations. Examples include training the recruitment panel, excluding the age information of candidates during the shortlisting process, and continuous monitoring (Drydakis et al., 2017; Lievens et al., 2012).

Case Study

Ageism in Recruitment: Patricia's Voice

'I have had this job for six years. I love the children and I love caring for them … The work can be difficult at times … But I'm drawn to the job, like a magnet. When the children returned to school after the first lockdown, you could see how much it meant to them … The biggest challenge at work … is the management and the staff … it is the way they treat me. I think I only got this job because they were desperate for staff … When I was going for interviews, I found myself having to explain … and prove myself, because of my age … I had to convince them that I'm fit enough to work. They would ask, "can you do this or can you do that?" or "that's going to be difficult for you". When this school offered me a job, I felt it was because they didn't have anyone else.

'Six years later, other staff have come and gone, and I am still here … When I applied for the job, I told them about my diabetes … But I think they didn't take much notice because they needed somebody like me to start straight away. I work hard … but I am always having to explain myself to managers and younger members of staff when there are things I can't do because of my condition. There is a lot of ignorance.

'They make me feel guilty or question my own ability. Because of this, I have sometimes gone to work when I did not feel well enough, or I am in pain … During the first lockdown I had to shield because of my condition … but when I returned to work in September, younger colleagues who are fit and healthy treated me like I had been on holiday and had a good break. But it really wasn't like that …

'I have another two years before I retire and the government says I am fit enough to work. We are coming into an era where more older people are working and staying for longer in their jobs, and many are in similar situations to me. I talk to other women at work who are older, and they feel like me. The way work is set up makes it difficult for us to do our jobs. But we have so much to offer.'

Centre for Ageing Better (https://ageing-better.org.uk/stories/patricias-voice-ageism-recruitment, accessed 17 July 2023)

Anna Paraskevopoulou

Conclusion: Ageism and the Future of Work

In the last 50 years, the United Kingdom has experienced many changes in terms of production processes and the ways services are organised. The workplace itself has experienced radical transformations, reflecting the demographic and social composition of the workforce, the type of jobs and contracts available, the way we search for jobs, the way in which we view work itself, and the way we protect our rights at work. The incorporation of age discrimination in the Equality Act 2010 is one example. However, despite change and new legislation, as the case study of Patricia (in the preceding section) shows, working people are still discriminated against on the basis of their age.

As a concluding remark, it is essential to consider age discrimination within the wider discussion on the future of work and the evolution of the workplace, characterised by demographic changes and rapid technological advances. There are both challenges and opportunities for organisations in terms of skills, the transfer of knowledge, and ways of working.

As the chapter demonstrated, to achieve **age justice** in the workplace it is important to understand that ageism and age discrimination are manifested in both the structures and the culture of organisations. A more collective approach is needed to address the issue. Developing the right training programmes, promoting age-friendly policies, and creating inclusive workplaces is imperative to tackle the present economic uncertainties and to inform future models that reduce inequalities and discrimination in the workplace.

STUDENT ACTIVITY

Consider the case study on Patricia.

1. Discuss the following:

   a. What are the main challenges that Patricia experiences in her workplace?
   b. Why is age a factor in this case study?
   c. What recommendations do you have to improve Patricia's situation?
   d. Identify the sentences that relate to the internalisation process.
   e. Discuss the effects of the internalisation process on Patricia.

To revise further the main points raised in this chapter, please engage with the following activities:

2. Discuss the different contexts and impacts, considering examples of age discrimination relating to:

   • individual level
   • organisational level
   • institutional level
   • unconscious bias.

3. What do we mean by good practice, and what good practice solutions can you suggest for Patricia's organisation?

4. Researchers found that older women from a BAME background experience discrimination during the hiring process more frequently than do other groups. Which theoretical approach is useful to advance this discussion, and why?

5. According to Furlong et al. (2018), 'the growth of non-standard working was the direct consequence of government policies since 1979 and the desire to improve economic performance through deregulation and increased flexibility for employers. This trend had significant implications for young workers who, in a context of rising youth unemployment, were increasingly under pressure to take non-standard forms of employment.'

Please discuss the following questions:

a. How widespread is non-standard employment in today's society?
b. Is there a link between non-standard employment and age discrimination?

Key Terms

Access to employment
refers to people's employment opportunities.

Advisory, Conciliation and Arbitration Service (Acas)
an independent public body that is funded by the government to provide employers, employees, and their representatives with
impartial advice on employment matters.

Age
one of the nine protected characteristics as defined by the Equality Act 2010. It refers to people belonging to a particular age or a range of ages (for example, 20- to 30-year-olds).

Age justice
the collective action to raise awareness on the systemic and institutional issues of ageism and age discrimination, and to promote collective action tackling it.

Ageism or age discrimination
occurs when people are treated less favourably because of their age. It usually affects young and old people, but anyone can be affected at any stage of their work life.

Barrier
refers to disadvantages for individuals or groups that share the same characteristics.

Discrimination
the unfair treatment of people in relation to protected characteristics (although people can be discriminated in other ways, too, for example, because of their weight or social class). Discrimination can be direct, indirect, and involve bullying and/or harassment.

Diversity

recognises that people are different in ways that are both visible and invisible and that these differences should be valued and respected.

Equality

is about ensuring that everyone has equal opportunities and equal rights regardless of the background or social characteristics.

Equality and Human Rights Commission

the UK's equality body; an independent organisation with prime responsibility to advise and encourage equality and diversity, help to eliminate discrimination, and promote human rights.

Inclusion

refers to the development of policies and practices in the working and social environment that are welcoming to everyone, recognising and celebrating differences and different needs.

Organisational culture

refers to beliefs, norms, values, attitudes, or underlying assumptions shared by people within the same organisation. These can define practices and processes within organisations.

Organisational structure

the way tasks and resources are organised within an organisation.

Prejudice

making assumptions and perpetuating stereotypes, judging people on how they look or on the type of group they belong to.

Stereotypes

views and beliefs about individuals belonging to particular groups, and labelling them in the same way. They can be positive or negative – however, the impact of stereotypes is usually negative.

Unconscious bias

relates to the unconscious beliefs and views we form about people or groups of people because of general societal prejudices. These can lead to positive or negative perceptions about people and can also influence decision-making.

References

Abrams, D., Swift, H., and Houston, D. (2018) *Developing a national barometer of prejudice and discrimination in Britain (119.)* London, Manchester, Cardiff, Glasgow: Equality and Human Rights Commission.

Achenbaum, W.A. (2015) 'A history of ageism since 1969'. *Generations: Journal of the American Society on Aging*, 39(3): 10–16.

Andersen, M.L., and Taylor, H.F. (2011) *Sociology: the essentials*, 6th edition. Belmont, CA: Wadsworth.

Ayalon, L., and Tesch-Römer, C. (2017) 'Taking a closer look at ageism: self- and other-directed ageist attitudes and discrimination'. *European Journal of Ageing* 14: 1–4.

Bal, A.C., Reiss, A.E., Rudolph, C.W., and Bates, B.B. (2011) 'Examining positive and negative perceptions of older workers: a meta-analysis'. *Journals of Gerontology Series B: Psychological Sciences and Social Sciences*, 66(6): 687–698.

Budd, J.W. (2011) *The thought of work*. Ithaca, NY: Cornell University Press.

Butler, R. (1975) *Why survive? Being old in America*. New York: Harper & Row.

Centre for Policy on Ageing (CPA) (2009) *Ageism and age discrimination in social care in the United Kingdom: a review from the literature*. London: Department of Health.

de Paula Couto, M.C., and Rothermund, K. (2019) 'Ageism and age discrimination at the workplace – a psychological perspective'. In M. Domsch, D. Ladwig, and F. Weber (eds), *Vorurteile im Arbeitsleben*. Berlin, Heidelberg: Springer Gabler. https://doi.org/10.1007/978-3-662-59232-8_4

Drydakis, N., McDonald, P., Bozani, V., and Chiotis, V. (2017) 'Inclusive recruitment? Hiring discrimination against older workers'. In A. Arenas, D. Di Marco, L. Munduate, and M.C. Euwema (eds), *Shaping inclusive workplaces through social dialogue*. Geneva: Springer, pp. 87–102.

Drydakis, N., Paraskevopoulou, A., and Bozani, V. (2023) 'A field study of age discrimination in the workplace: the importance of gender and race-pay the gap'. *Employee Relations*, 459(2): 304–327.

Fasbender, U., and Gerpott, F.H. (2021) 'To share or not to share: a social-cognitive internalization model to explain how age discrimination impairs older employees' knowledge sharing with younger colleagues'. *European Journal of Work and Organizational Psychology*, 30(1): 125–142.

Finkelstein, L., and Truxillo, D.M. (2013) 'Age discrimination research is alive and well, even if it doesn't live where you'd expect'. *Industrial and Organizational Psychology*, 6(1): 100–102.

Gendron, T.L., Inker, J.M.S., and Welleford, E.A. (2018) 'A theory of relational ageism: a discourse analysis of the 2015 White House Conference on Aging' *The Gerontologist*, 58(2, April): 242–250.

Gold, M., and Smith, C. (2023) *Where is the human in human resource management*, Bristol: Bristol University Press.

Guillén, L., and Kunze, F. (2019) 'When age does not harm innovative behavior and perceptions of competence: testing interdepartmental collaboration as a social buffer'. *Human Resource Management*, 58(3): 301–331.

International Labour Organization (ILO) (2013) *Report IV, Employment and social protection in the new demographic context*. International Labour Conference, 102nd session. Geneva: International Labour Office.

Jones, K., Arena, D., Nittrouer, C., Alonso, N., and Lindsey, A. (2017). 'Subtle discrimination in the workplace: a vicious cycle'. *Industrial and Organizational Psychology,* 10(1): 51–76. https://doi.org/10.1017/iop.2016.91

Kirton, G., and Greene, A.M. (2021) *The dynamics of managing diversity and inclusion, a critical approach*, 5th edition. Abingdon: Routledge.

Krekula, C., Nikander, P., and Wilińska, M. (2018) 'Multiple marginalizations based on age: gendered ageism and beyond'. In L. Ayalon and C. Tesch-Römer (eds), *Contemporary perspectives on ageism*. International Perspectives on Aging vol. 19. Berlin: Springer Open, 33–50.

Kulik, C.T., Perera, S., and Cregan, C. (2016) 'Engage me: the mature-age worker and stereotype threat'. *Academy of Management Journal*, *59*(6): 2132–2156.

Laczko, F., and Phillipson, C. (1990) 'Defending the right to work: age discrimination in employment'. in E. McEwen (ed.), Age: the unrecognised discrimination – views to provoke a debate. London: Age Concern England, pp. 84–96.

Li, J., Chu, C.W L., Lam, K.C.K., and Liao, S. (2011) 'Age diversity and firm performance in an emerging economy: implications for cross-cultural human resource management'. *Human Resource Management*, *50*(2): 247–270.

Lievens, F., Van Hoye, G., and Zacker, H. (2012) 'Recruiting/hiring older workers'. In W.C. Borman and J.W. Hedge (eds), *The Oxford handbook of work and aging*. Oxford: Oxford University Press, pp. 380–391.

Noon, M. (2018). 'Pointless diversity training: unconscious bias, new racism and agency'. *Work, Employment and Society*, *32*: 198–209.

Palmore, E. (2015) 'Ageism comes of age'. *The Journals of Gerontology Series B, Psychological Sciences and Social Sciences*, *70*: 873–875.

Paraskevopoulou, A., and McKay, S. (2015) *Workplace equality in Europe: the role of trade unions*. London: Routledge.

Sargeant, M. (2007). *Age discrimination in employment,* 1st edition. Abingdon: Routledge. https://doi.org/10.4324/9781315566184

Shore, L.M., and Goldberg, C.B. (2004) 'Age discrimination in the workplace' in R.L. Dipboye and A. Colella (eds), *Discrimination at work: the psychological and organizational bases*, 1st edition. Hove: Psychology Press.

Snape, E., and Redman, T. (2003) 'Too old or too young? The impact of perceived age discrimination'. *Human Resource Management Journal*, *13*(1): 78–89.

Stypińska, J., and Turek, K. (2017). 'Soft and hard age discrimination: the dual nature of workplace discrimination'. *European Journal of Ageing*, *14*(1): 49–61.

World Health Organization (2021) *Global report on ageism*. Geneva: World Health Organization.

Useful Websites

www.acas.org.uk/
https://ageing-better.org.uk/
www.ageuk.org.uk/
https://equalityhumanrights.com/en
www.equallyours.org.uk
www.ilo.org/global/lang--en/index.htm

chapter 7

Migrant Sex Work and Survival Sex

Dina de Sousa e Santos

Sex Work: Unpacking the Terminology

Sex work continues to be a problematic research area, and it is often excluded from debates about work, partly because of its invisible nature and also because of the fact that a lot of the actions associated with sex work are illegal. Prostitution in the UK is legal, but UK legislation is perplexing, because it states that **soliciting**, making money from prostitution, causing prostitution, or paying for sexual services are criminal offences (under the Sexual Offences Act 2003). Therefore, legislation indirectly criminalises women who work as sex workers as well as their clients. In fact, the terminology used in the current legislation only uses the term 'prostitution'. This approach, some argue, denies those that engage in these labours the right to see sex work as a form of work. This chapter unpacks some of these debates.

Sanders (2012) offers a range of examples in her book *Sex work: a risky business,* which illustrates the variety of practices that fall under the umbrella of 'sex work'. She interviews women who work in **indoor sex markets** in Birmingham, UK (licensed saunas, brothels, and working premises), as well as street prostitutes, but also discusses women from New York in the 1990s, who see sex work as 'careers and not a seedy part of their history but of their 'businesses' working out of five star hotels' (Sanders, 2012: 3). The type of work carried out by women working in five-star hotels is in some ways different from the women that the charity Streetlight UK supports in the UK. Working in a five-star hotel implies more safety for the worker and also possibly a higher income, whereas the women working in the streets tend to face a wider range of risks, less control over who they interact with (for example, they are more likely to be attacked by the local community, by other working women and by clients), and lower pay (Campbell and Sanders, 2021;

DOI: 10.4324/9781003314769-9

Sanders, 2017). Studies also show that streetwalkers are perceived as being in the lower ranks in the sex industry (Weitzer, 2005).[1] But categories can be misleading. The experiences of sex workers and their journeys into this type of work are not always easily classified; hence the need to continue researching and writing about these experiences to highlight the diversity of roles, sex workers' perceptions about the work that they do, as well as to identify the struggles that women face.

Workers' Rights

Regardless of where we stand on the morality of the sex work debate, and despite the fact that there are different perspectives on sex work as a career, the reality is that there are individuals whose only source of income is sex work. These individuals are indeed providing a service, and many see themselves as workers without rights.

Sex workers and the charities that work directly with them have different interpretations of what sex work means. For example, in their mission statement, StreetlightUK states that they are 'focused on providing women with tangible and material pathways out of a life of prostitution and violence' (StreetlightUK, 2023). StreetlightUK works with very vulnerable women who are materially deprived and who are 'powerless'. As the Director of StreetlightUK states on their website, 'Prostitution is often called the oldest "profession" – but it is not a career choice ... no little girl dreams of growing up to do this' (StreetlightUK, 2023). In contrast, the Sex Worker Advocacy and Resistance Movement (SWARM), a UK-based charity run by sex workers, has a different mission statement, which includes the fight 'for the rights and safety' of prostitutes and for the 'decriminalisation of sex work'. Despite their different approaches to sex work, the ultimate goal of these two charities is primarily to support women, with the distinction that StreetlightUK emphasises the psychological harms of sex work and aims to help women leave this type of work, while SWARM focuses on fighting for better working rights for sex workers, as they 'recognise sex work as work' (SWARM, 2023).

The existence of the charities mentioned above, as well as Beyond the Streets, **National Ugly Mugs,** and the English Collective of Prostitutes, all offering some type of support to women as well as launching a wide range of campaigns, is the highest indicator that sex workers are marginalised members of society who face multiple risks while at work. The English Collective of Prostitutes write on their website that sex workers are mostly mothers who resort to prostitution to survive. In their quest to fight for pensions, trade union membership, and the same rights as other workers in traditional employment, the English Collective of Prostitutes (in line with SWARM) are essentially campaigning for sex workers to have better working conditions. However, the concept 'work' itself also needs to go through its own analytical transformation to include a wider range of (hidden, unpaid, and non-organisational) services provided by women, and those in the informal market sector in many parts of the world who also contribute directly or indirectly to the economy.

For decades, feminists have questioned why the jobs that *women* have traditionally done (including domestic labour and emotional labour) are not valued in society. While sex work is separated from this debate, some argue that sex work is *de facto* a form of 'intimate labour' (Gutierrez-Garza, 2013). In fact, as Gutierrez-Garza suggests (2013: 22), 'categories of care, domestic and sex work [are] in a continuum'. Indeed, a closer examination of these roles reveals that the three (care, domestic, and sex work) are classed as 'intimate labour', because they involve working mostly in private spaces, and all rely on what the author calls 'intimate knowledge' about clients or patients in order to be able to provide a good service (Gutierrez-Garza, 201).

Postmodernists also challenge previous notions of work by making us consider the micro-experiences of individuals as they construct their own realities. As Maclean et al. (2016, cited in Bowden, 2018: 292) state, for postmodernists, 'what counts ... is the occurrences that happen "at the grassroots"'. Applying these ideas to sex work, it could be argued that including the voices of sex workers in a debate about work would enrich the understanding of how people 'create' their own employment opportunities and shape definitions of work. In his evaluation of the different meanings of work, Tony Watson (2008) concludes that most sociologists tend to focus on paid employment – a definition which he refutes, as it excludes a range of practices, including (this chapter adds) sex work which does not always involve working in a legal or fixed setting, and which does not always guarantee a regular source of income. Yet, the Global Network of Sex Work Projects (NSWP), an organisation which advocates sex workers' rights, emphasises that sex workers contribute to local and global economies. For instance, **migrant sex workers** send remittances to their countries of origin, and are often the breadwinners, with various members of their families dependent on their income.

The Vulnerability Continuum

Any discussion about sex work has to be cautious not to make generalisations. There are, indeed, women who claim to be empowered or rescued by sex work, but even these concepts can be argued from different angles. Are those that claim to be empowered truly empowered? On the other hand, there are women who are clearly exploited and enslaved by sex work. Therefore, how women experience sex work depends on a range of factors, including the routes into this type of work.[2]

When discussing sex work, there is a danger of aligning with only one side of the 'voluntary versus forced' debate that characterises much of the research in this field (Doezema, 2018). This chapter proposes that, apart from the extreme cases (women who are empowered and satisfied by their career choices, versus women who are trafficked and must be protected), there are women who do not fall neatly into the voluntary or the forced side. This chapter tells the stories of those who are less visible in the literature – migrant sex workers who turn to prostitution because of poverty, or who are in search of better opportunities. As Figure 7.1 indicates, those who claim to have made the conscious choice to go into sex work to support their families, and those who state that sex work is their only career

Dina de Sousa e Santos

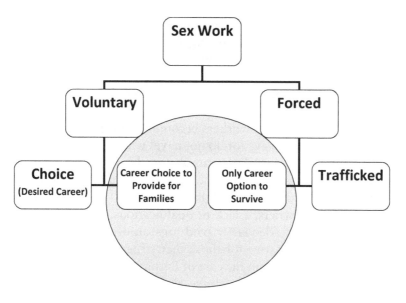

Figure 7.1 Migrant Sex Workers' Experiences

option, may sometimes be included in the same category. Therefore, it might be more productive to discuss not only whether women chose or not sex work but instead which group of sex workers are more vulnerable and in need of support.

In the case of the Latin American sex workers interviewed by Gutierrez-Garza (2013), what is particularly interesting is that most defined themselves as middle class in their country of origin (and they based this on factors such as home ownership, lifestyle, education, and employment status). For example, one owned a pharmacy. Despite their status in their countries of origin, all were vulnerable to unstable local economies. The stories presented by Gutierrez-Garza were different, yet strangely similar: some women lost their businesses, others lost their jobs, most accumulated large debts, and, due to the lack of governmental support in their home countries, they saw the UK as their only hope to make a new start. Yet, once in the UK, the women faced major hardships and, for some, who were illegal in the country, sex work became the only choice.

The Complexities of Understanding Sex Work

The campaign for sex workers' rights started in the 1970s (Campbell and O'Neill, 2013: xi), and in 1978, activist Carol Leigh coined the term 'sex work' at the Women Against Violence in Pornography and the Media meeting (Anonymous, 2022; Ditmore, 2011). These days, scholars and activists tend to adopt the term 'sex work' rather than 'prostitution', emphasising 'labour law and unionisation' (Campbell and O'Neill, 2013: xii).

It is impossible to know the exact number of sex workers in the UK, or in any other country. In 2016, the House of Commons estimated that there were 'around 72,800 sex workers in the UK' (House of Commons Home Affairs Committee,

2016), with a large number working in London, but StreetlightUK estimates that there are probably 105,000 people selling sex in the UK (StreetlightUK, 2023). This unknown figure is greater when we discuss migrant sex workers, as these statistics are harder to obtain. However, a report by PICUM[3] suggests that '65 percent of the sex worker population in Western Europe' are migrants (PICUM, 2019: 9).

To explain why some migrant workers become sex workers, it is also worth examining the skills that some have (or do not have) when they arrive in the UK and the legal status of the migrants. For example, not being able to speak English is one of the factors that explains why some legal and **illegal migrants** find sex work to be the only way of earning a living. Balfour and Allen (2014: 5) take this further and say that 'language barriers, a lack of qualifications, a lack of rights to work in the UK and the lack of adequately paid jobs on offer' could make sex work the only employment alternative for those that struggle to find a job with good remuneration. This could explain the case of Eastern European sex workers,[4] who until recently were able to enter, and leave, the UK due to the ease of movement that existed before Brexit. However, in the case of asylum seekers, and those that are either illegal migrants or whose asylum case has not been decided, research indicates that this could be 'the only means to make money' (Balfour and Allen, 2014: 5). These are the cases that could loosely be described as not just sex work but also **survival sex**.

The ideas presented here do not offer the full story for all migrant sex workers, because not all Global South sex workers are illegal and not all Eastern European women choose sex work because of the economic rewards. As for the type of work carried out by various nationalities, more research is needed to ascertain if there are any trends and patterns. For now, there is a clear consensus that there has been an increase in women travelling to 'richer countries from poorer and work in prostitution' (Thorbek and Pattanaik, 2002: 1). Another big problem that seems to obscure some discussions about migrant sex workers is that the issue of **sex trafficking** is sometimes intertwined with migrant sex workers, but some argue this distracts from the fact that there are migrants who *volunteer* to come to the UK (Campbell and O'Neill, 2013: xii) and those who choose sex work as a way to send wages back to their country of origin.

Survival Sex: Meanings and Causes

While during the COVID-19 lockdown, and due to strict social-distancing restrictions, sex workers struggled to meet clients and make a living, there is also enough evidence to suggest that the number of women[5] turning to prostitution to survive increased in the UK (Yasseri, 2021). Therefore, the pandemic and the post-pandemic period are strongly associated with survival sex, where the most economically vulnerable had to find ways to make ends meet. Within this social group, this includes not only students[6] turning to sex work, and mothers, but also migrants. What is clear from the literature is that women in low-skilled jobs were one of the groups more likely to turn to survival sex (Worden, 2020).

Dina de Sousa e Santos

For vulnerable women, who were already living on the breadline due to austerity cuts, COVID worsened their financial struggles. For those in zero-hour contracts, cash-in-hand arrangements, or who were self-employed, there was more job insecurity. In their research about the impact of the Job Retention Scheme on women, Jones and Cook conclude that women faced more job insecurity during the Coronavirus lockdown than men (Jones and Cook, 2021). Thus, it could be argued that, for women in 'atypical forms of employment', the insecurity was greater (Turn2us, 2020). Indeed, evidence from Turn2us's survey shows that these were the individuals that saw a greater 'drop in income' during the lockdown (Turn2us, 2020: 1). Job uncertainty and a lack of stable income due to the lockdown was, therefore, one of the reasons why women resorted to survival sex in large numbers. Yet the very act of turning to survival sex during the lockdown exposed them to many other problems, such as high-risk interactions and facing fines due to breaking lockdown rules (NUM, cited by the UK Parliament, 2020).

Migrant sex workers are one of the hardest groups to research. Hester et al. propose that this group 'may be suspicious of engaging in research funded by the Home Office, given its wider remit on immigration' (2019: 51); separating migrants in the sex industry from those who turn to survival sex is an even greater challenge. Therefore, while there is clear evidence that survival sex has increased, trying to estimate the number of migrants having to resort to survival sex in the UK is unfeasible. To gain a more valid picture, governmental data need to be analysed alongside non-governmental sources. Sex worker organisations give a good insight into the characteristics of the women they support, but even this approach has its limitations, because sex worker organisations tend to work within certain communities and are not approached by all sex workers; thus, they can only offer a snapshot, based on the women they are in contact with.

Survival sex is an act that destitute and marginalised individuals resort to. It highlights a desperate need to survive. Greene et al. (1999: 1406) define it as 'the selling of sex to meet subsistence needs'.

The debate about survival sex is further complicated when considering subsistence needs. This is particularly relevant in analysing migrant women's experiences, since they may be breadwinners for their families in their country of origin (Ehrenreich and Hochschild, 2004), so it might be the subsistence needs of their families, as well as their own needs, that prompt them to turn to this type of work.

Although it is impossible to come up with a one-size-fits-all definition of survival sex, it is possibly easier to distinguish survival sex from sex work by defining it in terms of what survival sex is not. Survival sex is not a career choice for women. Women who turn to it do so as they struggle with poverty. Another potential distinction between sex work and survival sex, although one that needs to be further theorised, is that some women who resort to survival sex do not define themselves as sex workers (Simon on the Streets, 2021). An important distinction made by the charity Simon on the Streets[7] is that, due to the sporadic nature of survival sex (women turn to it only when in desperate financial need), these women face higher risks as they work alone and do not have a network of support. To highlight the level of despair that they are dealing with, the charity mentions that they have supported women who had 'no ID, no bank account, no benefits and no access to the internet' (Simon on the Streets, 2021: para 5). Therefore, in desperate times, survival sex offers the only alternative for some women.

Survival sex is not just associated with the current cost of living crisis. Some associate it with the introduction of Universal Credit in the UK as part of the Welfare and Reform Act in 2012; other researchers, like Hanks (2020), link survival sex to strict immigration rules. As Hanks states: 'restrictive immigration policies limit the ability of migrants to secure employment across a range of "legitimate" and regulated sectors' (2020: 131). StreetlightUK also mentions in their 2021 report that immigration status could be a contributing factor leading some women to turn to prostitution during the lockdown. Citing the English Collective of Prostitutes, Worden (2020) also confirms the point that the financial circumstances of asylum seekers who have no right to work, and have 'to survive on £37.75 a week', is yet another potential reason why some migrant women turn to survival sex (Worden, 2020: para 7).

Migrant women involved in sex work or survival sex are not a homogeneous group. Yasseri (2021) carried out research of *Adultwork* and found that most of the profiles were of non-British-born sex workers, mainly Eastern Europeans. Likewise, in Platt et al.'s (2011) research on sex work in London, 61 per cent of the 268 participants were migrants, originally from 'Romania [30%], 19% from Lithuania, 17% from Poland, 7% from Latvia and Albania, 5.5% from the Czech Republic, and 4% from the Russian Federation. Two per cent or less originated from Bulgaria, Slovakia, Kosovo, Estonia, Moldova, Serbia and Tajikistan' (Platt et al., 2011: 378). Some studies indicate that Eastern European sex workers are economic migrants who work as sex workers, as this is 'more lucrative' than other informal jobs. Despite charging less than British sex workers, their pages have more views and they are able to come to the UK to work for a few weeks/months, which will give them enough income for their families (Yasseri, 2021). This has been partly confirmed by the CEO of POW Nottingham Limited,[8] who not only stated that there was an increase of Romanian sex workers in Nottingham, but also proved that women participate in various sectors within the sex industry:

> We hear so many different stories – some that have been sex workers in Italy and Germany and come to England because they believe it is lucrative. Some that have been in Nottingham working on the streets, some who have come for the purpose of sex work or who have come over and got into sex work and never been in it before. There are some people that I suspect are being controlled.
>
> (*Nottingham Post* interview; Jarram, 2017)

While the reason that women turn to sex work can be linked to wider structural issues in a particular country, there is also wider debate about 'global inequalities and exploitation of poor nations' that explains why some women desperately choose to go to the *wealthier* Global North (Thorbek and Pattanaik, 2002: 6), but equally important are representations of some countries in the Global North. The Global North is seen as a possibility for many, and, as Thorbek and Pattanaik

Dina de Sousa e Santos

point out, some migrant women see travelling to these countries as an investment. These women plan their work lives like 'entrepreneurs' and 'take risks and invest in order to earn good money (2002: 3).

The Risks of Sex Work and Survival Sex

Multiple studies have highlighted that one of the greatest problems faced by sex workers in general is violence. Whether they are street sex workers or in private premises, the danger is constant. In the case of illegal migrants, fear of deportation could prevent women from reporting to the police. As PICUM show in their report, sex workers are at risk of rape, violence, and murder (2019: 11). In fact, statistics published on the English Collective of Prostitutes website show that

> UK sex workers have the highest murder rate compared to women in other occupations. It is much safer to work indoors with others, but this is illegal. Sex workers are three times more likely to experience rape and other violence in countries where sex work is criminalised.
>
> (English Collective of Prostitutes, 2019)

This quote puts into perspective why, for almost 50 years, activists have campaigned to influence policy-makers to decriminalise sex work, to improve the working lives of women who are working voluntarily. A recent Home Office study of sex work showed that many sex workers are fearful when they go to work, and that is because they could be attacked by anyone: clients, public, and the police. If we add migration to the equation, then sex work becomes even more precarious.

There are also significant health risks associated with the role when it comes to women without the right to stay in the UK. Platt et al. found that 'migrant women were less likely to use contraceptives than UK-born women' (2011: 379), and a large number also had not had HIV screening in 12 months. This was also the group of sex workers that were less likely to be registered with the GP due to their migration status. The fact that these women are younger, and therefore have more clients, possibly has a link with a higher number of HIV infections and other sexually transmitted diseases.[9]

For Eastern European sex workers, Brexit has been the biggest concern, as immigration policies and greater surveillance have made their work lives more difficult (Campbell and Sanders, 2021). Hate crime has also increased since Brexit. For example, the NSWP (2017) reports that Eastern European sex workers have been victims of violence, discrimination, and threats of deportation, and Hanks (2020) discusses the discrimination faced by Romanian sex workers, not just because of their nationality, but, in the case of Roma Romanians, also because of their ethnicity.

Fear of violence has led some migrant sex workers to adopt a 'buddying system' – that is, they work with another person and choose to work indoors more (indoor sex markets) – but, as Connelly and the English Collective of Prostitutes (2021) point out, this strategy poses yet another risk, as the law stipulates that sex workers must not work together. Combined, all these factors contribute to the stress and anxiety associated with working as a sex worker. This has led some scholars and sex work organisations to ask whether decriminalisation would offer better working conditions for women. New Zealand, the first country to decriminalise prostitution in 2003, has been hailed a success story in terms of safety records (Abel and Armstrong, 2020). In their research on the experiences of sex workers in New Zealand, Abel and Healy (2021) indicate that decriminalisation has been 'successful in promoting sex workers' health, safety and wellbeing' (Abel and Healy, 2021: n.p.). Meriluoto et al. (2015) support some of the findings of this research, although they are careful to highlight that prostitution is still a 'risky business' in New Zealand (Meriluoto et al., 2015: 297).

A full discussion about sex work has to acknowledge the reasons why, for some, sex work is seen as the only career alternative. As mentioned previously, some women have no qualifications, others have no working documents, and that is the only work available. But some women struggling with mental health may see this as the only alternative means to make a living. Macioti et al. (2021) interviewed sex workers in four European countries, and found that: the majority of the women working in the UK also struggled with their mental health, some associated it with the stress of working as sex workers (violence, raids, discrimination), and, while a large number had mental health issues before they became sex workers, some also said that being able to earn their own money was beneficial to their mental health. More importantly, participants cited flexibility as one of the benefits of sex work – being able to work shorter hours, take time off, in other words, not being subject to the inflexible nature of traditional jobs. This also explains why a large number of sex workers are mothers, who turn to sex work to provide for their children (English Collective of Prostitutes, 2020).

The Legal Context

Sex workers are trapped in a web of legal insecurity, which has only become more intense since the Brexit referendum of 2016. Despite EU migrant sex workers being able to settle in the UK and 'claim self-employment status', migrant women face greater deportation and uncertainty than before, due to aggressive migration policies (Connelly and the English Collective of Prostitutes 2021: 4). In order to apply to settle in the UK, migrants need to provide evidence in support of their application, which acts as another barrier for migrant sex workers in the shadows of the economy. As Connelly and the English Collective of Prostitutes state:

> Since sex work is not widely recognised as 'legitimate' work in the UK, EU migrant sex workers may find it difficult to compile the documentation, including a record of waged labour, that is needed to apply for settled status in the UK and the EU settlement scheme.
>
> (2021: 4)

For those that achieve settled status, there is still no guarantee that they are legally safe. Because sex work has many 'illegal' practices attached to it, the women are still subject to other forms of control and therefore could be deported if they are caught committing a crime.

Scholars and activists fighting for sex workers' rights often argue that the lack of clarity around the distinction between the concepts 'sex trafficking' and 'sex work' has a negative impact on the legal rights of voluntary sex workers. This confusion harms the livelihoods of those who 'choose' to work as sex workers, as they face 'raids and rescue missions' under what Connelly calls the '**modern slavery** agenda' (Connelly and the English Collective of Prostitutes, 2021: 1). This surveillance in turn adds to the precarious nature of the sex industry. Mai et al. (2021) take this further and suggest that 'sexual humanitarianism' (which sees migrant sex workers as people in need of protection by various humanitarian and other international organisations, who fight to eliminate sex work) in fact causes more harm than good, as it denies agency yet also puts more women at risk of exploitation. Indeed, the lack of a legal migration status while working in a field without legal rights could make this type of work hazardous, risky, and women become victims of financial exploitation. For example, Balfour and Allen (2014: 12) suggest that vulnerable sex workers desperate to earn money could be *forced* to work longer hours, are less likely to use condoms, and often do not visit health services, as they fear being caught by the authorities or due to barriers to communicate in English.

Case Study

Migrant Sex Workers in the UK[10]

StreetlightUK received a call from Surrey Police at 3.45 p.m., requesting support from StreetlightUK as they identified a property with suspected trafficking victims. When arriving at the property, there were five individuals in the house (one male, four female) of Chinese origin, and a male and female were being arrested on suspicion of trafficking and prostitution offences.

One of the females, Woman X, informed StreetlightUK that she was being forced to have sex for money to pay off a debt of £30,000 to her traffickers back in China. Her husband had got into debt through gambling, and threats were made towards her husband and child. She was told that, if she did not pay this debt, she and her family would be killed. Woman X felt that she had no other choice but to come to the UK. Woman X was told when she came to the UK that she would be a waitress in a restaurant and that her debt would be paid. However, this was not the case and her debt increased every day. She was forced to work in massage parlours, which then led to being trafficked inside and out of London to men who would pay for sex.

Woman X was living in fear for herself and for her family, with no way of reducing her debt. She was scared of the authorities and was told that the police would kill her or send her back to China. Woman X was very fearful, but, with the support of StreetlightUK, agreed to be referred through the National Referral Mechanism (NRM)[11] process.

Most women will enter the sex industry in times of financial vulnerability. This is most certainly the case of Woman X, with whom StreetlightUK have been working.

Woman X told StreetlightUK that 'I thought I was coming to the UK to work in a restaurant or a nail bar to help pay off my husband's gambling debts.' In Woman X's case, she became involved in sex work because she was not earning enough money working in a restaurant, and every day the debt that she owed increased, to the point where she was told that she owed nearly £30,000. Woman X could not earn enough to pay off this debt, despite working long hours, so her situation had become intractable.

Conclusion

This chapter has examined the case of migrant sex workers in the UK, shedding light on the precarious lives that non-British-born women face while trying to make do and/or provide for themselves and their families. Sex work is, indeed, as one of Sanders' (Sanders and Hardy, 2013) titles suggests, the 'ultimate precarious labour', and it is so because it does not provide women long-term economic stability or decent working conditions (especially for street sex workers). It is unsafe in most cases and a danger to women's health, as women may develop a range of psychological, as well as other chronic illnesses as a result of lack of regulation and protection. Women who work as sex workers have no rights to a pension, do not have a steady flow of income, and are invisible service providers in society. The stigma associated with the job also prevents some women from visiting doctors or reporting crimes that they are victims of.

Migration adds further risks to sex work. Migrant sex workers face discrimination, often have language barriers, and, not only have no access to basic services, such as healthcare, but also have no protection from the police. Multiple charities are working either to help women exit sex work or to give them better working rights. To date, some of these efforts have not yielded the expected results, possibly because prostitution is a divisive matter, with sex worker organisations approaching it from different angles (some see it as work, others as female oppression).

This chapter has highlighted that, ultimately, poverty and lack of employment opportunities are directly associated with sex work and, in extreme cases of destitution, survival sex becomes their only option. Structural issues need macro solutions, but global issues are harder to tackle. Cash-stricken charities do an exceptional job every day in supporting a range of sex workers, not just women, and that was the focus of the chapter. However, to expect charities to *save* women from the effects of living in unequal global societies is unrealistic at best.

STUDENT ACTIVITY

1. Check your understanding.

   - What is meant by the term 'survival sex'?
   - Give two reasons why migrant women might turn to sex work in the UK.
   - Outline two explanations for the increase in 'survival sex'.
   - Outline and explain how some charities support sex workers in the UK.

Dina de Sousa e Santos

2. Case study analysis. Read the case study about migrant sex workers in the UK. Then explain:

- How do charities like Streetlight UK support migrant sex workers in the UK?
- Why is the definition and study of migrant sex workers problematic?

Practice Questions

Choose *one* question only to answer, then create a detailed plan.

- Sex work should be decriminalised to better protect all sex workers, not just migrant sex workers. To what extent do you agree with this statement?
- There is enough evidence to suggest that the cost of living crisis has made migrant women more vulnerable, causing them to consider "survival sex" as an option. Discuss.
- "Sex work" is a more suitable term than "prostitution" to explain the actions of all women who sell sex to make a living. Evaluate this view.

Key Terms

Illegal migrant
someone who is not a citizen of the UK and who does not have a valid visa (or other document) proving that they have the right to remain in the UK.

Indoor sex markets
private areas where sex work takes place in the UK, including licensed saunas, home, brothels, independent escorts, and privately rented premises.

Migrant sex worker
foreign-born individual who sells sex in exchange for money, goods, and services.

Modern slavery
an umbrella term that includes forced labour, sexual exploitation, and criminal exploitation. Modern slavery is a crime that includes human trafficking and implies forcing people to work against their will.

National Ugly Mugs (NUM)
a national organisation created with the aim of protecting sex workers. NUM uses digital reporting technology that enables sex workers, regardless of their type of work, to report any suspicious activity, therefore acting as a warning to the community.

Sex trafficking
a range of actions that culminate in transportation of a person from one country to another with the purpose of being exploited for sex.

Sex work
work in the sex industry, which includes indoor markets, street prostitution, and other forms of work performed by adults in exchange for money, goods, or other services.

Soliciting
when a sex worker tries to engage a client in the street or other public space.

Survival sex
a term that is associated with desperation, poverty, and having to perform sex work to survive.

Notes

1 While prostitution has traditionally been seen as a working-class job (Brock, 1998), research suggests that sex workers that work off the street have a higher level of education than street prostitutes, some have had professional jobs, and in general they have more stable jobs within the sex industry (Sanders, cited in Balfour and Allen, 2014). However, the internet and websites such as OnlyFans could make these class distinctions less clear.
2 This chapter focuses on women only, as statistics indicate that the vast number of sex workers are female.
3 The Platform for International Cooperation on Undocumented Migrants.
4 The number of Polish migrants in the UK increased after Poland joined the EU (with other central and Eastern European countries, EU8) in 2004. Various articles appeared during the pandemic highlighting increased numbers of Romanian women trafficked into the UK to work as sex workers. It is believed that most sex workers work independently, though.
5 Nicola Mai has written extensively about migrant male sex workers.
6 For research on students, see Simpson and Smith (2020).
7 Simon on the Streets is an outreach charity based in Leeds, Bradford, and Huddersfield. It offers practical and emotional support to homeless and vulnerable people in these areas.
8 POW Nottingham is a voluntary organisation that supports sex workers, ex-sex workers, individuals affected by sex work, and those at risk of exploitation. The wide range of services they provide includes: drop-in services (i.e. counselling, personal alarms, and condoms), as well as outreach services in the evening to provide food, hot drinks, clothing, and other practical forms of support.
9 The contributors also point out that migrant sex workers are less likely to have drug addictions.
10 Case study provided by StreetlightUK.
11 The National Referral Mechanism (NRM) is a system which allows first responders (i.e. NHS staff) to refer a person who has been identified as a victim (or suspected victim) of modern slavery to the NRM.

References

Abel, G., and Armstrong, L. (2020) *Sex work and the New Zealand model: decriminalisation and social change*. Bristol: Bristol University Press.

Abel, G., and Healy, C. (2021) 'Sex worker-led provision of services in New Zealand: optimising health and safety in a decriminalised context'. *Sex Work, Health, and Human Rights: 175–187*. https://doi.org/10.1007/978-3-030-64171-9_10

Anonymous (2022) 'Activist Carol Leigh, who coined term "sex work", dies at 71'. *Independent,* 18 November. Accessed 13 January 2023 from www.independent.co.uk/news/ap-san-francisco-leigh-hiv-carol-b2227735.html

Balfour, R., and Allen, J. (2014) 'A review of the literature on sex workers and social exclusion'. *HM Government.* Accessed 15 January 2023 from https://assets.publishing.service.gov.uk/government/uploads/system/uploads/attachment_data/file/303927/A_Review_of_the_Literature_on_sex_workers_and_social_exclusion.pdf

Bowden, B. (2018). *Work, wealth, and postmodernism: the intellectual conflict at the heart of business endeavour.* Cham, Switzerland: Palgrave Macmillan.

Brock, D.R. (2009) *Making work, making trouble: prostitution as a social problem.* Toronto: University of Toronto Press.

Campbell, R., and O'Neill, M. (2013). *Sex work now.* Abingdon: Routledge.

Campbell, R., and Sanders, T. (2021). 'Sex work, crimes and policing in the UK'. In R. Campbell and T. Sanders, *Sex work and hate crime: innovating policy, practices and theory.* Cham, Switzerland: Macmillan, pp. 29–49.

Connelly, L., and The English Collective of Prostitutes (2021). *EU migrant sex work in the UK post-Referendum.* https://prostitutescollective.net/wp-content/uploads/2021/05/Full-Report-EU-migrant-sex-work-in-the-UK-post-Referendum.pdf

Ditmore, M.H. (2011) *Prostitution and sex work.* Santa Barbara, CA: Greenwood.

Doezema, J. (2018). 'Forced to choose: beyond the voluntary v forced dichotomy'. In K. Kempadoo and J. Doezema (eds), *Global sex workers: rights, resistance, and redefinition.* New York: Taylor and Francis.

Ehrenreich, B., and Hochschild, A.R. (2004). *Global woman: nannies, maids, and sex workers in the new economy.* New York: Henry Holt and Company.

English Collective of Prostitutes (2019) 'Facts about sex work'. Accessed 22 July 2023 from https://prostitutescollective.net/facts-about-sex-work-sheet/

Greene, J.M., Ennett, S.T., and Ringwalt, C.L. (1999). 'Prevalence and correlates of survival sex among runaway and homeless youth'. *American Journal of Public Health,* 89(9): 1406–1409. https://doi.org/10.2105/ajph.89.9.1406

Gutierrez-Garza, A. (2013). 'The everyday moralities of migrant women: life and labour of Latin American domestic and sex workers in London'. PhD thesis. Accessed 1 February 2023 from http://etheses.lse.ac.uk/1067/1/Gutierrez_The_everyday_moralities_of_migrant_women.pdf

Hanks, S. (2020). 'Increased vulnerabilities: considering the effects of xeno-racist ordering for Romanian migrant sex workers in the United Kingdom'. *International Journal for Crime, Justice and Social Democracy,* 9(4). https://doi.org/10.5204/ijcjsd.1661

Hester, M., Mulvihill, N., Matolcsi, A., Sanchez, A., and Walker, S.-J. (2019). *The nature and prevalence of prostitution and sex work in England and Wales today.* Available at https://assets.publishing.service.gov.uk/government/uploads/system/uploads/attachment_data/file/842920/Prostitution_and_Sex_Work_Report.pdf

House of Commons Home Affairs Committee (2016) *Prostitution: third report of session 2016–17*. Available at https://publications.parliament.uk/pa/cm201617/cmselect/cmhaff/26/26.pdf

Jarram, M. (2017) '"Gigantic" rise in migrant sex workers in Nottingham'. *NottinghamshireLive*. Accessed 15 January 2023 from www.nottinghampost.com/news/local-news/gigantic-rise-migrant-sex-workers-886509

Jones, L., and Cook, R. (2021) *Does furlough work for women? Gendered experiences of the Coronavirus Job Retention Scheme in the UK*. The Global Institute for Women's Leadership/King's College London. Accessed 5 May 2023 from www.kcl.ac.uk/giwl/assets/does-furlough-work-for-women.pdf

Keay, L. (2022) 'Cost of living crisis pushing more women into sex work – and unable to refuse dangerous clients'. *Sky News*. Accessed: 26 April 2023 from https://news.sky.com/story/cost-of-living-crisis-pushing-more-women-into-sex-work-and-unable-to-refuse-dangerous-clients-12675932

Macioti, P.G., Geymonat, G.G., and Mai, N. (2021) 'What happens when sex workers actually need mental health support? Sex work and mental health – access to mental health services for people who sell sex in Germany, Italy, Sweden, and UK'. Available at swp.org/sites/default/files/65f262_75618d0bae824482bd9560929b677a59.pdf

Maclean, M., Harvey, C., and Clegg, S.R. (2016) 'Conceptualizing historical organization studies'. *Academy of Management Review,* 41(4): 609–632. https://doi.org/10.5465/amr.2014.0133

Mai, N., Macioti, P.G., Bennachie, C., Fehrenbacher, A.E., Giametta, C., Hoefinger, H., and Musto, J. (2021) 'Migration, sex work and trafficking: the racialized bordering politics of sexual humanitarianism'. *Ethnic and Racial Studies*, 44(9): 1607–1628. https://doi.org/10.1080/01419870.2021.1892790

Meriluoto, L., et al. (2015) 'Safety in the New Zealand sex industry'. *New Zealand Economic Papers, 49*(3): 296–317. https://doi.org/10.1080/00779954.2015.1041548

NSWP (2017) *Policy brief: sex work as work*. Available at www.nswp.org/sites/default/files/policy_brief_sex_work_as_work_nswp_-_2017.pdf

Platt, L., et al. (2011) 'Risk of sexually transmitted infections and violence among indoor-working female sex workers in London: the effect of migration from Eastern Europe'. *Sexually Transmitted Infections*, 87(5): 377–384. Available at https://doi.org/10.1136/sti.2011.049544

PICUM (2019) *Safeguarding the human rights and dignity of undocumented migrant sex workers*. Available at https://picum.org/wp-content/uploads/2019/09/Safeguarding-the-human-rights-and-dignity-of-undocumented-migrant-sex-workers.pdf

Sanders, T. (2012) *Sex work: a risky business*. Abingdon: Routledge.

Sanders, T. (2017) 'The risks of street prostitution: punters, police and protesters'. In M. Morash and M. Chesney-Lind (eds), *Feminist theories of crime*. Abingdon: Routledge, 97–111. https://doi.org/10.4324/9781315094113-5

Sanders, T., and Hardy, K. (2013) 'Sex work: the ultimate precarious labour?' *Criminal Justice Matters*, 93(10): 16–17. https://doi.org/10.1080/09627251.2013.833760

Simon on the Streets (2021) 'The realities women on the streets face: survival sex'. *Simon on the Streets.* Accessed 11 January 2023 from www.simononthestreets. co.uk/news/realities-women-on-the-streets-face-survival-sex

Simpson, J., and Smith, C. (2020) 'Students, sex work and negotiations of stigma in the UK and Australia'. *Sexualities,* 24(3): 474–490. https://doi. org/10.1177/1363460720922733

StreetlightUK. (2023) 'About us'. *StreetlightUK.* Accessed 12 January 2023 from www.streetlight.uk.com/about-us-4/

SWARM (Sex Worker Advocacy and Resistance Movement) Collective (2023) *SWARM Collective.* Available at www.swarmcollective.org/

Thorbek, S., and Pattanaik, B. (eds) (2002). *Transnational prostitution: changing patterns in a global context.* London: Zed Books.

Turn2us (2020) 'Coronavirus: exacerbating structural inequalities in the labour market and a looming rental crisis'. *Turn2us Org.* Accessed 5 May 2023 from www.turn2us.org.uk/T2UWebsite/media/Documents/Communications%20 documents/Coronavirus-widening-structural-inequalities-June-2020.pdf

UK Parliament (2020) 'Written evidence submitted by National Ugly Mugs (CVG0014)'. *UK Parliament.* Accessed 5 May 2023 from https://committees. parliament.uk/writtenevidence/8610/pdf/

Watson, T.J. (2008) *Sociology, work and industry,* 5th edition. London: Routledge.

Weitzer, R. (2005) 'Flawed theory and method in studies of prostitution'. *Violence Against Women, 11*(7): 934–949. https://doi.org/10.1177/1077801205276986

Worden, D. (2020). 'Sex work in a pandemic: criminalising survival'. *The Justice Gap.* Accessed 12 January 2023 from www.thejusticegap.com/sex-work-in-a-pandemic-criminalising-survival/

Yasseri, T. (2021) 'How sex work has been affected by the pandemic'. *The Conversation.* Available at https://theconversation.com/how-sex-work-has-been-affected-by-the-pandemic-160736

part 3

Organising People and Well-being at Work

chapter 8

Redistributing Power through the Democratisation of Organisation

Mark Green and Barry McNeill

Introduction

This chapter discusses growing demand for increased levels of democracy and participation in the ways that people are managed, and organisations are run. While many traditional ways of managing people rely on top-down forms of power, a growing number of organisations are moving away from conventional hierarchical structures into something more dynamic, where employees have greater autonomy over workplace practices. Redistributing power within organisations requires a different form of leadership, one that is more ethical, whereby voice and agency enable workers within an organisation to claim more power for themselves.

What is the **democratisation of organisation**? The word 'democracy' is derived from ancient Greek: *demos* means 'the people', and *kratos* refers to power. Literally, this translates to 'power of the people', where the role of governance is dependent on the will of the people being governed. Practically, this is evidenced in society where the system of government is voted into power by the members of that society. In democratic societies, for example, members of the public can vote, having some influence over who becomes elected to govern. This principle has resonance with the democratisation of organisations, where workers help to determine processes and decision-making in an organisation. While many nations around the globe use democratic systems to determine who and how a country is

DOI: 10.4324/9781003314769-11

governed, fewer organisations have historically embraced democracy as a part of their functioning.

Conventional thinking around organisational design, as well as legacy perspectives over organisational governance and what it means to lead, have resulted in a large proportion of organisations defaulting to traditional hierarchies and ways of operating (such as a layered top-down approach). Yet, these default structures have resulted in serious consequences, including: increased levels of economic inequality evidenced in ever-escalating executive reward schemes that vastly outpace entry-level salaries (Mishel and Wolfe, 2019); multiple layers of unproductive management and bureaucracy that slow down decision-making (Hamel and Zanini, 2020); and increasing levels of employee disengagement (Gallup, 2023. Despite this, there are numerous pioneering organisations emerging that offer a counter-approach: embracing democratisation to determine how a business operates for the benefit of a broader set of organisational stakeholders.

This chapter begins by contrasting two fundamentally different philosophies of management thinking: scientific management and the human relations movement. The analysis of these approaches continues by examining several examples of organisational pioneers who have embraced less conventional ways of operating companies, and discusses three key emerging themes. First, the chapter considers operating models that embrace entrepreneurship as an enabler of innovation, weighing the redistribution of risk to the workforce against increased power and autonomy. Second, it examines the role of information as a mechanism for control and raises the question as to whether greater transparency, which enables more autonomy and participation, overburdens employees with increased accountabilities. A call for ethical leadership is the third emergent theme, exploring how business leaders can harmonise the commitment to commercial interests within the context of escalating global environmental and humanitarian crises. The case study presented in this chapter looks at the work of Ricardo Semler, and the practices he adopted to redistribute power in his father's business, Semco Group, during the 1980s and beyond, and how these have influenced and shaped the 'new ways of working' movement. This chapter explores different perspectives on how power can be redistributed through the set-up of work organisations. It is necessary to examine the explicit and implicit contracting needed to redefine how decisions are made so that organisations can better engage employees actively to participate, take ownership, and provide greater accountability. To work effectively in this environment, ways of working, leading, coordinating and agreeing expectations need to be different, with a stronger focus on people and a greater emphasis on how people 'show up', day in, day out.

Traditional Systems of Work Organisation and Power: Taylorism and Fordism

Each of the industrial revolutions (see the following) has fundamentally shaped the dominant principles of how work is experienced today. Although society and the workplace have seen much change, many of the core dynamics of how organisations are designed remain rooted in the conventions in these legacy traditions. In the context of the growth of factories and demand for goods, industrialists became increasingly interested in achieving greater efficiency and output. Frederick Winslow Taylor (1856–1915) and Henry Ford (1863–1947) were two of the most prominent and influential industrialists, their approaches enshrined in the sociology of work literature as 'Taylorism' and 'Fordism'. Taylor wrote a key text called *The principles of scientific management* (1911), discussing how management could break down work tasks into repeatable activities that could be completed as efficiently and predictably as possible. From this perspective, power sat with managers, who were considered to know better than workers how work should be done, as their knowledge of the production process was greater than the workforce.

Inspired by scientific management, Henry Ford (the founder of the Ford Motor Company) sought to push efficiency to even greater levels by streamlining workflows to enable increased car production (Hounshell, 1988). One of his most significant innovations was the introduction of the assembly line, deskilling the art of building motor cars and driving up assembly speeds. To remove the 'wastage' of workers moving around the cars, he installed a continuous automatic conveyor belt in his plants, moving part-assembled cars past highly specialised workers at a pace that could meet his ambitious production goals. Many industrialists praised Ford for radically innovating car production to generate huge output. However, while these industrial achievements have provided innovation and economic wealth, sociologists studying work have highlighted the problems and side effects of Taylorism and Fordism.

Harry Braverman's book *Labor and monopoly capital: the degradation of work in the twentieth century* criticised scientific management for separating the labour process from the skills of workers, splitting the conception and execution of work, and using the 'monopoly over knowledge' (1974: 82) to control how work was done. Drawing on Marxist ideas, Braverman (1974) explained how workers became alienated from the product they produced, sitting on a factory production line and only working with one element, or part, of the production process. Perhaps the best example of this is Beynon's (1973) study *Working for Ford*, which documented the deskilling of car manufacturing in the UK, emphasising the stress of repeatedly performing mindless tasks thousands of times per shift. This management process and factory set-up led to job dissatisfaction, increased absenteeism, and greater levels of conflict and tensions between workers and management (Beynon, 1975).

Both Taylorism and Fordism applied **rationalist scientific methods** to drive greater productivity. At a basic level, if the task of digging a hole was broken into sub-tasks, scientific management would measure how long each of these tasks took to complete, determine the most efficient way to complete these tasks, and allocate accordingly. Tasks, split into smaller sub-tasks, would be allocated to one worker, such as digging dirt and filling a wheelbarrow, with another worker picking up other sub-tasks around emptying the wheelbarrow into the skip and making sure the digging worker could continue to work on filling up empty wheelbarrows. Even the optimum size of the shovel used to dig the hole would be analysed and addressed. The underlying belief in this process is that the ultimate goal of work is increased efficiency and output, and that control and power should sit with management, who can optimise these outcomes.

How did work evolve to this point? The first industrial revolution, of the 1830s and 1840s, began to transform rural, agrarian societies into industrialised, urban centres through the invention of machines and the discovery of steam power. The second industrial revolution, in the late 19th and early 20th centuries, saw a rapid acceleration in the growth of factories, driving mass production and increased innovation. Where working hours and conditions had been previously shaped by daylight hours and seasons, factory owners used electricity to extend working hours and generate more significant outputs. This period saw the birth of the large corporation, with the likes of John D. Rockefeller founding the Standard Oil Company, William C. Durant founding General Motors, and J.P. Morgan forming U.S. Steel (Davoudi et al., 2018). To grow, these corporations needed to employ large numbers of workers. However, with workforces with minimal education, lacking experience of working in production lines, and no standardised processes for managing large numbers of people, early factory work was chaotic. Corruption and abuse were rife, with men, women, and children forced to work in inhumane conditions for pitiful pay (Huberman and Minns, 2007; Organisation for Economic Cooperation and Development, 2021).

The first and second industrial revolutions contributed to, and accelerated, levels of inequality among workforces, many of which still exist today. The industrial revolutions also reveal that inequalities are evident not only in terms of economic gaps but also in long-term health outcomes, such as life expectancy, and even death and disease (Engels, 1887). There is much discussion in the literature about the relationship between power and inequality, with the producer/employee dimension being the most obvious of a plethora of drivers of inequality (Riaz, 2015).

A More Human-Centric Approach: The Human Relations Movement

While Taylorism grew in significance and popularity, another alternative movement gained traction: the **human relations movement**. Elton Mayo is one key theorist associated with human relations, though Mary Parker Follett's work on exploring power dynamics is of particular interest (Follett, 1925). Follett introduced a nuanced understanding between 'power over' and 'power with', advocating that managers and workers should co-create how they worked together, rather than management exerting power over workers, or workers (through unionisation) exerting power over management to drive outcomes. 'Power with' is a more collective form of power that emerges through strong collaboration, deep levels of trust, and the integration of how stakeholders work together. Follett, with her roots in social care, experimented with many of her ideas through the Settlement House Movement, an organisation focused on removing social poverty through bringing the rich and poor together in social proximity. Yet there are many more examples of organisations that experimented with collective models for social impact, such as the cooperative movement or Quaker organisations. One such example is the British chocolate manufacturer Cadburys, which, during Britain's industrial expansion, adopted a different approach from other factory owners by building a village for their workers with recreational facilities and essential amenities intended to improve workers' quality of life and health (Carnegie Medal of Philanthropy, 2005). The founder, John Cadbury, was an active campaigner for social justice and worker rights, and his legacy was taken forward through future generations to today. Others have questioned whether moving workers away from their homes to be embedded at their workplaces was non-exploitative.

McGregor (1960), a social psychologist, summed up the essence of these two opposing perspectives as Theory X and Theory Y. In his book *The human side of enterprise* (1960), he described Theory X as the idea that people are inherently lazy, dislike work, have little ambition, and, therefore, need management to achieve work outcomes through the threat of punishment and coercion. Alternatively, Theory Y assumes that people can be self-motivated and enjoy the challenge of work if managers create the right conditions. McGregor also argued that control measures become counterproductive, as often individuals will then seek ways to 'play the system'.

The tensions between traditional systems of power and the democratisation of organisation were brought into sharper focus during the pandemic and the subsequent global recovery. Workers' experiences differed, with significant variation between sectors, industries, and geography. Arguably, COVID-19 catapulted the world of work into embracing flexibility and new ways of working, with a broad acceptance of the viability for working-from-home patterns (see Chapter 1, Parry's 'Introduction'). However, there has been a rise in the use of workplace surveillance technology as a means of 'accepting' this flexibility (Morgan and Nolan, 2023), although not a new phenomenon (Ball, 2010). The response to 'bringing workers back to the office' (see Chapter 21, Felstead and Blakely's 'Changing Places of Work') typified traditional responses and the dominant system of power seen in scientific management and McGregor's Theory X. The narrative for many businesses was to revert to managerial hierarchies to exert power and define where 'work' can be done, in the office and under supervision.

Society and workplaces have evolved since early industrialisation, with the pace of change, complexity, and uncertainty ever-increasing. Dominant approaches to how organisations are run have not necessarily kept pace with wider and broader societal changes. Gallup's *State of the Global Workplace: 2023 Report* started to measure 'employee engagement' in 2009. Undertaken on an annual basis, the most recent analysis found a strong link between engagement and performance outcomes, such as retention, productivity, safety, and profitability. Engagement levels peaked in 2019, pre-pandemic, and the instances of people reporting stress, worry, anger, and sadness hit an all-time high in 2022, albeit in the context of geopolitical unrest and huge uncertainty post-pandemic. Against this backdrop, how can the democratisation of organisation and a shift towards greater power-sharing reverse such trends? The following three key emergent trends offer some insight into how leaders and practitioners can intentionally design organisations for increased employee engagement and participation.

Driving Innovation through Distributed Power and Entrepreneurship

Innovation in organisations is heavily shaped by power dynamics as decisions around the allocation of budgets and resources influence what ideas are progressed or killed. Enterprises adopt a range of different practices to encourage 'out of the box' thinking, such as innovation hubs and design centres. Yet, when leaders adopt a scientific management mindset, creativity becomes quickly constrained by attempts to achieve greater efficiency and optimise results, using tools such as standard operating procedures, defined specifications, or blueprints and tightly monitored processes. Attitudes towards risk and fear of making mistakes lead to a lack of willingness to put ideas forward. Where people do risk proposing new ideas, they face the need to compile detailed business cases, calculate complex return on investment projections and follow lengthy approval processes. While due diligence in investment decisions is valuable, such processes can overly favour risk aversion and suppress the innovative flair and responsiveness to market opportunity in the moment. One of the most quoted examples of lost opportunity is Intel's refusal to supply processors for Apple's iPhone in 2007. Ex-CEO (former chief executive officer), Paul Otellini, admitted his decision was based on inaccurate cost projections and overly conservative demand expectations (Gassée, 2013). Risk aversion cost the CEO his role, as well as costing Intel significant market share and billions in revenue.

One organisation that has used the distribution of power and democratisation to drive innovation is Haier Group Corporation, the manufacturer of home appliances and consumer goods. Based in Qingdao, China, Haier has over 84,000 employees, with over a quarter of them outside China. Their unique culture, business, and operating model is defined as **Rendanheyi**, a word which breaks down to mean: *Ren* ('each employee'); *Dan* ('the needs of each user'), and *HeYi* (referring to the *connection* between each employee and the needs of the user) (Frynas et al., 2018). In practice, this means that employees are treated more as entrepreneurs than employees, with the parent organisation acting as an investment platform supporting an ecosystem. Instead of having a traditional, hierarchical structure, Haier is made up thousands of micro-enterprises; these small, autonomous units are either customer-facing (just over 200) or internal, support functions delivering a service to their customer (circa 3,800).

The Rendanheyi philosophy not only distributes power but also risk. The success or failure of a micro-enterprise is determined by 'market-based dynamics', or the market's willingness to pay for an innovation, rather than the decisions of leadership teams, or innovation committees. If the team in a micro-enterprise wish to prototype a new innovation and take it to market, they have to raise funds, source the support, and market-test to prove feasibility. They use open-source technology

Mark Green and Barry McNeill

and crowdsourcing of ideas to develop deep customer insight, innovate, and validate market demand before funding new innovations.

Haier did not always operate this way; it has gone through many organisational developmental stages since the 1980s. Its early 'command and control' top-down structure focused on embedding a quality standard and a need to strive for excellence. From 1991 to 1998, the organisation morphed from a singular structure, diversifying beyond one product to multiple lines – a more product-led structure. From 1998 onwards, Haier became more complex, structuring the organisation around product categories and across numerous geographies, a structure commonly known as a **matrix organisation**. In 2005, they adopted an inverted pyramid structure, where customer-facing teams were at the top of the organisation, *served* by support functions and ultimately by the leadership team. It was only in 2012 that the entrepreneurial ecosystem began to emerge and Rendanheyi was born.

The philosophy of Rendanheyi offers employees the opportunity to become entrepreneurs and have greater control over their own destiny, reframing the employer–employee relationship. Within traditional organisational models, the risk involved in investing in new product innovations is held by the business owners. As the source of capital and funding, owners then 'deserve' a greater share of the reward, while workers' skills and contribution are rewarded through wages. Rendanheyi redistributes power and autonomy to the workforce, yet also redistributes risk and market volatility. New innovations and ideas are always susceptible to market acceptance and demand, yet, through reframing employees into entrepreneurs, teams and individuals are much more exposed to the risk and reward dynamics of the market. Should an innovation not be successful, the entrepreneurial team or individual needs to adapt quickly to survive. Haier has processes in place to mitigate the potential impact, by providing a minimum pay guarantee for six months should a micro-enterprise's entrepreneurial venture prove unsuccessful. Yet, this raises questions around the impact on people. To what extent does the shift from employee to entrepreneur create greater levels of individual stress? Is this kind of environment right for everyone? What kind of learning and development do people need to become more effective at entrepreneurial thinking, market research, and product development? How sustainable is this organisational approach if individuals fail to interpret the needs of the market effectively enough?

To date, for Haier and other organisations experimenting with Rendanheyi (Kosman, 2021), the sense is that this model can bring significantly greater levels of innovation and adaptation to the needs of the customer and market. The key to Haier's huge transformation was an ongoing adaptation and evolution of ways of thinking and working that span over 35 years. Democratisation did not happen overnight. Instead, it started as an idea, from a leadership team who wanted to shift how people contributed and who began to experiment with how to organise and coordinate innovation on a mass scale. From this point forward, trust, alternative controls, and participation became the central forces around which experimentation and iteration enabled true innovation.

Increasing Autonomy and Participation through Transparency

Ignorance can be positioned as a counterargument to democracy: to what extent can people vote democratically on topics where they have insufficient understanding of the implications of a decision? To enable greater levels of autonomy and participation, it is therefore essential that information is freely shared and transparent across organisations. However, many organisational leaders and managers believe it is important to filter the information that is shared with their people.

More human-centric, progressive organisations manage the employee relationship in a more mature and sensible way instead, and work openly to enable more creative, participative solutions to come to the fore. One example where a CEO has adopted radical transparency was at FAVI, the French brass foundry (Laloux, 2014). Faced with a sharp decline in global car orders following the first Gulf War, in August 1990, the metal manufacturing business was in deep financial trouble. The CEO pointed out one approach that appeared relatively straightforward: 'fire the temp workers' (Laloux, 2014: 104). Yet, as a company that had traditionally treated temporary workers and employees equally, and recognising the importance of the front line in delivering value to their customers, the CEO did not want to break the underlying cultural norms. Instead, the CEO shared the situation with the workforce in a public town-hall meeting where team members volunteered to work a reduced working month and receive lower salary to ensure that costs could be adequately managed until business picked up again.

This raises the question as to whether it was fair to redistribute the additional pressure for this decision to the full workforce. By sharing information and being transparent, the CEO ultimately shared the burden of accountability with the collective workforce, with everyone becoming responsible for making the best decision. The employees at FAVI made a collective decision about what was the right thing to do, although one could question if this would be the best situation for everyone in any organisation. This example illustrates the power of being transparent about business challenges by enabling the workforce to co-create a collective decision that protected the full organisation and all its members – both temporary and fully employed.

Another organisation that has embraced transparency to support greater participation in decision-making is the Argentinian software development firm 10Pines (Semco Style Institute, 2022). Founded in 2009, the company adopted a human-centric approach to business, growing rapidly because of their open, collaborative culture. To support participative decision-making, three key interdependent policies are in place: a transparency of information policy (also known as open-book management), a training policy, and a profit-sharing policy. Creating transparency ensures that everyone can access the information needed to make decisions. The information needs to be easily understood, enabled by the training policy. 10Pines even promotes full transparency and openness with salaries, by encouraging staff to set each other's salaries, which are decided three times a year at the company's 'rates meeting'. The discussions include everyone except new hires still on probation. Employees (or mentors on their behalf) can put themselves forward for a pay rise, which is then openly debated. By sharing clear and correct information with everyone, people can then have balanced conversations and reach well-informed conclusions.

There are important considerations when aiming to enable this level of transparency within organisations. First, there is little point in sharing information if individuals are unable to understand or appreciate it fully. Therefore, combining transparency with relevant training and development is essential to ensure people can contribute meaningfully. It is also critical that people are able to openly discuss topics and propose ideas, without fear of repercussion or being brushed to one side. This condition is highly dependent on the levels of trust and psychological safety within the team climate or company culture to enable open conversations about the issues and ways forward (Edmondson, 2018).

Adopting Ethical Leadership for a Modern Workplace

The debate about the tensions between the commercial drivers of capitalism and the broader needs of workers and customers has been going on for centuries. Political philosophies and ideologies have been shaped around these two opposing views, with policy-makers seeking to favour the needs of either business or society. On the one hand, favouring business interests tends to lead towards wealth accumulation for business owners or landowners, while a more society-focused approach means considering the wider needs of all the members of society, including the most vulnerable in need of support. As this debate has continued to rage, there has been an increased focus on whether business should not just maximise value for shareholders alone, but also have a responsibility to benefit society.

Strongly opposed to the idea that business should exist for any other purpose than to increase profits, Milton Friedman's *New York Time Magazine* article (1970) heavily criticised the concept of socially responsible business. Yet, despite Friedman's best efforts, business leaders have since, in some cases reluctantly, woken up to the need to adopt a wider range of stakeholder perspectives beyond just the needs of the shareholder alone. Organisations have increasingly adopted corporate social responsibility policies, including practices to minimise their environmental impact or to support charitable activities that benefit their local community or wider society. During the 1990s and since, the public has become increasingly focused on protecting our planet, which has given rise to the **sustainability agenda.** Often under the pressure of public scrutiny, organisations gradually adopted more sustainable working practices, with the concept of the 'Triple Bottom Line' gaining credibility from around the mid-1990s (Elkington, 1994), arguing that the purpose of business was not just about profit, but also about people and the planet. The proposed methodology challenged business to move beyond financial accounting to consider the human and societal impact of organisations, as well. This shift in thinking has opened up a colossal growth market, with the global green technology and sustainability market projected to peak at $417.35 billion by 2030 (Laricchia, 2023). Yet, with continued failure to address climate change pledges, questions about the impact must continue to be raised (see also Chapter 19, Sahin-Dikmen's 'Climate Change and Work').

To take the decision to sacrifice profitability in favour of societal and humanitarian need, leaders have to step up to a higher, ethical standard and expectation. One of the most extreme examples of this type of leadership is the founder of the outdoor clothing retailer Patagonia, Yvon Chouinard. Patagonia has a long history of making business decisions based on purpose and broader societal values, rather than purely commercial factors, achieving great success alongside this commitment to broader purpose (Minnaar and Morree, 2019). One well-known example is when Patagonia produced an advertising campaign for Black Friday (the day when retailers begin to promote huge sales), advising people not to buy their clothing, to avoid over-consumerism. This approach rejects that there must necessarily be a trade-off between purpose or profit and argues that leaders can find a way to achieve both purpose and profit (Edmans, 2020). Much of the evidence from research on the links between purpose and organisational performance demonstrates that businesses that are driven by a broader purpose and achieve greater levels of financial success as people show greater levels of commitment and loyalty to want to continue to work with them (Edmans, 2020).

In 2022, Yvon Chouinard took ethical leadership further by committing that all future Patagonia profits be donated to saving the planet (McCormick, 2022). Such action may be unrealistic for most organisations, but ethical leadership can be evidenced through a commitment to daily decisions that create an environment where people can thrive and do their best work. Creating organisations that are more inclusive, enable greater levels of participation, distribute decision-making and power supports more human-centric work environments.

Case Study

Pioneering the New Ways of Working Movement with Ricardo Semler and the Semco Style Institute

The New Ways of Working Movement has its origins in the 1980s, when 21-year-old Ricardo Semler took majority ownership of his father's business, Semco. The business at that point was predominantly a mixer and agitator supplier in São Paulo, Brazil. With 90 per cent of the business focused on the maritime market, and Brazil's shipbuilding industry in rapid decline, Semco was on the brink of bankruptcy. On his first day as CEO, Ricardo Semler fired 60 per cent of the top managers, to remove additional bureaucratic layers: a crisis move to shift Semco in a new direction.

His approach became hallmarked by delegating decision-making power to the workforce. He moved away from the traditional model of hierarchy and power, towards a more ethical, inclusive form of leadership, and continually questioned the traditional, conventional, accepted ways of leading organisations. Semler's approach to challenging and dismantling traditional business practices continued as he dismantled Semco's previous ways of working, where they discouraged flexibility and bolstered complacency.

Mark Green and Barry McNeill

Ricardo's philosophy blended elements of neoliberalism with a focus on personal freedom, individualism, and competition. He also borrowed from the theories of *socialism*, where decisions about production are determined by democratic process and social controls (Gilabert and O'Neill, 2019) as opposed to a capitalist standpoint. Semler implemented alternative controls, encouraging workers to self-govern by interviewing and electing their coordinators (line managers) and operating in more self-managed ways.

Ricardo and his company gained international recognition for the way they forged a partnership with employees, where power was shared, control relinquished, and organisational structures replaced with democracy. Democratising the workplace through distributing and sharing power were core to Ricardo's vision for partnering with the workforce. In contrast to Fordism or Taylorism, which are famed for breaking down the process of manufacturing into its constituent components and, in the process, deskilling people, Semco's factories are often described as 'messy'. People are organised in multi-skilled clusters or teams, assembling complete products, as opposed to isolated parts.

Over the next two decades, Ricardo grew the company from 90 to 5,000 employees and raised the company's annual revenue from $4 million to $212 million. The Semco Group grew at an average rate of 47 per cent per annum and achieved a low employee turnover rate of just 2 per cent under Ricardo's leadership. In the early 2000s, employee surveys rated Semco as the best company to work for in Brazil and it had a substantial waiting list of people wanting to work for the company. Beyond his best-selling publications, Ricardo Semler's TED Talks have been viewed by millions and he has shared his learning and insights as a professor of Leadership at MIT's Sloan School of Management.

The establishment of the Semco Style Institute (SSI), which began operations in 2016 in the Netherlands, enabled the Semco principles and supporting framework to be co-defined. The principles were drawn from the way Ricardo and the Semco Group grew and developed from the 1980s. The principles of trust, alternative controls, self-management, extreme stakeholder alignment, and creative innovation were defined as the essence of what made Semco's journey unique. Today, SSI is active in more than 30 countries and actively supports multiple organisations, from ABN Ambro, a retail bank in the Netherlands, to Pragma, a South African engineering company, and the Japanese digital marketing agency Exidea.

Conclusion

While successful organisations need to have a clear sense of vision, mission, and purpose, they must be able to adapt, in order to continue to deliver as society, market needs, and customer expectations change. While organisations must adapt, the people within them must do so, too. But people are deeply complex. They have highly individualised and unique needs, and, as the individual relationship that people have with their workplace evolves, so does the management of those relationships.

Complex, adaptive systems, such as climate, cities, or organisations, cannot be controlled by the fragmentation and tight management of isolated tasks or entities. Instead, they must be nurtured, to enable each part of the system to flourish for the benefit of the whole system. They do not tend to sit in perfect equilibrium; instead, complex, adaptive systems are in constant flow and dynamic adaptation. The role of leadership in this environment is to facilitate that dynamic adaptation through enabling ongoing participation, creating the conditions where people are included, feel able to contribute, voice concerns, and take autonomous decisions that not only serve their own interests but are aligned to meet the interests of the complex stakeholder environment.

This chapter has explored the dynamics of power and power distribution in organisations. Traditional organisational models have two key philosophies: the rational thrust of Taylorism designed to optimise efficiency, versus the people-centric values of the human relations movement. This is not a new debate, but one that the global pandemic and the need for stability post-pandemic has thrust squarely back up the agenda. The ever-increasing divide between those at the top of society and those trying to make ends meet places a stronger ethical expectation upon what it means to be a leader, and how these leaders can be nurtured to be less driven by self-interest and power and more concerned about protecting the interests, needs, and aspirations of the wider ecosystem and society.

STUDENT ACTIVITY

Consider two very different workplace environments: one which is highly bureaucratic, with lots of rules and processes to support these rules, lines of approval, sign-off requirements; and a second, which is very agile, dynamic, fast-paced, where people can make independent decisions themselves.

Research some examples of the two different types of organisations you have identified ('traditional and bureaucratic' versus 'modern and agile'). To help you begin to understand their culture and environment better, review their websites, annual reports, and other literature or news about them.

- What can you identify that helps you get a feel for what it would be like to work in any of these organisations?
- How much structure or bureaucracy do you think there might be? What indicators could you look out for? How might these factors influence the experience of work in this environment?
- What can you infer about leadership in each of these organisations? What are leaders required to do to be effective in each of these environments?
- From what you know about your own working style, your preferences and needs, what kind of environment would you prefer to work in? Why?

Practice Questions

- In what ways can Fordism and Taylorism be applied to some contemporary forms of work?
- How might democratisation of organisation provide more autonomy to individual workers?
- Drawing on Braverman's book *Labor and monopoly capital: the degradation of work in the twentieth century* (1974), explain how modern workers might feel alienated from the product or service they produce? Use contemporary work examples only.

Key Terms

Democratisation of organisation
a system of work organisation in which employees have more agency (more say) and more equal involvement in decision-making. Processes and decision-making are more democratic.

Fordism
an approach to work directly associated with the car manufacturer Henry Ford (1863–1947), in which assembly lines were key to the speed and accuracy in which a Ford car could be manufactured. Fordism refers to that 'assembly-line' philosophy, which still exists across many forms of work today.

Human relations movement
an alternative philosophy of work to scientific management, prioritising the importance of meeting the needs of individuals and creating supportive environments where people are protected and cared for. Elton Mayo (1880–1949) and Mary Parker Follett (1868–1933) were two key pioneers in the human relations movement.

Matrix organisation
a work structure where team members report to multiple leaders; to a project manager as well as their line manager or department head. This management structure is often used in companies to create new products and services without realigning teams.

Rationalist scientific methods
approaches in science that seek to focus on a 'means to an end', such as the use of technology to speed up work tasks.

Rendanheyi
a Chinese business philosophy pioneered by the product manufacturing firm Haier Electronics, designed to enable entrepreneurship from within a large corporate

structure. The approach breaks larger organisations into small, interdependent business units using technology and platforms to enhance collaboration and co-working.

Socialism
a political and economic theory focused on how communities and societies come together to take collective responsibility for decisions of production, distribution, and exchange of value.

Sustainability agenda
an international approach to climate change and global warming, which requires minimising our carbon footprint to provide a greener and more sustainable future.

Taylorism
a work approach focused on the scientific management of work tasks, such as analysing time taken to perform a work activity and breaking down the activity into smaller tasks. Frederick Winslow Taylor (1856–1915) wrote a key text called *The principles of scientific management* (1911), from which the idea of Taylorism emerges.

References

Ball, K. (2010) *Workplace surveillance: an overview.* London: Routledge.

Beynon, H. (1973) *Working for Ford.* London: Allen Lane.

Beynon, H. (1975) *Car making: an industry at war with its workers.* London: New Society.

Braverman, H. (1974) *Labour and monopoly capital: the degradation of work in the twentieth century.* New York: Monthly Review Press.

Carnegie Medal of Philanthropy (2005) 'The Cadbury family: a sweet tradition of giving'. Accessed 17 September 2023 from www.medalofphilanthropy.org/the-cadbury-family-a-sweet-tradition-of-giving

Davoudi, L., McKenna, C., and Olegario, R. (2018) 'The historical role of the corporation in society'. *Journal of the British Academy*, 6(s1): 16–47.

Edmans, A. (2020) *Grow the pie: how great companies deliver both purpose and profit.* Cambridge: Cambridge University Press.

Edmondson, A. (2018) *The fearless organization: creating psychological safety in the workplace for learning, innovation, and growth.* Oxford: Wiley.

Elkington, J. (1994) 'Towards the sustainable corporation: win-win-win business strategies for sustainable development'. *California Management Review, 36:* 90–100.

Engels, F. (1887) *The condition of the working class in England.* New York: John W. Lovell Company.

Follett, M.P. (1925) *Power, dynamic administration: the collected papers of Mary Parker Follett.* London: Routledge.

Friedman, M. (1970) 'The social responsibility of business is to increase its profits'. *New York Times Magazine*, 13 September, 17. Available at www.nytimes.com/1970/09/13/archives/a-friedman-doctrine-the-social-responsibility-of-business-is-to.html

Frynas, J.G., Mol, M.J., and Mellahi, K. (2018), 'Management innovation made in China: Haier's Rendanheyi'. *California Management Review*, 61(1): 71–93.

Gallup (2023) 'State of the global workplace: 2023 report'. Accessed 23 May 2023 from www.gallup.com/workplace/349484/state-of-the-global-workplace-2022-report.aspx

Gassée, J.L. (2013) 'Intel is under new management – and it's already starting to show'. *Guardian*. Accessed 4 July 2023 from www.theguardian.com/technology/blog/2013/nov/04/intel-new-management-smartphone

Gilabert, P., and O'Neill, M. (2019) 'Socialism'. *The Stanford Encyclopedia of Philosophy*, ed. Edward N. Zalta. Accessed 4 July 2023 from https://plato.stanford.edu/entries/socialism/#SociCapi

Hamel, G., and Zanini, M. (2020) *Humanocracy: creating organizations as amazing as the people Inside them*. Brighton, MA: Harvard Business Review Press.

Hounshell, D. (1988) 'The same old principles in the new manufacturing', *Harvard Business Review*, November. Accessed 18 October 2023 from https://hbr.org/1988/11/the-same-old-principles-in-the-new-manufacturing

Huberman, M., and Minns, C. (2007) 'The times they are not changin': days and hours of work in old and new Worlds, 1870–2000'. *Explorations in Economic History*, 44(4): 538–567.

Kosman, M. (2021) 'Rendanheyi now a frequently mentioned term in business globally'. *BusinessWire*, September 27. Accessed from www.businesswire.com/news/home/20210927005313/en/Rendanheyi-Now-a-Frequently-Mentioned-Term-in-Business-Globally

Laloux, F. (2014) *Reinventing organizations*. Brussels: Nelson Parker.

Laricchia, F. (2023) 'Green technology and sustainability market size worldwide from 2022 to 2030'. *Statista*. Accessed 4 July 2023 from www.statista.com/statistics/1319996/green-technology-and-sustainability-market-size-worldwide

McCormick, E. (2022) 'Patagonia's billionaire owner gives away company to fight climate crisis'. *Guardian,* 5 September. Accessed 4 July 2023 from www.theguardian.com/us-news/2022/sep/14/patagonias-billionaire-owner-gives-away-company-to-fight-climate-crisis-yvon-chouinard

McGregor, D. (1960) *The human side of enterprise*. New York: McGraw-Hill. Annotated edition, 2006.

Minnaar, J., and Morree, P.D. (2019) *Corporate rebels: make work more fun*. Corporate Rebels. Eindhoven: Corporate Rebels Nederland B.V.

Mishel, L., and Wolfe, J., (2019) 'CEO compensation has grown 940% since 1978'. *Economic Policy Institute*, 14 August. Accessed from www.epi.org/publication/ceo-compensation-2018/

Organisation for Economic Cooperation and Development (2021) *How was life?* Vol. 2, *New perspectives on well-being and global inequality since 1820*. Paris: OECD Publishing.

Riaz, S. (2015) *Bringing inequality back in: the economic inequality footprint of management and organizational practices*. India: Sage Publications.

Semco Style Institute (2022) 'Understanding the difference between equal and fair: Semco Style Stories with 10Pines, Argentina'. Accessed 4 July 2023 from https://semcostyle.com/semco-style-stories-10pines/

Taylor, F.W. (1911) *The principles of scientific management*. London: Routledge.

chapter 9

Women Leaders in Male-Dominated Industries

Julia Hansch and Natalie Janning-Backfisch

Introduction

The phenomenon 'think manager – think male' has embedded itself in the human consciousness as a culturally overarching set of beliefs (Schein et al., 1996: 39). According to Schein et al. (1996) qualities expected of leaders tend to resemble those associated with men. This notion manifests itself in the preference of male leaders over female ones, since the latter are confronted with prejudice as well as stereotypes (Powell, 2012). While men are perceived to possess agentic traits (pertaining to self-assertion and independence), which are mostly used to describe a successful manager, women are usually not associated with these traits, due to **gender stereotypes**. Gender stereotyping is a significant issue obstructing the career progressions of women in management. These so-called agentic traits include, for example, characteristics such as being direct, frank, aggressive, dominant, assertive, self-confident, vigorous, skilled in business matters, and so on which are highly associated with (male) managers. Women are more closely seen as caring, helpful, intuitive, neat, harmony-seeking and aware of others' feelings (Ryan et al., 2011). Schein's 'think manager – think male' attitude, dating back to the 1970s, is still very much in existence today. In contrast, perceptions of women leaders have, among other things, revolved around their ability to deal with crises. The notion of 'think crisis – think female' (Ryan et al., 2011: 472) is premised on the idea that female leaders can manage difficult situations better than male leaders. Gender stereotypes distort how women and men view themselves and are viewed by others, particularly hindering the work success of women, since both employer and

DOI: 10.4324/9781003314769-12

employees tap into the cultural image of women having fewer of the **leadership** qualities required for the world of work.

Markets and ways of working are changing, yet for decades many companies have relied on the same management line-up – men of the same age, the same background, and similar education (AllBright, 2019). This approach and the corresponding attitude have led to an underrepresentation of women in executive bodies and management positions. Despite significant labour market progress over the last decades, women remain heavily underrepresented in high-earning, high-status occupations (Bertrand et al., 2018). One way of analysing this is to look at the gender pay gap (see Chapter 3 for an introduction to this). The EU Commission has been tracking ender pay gaps for years and has an extensive database on the subject. The gender pay gap in the EU has changed only minimally over the last decade, with women earning an average 12.7 per cent less per hour than men in 2021. Until recently, the gender pay gap in Germany has been typically worse than the EU average, locked in at over 20 per cent.

In Germany, like other countries around the globe, the gender pay gap occurs simultaneously with the overrepresentation of women in relatively low-paying sectors, such as care, health, and education. Highly feminised jobs tend to be systematically undervalued – in Europe and most countries around the world. The greater the attention given to combating such conditions, the more the gender pay gap itself will be combated. Germany has long had much less political focus on gender equality compared to, for example, the Nordic EU countries, and this could be one of the reasons for the significant gender pay gap in Germany. In addition, as in other European countries, today there is still an unequal division of labour in the home, with women spending more time on unpaid work (childcare, caring for older people, doing domestic chores). The *perception* of women as needing to care for children has a powerful influence, with employers themselves often cautious about employing women in highly paid management roles, in case they need 'time off' for childcare reasons. To help change these ideas and improve arrangements for those with children, the EU promotes equal sharing of parental leave and flexible working time arrangements (see also Chapter 10, 'Work–Life Balance').

An unacknowledged barrier to progress in a career or industry has been called 'the glass ceiling'. Women often try to be promoted, but many can never reach the top positions, simply because of their gender. Generally, access to top management or board positions is still very difficult for women. Over a five-year period in Germany's corporate sector, there was only a small increase in women occupying the C-level positions (CEOs/chief executive officers, CFOs/chief financial officers, etc.), from just under 5 per cent in 2015 to 7 per cent in 2020. The higher up the management ladder, the bigger the pay gap between men and women tends to be, and in the EU the largest difference in hourly earnings was found in the management group: 23 per cent lower earnings for women than for men (Statistisches Bundesamt, 2021). However, some policies around pay can make a difference. For example, in companies that are being regulated by a mandatory gender quota, women hold 30 per cent more board positions than those in companies without such a mandatory quota (Anonymous, 2020). Typically, Germany has lagged

　　　　　　　　　Julia Hansch and Natalie Janning-Backfisch

behind many countries from around the globe. For example, in both New Zealand and France, more than 40 per cent of board members are female (Egon Zehnder, 2020). In 2020, only 14 per cent of the board members of the 100 biggest German companies were female (Kirsch and Wrohlich, 2021). In general, the proportion of women in leadership in Germany and in many other parts of the globe remains very low, with only one third of all managers in 2021 being female (Statistisches Bundesamt, 2021).

The rest of this chapter discusses the ways in which the pandemic **crisis** and other global events have changed the working world of the industry for women. For example, it will look at how the circumstances will change the perception of leaders in the traditional logistics industry in countries like Germany. Will there be more opportunities for women, or will logistics become even less diverse? In addition, the **competencies** associated with 'good leadership' today will be addressed.

Changing Perceptions of Women Leadership

Both the perception of women in leadership positions and the way companies are led by men and women are changing. Across Germany, recent trends show that more and more women are occupying management positions. An indication is the gender pay gap, on which scale Germany has moved from being ranked 10th (from 146 countries) in 2022, to 6th in 2023 (World Economic Forum, 2023). Other studies in Germany also reveal how women in top management positions at DAX (stock market index) companies earn more on average (approximately 1 per cent) than their male counterparts (Barwitzki, 2020). These recent developments in Germany (and other parts of the world) indicate that gender-based ideas about leadership are changing. Although there is still a long way to go to achieve gender balance in leadership positions in countries like Germany, a shift in mindset appears to be happening. For example, since organisations worldwide have been facing a global **crisis** due to the COVID-19 pandemic – and, more recently, Russia's war on Ukraine – the preference for female **leadership competencies** in times of crises (Ryan et al., 2011) could change the perception of women as leaders. The 'think crisis – think female' association seems to reverse the conventional assumption of 'think manager – think male' (Gartzia et al., 2012: 621), since studies suggest that female leaders are perceived to better navigate through a time of crisis than men (Gartzia et al., 2012).

In the past few years, researchers have found that women have a better chance of breaking through glass ceilings when an organisation is facing a crisis—thus finding themselves on what experts call the 'glass cliff' (Ryan and Haslam, 2005). As long as a company headed by men performs well, there's no perceived need to change its pattern of male leadership. Only if male leaders have manoeuvred an organisation into trouble is a switch to a female leader preferred, since the chance of failure is already high. The 'glass cliff' here represents the fragility of the situation as well as the 'deep fall' that is imminent in the event of failure. This phenomenon might have led to an accelerated rate of promoting female leaders during the COVID-19 pandemic in Germany.

The Example of Logistics: A 'Man's World'

The logistics industry is the third largest employer in Germany. Logistics is the process of planning and executing the efficient transportation and storage of goods from the point of origin to the point of consumption. Thus, logistics organises the modes of transport (by air, sea, road, rail, etc.) from the sellers to the producers and the customers. Located in the middle of Europe, Germany is the continent's largest economy and most important logistics hub, offering world-class infrastructure and cutting-edge logistics services. The location provides companies with opportunities for convenient Europe-wide distribution and easy access to the EU's 500 million consumers. However, the logistics industry in Germany is still largely a 'man's world', with men dominating the job market and holding most of the managerial and highly paid positions. In 2019, only 18.6 per cent of the top 100 German logistics companies had at least one woman on their management board (Bundesvereinigung Logistik, 2019).

Many companies specialise in logistics, providing the service to manufacturers, retailers, and other industries with a large need to transport goods. Some own the full range of infrastructure, from planes to trucks, warehouses, and software, while others specialise in one or two parts. Historically, logistics has predominantly been a male sector for male workers, so much so that, even today, people often talk about the 'postman' or 'delivery man' without anticipating that it may well be a 'postwoman' or 'delivery woman'. (See Chapter 2 on taken-for-granted assumptions of work.) Even the terms 'driver' or 'pilot' are usually assumed to be male. Companies like FedEx, UPS, and DHL are just some of the well-known logistics providers, where most workers doing the deliveries are male, although more and more women are taking on these roles. Amazon has been entering the logistics market in many countries, not only by selling goods but also services including storage, retail services, and goods delivery. While there is a mixed-gender workforce at Amazon, there is still a gendered division of labour, with men dominating the warehouse positions, as well as supervisory and management roles (Amazon Workforce Data, 2022).

One challenge for women occupying leadership positions is that they face forms of sexism when entering male-dominated industries (Rubin et al., 2019). Sexism in the workplace includes derogatory comments, objectification, sexist humour or jokes, overfamiliar remarks, silencing or ignoring people. It may also include gratuitous comments about dress and physical appearance, sexist body language, lack of respect, and masculine practices which intimidate or exclude women and favour fellow men. This might, for example, involve some lorry drivers showing pictures of scantily clad women in canteen rooms or inside the cabin space of vehicles. Sexist assumptions and practices can hold employees back and channel them into the wrong roles. Women may be shut out of senior positions or diverted into roles seen to require stereotypically 'feminine' skills. For instance, they are often expected to take on assistant, secretarial, or managerial tasks within logistics firms. This is a waste of human resources and is thus inefficient for logistic businesses. Sexism can seriously harm employees; sexist expectations and behaviours negatively affect employees' performance, sense of belonging, mental health, and job satisfaction. Sexist behaviour and practices, when frequent and normalised, have been shown to be as detrimental to employees' occupational well-being.

Since logistics is commonly viewed as a male-dominated industry, the proportion of women within the logistics industry is rather low, both at the executive level and among lower ranks of the industry. In 2018, the share of women in the first management level of German logistics companies was only 18 per cent, while 23 cent of the total workforce was female (Kohaut and Möller, 2019). Similarly, most companies do not have a single woman on board level (four out of five management teams are strictly male). Women also still lack opportunities for development in logistics. Only recently, Sabina Jeschke, one of the two female board members of Deutsche Bahn, left the state-owned company after a three-year tenure for this reason (Manager Magazin, 2021). In logistics, as well as in other industries, there is a significant call for a more diverse and (gender) balanced leadership.

Gendered Leadership Competencies: Agentic and Communal Traits

To facilitate an examination of leadership competencies, it is first necessary to define the term 'leadership'. In this chapter, leadership competencies are defined as personality traits, skills, values, knowledge, capacities and capabilities that facilitate one's ability to perform leadership tasks (Wisittigars and Siengthai, 2019). They are generally seen as highly dependent on the contextual components; thus there is no 'one size fits all' approach to leadership (Haddon et al., 2015: 613). According to Ryan et al. (2011: 471), good leadership is characterised by a 'match between leader characteristics and the features of the situation that a leader confronts'. For instance, cultural and social values can influence the leadership behavioural preferences (Sharif, 2019). Furthermore, the organisational environment plays an important role in the perception of effective leadership, as this can significantly vary from 'normal' times compared to times of crisis (Haddon et al., 2015: 613). Savaneviciene et al. (2014) grouped leadership competencies into three components: self-management competencies, business management competencies, and people management competencies. These three competencies enable leaders to adapt to rapidly changing circumstances and achieve both efficient business communication and effective people management, especially during a crisis.

Perceptions around leadership competencies are gendered. Studies reveal that people still associate stereotypically masculine character traits and competencies with successful leadership (Powell, 2012). Men are usually said to possess so-called **agentic traits**, such as assertiveness, task-orientation dominance, and ambition, which led to these qualities being perceived as stereotypical competencies required for leaders (Griffiths et al., 2019: 33). Women, on the other hand, are seen as 'affectionate, helpful, kind, … and gentle' (Eagly and Karau, 2002: 574) which are classified as **communal traits** (pertain to concern for others and interpersonal sensitivity). In some studies of leadership perception, 'men rate themselves as significantly more effective than women rate themselves' (Paustian-Underdahl et al., 2014: 1129).

One leadership style that is highly sought after today, transformational leadership, seems to be the result of using a skill set pertaining to the use of both masculine and feminine leadership skills. Both female and male managers who are capable of taking advantage of both masculine and feminine skills and features tend to be seen as transformational leaders (Kark et al., 2012), yet such a style of leadership is usually associated with women (Eagly et al., 2003). Transformational leadership is a style that can inspire positive changes in those who follow. Transformational leaders are generally energetic, enthusiastic, and passionate. Not only are these leaders concerned and involved in the process, but they are also focused on helping members of the group succeed. Examples of transformational leaders can be politicians, such as Barack Obama or Nelson Mandela; reformers, such as Mahatma Gandhi; or managers, such as Steve Jobs. There are also many inspiring female transformational leaders, of course, including politicians such as Jacinda Ardern, media executive Oprah Winfrey, and managers such as Sheryl Sandberg.

Gender thus affects leadership in many aspects. Whether men and women lead in a different way is still a highly debated issue. However, the major effect of gender on leadership is that women are *presumed* to be less competent and less worthy to hold leadership positions, like management board positions (Eagly and Johannesen-Schmidt, 2001). In some research studies, a larger proportion of women than men have indicated a preference for a male leader (Powell, 2012), revealing that many women also perceive men as having the best competencies for leadership.

Leadership During Crises

A crisis is characterised by 'a low-probability, high-impact event that threatens the viability of the organisation and is characterised by ambiguity of cause, effect, and means of resolution, as well as by a belief that decisions must be made swiftly' (Pearson and Clair, 1998: 60). Further, a crisis can have substantial negative effects on those affected by it like stress, fear, physical and mental health problems (Dückers et al., 2017). Crises can either arise internally – for instance, through 'moral or ethical failures, an unanticipated change in leadership, poor oversight, product failures' – or through external factors, like 'environmental disasters due to acts of nature, pandemic threats, targeted public acts, stock market crashes' (Bowers et al., 2017: 555).

In order to overcome crisis-related challenges effectively, Boin et al. (2016) suggest that leaders should pursue the following six tasks: sense-making, decision-making, coordination, meaning-making, account-giving, and learning. Sense-making requires that managers unfold unknown situations adequately, given the scarce information. Decision-making requires critical decision-making at a strategic level. Coordination refers to the internal coordination and the allocation of capacities and resources. Meaning-making is about providing an explanation of the cause of the crisis, as well as the effects and necessary reactions. The fifth task, account-giving, requires that responsibilities are clarified and accepted without engaging in scapegoating. Learning involves critical assessments of one's own actions, and the ability to draw conclusions for future performance out of it, during and after the crisis. In order to pursue these tasks, certain competencies are needed. Competencies are characterised as self-organised, individual, situational, able to transform, and closely related to action (Janning-Backfisch, 2018; Kanning, 2009). Leaders must be self-organised subjects in organisations. Self-organised activities are necessary to anticipate the challenges of such crises in a flexible and dynamic way (Erpenbeck, 2002; Janning-Backfisch, 2018). Competencies are not directly empirically observable, but their indicators can be observed in individual behaviour (Heyse, 2007).

The Prominence of Female Leadership

One prominent question that arises is to ask which competencies are needed for good leadership during crises. Can 'female leadership' be seen as an advantage? In a study of female leadership during times of crisis, Hougaard et al. (2022) found that women leaders were more equipped at managing workers than their male counterparts. For their research, they conducted a multi-year study with managers and employees from approximately 5,000 companies in almost 100 countries. The aim of the study was to determine how managers can be effective while making difficult decisions or giving negative feedback. They distilled the analysis into two main traits: *wisdom*, the courage to do what needs to be done, even when it is difficult; and *compassion*, the care and empathy shown towards others, combined with the intention to support and help. Both traits have been shown to be important, but in combination they are exceptionally well received: job satisfaction is 86 per cent higher for an employee who works for a wise and compassionate leader than an employee who does not. Looking at gender, the authors find that more than half of the female leaders were being perceived as possessing both traits, compared to roughly a quarter of male leaders. During the pandemic and other recent crises, leaders were called on to navigate their teams through waves of grief, anxiety, and uncertainty, to help protect their (mental) health, and to provide a better working environment for all.

Female leadership is changing the world of work. In contemporary workplaces, many women are being favoured for their inclusive and empathetic activities, and the harsh masculine qualities of the corporate world are becoming outdated and unwanted. This change favours women who wish to succeed in management roles. Furthermore, employers with an emphasis on improving environmental, social, and governance (ESG) factors require leadership which can perform and deliver what is needed in the modern workforce (Ahmad et al., 2023). And many women are seen as having these qualities of leadership. This becomes especially important for the younger **generation**, Generation Z (the generation following the Millennials), since corporate jobs will require an understanding of many environmental and social issues. Many organisations place women's leadership at the heart of this ambition. Having experienced 9/11, the 2008 recession, and an escalating climate crisis as important moments in their upbringing, Generation Z-ers have grown up seeking stability in their lives, including in their working careers. This sentiment was exacerbated for those graduating from 2019 to 2021, and having to endure one of the most volatile employment markets in the wake of the COVID-19 pandemic. In addition, they were impacted by the associated economic uncertainty and had to adjust their learning behaviour and social expectations.

At the same time, Generation Z-ers are on track to be the most qualified generation in history – in 2018, in the US, 57 per cent of 18- to 21-year-olds were in higher education, compared to 52 per cent of Millennials and 43 per cent of Gen X-ers at the same age (Dennington, 2021). Because of these world-shaping events, much of Generation Z feels a drive to enact positive change in the world. As the most diverse generation so far, diversity and inclusion initiatives are important to them, as well as a deep concern for the climate crisis and increasing access to mental health support and resources (Scholz, 2014). These needs can be met by leaders who exhibit not only agentic traits, but also put emphasis on caring, purpose, and vision. Krivkovich et al. (2022: 50) say that 'the COVID-19 crisis and racial reckoning of 2020 pushed corporate America to reimagine the way we work … Women are ambitious and hardworking. They're more inclusive and empathetic leaders.' Thus, the perception around female leadership is changing. Women are seen as possessing different qualities, ones which are ideal for leadership of the future.

Case Study

Male-Dominated Logistics Company in Crisis – Bavaria, Southern Germany

Bettina Nicols is Managing Director at Transpoxit, based in Rosenheim, southern Germany. She has been in this position since February 2018, exactly two years before the COVID-19 pandemic crisis reached Europe and most of the globe. In conversation, she says that over a few days, all the processes of her daily work changed. From one moment to the next, most European countries closed their borders and only allowed Transpoxit's trucks to pass after strict application procedures. The majority of German companies are SME (small or medium-sized). The medium-sized company Transpoxit, founded by several production companies from southern Bavaria, does most of its business transporting raw materials from Germany to Southern and Eastern Europe. Since the supply of raw materials from Asia began to falter in spring 2020, the company and its business partners were struggling.

From the beginning, it was crucial for Bettina to remain in transparent discussions with employees. The male-dominated workforce consisted mostly of truck drivers, many of them from Eastern European countries: 'Nobody knew what was coming! Both economically and socially, my management and I felt like we were in an empty space. We had to decide from day to day what to do; how we could implement the special regulations that were different from country to country and from customer to customer.'

Julia Hansch and Natalie Janning-Backfisch

Although the workforce is dominated by mostly conservative men, Bettina, as a female boss, is popular. This is mainly due to her consistency and determination, says Timo Miller, sales representative at Transpoxit: 'She also has no problem telling people what she thinks, be it employees or business partners. She doesn't let herself be intimidated and always tries to reconcile differences of opinion in a respectful way.'

Even during the most challenging periods of the pandemic, Bettina kept a cool head and established clear priorities, consistently putting the well-being of her employees first. However, this approach did not always align with some business partners, who insisted on uninterrupted transportation and seamless business operations regardless of the circumstances. During these uncertain times, she demonstrated great empathy towards her employees' needs. For Bettina, the primary objective was not solely short-term profitability, but rather the company's enduring sustainability and its employees' welfare. Consequently, she devoted significant attention to the social aspect of ESG (environmental, social, and governance) considerations. Bettina anticipated that these efforts would, ultimately, yield personal benefits in the long run.

Despite the dissenting views of her business partners, Bettina decided – particularly in the case of foreign drivers – that it was necessary for them to return to their families: 'No one knew how hard it would hit health-wise. Anyone could have died from the virus.' Another haulage company from the neighbouring town relied on continuing to operate all their trips. Initially, this approach proved effective, and the workload was more than full. However, when the (male) manager attempted to prevent the employees from going home to their families in Eastern Europe, to be there for them, they left regardless. To this day, none of the drivers have returned ... And, due to the already severe shortage of drivers, the company continues to face considerable challenges, even after the COVID-19 peak. Bettina's employees, on the other hand, have been (and are still) treating her with a lot of respect, and expressing their gratitude for her understanding with their continued good performance. This case study shows that there is a difference between how male and female leaders manage organisations in times of crises. Women leaders like Bettina Nicols possess many of the much-needed traits required in modern times.

Conclusion

Germany's logistics sector is the country's third largest industry, employing approximately 3 million people. Despite being such a vital part of the economy, the industry lacks fair representation of women in leadership positions – i.e. logistics is still 'a man's world'. During the pandemic, a lot has changed in terms of leadership, and female leaders are being sought after for their empathetic and authentic leadership behaviour. Therefore, it is necessary to have a look at leadership and leadership competencies in times of crisis, and to ask whether the perception of leaders has changed during the COVID-19 pandemic, as an example of a worldwide crisis. Companies within the logistics industry should use research results to make better use of the potential of female leaders. The logistics industry can use these data to eliminate the gender gap, be it in career advancement, pay, or leadership opportunities. The first steps to answer these questions have been taken, but many facts still need to be uncovered and discussed, and time will tell whether we will be experiencing a significant shift in (logistics) companies' leadership.

STUDENT ACTIVITY

- Which competencies do you know, and which are particularly important for 'good leadership'?
- Look at the definition used in this chapter to define leadership. Consider how much perceptions of leadership have changed in, or during times of, crises (e.g. the COVID-19 pandemic).
- Consider whether you have perceived competencies in successful leaders. What competencies would be particularly important to you in a leadership role?
- Imagine the peak of one crisis – for example, the recent COVID-19 pandemic. What situations in the context of your job or your educational life changed or were changing during this time? Think about the manager to whom you reported, or the professor who led your courses. Did this leader manage this special situation in a way that you felt comfortable with? Indicate whether it was a female or male leader. Do you think someone form the opposite sex would have done better, or not as well? What is the reason for this? How would you justify that female leaders are perceived differently to male leaders?

Practice Questions

- Is female leadership in a crisis more successful than male leadership? Give examples.
- Which industries do you know as male-dominated? What are the challenges they pose for women?
- Do you still believe in 'think manager, think male'?
- Will environmental, social, and governance (ESG) factors continue to play a major role, now that the pandemic is officially over?
- What is the dominating gender of leaders in the industry you plan on working in? How might this limit or facilitate your success?
- Imagine you get a job as a human resources director. One of your first tasks is to create a requirements profile for leaders in your company, and you think it is important the company is well prepared for crises. What does your requirements profile look like?

Key Terms

Agentic vs. communal traits
research has demonstrated that men are often stereotyped as agentic, and women are stereotyped as communal. Therefore, the perceived importance of agentic

Julia Hansch and Natalie Janning-Backfisch

versus communal traits for success in business may contribute to gender biases. According to Twenge, women are more communal than men, but there are actually no gender differences in agentic traits (Twenge, 2009).

Competency
a competence can be defined as the quality or state of having sufficient knowledge, judgement, skill, or strength for a particular task or in a particular respect. Thus, competency means capability. Heyse (2007) defines competencies as personal prerequisites to self-organise in order to accomplish new, non-routine tasks.

Crisis
'a low-probability, high-impact event that threatens the viability of the organisation and is characterised by ambiguity of cause, effect, and means of resolution, as well as by a belief that decisions must be made swiftly' (Pearson and Clair, 1998: 60).

Gender stereotypes
many people hold prejudices regarding the attributes of different genders. Gender stereotyping describes these overgeneralised characteristics and behaviours ascribed to people based on their identifiable gender. This includes, for example, the assumption that women typically possess more communal traits compared to men.

Generation
a group of a population born in a certain period. This group has similar experiences from their environment (social, economical, political, technological); the individuals of these group socialise in a similar way and represent similar values and attitudes which shapes their behaviour.

Leadership
in the economic context, leadership encompasses much more than the sheer administration of an organisation. Leadership is the ability of an individual or a group of individuals to influence and guide followers or other members of an organisation. Leadership can be discussed in terms of traits or characteristics, behaviour and the situational context. In particular, the characteristics of the leader, who has the ability to guide other people on the basis of his or her personality, are associated with (perceived) leadership (Peters, 2015).

Leadership competencies
according to Boyatzis (2008), leadership competencies are 'personality traits, skills, values, knowledge, capacities and capabilities that facilitate one's ability to perform leadership tasks' (Wisittigars and Siengthai, 2019).

References

Ahmad, H., Yaqub, M., and Lee, S.H. (2023) 'Environmental-, social-, and governance-related factors for business investment and sustainability: a scientometric review of global trends'. *Environment, Development and Sustainability*. Accessed 18 August 2023 from https://doi.org/10.1007/s10668-023-02921-x

AllBright (2019) *Entwicklungsland: Deutsche Konzerne entdecken erst jetzt Frauen für die Führung*. Stockholm and Berlin: AllBright Stiftung GmbH.

Amazon Workforce Data (2022) 'Our workforce data'. Accessed 11 August 2022 from www.aboutamazon.com/news/workplace/our-workforce-data

Anonymous (2020) 'Studie & Ranking: WoB-Index 185'. *FidAR Analytics*. Accessed 11 June 2020 from www.fidar.de/wob-indizes-studien/wob-index-185/uebersicht.html

Barwitzki, M. (2020) 'Weibliche Dax-Vorstände verdienen mehr als männliche'. Accessed 29 May 2021 from www.finance-magazin.de/finanzabteilung/gehalt/weibliche-dax-vorstaende-verdienen-mehr-als-maennliche-2069201/

Bertrand, M., Black, S.E., Jensen, S., and Lleras-Muney, A. (2018) 'Breaking the glass ceiling? The effect of board quotas on female labour market outcomes in Norway'. *Review of Economic Studies*, 86(1): 191–239.

Boin, A., Hart, P. 't, Stern, E., and Sundelius, B. (2016) *The politics of crisis management: public leadership under pressure*, 2nd edition. New York: Cambridge University Press.

Bowers, M.R., Hall, J.R., and Srinivasan, M.M. (2017) 'Organizational culture and leadership style: the missing combination for selecting the right leader for effective crisis management'. *Business Horizons*, 60(4): 551–563.

Boyatzis (2008) 'Competencies in the 21st century'. *Journal of Management Development*, 27(1): 5–12.

Bundesvereinigung Logistik (2019) 'Begleitende Publikation zur Session "Männerdomäne?! Chancen für und mit Frauen in der Logistik"'. Accessed 15 August 2023 from www.bvl.de/schriften/schriften/begleitende-publikation-zur-session-maennerdomaene-chancen-fuer-und-mit-frauen-in-der-logistik

Dennington, A. (2021) 'Gen Ztressed: A new generation of college students'. Accessed 11 August 2023 from https://timelycare.com/blog/generation-z-college-students/#:~:text=Generation%20Z%20students%20are%20on,Gen%20Xers%20at%20similar%20ages

Dückers, M.L.A., Yzermans, C.J., Jong, W., and Boin, A. (2017) 'Psychosocial crisis management: the unexplored intersection of crisis leadership and psychosocial support'. *Risk, Hazards & Crisis in Public Policy*, 8(2): 94–112.

Eagly, A.H., and Johannesen-Schmidt, M.C. (2001) 'The leadership styles of women and men'. *Journal of Social Issues*, 57(4): 781–797.

Eagly, A.H., Johannesen-Schmidt, M, and Van Engen, M.L. (2003) 'Transformational, transactional, and laissez-faire leadership styles: a meta-analysis comparing women and men'. *Psychological Bulletin, 129*(4): 569–591.

Eagly, A.H., and Karau, S J. (2002) 'Role congruity theory of prejudice toward female leaders'. *Psychological Review, 109*(3): 573–598.

Egon Zehnder (2020) '2020 Global Board Diversity Tracker: Who's really on board?' Available at www.egonzehnder.com/global-board-diversity-tracker-2020

Erpenbeck, J. (2002) 'Kompetenz und Performanz im Bild moderner Selbstorganisationstheorie'. Dokumentation 4, BIBB-Fachkongress 2002. *Berufsbildung für eine globale Gesellschaft Perspektiven im 21. Jahrhundert*. Accessed 29 May 2021 from https://ams-forschungsnetzwerk.at/downloadpub/erpenbeck_03_4_2002.pdf

Gartzia, L. Ryan, M.K., Balluerka, N., and Aritzeta, A. (2012) 'Think crisis – think female: further evidence'. *European Journal of Work and Organizational Psychology*, 21(4): 603–628.

Griffiths, O., Roberts, L., and Price, J. (2019) 'Desirable leadership attributes are preferentially associated with women: a quantitative study of gender and leadership roles in the Australian workforce'. *Australian Journal of Management*, 44(1): 32–49.

Haddon, A., Loughlin, C., and McNally, C. (2015) 'Leadership in a time of financial crisis: what do we want from our leaders?' *Leadership & Organization Development Journal*, 36(5): 612–627.

Heyse, V. (2007) 'Strategien – Kompetenzanforderungen – Potentitalanalyse'. In J. Hansch (2021) *Corporate Governance für internationale Konzerne*. In V. Heyse and J. Erpenbeck (eds), *Kompetenzmanagement: Methoden, Vorgehen, KODE® und KODE®X im Praxistest*, Münster: Waxmann, 11–180.

Hougaard, R., Carter, J., and Afto, M. (2022) 'When women leaders leave, the losses multiply'. *Harvard Business Review*. Accessed 28 August 2023 from https://hbr.org/2022/03/when-women-leaders-leave-the-losses-multiply

Janning-Backfisch, N. (2018) K*ompetenz- und Qualifikationsanforderungen in der Logistik: Empirische Analyse betrieblicher Anforderungen mit Fokus Baden-Württemberg und Bayern*. Wiesbaden: Springer Gabler.

Kanning, U.P. (2009) *Diagnostik sozialer Kompetenzen*: 2., *aktualisierte Auflage*. *Kompendien psychologische Diagnostik,* Vol. 4. Oxford: Hogrefe.

Kark, R., Waismel-Manor, R., and Shamir, B. (2012) 'Does valuing androgyny and femininity lead to a female advantage? The relationship between gender-role, transformational leadership and identification'. *Leadership Quarterly*, 23(3): 620–640.

Kirsch, A., and Wrohlich, K. (2021) Mehr Frauen in Spitzengremien großer Unternehmen, Dynamik aber verhalten – gesetzliche Vorgabe könnte Schwung bringen'. *DIW Wochenbericht*, 3: 22–35.

Kohaut, S., and Möller, I (2019) Frauen in leitenden Positionen: leider nichts neues auf den Führungsetagen. *IAB Kurzbericht,* 23. Nuremberg: Institut für Arbeitsmarkt- und Berufsforschung (IAB) der Bundesagentur für Arbeit.

Krivkovich, A., Yee, L., Liu, W., Rambachan, I., Robinson, N., Nguyen, H., and Williams, M. (2022) *Women in the Workplace 2022*. New York: McKinsey & Company.

Manager Magazin (2021) 'Abgang nach rund drei Jahren: deutsche Bahn verliert Digitalchefin Sabina Jeschke'. *manager magazin*, 18 February. Accessed 13 May 2021 from www.manager-magazin.de/unternehmen/deutsche-bahn-sabina-jeschke-verlaesst-den-konzern-a-38707de0-fab3-4e0f-be5b-e7b11ed63f49

Paustian-Underdahl, S.C., Walker, L.S., and Woehr, D.J. (2014) 'Gender and perceptions of leadership effectiveness: a meta-analysis of contextual moderators'. *Journal of Applied Psychology*, 99(6): 1129–1145.

Pearson, C.M., and Clair, J.A. (1998) 'Reframing crisis management'. *Academy of Management Review*, 23(1): 59–76.

Peters, T. (2015) *Leadership: traditionelle und moderne Konzepte mit vielen Beispielen*. Wiesbaden: Springer Gabler.

Powell, G.N. (2012) 'Six ways of seeing the elephant: the intersection of sex, gender, and leadership'. *Gender in Management: An International Journal*, 27(2): 119–141.

Rubin, M., Paolini, S., Subašić, E., and Giacomini, A. (2019) 'A confirmatory study of the relations between workplace sexism, sense of belonging, mental health, and job satisfaction among women in male-dominated industries'. *Journal of Applied Social Psychology*, 49: 267–282.

Ryan, M.K., and Haslam, S.A. (2005) The glass cliff: evidence that women are over-represented in precarious leadership positions'. *British Journal of Management*, 16: 81–90.

Ryan, M.K., Haslam, S.A., Hersby, M.D., and Bongiorno, R. (2011) 'Think crisis–think female: the glass cliff and contextual variation in the think manager-think male stereotype'. *Journal of Applied Psychology*, 96(3): 470–484.

Savaneviciene, A., Čiutienė, R., and Rūtelionė, A. (2014) 'Examining leadership competencies during economic turmoil'. *Procedia – Social and Behavioral Sciences*, 156: 41–46.

Schein, V.E., Mueller, R., Lituchy, T., and Liu, J. (1996) 'Think manager – think male: a global phenomenon?' *Journal of Organizational Behavior*, 17(1): 33–41.

Scholz, C. (2014) *Generation Z: wie sie tickt, was sie verändert und warum sie uns alle ansteckt*. Weinheim: John Wiley and Sons.

Sharif, K. (2019) 'Transformational leadership behaviors of women in a socially dynamic environment'. *IJOA*, 27(1): 1–27.

Statistisches Bundesamt (2021) 'Frauen in Führungspositionen'. Accessed 18 April 2021 from www.destatis.de/DE/Themen/Arbeit/Arbeitsmarkt/Qualitaet-Arbeit/Dimension-1/frauen-fuehrungspositionen.html

Twenge, J.M. (2009) 'Status and gender: the paradox of progress in an age of narcissism'. *Sex Roles: A Journal of Research*, 61(5–6): 338–340.

Wisittigars, B., and Siengthai, S. (2019) 'Crisis leadership competencies: the facility management sector in Thailand'. *Facilities*, 37(13/14): 881–896.

World Economic Forum (2023) Global Gender Gap Report 2023. Accessed 19 August 2023 from www.weforum.org/reports/global-gender-gap-report-2023/in-full?_gl=1*t7fm65*_up*MQ..&gclid=CjwKCAjw44mlBhAQEiwAqP3eVi50Fb5jqfROPSdI9PBF8IPFJUTIUAW8hDfuGP3_97zvC24V2QIZHxoCSjQQAvD_BwE

chapter 10

Work–Life Balance
Mengyi Xu and Clare Kelliher

Conceptualisation of the Work–Life Balance

Researchers, policy-makers, and practitioners have tended to place emphasis on **work–life balance** as a means to enhance employee well-being. Work–life balance concerns the relationship between the work and non-work aspects of people's lives. It may seem easy to understand at face value, but an established definition is lacking in the literature (Kelliher et al., 2019). One reason for this is because the work and non-work domains have evolved. 'Work' traditionally refers to full-time, permanent employment based on the 'standard employment relationship' (Bosch, 2004). The consideration of 'life' has often been seen as interchangeable with 'family', particularly for women with dependent children. Yet, over the past few decades, the scope of what is considered in the work and non-work domains has changed and developed in a more holistic way. A contemporary understanding of work needs to incorporate diverse arrangements and employment relationships, such as part-time and gig economy work. More diverse life patterns may mean that people wish to balance other aspects of their non-work lives with work in addition to family responsibilities, including, for example, leisure activities, community involvement, volunteering, and supporting extended families (Kelliher et al., 2019).

The other reason lies in the problematic definition of 'balance'. Traditional research uses work–life conflict and work–life enrichment as representative components and distinctive dimensions in understanding work–life balance (Greenhaus and Beutell, 1985; Greenhaus and Powell, 2006). However, this conceptualization becomes challenging when examining the antecedents and consequences of work–life balance. Grzywacz and Carlson (2007: 463) highlight that '**work–family conflict** and **work–family enrichment** occasionally share antecedents that have similar rather than opposite effects'. For instance, reduced working hours may alleviate work–life conflict but could weaken enrichment due to fewer pay and career opportunities. A complex workload may induce conflict but enhance job enrichment through skill acquisition and problem-solving capabilities. This complexity arises

DOI: 10.4324/9781003314769-13 147

when organizations aim to improve employees' work–life balance by increasing enrichment through heightened work demands, inadvertently increasing work–life conflict. Carlson et al. (2006) argue that work–family balance transcends the absence of conflict and the presence of enrichment.

Furthermore, some definitions imply balance as an equal distribution of time, energy, and commitment between the work and non-work domains (Greenhaus et al., 2003). However, this overlooks the diverse ways individuals may manage their multiple roles and where they allocate priority, rather than seeing them as equal. Greenhaus and Allen (2011) propose work–life balance as an overall appraisal of how individuals' satisfaction in their work and non-work roles are consistent with their priorities at any given time. Therefore, how individuals perceive work–life balance and prioritise their work and non-work roles and activities in their personal context is critical to understanding their work–life balance experience.

Perception of the Work–Life Balance

How work–life balance is understood may be shaped by multiple factors at the national, organisational, and temporal levels. At the national level, the opportunities and constraints stemming from legal, economic, and social structures can influence individual perceptions and how they experience the work and life interface and organisational support (Le et al., 2020; Ollier-Malaterre and Foucreault, 2017). For example, as early as 2000, the UK government promoted a framework, the 'work–life balance campaign', which encouraged employers to introduce family-friendly practices to assist employees in improving the balance between their work and lifestyles while allowing them to fulfil their business goals. This was subsequently embedded in legislation, with the 'right to request **flexible working**' provisions introduced for parents and extended to cover all employees in 2014, alongside the strengthening of maternity and paternity leave rights in 2021. Similarly, since 2017, European countries such as France, Italy, Spain, and Ireland, have implemented the right of employees to disconnect from work-related technology outside of working hours. While there have been some controversies regarding how these provisions can be implemented in practice, the evidence shows that they had a positive and beneficial influence on employees' work–life balance (Kossek et al., 2022).

Unlike much of the industrialised West, Asian developing countries like China and India tend to have given less consideration to work–life balance and, to date, only limited flexible working and family-friendly work policies are available to employees (Le et al., 2020). Significantly, national culture shapes an individual's expectations and perceptions of work–life balance and consequently influences an individual's work–life experiences. The gendered culture of work and care roles are relevant to the work–life interface. For instance, in countries like Italy and Portugal, a common pattern can be observed, where men are primarily involved in paid work, while women are primarily engaged in non-work roles (Lewis, 2009). Another aspect of culture that affects the work–life interface is the relationship

Mengyi Xu and Clare Kelliher

between individuals and groups. Countries of collectivist cultures (e.g. China and India), as opposed to individualist cultures (such as the US and UK), should experience less work–life conflict. This is mainly because work is viewed as a form of self-sacrifice that brings honour to the family. In addition, the emphasis on high performance-oriented culture or human-oriented culture also plays a significant role. In cultures that prioritize high performance and competitiveness, individuals may experience greater work–life imbalance. On the other hand, in cultures that value a more human-oriented approach and emphasize the well-being of individuals, there may be a higher likelihood of achieving work–life balance (Ollier-Malaterre and Foucreault, 2017).

Taking the Chinese context as an example, rapid economic development has given employees access to higher incomes. However, it has also resulted in increased stress, due to long working hours and intensification of performance requirements, brought about by the move to marketisation in the Chinese economy. While growing legal protection requires employers to pay attention to employees' leave entitlement and well-being, there is little regulation from the government and/or initiatives on work–life balance and flexible working from employers. Advocacy of work–life harmony is often in conflict with an established 'sacrificing oneself for one's work' culture. This paradoxical situation explains, to some extent, why Chinese employees tend not to be sensitive to work–life conflict, instead seeing it simply as 'as a matter of fact' (Xiao and Cooke, 2012).

At the organisational level, formal regulations and culture affect employees' work–life balance perceptions and experiences (Daverth et al., 2016; Kossek et al., 2022). Formal regulation can take the form of legislation and government policies, such as the right to request flexible working and company work–life initiatives such as hybrid working and on-site childcare facilities. Negotiation between the employee and line managers over working arrangements also directly affects employees' work–life balance – for example, where managers can grant temporal flexibility and leave if employees need to deal with a personal emergency. Research shows that informal arrangements between employees and their line managers are widespread and may be better able to accommodate individual work–life preferences (de Menezes and Kelliher, 2017). In addition, an individual's work–life balance is likely influenced by what is normative, feasible, and socially acceptable in the particular workplace (Lewis and Beauregard, 2018). Organisational culture, such as long working hours and **'ideal worker norms'**, could be detrimental to the legitimacy and use of work–life policies. By contrast, a supportive **work–life culture** can foster the uptake of work–life policies and practices (Daverth et al., 2016).

At the temporal level, the meanings of work–life balance can shift and evolve in response to specific events and changes in specific places (Lewis and Beauregard, 2018). This is due to the dynamic nature of work and personal lives, which are influenced by technology, social norms, and economic conditions. For example, the COVID-19 pandemic significantly impacted work–life balance, as many employees were forced to work from home and juggle work and personal responsibilities in new ways (see the Introduction, Chapter 1). This shift resulted in a greater concern for work–life balance and interest in flexible work arrangements, with the blurring of boundaries between work and personal life and the need for better support systems to help employees manage their responsibilities (Kossek et al., 2022). The evolving nature of the work–life balance underscores the importance of ongoing research and adaptation of work–life balance policies and practices and culture to reflect the changing needs and realities of the workforce.

Why Organisations Manage Work–Life Balance

There are three main rationales for organisations to help employees achieve a better work–life balance. First, many organisations draw on a 'business case' for implementing better work–life balance practices. Organisational support for employees' work–life balance can be seen as a win–win situation by improving employees' lives and concurrently boosting organisational performance. Effective support for work–life balance is also seen as helping organisations attract and retain a more diverse range of employees, reduce absenteeism and turnover caused by conflicting demands, and increase employee commitment through feeling valued by their employer, potentially contributing to organisational success (Kelliher et al., 2019).

Second, there is a 'legal case' for facilitating a satisfactory work–life balance, since the employer must follow the external form of job regulations making appropriate policies and practices to manage the workforce. Legal regulation of working hours and the right to flexible working arrangements is linked to work–life balance. In particular, the latter has grown in significance in recognising employees' desire for a better work–life balance and the need for greater protection of workers who work non-standard hours, often due to non-work commitments. For example, a recent extension of the legal provisions in the UK allowed employees to request flexible working arrangements, such as part-time working, changes to start and finish times and compressed hours, without a minimum qualification period of employment. Similarly, in Australia, the Fair Work Act 2009 allows parents and carers to apply for flexitime options. Moreover, indirect legal requirements, such as 'duty of care', where an employer has a duty to protect the health, safety, and welfare of their employees and others who might be affected by their work activities, are also crucial to employees' work–life balance. In the Netherlands, employers have a statutory duty to take care of employees' safety and health, both physical and psychosocial, including work–life balance. Accordingly, governments have been proactive in encouraging employers to consider how employer and employee needs can be matched, and to offer the best possible working conditions for employees.

Third, there is a 'social case' for managing employees' work–life balance, meaning that understanding and caring for employees' work–life balance can be seen as a demonstration of corporate social responsibility (Been et al., 2017). Organisational leaders are expected to recognise their responsibilities in an effort to ensure that their employees do not work in a way that unduly interferes with their personal lives, leading to a detrimental impact on individual well-being and social inequality in terms of gender and class (Álvarez-Pérez et al., 2020).

Mengyi Xu and Clare Kelliher

How Organisations Manage Work–Life Balance

Managing work–life balance generally involves a formal approach, such as work–family/life policies and practices and contextual support, including fostering a positive work–life culture and the provision of support from managers and co-workers (Daverth et al., 2016; Kossek et al., 2022).

Formal approaches to managing work–life balance may originate from two main channels: statutory entitlements and company initiatives. First, governments enact statutory regulations and social policies related to employees' work–life balance, which serves as a foundation for organisations to set up work–life balance policies and practices (Ollier-Malaterre and Foucreault, 2017). Second, organisations may 'top up' these policies by initiating work–life balance practices to benefit employees for 'business case' (Kossek et al., 2022). Exemplar definitions and categories of work–life balance policies and practices can be found in Table 10.1 below.

Table 10.1 The Definition and Categories of Work–Life Balance Policies and Practices

Definition	*'Any organisational programmes or officially-sanctioned practices designed to assist employees with fulfilling paid work with other fundamental life roles such as family, education or leisure.' (Ryan and Kossek, 2008: 295)*		
Content and categories	Flexible working arrangements	Flexible working hours	Part-time work is usually defined as regular paid employment with fewer hours than the average full-time work. Flexitime permits employees to vary their start and finish times, provided that their contracted number of hours are worked. Job sharing involves sharing a full-time job between two employees. A compressed working week is where employees work the total number of weekly or monthly hours but over fewer days than is the workplace norm, e.g. total hours worked over four days instead of five.
		Flexible workplace	Remote working: working away from the workplace (e.g. at home or in other locations)
	Leave entitlement	Statutory maternity leave, paternity leave, family leave	
	Caring support	On-site childcare and financial/informational assistance with childcare and elder-care services	
	Support and well-being programme	Employee Assistance Programme (EAP), including facilities such as an on-site gym, stress management programme, employee counselling schemes	

Source: drawing on Ryan and Kossek (2008: 295).

While formal approaches to managing work–life balance are increasingly on employer agendas, the evidence is mixed regarding whether policies and practices enhance job performance by reducing work–life conflict (de Menezes and Kelliher, 2011). Understanding employee perceptions of work–life balance policies and practices is crucial in explaining work-related outcomes. If employees view the practices as unfair, unresponsive, or unhelpful, they may be less likely to engage with the organisation and may seek opportunities elsewhere. By contrast, if employees view the practices as supportive, effective, and transparent, they may be more likely to be satisfied with their jobs, motivated to perform at a high level, and committed to the organisation's goals. Therefore, availability, their experiences, and the effectiveness perceived by employees could be key indicators in identifying the effect of work–life balance policies and practices (Kossek et al., 2022).

The availability of work–life balance opportunities may be limited if employers only develop policies and practices symbolically without effective implementation (Williams et al., 2021). Even if the policies and practices are made available, not all members of the workforce may be aware of them and have equal *access* to these policies and practices (Beauregard, 2014). Research on the implementation of work–life balance policies and practices has shown that they are often seen as catering to the needs of specific groups in the workforce, such as working mothers, often the primary caregivers for children and other dependants, and knowledge workers who have high levels of education and in professional and/or managerial roles (who may be more able to negotiate and benefit from these policies and practices). Other groups, like working fathers and employees who live alone, are often seen to be neglected in these policies (see Gatrell et al., 2022; Wilkinson et al., 2018). Inequality in being able to access policies and practices may challenge perceptions of organisational justice and workplace inclusion (Kelliher et al., 2019; Beauregard, 2014).

Even for employees who perceive that work–life balance policies and practices are available, there may be concerns about the potential consequences, making them hesitant to use them. For example, employees may fear facing financial problems if they take (unpaid) parental leave or reduce their hours; remote working could limit employees' workplace networking, viability, and social capital accumulation and create barriers to career development and promotion due to reduced 'face time' in the workplace. In addition, the '**flexibility paradox**' raised by researchers (Cañibano, 2019) argues that when workers gain more control over when and where they work, they often end up working harder and longer. Organizational performance pressure may drive employees to intensify their work efforts, dedicating extended hours to bolster their competitive edge and capitalize on market opportunities in alignment with the 'ideal worker norm'. This **work intensification**, stemming from performance pressures, can extend to part-time employees who may face expectations of a workload equivalent to that of full-time positions(Kelliher and Anderson, 2010).

To enable employees to use work–life balance policies and practices effectively, informal approaches to managing work–life balance, including cultural, managerial, and co-worker support, play crucial roles (Daverth et al., 2016). Work–life culture can be defined as 'shared assumptions, beliefs, and values regarding the extent to which an organisation supports and values the integration of employees' work and family lives' (Thompson et al., 1999: 416). Culture signals the approach of an organisation to valuing the employees' work–life balance and includes the extent to which they are aware and willing to support employees' responsibilities beyond the workplace. This might be signified by the accommodation of employees' family and personal commitments; managers being willing and able to support employees' work–life balance; and employees feeling able to use the work–life balance policies and practices open to them (Daverth et al., 2016). Research shows that a supportive work–life culture can increase the uptake rate of work–life balance policies and practices, which is associated with lower work-family conflict (Talukder, 2019), enhanced job attitudes (Beauregard and Henry, 2009), and employee retention (Lamane-Harim et al., 2021).

Work–life culture is often cultivated and transmitted at the group level, where managers and co-workers play a significant role in supporting employees. **Managerial support** is 'the extent to which managers were supportive and sensitive to employees' family responsibilities' (Thompson et al., 1999: 417). Line managers can play a critical role in the effective implementation of work–life balance policies and practices, ensuring employees feel able to utilise them. They can also help identify and address barriers that employees may face in achieving a satisfactory balance between work and life. Managers can also act as role models by overtly prioritising their own work–life balance and encouraging employees to do likewise. Positive managerial support fosters more positive employee attitudes and is thus identified as an important determinant of employee commitment and turnover intentions (Lamane-Harim et al., 2021). However, perceived differentiation and favouritism may arise from managers providing 'support', which could counter the positive effects of work–life balance policies and practices by raising concerns over organisational justice (Beauregard, 2014).

Co-worker support involves sharing knowledge and expertise, providing encouragement and tangible assistance and showing appreciation. While co-worker support remains understudied, Koessek et al. (2022) contend that such support significantly impacts the workplace environment and work–life balance, empowering individuals to effectively navigate multiple responsibilities.

The interaction of formal and informal approaches to managing work–life balance may create a benign cycle in employees' work–life experience; the **perceived availability of work–life practices** and policies can be enhanced with a supportive work–life cultural context, and, in turn, with the take-up of policies and practices, the cultural context can be strengthened, thus facilitating greater work–life balance in the workplace (Daverth et al., 2016). In the following case study, the interplay between these two approaches and the potential work-related outcomes are discussed in the context of managing work–life balance in a Chinese organisation.

Case Study

Managing Work–Life Balance: Beyond Management Consulting Ltd in China

Background

Paying attention to facilitating employees' work–life balance is urgent for many Chinese organisations. Many Chinese employees were inured to extremely long working hours (e.g. the normalised '996' working hour pattern, meaning working from 9.00 a.m. to 9:00 p.m., six days per week, i.e. 72 hours per week), and the long-standing expectation of 'sacrificing oneself for one's work' culture (Xiao and Cooke, 2012). Meanwhile, the increasing living costs and caring responsibilities of working-age employees peaked following the ending of the one-child policy and a rapidly ageing society (Zhang et al., 2020). Such work–life tensions among employees would leave a twin threat of changes for organisations to deal with, affecting employee engagement, talent attraction, and talent retention. Instead of accepting stressful jobs and work–life tensions as they used to, employees started pushing back from the 'hustle' workplace to chill out, or directly resigning from jobs for their 'inner peace'. However, unlike many Western developed countries, few formal policies and practices related to work–life balance were initiated and implemented in Chinese organisations to address these issues. Jun, the CEO of Beyond Management Consulting in Shanghai, China, has keenly captured the company's employees' work–life challenges and decided to practise flexible work arrangements for employee engagement and retention.

Flexible Work Arrangement Trials in Beyond Ltd

Beyond Ltd is a management consulting firm that endeavours to provide audit, assurance, tax, and consulting services at a cost lower than the leading consulting firms. In 2012, Jun co-founded the company, and to date the company has grown to 97 employees, and is headquartered in Shanghai, serving clients in East and Southeast Asian areas. The mission statement of Beyond is 'delivery beyond expectation service to clients'. Beyond always puts a high priority on its employees – known as 'Beyonders' – and values their talent and well-being to deliver the mission.

In 2022, Jun noticed several employees resigning for reasons of work–life conflict. Therefore, after discussing with their HR department, he proposed a flexible working arrangement, to avoid future talent turnover. The basis of this was allowing employees to work from home and choose their working hours, as long as they delivered the task. All employees can request flexible working arrangements, as they wish, subject to the line manager's approval. Since the trial launched in September 2022, it has been observed that some employees appreciate the policy and plan to use it to balance personal and working life; line managers often grant this flexibility depending on business needs, and usually client-facing specialists in each department must show up during regular 9 a.m. to 5 p.m. office hours. Meanwhile, more problems are occurring in the implementation, as the following example illustrates.

Is the Flexible Work Arrangement Limited to Female Employees?

Rui, a consultant with a 1-year-old child, was among the first employees to use the flexible working arrangement. She chose to work late afternoon and evening while her husband cared for their baby. She always completes tasks promptly. Xing works with Rui as a client-facing specialist. Considering Rui's working hours, Xing tended to check Rui's work in the morning before sending it off to clients. However, Xing found that Rui's work usually needed amendments, but he was unable to reach Rui to get her to make them. Xing made these changes himself and sent them to the client on time.

Xing came to Jun saying that some employees are not reachable during regular office hours, which led him to complete tasks, regularly outside of his responsibility and office hours. Xing also shared his personal issues with his sick dad in the hospital, asking Jun to allow him to work flexibly so he could care for his father. Jun tried to convince Xing to take several leaves of absence instead, given the nature of his role. Disappointed by his reply, Xing implied that he had got a job offer from another competitor company. Jun remained calm and asked to meet and discuss on another occasion, to give him time to assess the overall situation. Xing stepped out the Jun's office, mumbling, 'Is the flexible work arrangement only limited to female employees with childcare?'

Jun pondered over the conversation and wondered if adopting this flexible working arrangement was wise. However, it allowed employees to achieve a better work–life balance, which could have led to increased work engagement and productivity. On the other hand, it could confuse communication, as in Rui and Xing's case. It could also lead to tensions between employees: some might feel they are taking on extra work because of the flexible working arrangement of their colleagues. Jun decided, therefore, to step back and evaluate the company's current policies and guidelines around flexible working arrangements and support employees' work–life balance effectively and fairly.

Conclusion

Work–life balance concerns the relationship between the work and non-work aspects of individuals' lives. As discussed in the chapter, this seemingly straightforward term is actually complicated and dynamic. On the one hand, the domains of work and non-work have evolved by including a broader consideration of work and non-work activities; on the other hand, it is challenging to establish the meaning of 'balance' in time, involvement, and satisfaction across multiple roles and life domains. How employees perceive 'balance' between work and personal life in diverse contexts influences whether they see balance as feasible and attainable, the support they expect or would like, and the 'choices' they can make. Therefore, more needs to be known about the meaning and inclusiveness of the work–life balance concept by researching those working in non-standard work contexts and those where childcare is not the dominant, or sole, element of 'life'. In addition, more longitudinal research is needed to track how the meanings of work–life balance change over time within a given context, to understand the dynamic in greater depth.

Multiple intersecting contexts at national, organisational, and individual levels critically affect employees' perceptions of work–life balance. This chapter examined different national contexts to show how the national legal, economic, and social structures and cultural values can influence individual perceptions and experiences of the work–life interface and organisational support for non-work (Le et al., 2020; Ollier-Malaterre and Foucreault, 2017). In particular, the chapter discussed how work–life balance is perceived in a less well-researched country, China. Its specific economic, institutional, and sociocultural characteristics provide potentially novel and fertile perspectives for the work–life balance discourse in the global context. How work–life balance is viewed in different contexts raises important questions for both scholarship and practice regarding how and why the meanings of work–life balance might vary cross-culturally.

Organisations play a crucial role in shaping employees' work–life perception and experience for 'business', 'legal', and 'social' cases. When institutionalising work–life balance policies and practices, scope to nurture and develop a supportive work–life culture is needed to enable and strengthen the policy implementation, generating more positive work attitudes and behaviours. However, business pressures, cost concerns, lack of work–life balance awareness, and potential career penalties can constrain the effect of managing the work–life balance for employees. In addition, our understanding of managing employees' work–life balance in less regulated settings and emerging economies remains very limited. Scholars and practitioners could usefully focus on managing the work–life balance in a non-Western context. The case study in this chapter has explored whether the prevalent work–life balance practice – flexible working arrangement in the West – can be implemented effectively in China, where limited awareness and regulations have developed in managing the work–life balance. This case study leads to further discussions and reflections on the importance of developing contextualised policies and practices to address the work–life tension facing employees in particular national, organisational, and temporal contexts.

STUDENT ACTIVITY

Based on the case study earlier, answer the following questions.

1. Is it wise to offer flexibility to the workforce in a Chinese organisation like Beyond Ltd? Please discuss in terms of business, social, and legal cases.
2. Should Beyond Ltd repeal the initiative and return to traditional office work hours? If it does, how will it ensure that talent will be retained?
3. If Beyond Ltd chooses to continue the flexible work arrangements, what would the firm need to do to change the perceptions of employees using the flexible working arrangement? Moreover, what could be the best options for maintaining a sense of harmony among employees and clients?
4. Is there a possibility of popularising a flexible work arrangement widely in a national context, like China, with limited legal regulation on work–life rights? Critically analyse the possibility, and any challenges.

Practice Questions

1. Brainstorming activity: decipher how your work–life balance is formed.

   - Think about, and write down, any factors from national, organisational, family, professional, or individual levels that affect your experience of the work–life balance.
   - Select four dominant factors that affect your work–life balance and explain why they are influential.
   - After reflecting on these factors, summarise how you feel about your work–life balance.

2. As a people or HR manager, how would you design a work–life balance improvement arrangement for yourself and your team, respectively?
3. As the COVID-19 pandemic has accelerated work flexibility, hybrid working – which entails a mix of office-based and remote working – has become a firmly established option for many organizations (Xu, 2023). How does this way of working affect employees' work–life balance? And how might organisations wish to apply hybrid working to ensure it works effectively?

Key Terms

Flexibility paradox
this illustrates the potential downsides and risks of flexible working. Flexible working does not always provide employees with a work–life balance and positive well-being. Instead, it can blur the lines between work and life. This means workers are expected to do overtime in return for greater control over when and where they work, or feel they are being done a favour by being given more flexibility, which makes them feel they have to work harder and longer, with work encroaching on family life.

Flexible work
refers to working arrangements which differ from what has traditionally been seen as a standard way of working, typified as full-time, permanent, at a designated workplace, and at defined times. Most commonly, flexible working involves changing where and when work is done and the amount of time worked, although some definitions include a more comprehensive range of arrangements. The emerging form of flexible working – hybrid working – combines a part-remote and part-office schedule.

Ideal worker norm
emphasises firm boundaries between work and personal life, guided by the assumption that devoted full-time employees either do not have outside responsibilities or have someone to take care of any such responsibilities for them.

Managerial support
in the context of managing work–life balance is referred to as the extent to which managers are supportive and sensitive to employees' family responsibilities.

Managers can offer emotional support (e.g. talk to employees about their family and personal commitments), instrumental support (e.g. interpret policies and practices in a way that responds to an individual employee's work and family needs), lead by example, offer creative work–life balance management (e.g. strategically and innovatively restructure work to facilitate employee effectiveness on and off the job).

Perceived availability of work–life practices
pays attention to what extent employees are aware of the availability of work–life balance practices in their organisations. Due to the knowledge gap, employees do not equally know about and use the available work–life practice. Perceived availability, compared to the availability of the practices, is identified as a more important predictor of several behavioural outcomes, such as employees' take-up of these practices.

Work–family conflict
a form of inter-role conflict in which the role pressures from the work and family domains are mutually incompatible in some respects. The conflict could come from either side: work interference with family (WIF), and family interference with work (FIW).

Work–family enrichment
the extent to which experiences in one role improve the quality of life in the other. The enrichment could come from either side: work enriches family, and family enriches work.

Work intensification
can refer to the work effort or pace required in a job ('intensive work intensification') or the number of hours required ('extensive work intensification'). It can be an organisational tool to increase the productivity of an existing workforce. However, work intensification could negatively impact employees' well-being and work–life balance (i.e., exhaustion, burnout, stress).

Work–life balance
an overall appraisal of how individuals' effectiveness and satisfaction in work and personal roles are consistent with their life values at a given time and in context.

Work–life culture
also known as work–family or work–home culture, this is the shared assumptions, beliefs, and values regarding how an organisation supports and values the integration of employees' work and family lives.

References

Álvarez-Pérez, M.D., Carballo-Penela, A., and Rivera-Torres, P. (2020) 'Work-life balance and corporate social responsibility: the evaluation of gender differences on the relationship between family-friendly psychological climate and altruistic behaviors at work'. *Corporate Social Responsibility and Environmental Management*, 27(6): 2777–2792.

Beauregard, T.A. (2014) 'Fairness perceptions of work–life balance initiatives: effects on counterproductive work behaviour'. *British Journal of Management*, 25(4): 772–789.

Been, W.M., den Dulk, L., and van der Lippe, T. (2017) 'A business case or social responsibility? How top managers' support for work–life arrangements relates to the national context'. *Community, Work & Family*, 20(5): 573–599.

Bosch, G. (2004) 'Towards a new standard employment relationship in Western Europe'. *British Journal of Industrial Relations*, 42(4): 617–636.

Brough, P., Timms, C., Chan, X.W., Hawkes, A., and Rasmussen, L. (2020) 'Work–life balance: definitions, causes, and consequences'. In Töres Theorell (ed.), *Handbook of socioeconomic determinants of occupational health: from macro-level to micro-level evidence*. Cham, Switzerland: Springer, 473–487.

Cañibano, A. (2019) 'Workplace flexibility as a paradoxical phenomenon: exploring employee experiences'. *Human Relations*, 72(2): 444–470.

Carlson, D.S., Kacmar, K.M., Wayne, J.H., and Grzywacz, J.G. (2006) 'Measuring the positive side of the work–family interface: development and validation of a work–family enrichment scale'. *Journal of Vocational Behavior*, 68(1): 131–164.

Daverth, G., Hyde, P., and Cassell, C. (2016) 'Uptake of organisational work–life balance opportunities: the context of support'. *International Journal of Human Resource Management*, 27(15): 1710–1729.

de Menezes, L.M., and Kelliher, C. (2011) 'Flexible working and performance: a systematic review of the evidence for a business case'. *International Journal of Management Reviews*, 13(4): 452–474.

de Menezes, L.M., and Kelliher, C. (2017) 'Flexible working, individual performance, and employee attitudes: comparing formal and informal arrangements'. *Human Resource Management*, 56(6): 1051–1070.

Gatrell, C., Ladge, J.J., and Powell, G.N. (2022) 'A review of fatherhood and employment: introducing new perspectives for management research'. *Journal of Management Studies*, 59(5): 1198–1226.

Greenhaus, J.H., and Allen, T.D. (2011) 'Work–family balance: a review and extension of the literature'. In J.C. Quick and L.E. Tetrick (eds), *Handbook of occupational health psychology*. Washington, DC: American Psychological Association, 165–183.

Greenhaus, J.H., and Beutell, N.J. (1985) 'Sources of conflict between work and family roles'. *Academy of Management Review*, 10(1): 76–88.

Greenhaus, J.H., and Powell, G.N. (2006) 'When work and family are allies: a theory of work–family enrichment'. *Academy of Management Review*, 31(1): 72–92.

Greenhaus, J.H., Collins, K.M., and Shaw, J.D. (2003) 'The relation between work–family balance and quality of life'. *Journal of Vocational Behavior*, 63(3): 510–531.

Grzywacz, J.G. and Carlson, D.S. (2007) 'Conceptualizing work–family balance: implications for practice and research'. *Advances in Developing Human Resources*, 9: 455–471.

Kelliher, C., Richardson, J., and Boiarintseva, G. (2019) 'All of work? All of life? Reconceptualising work–life balance for the 21st century'. *Human Resource Management Journal*, 29(2): 97–112.

Kossek, E.E. (2016) 'Managing work–life boundaries in the digital age'. *Organizational Dynamics*, 45(3): 258–270.

Kossek, E.E., Perrigino, M.B., and Lautsch, B.A. (2022) 'Work–life flexibility policies from a boundary control and implementation perspective: a review and research framework'. *Journal of Management*, 49(6).

Lamane-Harim, J., Cegarra-Leiva, D., and Sánchez-Vidal, M.E. (2021) 'Work–life balance supportive culture: a way to retain employees in Spanish SMEs'. *International Journal of Human Resource Management*, 34(4): 1–31.

Le, H., Newman, A., Menzies, J., Zheng, C., and Fermelis, J. (2020) 'Work–life balance in Asia: a systematic review'. *Human Resource Management Review*, 30(4): 100766.

Lewis, J. (2009) *Work–family balance, gender and policy*. Northampton, MA: Edward Elgar.

Lewis, S., and Beauregard, T.A. (2018) 'The meanings of work–life balance: a cultural perspective'. In K. Shockley, W. Shen, and R. Johnson (eds), *The Cambridge handbook of the global work–family interface*. Cambridge Handbooks in Psychology. Cambridge, UK: Cambridge University Press, pp. 720–732.

McCarthy, A., Darcy, C., and Grady, G. (2010) 'Work–life balance policy and practice: understanding line manager attitudes and behaviors'. *Human Resource Management Review*, 20(2): 158–167.

Ollier-Malaterre, A., and Foucreault, A. (2017) 'Cross-national work–life research: cultural and structural impacts for individuals and organizations'. *Journal of Management*, 43(1): 111–136.

Ryan, A., and Kossek, E. (2008) 'Work–life policy implementation: breaking down or creating barriers to inclusiveness'. *Human Resource Management*, 47: 295–310.

Talukder, A.K.M.M.H. (2019) 'Supervisor support and organizational commitment: the role of work–family conflict, job satisfaction, and work–life balance'. *Journal of Employment Counseling*, 56(3): 98–116.

Thompson, C.A., and Prottas, D.J. (2006) 'Relationships among organizational family support, job autonomy, perceived control, and employee well-being'. *Journal of Occupational Health Psychology*, 11(1): 100.

Thompson, C.A., Beauvais, L.L., and Lyness, K.S. (1999) 'When work–family benefits are not enough: the influence of work–family culture on benefit utilization, organizational attachment, and work–family conflict'. *Journal of Vocational Behavior*, 54(3): 392–415.

Valcour, M., Ollier-Malaterre, A., Matz-Costa, C., Pitt-Catsouphes, M., and Brown, M. (2011) 'Influences on employee perceptions of organizational work–life support: signals and resources'. *Journal of Vocational Behavior*, 79(2): 588–595.

Wilkinson, K., Tomlinson, J., and Gardiner, J. (2018) 'The perceived fairness of work–life balance policies: a UK case study of solo-living managers and professionals without children'. *Human Resource Management Journal*, 28(2): 325–339.

Williams, P., Cathcart, A., and McDonald, P. (2021) 'Signals of support: flexible work for mutual gain'. *International Journal of Human Resource Management*, 32(3): 738–762.

Xiao, Y., and Cooke, F.L. (2012) 'Work–life balance in China? Social policy, employer strategy and individual coping mechanisms'. *Asia Pacific Journal of Human Resources*, 50(1): 6–22.

Xu, M. (2023) 'Hybrid working'. In S. Johnstone, J. Rodriguez, and A. Wilkinson (eds), *Encyclopedia of human resource management*, 2nd edition. Cheltenham: Edward Elgar Publishing, 297–298.

Zhang, M., Foley, S., Li, H., and Zhu, J. (2020) 'Social support, work-family balance and satisfaction among Chinese middle-and upper-level managers: testing cross-domain and within-domain effects'. *International Journal of Human Resource Management*, 31(21): 2714–2736.

chapter 11

Well-being and Mental Health at Work

Maria Hudson

Introduction

Global policy has increasingly prioritised the importance of **mental health** (World Health Organization, 2022). This chapter builds understanding of mental health and well-being at work. The World Health Organization (WHO) defines mental health as 'a state of mental well-being that enables people to cope with the stresses of life, realize their abilities, learn well and work well, and contribute to their communities' (WHO, 2022). This broad definition recognises that there is a continuum of mental health (WHO, 2022).

The chapter draws on a range of examples including the Global North (UK and Europe) and Global South (including insights into experiences in Bangladesh, India, and Ghana). It begins with a consideration of why mental health matters, reflecting on the extent of mental health problems, their situated context, and the social and economic costs. The discussion suggests that work can promote mental health and well-being as well as harm it, and that difference and intersectional experience may be important in understanding the dynamics of this. Outlining the range of factors that might negatively impact mental health and well-being, the chapter engages with **stigma** and influences beyond and within the workplace. It considers evidence that the UK is experiencing anxious organisations and a more anxious society in which structural factors and the pandemic context are complicit.

The discussion then moves onto a consideration of different models of disability and mental health, including the **biomedical and social models**. Some of the controversy that surrounds the social model of disability and its relevance to people with mental health problems is reflected upon. Concepts of the ideal worker and **ableism** are introduced through a review of recent research on disabled people's

DOI: 10.4324/9781003314769-14

experiences in ableist work contexts. An ongoing workplace support gap is identified as contributing to the disadvantage and marginalisation of people with mental health problems.

The chapter then considers what needs to happen to improve the workplace experience of people with mental health problems. It examines the imperative of providing a workplace culture that helps people with mental health problems feel comfortable with disclosing them as a step in accessing support, including through **reasonable adjustments**. The role of a range of organisational stakeholders is drawn out, including line managers bridging a policy–practice gap, greater recognition and support for the role of co-workers, the value of learning from lived experience of mental health problems, and also the importance of senior leadership and, where present, HR managers. The chapter then turns to an exploration of the management of mental health at work in a case study of a medium-sized enterprise in England. This provides an opportunity to reflect on some of the issues raised in the chapter, generating insights into the difference that effective interventions can potentially make, as well as challenges that workplaces might encounter in trying to improve mental health policy and practice.

Addressing Mental Health at Work: Why Does it Matter?

It is common for people to have mental health problems. A report from the independent Mental Health Taskforce to the National Health Service in England (2016) notes that each year one in four adults experience at least one diagnosable mental health problem. Examples of common mental health problems include anxiety, phobias, obsessive compulsive disorder, depression, and panic disorder. In England the number of people experiencing such issues has been on an upward trajectory, though across all age groups there is a higher incidence of mental health problems experienced by women (Whitty, 2021). Mental health problems need to be explored in their situated context. For example, they can be a symptom of the menopause which may manifest in mood swings and anxiety. In addition, women are overrepresented in unpaid and paid care-giving roles within the family and frontline health and care services. Such roles can have a heavy toll for health and well-being, including through stress, anxiety, and isolation. In response to poorer mental health among women in 2017, the UK government set up a Women's Mental Health Taskforce which started to provide greater recognition of the influence of women's roles as mothers and carers and the impact of domestic violence and abuse (Department of Health and Social Care, 2018). This engagement with household dynamics helps to bring to the fore how structural issues may impact on mental health. The need for action in relation to these issues is arguably all the greater given that the economic consequences of the pandemic may disproportionately affect women in lower-paid and undervalued work.

Further evidence of gendered challenges for the management of mental health and well-being has emerged in the Global South. Venkataraman and Venkataraman

(2021) explored reflections of working women during the lockdown in Vadodara, Gujarat, Western India. These scholars report on how the research participants conveyed multifaceted roles during the lockdown, combining paid work and childcare, and this was not acknowledged or valued by people around them, contributing to a sense of loneliness and emotional turmoil. Similar findings emerged in a study of experience in Ghana, finding that women trying to combine family, care-giving, and career roles experienced stress, with the greatest impact on overall well-being experienced by those without social support (Akuoko et al., 2021).

The situated context of mental health and well-being can be particularly challenging in low-income countries. Bangladesh has experienced a growth in the labour market participation of women since the 1980s and Akhter et al. (2017) have drawn attention to the neglect of mental health issues and how structural factors may impact on mental health. Women from low-income families in rural areas experienced changing gender roles arising from taking up paid work in the ready-made garment industry. They moved away from their families to do so, leaving their children in the care of grandparents (Akhter et al., 2017). The research evidence suggested that stress, anxiety, and suicidal thoughts arose due to women's separation from their children, as well as the nature of the work: sewing machine operators working for 10–12 hours per day, often for seven days a week with little holiday. A lack of health system support for their well-being appeared to be exacerbating the situation (Akhter et al., 2017).

The mental health of young people is also a source of concern. The growth in young people with mental health problems is a global phenomenon, and there is a care and support gap in both low- and high-income economies (World Health Organization, 2022). In England, for example, following the COVID-19 pandemic, the percentage of young people aged 17 to 19 estimated to have a probable mental health problem rose from 10 per cent to 26 per cent, and there is concern about services not meeting demand (National Audit Office, 2023).

Having a mental health problem can have a deleterious impact on life chances. People with mental health problems are persistently overrepresented among the unemployed and economically inactive (Hudson et al., 2009; Thornicroft, 2006). However, work has long been recognised as being important to mental health and well-being. A rethinking of recovery in mental health presents 'work as a significant stage in the journey to recovery, rather than recovery as a necessary precursor to work' (Secker et al., 2005: 65, cited in Hudson et al., 2009: 7). Both unemployment and poor-quality employment can have a negative impact on mental health. It is not as simple as finding people work. The sustainability of employment outcomes is important, including in a context where people with a long-term mental health problem, which may fluctuate, might need in-work support in managing periods of poor mental health and well-being. However, that sustainability can be elusive in a context in which stigma, discrimination, and marginalisation are part of everyday experience around mental health. In January 2017, then UK Prime Minister Theresa May commissioned *Thriving at work: Stevenson/Farmer review of mental health and employers* (Stevenson and Farmer,

2017), which noted that, while there had been a growth in the number of people with mental health problems in work in the UK, and that while 'good work is good for mental health', a significant number were 'struggling emotionally, off sick, less productive, or leaving employment' (Stevenson and Farmer, 2017: 15).

Research continues to demonstrate that poor mental health is costly. For example, Farmer and Stevenson (2017) reported that annually 300,000 people with a long-term mental health condition in the UK were leaving paid employment. A recent study of the economic case for investing in the prevention of mental health conditions in the UK provided the 'conservative' estimate that poor mental health was costing the UK economy at least £117.9 billion annually (McDaid et al., 2022). It has been estimated that there is a cost of $1 trillion to the global economy due to depression and anxiety, mostly linked to lost productivity (WHO and ILO, 2022). Those costs have a social dimension. In recent years, public health globally has been dominated by COVID-19. In this period, a Chief Medical Officer's report for England recognised that short-term negative effects include significant negative mental health impacts, for example, due to loneliness and isolation during lockdown (Whitty, 2021). The World Health Organization Europe identifies three phases that map the social and economic impacts from COVID-19, conveying an escalation of mental health impacts: increases in levels of stress and anxiety in the first phase; as part of the second phase, mental health problems; and long-term ill-health forming part of the third (Welsh Government, 2021). A labour market change which perhaps aligns with this includes the huge dip in economically active older workers since the start of the pandemic – whom the Office for National Statistics are following in their Over 50s Lifestyle Survey (Office for National Statistics, 2022).

Anxious Organisations and Nations?

Our experiences within and outside of paid work contribute to, and impact on, our mental health and well-being throughout our lives. Qualitative case studies undertaken by the author across UK public, private, and voluntary sector employers in 2016 suggested that a range of factors within and beyond the workplace were contributing to mental health problems. Outside work, these factors included: bereavement, relationship breakdowns, and family problems; addiction; finance, debt, and housing issues; and genetics. In the majority of cases, such influences were felt to be beyond the control and influence of employers (Hudson, 2016). At the same time, research participants perceived that there was a growing awareness of mental health, accompanied by increased acknowledgement of the need for employers to be mindful of the circumstances and challenges facing individuals in their lives outside of paid work.

Current socioeconomic and demographic changes in the workforce – for instance, the cost-of-living crisis and growth in older workers and the demands on carers – suggest that the interfaces between private lives and workplace experience are increasingly interlinked. The **anxious organisation** has been discussed in terms of personality conflicts and destructive organisational politics (Miller, 2019).

However, broader trends towards work intensification (and, as will be discussed in the following text, atypical work), which it is assumed are beneficial for organisational productivity, have less well-documented impacts around mental health. The author found that, while organisational change is normal, downsizing, growing workloads, and pressure at work showed signs of impacting negatively on mental health, and stress at work contributed to staff resignations (Hudson, 2016). While stress tends not to be classified as a medical condition, it can have serious health consequences and cause, or exacerbate, other mental health problems, such as anxiety. The anxious organisation reflects ongoing employer struggles to manage change effectively, alongside an increasing pressure for improved organisational performance that fed into workers feeling unable to cope. Management culture echoed the anxiety rather than contained it. Challenging workplace contexts are ongoing. Reports of an escalating mental health crisis in the National Health Service, with doctors and nurses feeling 'brutalised' and burnt out, provides a stark example (Savage, 2022). Healthcare workers from ethnic minority backgrounds have been disproportionately affected (Qureshi et al., 2022).

Clark and Wenham (2022) have raised the question of whether Britain has become an 'anxiety nation', with anxiety becoming a more prominent mental health problem. These authors highlight the fragile underpinning of material life for a substantial section of the population, and its contribution to poor mental health. The Understanding Society survey is the largest annual longitudinal household panel study of its kind and has been providing evidence on life changes and stability since 2009. Undertaking new analysis of this survey, Clark and Wenham (2022) analysed twelve indicators which provided strong evidence that a more insecure society is linked to a more anxious society. For example, they found that mental distress was higher for renters than for homeowners, and that insecure work was a marker of mental distress. The authors tentatively suggest 'the overriding importance of assets and debts in mental health, with work playing a secondary, but still important role' (Clark and Wenham, 2022: 32).

As Clark and Wenham (2022: 32) imply, there is a need for more research on the links between insecure work and mental health. Irvine and Rose (2022) provide some answers in a scoping review and thematic synthesis of the relationship between precarious employment and mental health (see also Chapter 5, 'Precarious and Gig Work in the Global Economy'). The focus is on what they describe as 'objectively insecure' forms of employment, engaging with temporary agency, fixed-term, casual, zero-hours, and gig work (Irvine and Rose, 2022: 3). Adopting a broad definition of mental health, their literature search terms included 'stress', 'anxiety', and 'depression', and Western sociocultural understanding such as 'well-being' and 'lived experience' (Irvine and Rose, 2022). Outlining their approach to the thematic synthesis of their findings, Irvine and Rose describe how they mapped four 'core experiences' of precarious employment; that is, financial instability, temporal uncertainty, marginal status, and employment insecurity. Each led to economic, sociorelational, behavioural, and physical experiences of, and responses to, precarious employment. Via a range of routes involving dynamics around work–family conflict and deprivation, a variety of mental health effects were found, including 'stress, anxiety and depression' and 'low morale, low self-esteem, frustration and guilt' (Irvine and Rose, 2022: 8). As the authors note, there is lack of research on how people living with long-term mental health conditions experience precarious employment.

Different Perspectives on Mental Health and Mental Illness

Mental health and mental illness continue to be contested concepts and the UK context is a good example of this (Beresford, 2002). The dominant understanding of mental health has been the biomedical model, with its emphasis on the individual's illness, their impairment and limitations, and the roles of psychiatric care and medication as a treatment response. Beresford (2002) argues that stigma has been complicit in labelling mental health service users as a danger to society. He suggests that mental health service users and progressive practitioners have an important role in challenging that stigma and biomedical approaches. Some mental health service users have drawn on a social model of disability, which highlights the significance of discrimination and social exclusion in their everyday lives. The focus shifts from the individual (and the notion of impairment) to the contexts in which people with mental health problems are living their everyday lives. This may help in addressing barriers to inclusion, for example, by discouraging **presenteeism** and encouraging more flexible support to facilitate employment retention for people with fluctuating mental health problems, including return to work policies that support sustainable outcomes.

Subsequent research by Beresford et al. (2010) found that some people with mental health problems want to distance themselves from disabled people because it may be implied that they have a permanent impairment. The researchers express concern that mental health service users might be disadvantaged by this, given the rights-based policies that have been emerging in relation to disabled people. Where the links between mental health and disability are salient, for example, is how, if a person's mental health problem means that they are disabled under UK anti-discrimination legislation, they can potentially get support at work from their employer in the form of reasonable adjustments. Under the Equality Act 2010, a mental health problem is considered a disability if it has a long-term effect on a person's normal day-to-day activity – for example, the ability to interact with other people or to work at particular times. The problem is 'long-term' if it lasts, or is likely to last, twelve months.

To support progressive and nuanced policy and practice, it is arguably important to recognise that 'mental health is not a binary state: we are not either mentally healthy or mentally ill' (World Health Organization, 2022: 35). People with mental health problems can have high levels of mental health well-being when those problems are well-managed. Public policy debates are beginning to take a human rights approach that considers the need to imbue health and well-being interventions with ethical and equity considerations (Berghs et al., 2019). In this vein, recent criticisms of the medicalised framing in the UK welfare system have argued for a more holistic assessment of capacity for work, engaging with the range of social, personal, and economic circumstances, and types of support, that may influence an individual's prospects for sustainable employment outcomes (Irvine and Haggar, 2023).

The Ideal Worker and Organisational 'Fit'

As already outlined, mental health problems can be a disability potentially providing a pathway to protection under UK anti-discrimination law. When people feel that access to workplace support has been unfairly discriminatory, they can try to take a claim to a judicial body with responsibility for workplace justice called an employment tribunal (ET). Foster and Wass (2013) undertook an analysis of four ET claims taken forward by employees. In so doing, these researchers provided a critical perspective on employers' perception of an ideal worker. For example, they discuss the case of a police constable in South Yorkshire Police who experienced chronic anxiety syndrome, which prevented him from undertaking face-to-face contact with the public. Initially he was given a back-office role on a community service desk. However, within a couple of years work reorganisation led to a job description change requiring all those in his team to undertake face-to-face interactions with the public and clients. A subsequent chain of events saw him placed in an unsatisfactory performance procedure, which prompted a period of sickness absence followed by medical retirement. This case was used to help illustrate how employers' assumptions, ideas and behaviour – for example, inflexible job descriptions – marginalise and disable people with an impairment.

Disabled people do exercise agency, as illustrated in the research of Jammaers et al. (2016), who explored their efforts in the context of ableist discourses of disability as lowering productivity. Echoing notions of the ideal worker, ableism presumes able-bodiedness in workplace practices and social relations, and casts disabled people as less employable and capable. These scholars undertook a discourse analysis of in-depth interviews with thirty disabled employees in Belgium, to explore how they tried to construct positive identities in their workplaces. Research participants were found to display a variety of responses to being constructed in terms of what they were unable to do. Some participants proactively tried to create a work environment that supported their productivity – for example, advance booking of a meeting space more suitable to their disability. Others tried to redefine the meaning of productivity. For example, a woman with chronic depression emphasised her high motivation to perform well during periods of good mental health (Jammaers et al., 2016). Participants again challenged the meaning of productivity by presenting their lived experience of disability as an advantage in building understanding and empathy for colleagues and clients who were unwell (Jammaers et al., 2016).

While the research of Jammaers et al. (2016) implies that people with mental health problems may not be passive victims in the face of challenges encountered, and arguably urges us to move towards a more moral economy, the evidence base suggests a mental health and well-being support gap. This may be exacerbated by the reluctance of a person with a mental health problem to disclose it and by the fact that mental health problems can be less visible than physical ones. Human resource management (HRM) can be more reactive than proactive, as found in research on the experiences of disabled academics in the higher education sector (Sang et al., 2022).

Managing Mental Health and Well-being at Work

Workplaces still have much to do to improve how mental health and well-being is managed at work. Employers need to engage with people, policies, processes, and mental-health-related support services. Support needs to be tailored, acknowledging that there are a variety of mental health problems that vary in severity. Looking at the UK experience, examples of interventions that may help include consciousness raising around the importance of talking about mental health and learning from people with lived experience of mental health problems. Training and support are needed, particularly for line managers, to help build skills and confidence in recognising signs of mental health problems, fostering conversations that may support disclosure and signposting to relevant support and services. The role of other social actors, including co-workers and senior leaders, should not be neglected. It is important that interventions are sensitive to workplace circumstances, which vary across organisations of different workforce size.

Recent years have seen UK mental health charities spearhead several high-profile campaigns aiming to challenge the stigma and discrimination faced by people with mental health problems. The campaigns have encouraged more workplace conversations about mental health that may be beneficial for nurturing workplace cultures that erode fears surrounding disclosure of mental health problems and encourage self-care and care for others. This has included days and weeks designated for organisations to run initiatives raising mental health consciousness and awareness. Learning from innovative HRM practice in the mental health services sector, Wang et al. (2023) are among those advocating the organisational benefits of employing people with experience of mental health problems in roles that can have a positive influence on workplace practices and cultures. People feed their lived experience into the inclusive design and delivery of mental health services (Wang et al., 2023).

Poor management needs to be addressed. The Chartered Institute of Personal Development (CIPD) 'health and wellbeing at work' survey, carried out across a range of organisation sizes in 2022, found a positive UK workplace impact of the pandemic in the form of greater employer focus on well-being, including people's mental health. However, only a minority of organisations provided guidance and training for line managers to help people with health problems avoid absence and stay in work. This is despite most organisations surveyed indicating that they relied upon line managers to manage both short- and long-term absence (CIPD, 2022). **Mental Health First Aid** courses have become part of the training landscape in the UK, engaging with the signs of mental health problems and how to respond. A subsequent CIPD health and well-being survey found that two-thirds of respondents were training staff in Mental Health First Aid (CIPD, 2023).

As discussed earlier, workplace adjustments are an important part of mental health support, with the potential to help facilitate equitable employment experiences. While numerous countries have placed a legal duty on employers to make reasonable adjustments/accommodations for disabled people, in low- and middle-income countries there has been a lack of focus on promoting social rights (Read et al., 2020). In discussing the negative work experiences of people with mental health diagnoses in Ghana, Read et al. (2022) suggest social activism is needed to promote the rights of people with mental health problems and mobilise change.

The implementation of adjustments can be pivotal in supporting a sustainable return to work after a period of mental-health-related absence, not least for people with more severe mental health problems. Despite progress on social rights in the UK, there is room for improvement. Foster (2007) undertook a qualitative study of employee experiences of disability and the negotiation of adjustments in the public sector workplace. She found that managers lacked understanding of their legal obligations to employees. Greater line manager training in this area may support an organisational approach that recognises that proactive tailored adjustments made for people with mental health problems, in discussion with them, to support their inclusion, must be a part of everyday working life.

HR managers have a role in the proactive action needed to foster workplace equity and inclusion. This might be aided by having influence within senior management teams. A strong understanding of mental health can help to foster a leadership approach that creates a climate for people to talk about their mental health and well-being and access appropriate support. As in many areas relating to equality and diversity, transformational leadership is potentially important in cultivating a shared vision and supporting the building blocks of sustainable change. This includes providing access to internal or external employee assistance programmes with trained mental-health-related professionals. The author found that designating a senior manager with responsibility for overseeing the development of mental health policy and practice could be beneficial for progress on inclusion (Hudson, 2016). Where there are signs of damaging workplace contexts – for example, in the form of 'anxious organisations' that may be complicit in poor mental health – it is important that the structural and material conditions that may impact mental health are also addressed.

Smaller organisations are unlikely to have HR managers and, on a day-to-day basis, co-workers may have an important support role for people with mental health problems. However, what works for managing workplace mental health can be a complex issue. Recent research on managing people with mental health problems in UK small and micro-workplaces has described a difficult balancing act in which emerging tensions are rarely resolved (Suter et al., 2023). For example, while co-workers can be empathetic in providing workplace support and adjustments for colleagues with mental health problems, this can be an emotional strain and, alongside work pressures, they can experience harm to their own mental well-being (Suter et al., 2023).

Case Study

The Introduction of Mental Health First Aid in FamCo, a Case Study from the Project Sharing Better Practice in the Management of Mental Health at Work with Employers in the County of Essex[1]

A few years ago the human resources (HR) manager at FamCo attended an external Mental Health First Aid training course which emphasised that looking after mental health is as important as caring for physical health. FamCo was a medium-sized family-run business in England, with 150 workers. The HR manager was proactive in taking the course, due to her awareness of FamCo's lived experience of mental health. FamCo had a small senior management team (SMT), which included the sole HR manager, who felt that there was a gap in the SMT understanding of the lived experiences of the manual workforce. For some staff, the working conditions were hard and unpleasant, with long working hours and a lack control over the pace of work. The HR manager felt that this work context was having a knock-on effect on mental health and well-being. Moreover, relationship breakdowns, debt, and gambling were all complicit in staff experiencing mental health problems. The HR manager was concerned about a high degree of presenteeism.

Historically the FamCo HR management offering was reactive, including in relation to mental health. While the company had an external occupational health provider, their focus was on physical health, although workers were signposted to external mental health support where a need was identified. Feeling that FamCo could and should improve the management of mental health after taking the Mental Health First Aid course, the HR manager designed a two-hour Mental Health First Aid training session. This was targeted at colleagues who staff might approach if they had a problem – for example, team leaders and forklift trainers. Delivering this training was a real eye-opener for the HR manager, as she discovered that some participants were already having some conversations with co-workers about their mental health. Given the small numbers of staff in work teams, it was often easy for them to get to know each other and pick up on when someone was feeling ill. The Mental Health First Aid course was also an eye-opener for some of the participants, who were given the opportunity to reflect on how people management is more than about managing workload (important as that might be), but also about caring for colleagues and signposting them to the support they needed.

The HR manager worked on providing opportunities for disclosure of mental health conditions at the start of employment and encouraged colleagues to approach each other and speak about their own mental health problems. She had been open about her own mental health and found this to make her more approachable. While good relationships at work were felt to be very important in supporting disclosure, some negative and dismissive mindsets about mental health remained. In addition, the HR manager felt that it had been easier to make reasonable adjustments for people with mental health problems on the retail side of the business, compared to in manufacturing. For example, in retail it was possible for staff to swap days, and easy to decrease and increase hours, including getting additional staff in for peak periods. A part-time working culture in retail was felt to make this more acceptable. Despite such challenges, an increase in the disclosure of absence related to mental health problems at FamCo was seen as a sign of less stigma surrounding mental health, supported by a more proactive approach to its management.

Conclusion

This chapter has shown that poor mental health and well-being has significant economic and social costs. We all have mental health, and it is common for people to experience problems, influenced by factors within and beyond the workplace and events across the life course. Biomedical and social models provide contrasting recommendations for the amelioration of those problems. There is much that workplaces can do to challenge **ableist norms**, help bridge the workplace support gap for people with mental health problems, and foster the equitable management of difference.

Key learning points from the FamCo case study include having a mental health champion with lived experience of mental health can help to foster organisational change through their leadership and commitment. If the champion is part of the senior management team, this can further help to facilitate change. There needs to be sensitivity to how people's mental health can fluctuate. Line managers and co-workers need to be aware of this in being part of networks of support for inclusion and signposting to support where needed. Having Mental Health First Aid embedded in the organisation, while not a panacea for the challenges of managing mental health at work, can increase emotional intelligence and literacy around mental health and, in so doing, enable manager and co-worker support for colleagues with mental health problems.

STUDENT ACTIVITY

Vignette[2]

Sally has been a long-standing, respected and valued member of staff at a further education college. However, she has been absent from work for four months due to mental health problems, in part influenced by the menopause alongside the pressures of juggling work and looking after ageing parents. Her employer has a broad set of policies in place that are widely and effectively implemented and actively supported by the executive management team. However, in this instance Sally has received no contact from her colleagues or management within her department throughout her period of absence. Through engaging with support provided by her GP, local mental health team and mental health charities, Sally feels she has reached a point where returning to work would assist in her continuing recovery. This view is supported by her care team. Sally has a latent fear and reluctance to

Maria Hudson

return to work, given the lack of communication she has had with her employer. She is concerned about what might have changed and how her co-workers will treat her.

To allay some of her concerns, Sally has identified and accessed the company's relevant mental health policies on the internal company intranet. As per policy, Sally reached out to human resources and advised them of her desire to return to work. Sally's departmental manager and human resources agreed a return date between them, but failed to discuss appropriate workplace adjustments that might need to be made. Sally was not a party to these discussions. Upon returning to work, it becomes apparent to Sally that the expectation of her departmental team is that she will pick up where she left off. It becomes clear to her that there has been no discussion of reasonable adjustments. Work expectations prove to be too much for Sally and her mental health deteriorates to the extent that she is again signed off from work. Through a casual conversation with one of Sally's co-workers, a mental health champion from the company reaches out to Sally and provides her with an opportunity to share her experience and engage in a new initiative to refine policy and procedures in respect of returning to work. This results in renewed firm-wide training with regards to people reintegrating into the workforce following a period of absence, and the promotion of positive management of their mental health.

Discussion Questions

1. Despite a supportive culture and management within the firm, what went wrong? How did this impact on Sally?
2. Reflecting on her experience, including her life and work contexts, what might have been better done to support Sally?
3. How can active communication facilitate a transition back to work?
4. What benefits could be gained by inclusion of those with lived experience in the formulation of mental health policy?

Practice Questions

- What are the business and human cases for better management of mental health at work?
- Why might it be important to take an intersectional approach in an effort to understand workplace mental health?
- What is the difference between the biomedical and social models of disability?
- Why might ableism be problematic for the quality of working life of people with mental health problems?
- What can be done to improve the management of mental health at work? How can different stakeholders (for example, organisational leaders, HR managers, line managers, co-workers, and people with mental health problems) make a difference?

Key Terms

Ableism
the discrimination and social prejudice against disabled people, underpinned by a belief that typical abilities are superior.

Ableist norms
shared social beliefs about how society should be organised that do not recognise the needs of disabled people, instead presuming able-bodiedness.

Anxious organisation
where an organisation experiences an ongoing struggle to manage change effectively, an increasing pressure to perform better, and a management culture that mirrors the anxiety in the workforce rather than contains it.

Biomedical model of disability
emphasises the individual's mental illness, their impairment and limitations,and the roles of psychiatric care and medication as a treatment response.

Mental health
a state of mental well-being that empowers people to cope with the stresses of life, fulfil their capabilities, learn and work well, and contribute to society.

Mental Health First Aid
a training course which raises people's awareness of how to identify, understand, and help someone who may be experiencing a mental health problem.

Presenteeism
when an individual comes to work even though they are not feeling well enough to work.

Reasonable adjustments
changes an employer makes to remove or reduce a disadvantage related to someone's disability – for example, modifying a person's working hours.

Social model of disability
describes people as being disabled by barriers in society, not by impairment or difference.

Stigma
negative attitudes and beliefs about a particular group. Stigma is often attached to a person labelled with mental illness.

Notes

1 This case study draws on research undertaken as part of an Employer Action Learning project, 'Sharing better practice in the management of mental health at work with employers in the county of Essex', which was funded by the University of Essex Economic and Social Research Council Impact Acceleration Account.
2 This exercise draws on a vignette co-produced with Brentwood Community Print, an organisation that was run by people with mental health problems and supporting

people with mental health problems. It is part of work undertaken on the project 'Sharing better practice in the management of mental health at work with employers in the county of Essex'.

References

Akhter, S., Rutherford, S., Akhter Kumkum. F., Bromwich, D., Anwar, I., Rahman, A., and Chu, C. (2017) 'Work, gender roles, and health: neglected mental health issues among female workers in the ready-made garment industry in Bangladesh'. *International Journal of Women's Health*, 9: 571–579.

Akuoko, P.B., Aggrey, V., and Mengba, J.D. (2021) 'Mothering with a career during a pandemic: the case of the Ghanaian woman'. *Gender, Work & Organization*, 28: 277–288.

Berghs, M., Atkin, K., Hatton, C., and Thomas, C. (2019) 'Rights to social determinants of flourishing? A paradigm for disability and public health research and policy'. *BMC Public Health*, 19: 1–7.

Beresford, P. (2002) 'Thinking about "mental health": towards a social model'. *Journal of Mental Health*, 11(6): 581–584.

Beresford, P., Nettle, M., and Perring, R. (2010) *Towards a social model of madness and distress? Exploring what service users say*. York: Joseph Rowntree Foundation.

CIPD (2022) *Health and well-being at work*. London: Chartered Institute of Personnel Development.

CIPD (2023) *Health and well-being at work*. London: Chartered Institute of Personnel Development.

Clark, T., and Wenham, A. (2022) 'Anxiety nation: economic insecurity and mental distress in 2020s Britain'. Joseph Rowntree Foundation, 1–54. Accessed 28 September 2023 from www.jrf.org.uk/report/anxiety-nation-economic-insecurity-and-mental-distress-2020s-britain

Department of Health and Social Care (2018) *The Women's Mental Health Taskforce*, final paper. Accessed 28 September 2023 from https://assets.publishing.service.gov.uk/government/uploads/system/uploads/attachment_data/file/765821/The_Womens_Mental_Health_Taskforce_-_final_report1.pdf

Foster, D.J. (2007) 'Legal obligation or personal lottery? Employee experiences of disability and the negotiation of adjustments in the public sector workplace'. *Work, Employment & Society*, 21(1): 67–84.

Foster, D., and Wass, V. (2013) Disability in the labour market: an exploration of concepts of the ideal worker and organisational fit that disadvantage employees with impairments. *Sociology*, 47(4): 705–721.

Hudson, M. (2016) *The management of mental health at work*, 1–72. London: Acas. Accessed 28 September 2023 from www.acas.org.uk/management-of-mental-health-at-work

Hudson, M., Ray, K., Vegeris, S., and Brooks, S. (2009) *People with mental health conditions and Pathways to Work*, 1–133. Research Report No 593. Norwich: Department for Work and Pensions.

Irvine, A., and Haggar, T. (2023) 'Conceptualising the social in mental health and work capability: implications of medicalised framing in the UK welfare system'. *Social Psychiatry and Psychiatric Epidemiology*: 1–11.

Irvine, A., and Rose, N. (2022) 'How does precarious employment affect mental health? A scoping review and thematic synthesis of qualitative evidence from western economies'. *Work, Employment and Society*, p.09500170221128698.

Jammaers, E., Zanoni, P., and Hardonk, S. (2016) 'Constructing positive identities in ableist workplaces: disabled employees' discursive practices engaging with the discourse of lower productivity'. *Human Relations*, 69(6): 1365–1386.

McDaid, D., Park, A-La., Davidson, G., John, A., Knifton, L., McDaid, S., Morton, A., Thorpe, L., and Wilson, N. (2022) *The economic case for investing in the prevention of mental health conditions in the UK*, 1–114. Accessed 28 September 2023 from http://eprints.lse.ac.uk/114286/1/McDaid_the_economic_case_for_investing_published.pdf

Mental Health Taskforce (2016) *The Five Year Forward View for Mental Health: a report from the independent mental health taskforce to the NHS in England*, February 2016. Available at www.england.nhs.uk/wp-content/uploads/2016/02/Mental-Health-Taskforce-FYFV-final.pdf

Miller, J. (2019) *The anxious organisation: why smart companies do dumb things*, 3rd edition. Miami, FL: Vinculum Press.

National Audit Office (2023) *Progress in improving mental health services in England*, 1–70. Accessed 28 September 2023 from www.nao.org.uk/reports/progress-in-improving-mental-health-services-in-england/

Office for National Statistics., 2022. 'Reasons for workers aged over 50 years leaving employment since the start of the coronavirus pandemic: wave 2'. Accessed 28 September 2023 from www.ons.gov.uk/employmentandlabourmarket/peopleinwork/employmentandemployeetypes/articles/reasonsforworkersagedover-50yearsleavingemploymentsincethestartofthecoronaviruspandemic/wave2

Qureshi, I., Gogoi, M., Al-Oraibi, A., Wobi, F., Chaloner, J., Gray, L., Guyatt, A.L., Hassan, O., Nellums, L.B., Pareek, M., and UK-REACH Collaborative Group (2022) 'Factors influencing the mental health of an ethnically diverse healthcare workforce during COVID-19: a qualitative study in the United Kingdom'. *European Journal of Psychotraumatology*, 13(2): p.2105577.

Read, U.M., Sakyi, L., and Abbey, W. (2020) 'Exploring the potential of a rights-based approach to work and social inclusion for people with lived experience of mental illness in Ghana'. *Health and Human Rights*, 22(1): 91–104.

Sang, K., Calvard, T., and Remnant, J. (2022) 'Disability and academic careers: using the social relational model to reveal the role of human resource management practices in creating disability'. *Work, Employment & Society*, 36(4): 722–740.

Savage, M. (2022) '"Brutalised and burnt out" NHS hospital staff take 8m mental health sick days in five years'. *Guardian*, 17 April. Accessed 28 September 2023 from www.theguardian.com/society/2022/apr/17/brutalised-and-burnt-out-nhs-hospital-staff-take-8m-mental-health-sick-days-in-five-years

Stevenson, D., and Falmer, P. (2017) *Thriving at work: the Stevenson/Farmer review of mental health and employers*. Accessed 28 September 2023 from www.

gov.uk/government/publications/thriving-at-work-a-review-of-mental-health-and-employers

Suter, J., Irvine, A., and Howorth, C. (2023) 'Juggling on a tightrope: experiences of small and micro business managers responding to employees with mental health difficulties'. *International Small Business Journal*, 41(1): 3–34.

Thornicroft, G. (2006) *Shunned: Discrimination against people with mental illness*. Oxford: Oxford University Press.

Venkataraman, A., and Venkataraman, A. (2021) 'Lockdown & me …!! Reflections of working women during the lockdown in Vadodara, Gujarat-Western India'. *Gender, Work & Organization*, 2: 289–306.

Wang, Y., Byrne, L., Bartram, T., and Chapman, M. (2023) 'Developing inclusive and healthy organizations by employing designated lived experience roles: learning from human resource management innovations in the mental health sector'. *International Journal of Human Resource Management*, 34(10): 1973–2001.

Welsh Government (2021) *Protecting our health: our response in Wales to the first phase of COVID-19 – special report*. Accessed 28 September 2023 from www.gov.wales/sites/default/files/publications/2021-01/chief-medical-officer-for-wales-special-report.pdf

Whitty, C. (2021) *Chief Medical Officer's annual report 2020: health trends and variation in England*. London: Department of Health, 1–107. Accessed 28 September 2023 from www.gov.uk/government/publications/chief-medical-officers-annual-report-2020-health-trends-and-variation-in-england

World Health Organization (2022) *World mental health report: transforming mental health for all*, 1–296. Accessed 28 September 2023 from www.who.int/publications/i/item/9789240049338

World Health Organization and International Labour Organization (2022) *Mental health at work: policy brief*, 1–20. Accessed 28 September 2023 from www.ilo.org/wcmsp5/groups/public/---ed_protect/---protrav/---safework/documents/publication/wcms_856976.pdf

Useful Websites

www.acas.org.uk/reasonable-adjustments
www.accessliving.org/
www.disabilityrightsuk.org/social-model-disability-language
mhfaengland.org/
www.mentalhealth.org.uk/
www.mind.org.uk/
https://whatworkswellbeing.org/
www.who.int/news-room/fact-sheets/detail/mental-health-at-work

part 4

Digitalised Work

chapter 12

Digitalised Work

Garfield Benjamin

Introduction

This chapter discusses **digitalised work**. In societies where information and communication technologies, digital platforms, data, and artificial intelligence shape the ways in which people work, the activities they engage in are often described as digital work, digitalised work, or digital labour. Traditional jobs like manufacturing have become digitalised in the way automation replaces human tasks and the whole process is managed by computer algorithms. Other jobs, like teaching, have become digitalised in the sense that course content is uploaded to a digital platform, students engage with online material, and coursework is assessed and feedback given online. Most jobs today have been digitalised in some form or another. But **digital work** also includes an emergence of new jobs and ways of working born out of the digital economy. Examples include digital product managers, website developers, bloggers, social media managers, data analysts, and influencers. They work not with materials but with likes, swipes, and clicks.

Behind every action on a device lies a range of invisible types of work that make every click or swipe possible. This chapter discusses the different types of labour that support **digital societies** and the increasingly digital economy. Digital technologies require huge amounts of work to build and to function – this can be digging metals out of the ground or designing the systems that govern people's lives – but they are not always familiar types of labour, and not a lot of this labour is visible to people as they use their devices, networks, and other systems. It's important to think about types of work that is it not often possible to see. Compared to traditional forms of labour, much of which was apparent in factories, farms, or other visible places, work today is increasingly invisible (Crain et al., 2016). As economies and systems become more complex and more global, a lot of work becomes hidden. It is not always easy to see the full details of supply chains behind the things people buy – and with digital services this becomes even more hidden.

DOI: 10.4324/9781003314769-16

This chapter examines some of the different types of invisible labour that make up *digital work*, work that is done directly on digital platforms or enables those platforms to function. This is less about making physical products and instead about services, cultural products, and intellectual property. It includes exploring people's ideas, computer codes, creative content, and the work that goes on to support all of these. This chapter also considers *digitalised work*, how digital technologies shape the ways people work, and how such technologies can operate in ways that increase and automate inequality (Eubanks, 2018). This often continues along social class lines as well as encompassing other forms of marginalisation and discrimination such as gender, race, location, sexuality, and disability.

This chapter will start with a discussion of the connected systems that make digital technologies possible. These can include physical features like servers, devices, and cables, but also immaterial aspects like the protocols and code that make computers run and allow them to communicate with each other. It includes the design and content of every app or webpage people use or visit, and it includes the data and algorithms (the instructions that tell computers what to do) that go on in the background. The chapter then examines the effects of online systems on the ways people work. This includes the way that platforms manage and track existing jobs, and the new forms of work that have emerged on platforms like social media. The discussion will then turn to the less tangible and often unpaid elements of work online that relate to community and resistance. It takes hard work to build communities and digital activism, or to work within and against oppressive and exploitative systems. The chapter includes a case study of online content moderators in India, who work long hours for low pay with little support to keep people's online feeds clean of offensive or harmful content. Digital technologies can provide new ways of doing sociology, be that online behaviours as a topic of study, methods like netnographies or big data analysis, or new ways of engaging with and thinking about social issues (Lupton, 2014; Marres, 2017). They can also create new problems that sociologists need to think about, though – the inequalities that emerge. It is these inequalities which form the focus of this chapter.

Digital Work and Invisible Labour

Behind every click or swipe on any device is a huge network of people, practices, and processes that are never seen. Every digital connection is the result of huge amounts of labour. But the work that goes into these systems is hidden away, or just so far removed from most people's daily experiences that they can be thought of as different types of **invisible labour**. The work – and the harms, including bias, discrimination, and exploitation – of digital societies is unevenly distributed. While the benefits are seen more strongly in the Global North, or among already privileged groups, it is most often marginalised workers in poorer nations who are made invisible in the supply chains of production, as components and jobs are transported around the globe, from mines to factories to tech company offices where code is written, and on to the distributed outsourcing of data work.

Garfield Benjamin

A lot of this involves traditional material labour, making physical devices. Storing data 'in the cloud' – the idea that information is held not on devices but on services online – really involves vast networks of cables, servers, and other 'things'. All these different types of hardware require creating, and each come with a variety of costs. The extraction of materials, including precious or 'rare earth' metals, is a hazardous form of labour. Workers around the globe are needed to extract and transport these important metals.

In the Baotou region of Inner Mongolia (China), the extraction of rare metals needed to produce digital devices like phones or smart TVs has created a toxic lake (Ly, 2023). The manufacture of components requires labour to make, build, and transport electronic goods, often at low pay. Maintaining the networks that run platforms and the Internet requires constant work by engineers with practical experience. Even getting rid of electronic goods requires huge amounts of labour, whether that is in recycling plants, or the thousands of workers sifting through dangerous conditions in places like the Agbogbloshie dump in Accra, Ghana, where thousands upon thousands of devices are sent for recycling and disposal (Little and Akese, 2019; Otu, 2021). All these forms of labour are essential for the **infrastructure** of the digital world to function. But they often put additional pressures on those in already marginalised working conditions, particularly in the Global South. The entire process has huge costs in terms of human labour and environmental harm (see Chapter 19, Sahin-Dikmen's 'Climate Change and Work'). People do not usually see or think about these costs or this type of work when they use devices on a day-to-day basis. These workers, many exploited in systems of child labour and modern slavery (Banerjee, 2021), are made invisible by the global supply chains that bring people the latest iPhone, TV, or smart toaster.

A lot of digital work instead falls under the category of **immaterial labour**. Sometimes called intellectual labour or knowledge work, immaterial labour is work that does not produce 'things'. It is not 'productive' in the strictest sociological sense, even though it involves lots of work. Immaterial labour is about information and communication. It includes jobs like advertisers, writers, service providers, and content creators, as well as a whole range of jobs essential for digital technologies to work. From the firmware and operating systems that allow a device to function, through to software, web design, and analysis, there are many immaterial jobs at work. For example, there are an increasing number of jobs related to the collection or use of 'data'. The UK government lists data scientists, data engineers, data analysts, data ethicists, and other related jobs as distinct roles within the broader 'data job family' within the public sector (CDDO, 2023). Each one is part of the daily rhythms of a data-driven economy.

But, while this work is considered immaterial, it is also often made invisible. This goes beyond the fact that the work of each individual programmer is not seen each time an app is opened. It is an issue of inequality and marginalisation. Not only do technologies tend to serve the interests of power, but the major stories the media tell about technology tend to be those of white, rich, heteronormative men in the Global North. Achievements made by other people from other places have historically been erased from the image of technology. For example, Hicks (2017) shows how the pivotal role of women in designing and operating the first computers has been mostly ignored from how this history is presented. Similarly, McIlwain shows how black software designers in the early web of the 1990s were innovating and adapting to different community needs but remain hidden from the mainstream stories focusing on the (usually white, male) famous figures at companies like Apple and Google (McIlwain, 2019). Today, D'Ignazio and Klein show how terms like tech 'unicorns' and programming 'wizards' are applied to those from privileged backgrounds who get to make decisions and announcements about the direction of technology, usually those privileged by class, gender, race, or geography. Meanwhile, data 'cleaners' and 'janitors' are the marginalised workers (often women, people racialised as minorities, and/or people from the Global South) who make systems actually work (D'Ignazio and Klein, 2020). The same people (wealthy white men in the Global North) are taking credit for the work of others, perpetuating privilege and exacerbating inequality.

Today, there is a huge boom in digital platforms, online systems, the use of data in all kinds of sectors, and an increase in interest (and funding) in computer tools like AI (artificial intelligence) and algorithms to make decisions and automate or support other forms of work. Sometimes this comes with risks of people losing their jobs as computers replace them. But it is more often the case that human workers get shifted onto the tasks needed to make these computer systems run. While this has historically been uneven, replacing those deemed lower skilled, AI is pushing automation further, challenging immaterial labour roles like content creation, journalism, and other areas that could potentially be replaced by AI. An example is the rise of generative AI, systems based on huge datasets of written texts that turn a chatbot into attempts to create convincing conversations and text. Be it news stories, legal documents, or student essays, these systems claim to replace human work. But what they really do is make something that only 'sounds' like text written by humans; it is often filled with errors like fake references or made-up facts. Those who design and use these systems can expect substantial pay cheques, while those whom the systems replace see their entire profession at risk.

At the other extreme is **ghost work** (Gray and Suri, 2019), immaterial labour that is usually invisible. This type of invisibility is particular to technology and is seen most prominently in 'big tech companies like Google and Amazon. A lot of 'smart' technologies like AI are in fact not very smart at all. They work by taking large amounts of data and using this to make guesses based on calculations. Every stage of this requires human input. The data needs tidying up, sorting, and labelling in ways that make human concepts capable of being processed by a computer. The AI algorithms not only need to be designed with expertise, but lots of repetitive labour is necessary to correct the many errors that happen as the technology is improved. When computers make mistakes (which is a lot, when thinking about complex social issues), it is usually up to low-paid human workers to step in and check or correct things. These workers tend to go unseen, which maintains the myth that technology is going to solve society's problems. But it services powerful

Garfield Benjamin

technology companies, and often leads to precarious work and exploitation (see the discussion in Chapter 5, McDonough and Pearson's 'Precarious and Gig Work in the Global Economy').

Digital Platforms and Platform Workers

In Srnicek's (2017) book *Platform capitalism,* a 'platform' is described as an intermediary that produces network effects. This means a platform positions itself between users (which can include customers, advertisers, makers, service providers, and others), but also positions itself as the place where work happens. **Platform capitalism** describes how platforms become networks and are social structures. They are also prone to becoming monopolies – just think about the continued dominance of a few major social media platforms as sites of all kinds of work and other activities simply because that is where users are. Importantly, although platforms like to show themselves as neutral, an empty space for people to use, they are far from neutral. They have been designed in particular ways, and subsequently they encourage certain kinds of interaction and discourage others. They control behaviours and embed values. This shapes what can be done on a platform, a politics of design that shapes the nature of work that happens on or through the platform.

Noble, in her book *Algorithms of oppression* (2018), outlines the intersection of race and gender in the ways that online platforms oppress marginalised groups. She highlights issues like Google image search showing racist and sexist depictions of different jobs. For example, doctors, lawyers, CEOs, and professors are most often shown as white older men, while a search for 'unprofessional hair' showed a variety of African and African-American women's styles. Noble goes on to write about the impact of social media platforms on small businesses, particularly those from these marginalised communities. Whereas black-owned hairdressers might have once relied on word of mouth within a community for customers, platformisation has not always offered a direct way to connect with clients. Instead, it funnels users into a homogenising system of reputation and privilege. Success is defined by those who are already successful, made quantifiable through the mediation of search and social platforms. This rewards those who conform to mainstream styles and needs and excludes others. Social media is a huge site for advertising, whether that is big brands reaching a global audience, small local businesses trying to expand, or individual creators and freelancers hoping to make it big. Traditional measures of success are replaced with platform metrics like views, likes, and shares. It is an **attention economy** (Crogan and Kinsley, 2012; Goldhaber, 1997) of audience, reach, reputation, and engagement.

A lot of ghost work is dedicated to developing and maintaining digital platforms. But this type of work is also managed by platform algorithms. Amazon's Mechanical Turk platform has played an important role in the way that data and AI systems have been developed (Sadowski, 2022; Stephens, 2023). Like Task Rabbit for computing micro-jobs, it assigns parts of tasks, like labelling data or fixing problems, to human workers all over the world. The pay rates are often exploitative, using tactics like paying per task rather than per hour, while the work of Gray and Suri (2019) showed that 30 per cent of ghost workers reported not being paid for tasks (see also the open source coders discussed by Taylor in Chapter 15, 'Unpaid Work'). An additional risk of working for a platform like this is that people are required to be 'always on', ready to jump in and provide labour, all managed and tracked automatically. These workers might be distributed all over the world or, in positions of precarity (Bates et al., 2023; Kassem, 2023; Le Ludec et al., 2023), their exploitation far removed from those who benefit from their labour.

Platform work acts like a new form of outsourcing that attempts to hide the exploitation, particularly the locations where tasks are being carried out. While people tend to notice if a factory moves from the UK to India, if tasks are instead moved onto a platform, it hides the story behind the labour. There are also global legal implications. Platform work is often less regulated, so shifting labour onto a platform – particularly if it is international – can be a way of avoiding labour laws relating to hourly pay and working conditions. It is used by companies to escape responsibility for those doing work for them. And workers often do not know who they are working for, or what kind of system they are contributing to. It could be a research study to tackle inequality or part of developing a new defence system.

Platforms like Uber and Airbnb put huge amounts of effort into lobbying to allow their platforms to operate in a particular city. Politicians like French President Emmanuel Macron were shown to have been part of this plan, in France and across Europe, pushing through Uber's licence to operate (Davies et al., 2022). But within this gig economy platforms position themselves not as employers but as facilitators. There have been ongoing legal disputes around whether these workers count as employees and deserve protections like minimum wage and holiday pay, as with one case taken to the UK Supreme Court (see Russon, 2021).

As more and more people started working from home during the COVID-19 pandemic, their work was often managed through platforms of one type or another, adopted as a communication tool by human managers. As noted in later chapters of this text (for example, Chapter 21, 'Changing Places of Work', by Felstead and Blakely, who discuss working from home during COVID-19), this changed working relationships. Employers and managers could no longer check in with, or check up on, their employees like they could in the office. This had an impact on how workers were managed. Without in-person contact, platforms stepped in. Tools ranged from virtual meeting platforms to productivity management software, to full activity tracking. Platforms enabled this shift into full worker surveillance, just as systems with bias against people with dark skin or neurodiverse people would be marginalised by exam monitoring software (Coghlan et al., 2021).

Jobs using social media are also new forms of digital work (see Chapter 14, 'Blogging and Online Work', by Parry and Hracs). As companies are expected to maintain social media presence, social media managers are a new form of public relations job. These roles have been slowly recognised as work, but there are inequalities in perception, as they are often gendered as roles for women, compared to the more male perceptions of the roles of analyst, designer, and engineer (Duffy

Garfield Benjamin

and Schwarz, 2018). Creators have similar issues of perception. What often started as hobbies on platforms like YouTube and Instagram have become a huge economy of influencers and content creators. This has also had issues with a lack of regulation, with big names running into problems from creating harmful content in the constant chase for more engagement. YouTuber and influencer PewDiePie (Felix Kjellberg) has attracted repeated criticism for racist, anti-Semitic, and sexist comments. Logan Paul was removed from YouTube's Preferred channel list after showing a suicide victim at the Aokigahara forest in Japan on his channel. More recently in 2023, a TikToker known as Mizzy (Bacari-Bronze O'Garro) has flirted with legal boundaries through pranks that have escalated to threats, stealing dogs, and walking into people's homes uninvited. For most creators, though, it is a hard slog to gain and maintain reputation that is profitable. For every online celebrity, there are thousands of people trying to develop enough of a following to generate income. People are being pushed to enter exploitative industries under the promise of new digital jobs, often putting in huge amounts of unpaid work to build a reputation while exposing themselves to complex harms, economically and personally.

Digital Communities and Activism

To deal with the harms of platform work, additional work is required. Those who are victimised by online abuse must deal with the emotional burden of their own feelings and responses, manage how they react in full view of others, and have the extra steps of avoiding, reporting, and dealing with online harms. The alternative is to close off some modes of communication or opportunities. Think about the impact of a small business owner having to shut down a social media account if they start receiving torrents of sexist, racist, ableist, or anti-LGBTQ+ abuse. This type of work again falls on existing lines of marginalisation, an increased burden for women (Ahmed, 2017; D'Ignazio and Klein, 2020), queer and trans folk (Guyan, 2022; Skinner-Thompson, 2020; Spade, 2015), people from racialised minorities (R. Benjamin, 2019), disabled people (Hamraie and Fritsch, 2019) and from those whose experiences intersect with these groups (Bailey, 2021; Noble, 2018). This occurs on an individual level, but also on a social one. Data, AI, and platforms can make discrimination worse. For example, the use of algorithms in job hiring processes can lead to issues of inequality (Kelly-Lyth, 2021), with particular impact on dimensions like ageism (Stypinska, 2023), as well as those already mentioned. Sociologists, activists, lawyers, politicians, and tech employees need put effort into challenging these systems. But the burden of proof often rests on the marginalised, while big corporations and governments continue to push technologies with little to no regulation or enforcement.

While many digital technologies can exploit and marginalise people, those same technologies can also provide ways of building communities and politics. Sharing awareness of harms and tactics to overcome them, can lead to new forms of participating in digital society (Carmi et al., 2020). Online platforms can help with **#hashtag activism**, which can lead to superficial levels of engagement, sometimes called 'clicktivism', but they can also be used as rallying points to action on social issues (Jackson et al., 2020). While this can include organising campaigns like Black Lives Matter, MeToo, and environmental protests, it can also help organise to resist unjust technologies. The 2020 protest by UK teenagers against biased exam grade algorithms led to meaningful change, as the government was forced to reverse its decision and use teacher-assigned grades. The physical protests were organised through platforms, but news also spread through social media, including the hashtag #FuckTheAlgorithm, building a new awareness and politics around digital society (Benjamin, 2022).

Resistance also happens at an individual level, repurposing technologies to protect marginalised people. Digital tools can be used to confront and get around the ways society makes certain types of work invisible (see Chapter 13, 'Sex Work in the Digital Age', by Rand). The platformisation and surveillance of many jobs leads to new tactics in response. For example, gadgets have been developed or hacked together to trick step counters, to get lower insurance premiums by giving the impression of a healthier lifestyle. Vibrating widgets have been attached to computer mice to give the impression of constant work activity. Workers share tips to game surveillance systems to satisfy the metrics required by platforms while getting on with the more important or human parts of a job (or not) (G. Benjamin, 2019). These practices of 'tactical resistance' against algorithms become part of many people's everyday work (Treré, 2018). Platforms offer alternative ways of communicating, not only with clients but in building community and support networks, like the origins of the MeToo movement as online support for abuse survivors. Advice can be shared, support offered or found. The work that goes into data production can be repurposed by individuals and communities to present a case for change. But this takes effort.

The work of dealing with digital labour is an individual and collective effort. It can be helping a colleague work around job performance metrics, or it can be building a movement to resist oppressive technological systems (McQuillan, 2022). Whatever it is, the work is constant and there is always more to do.

Case Study

Digital Workers: The Exploitation of Content Moderators in India

What is seen on social media platforms is a product of user content mediated by the platform algorithms, based on the data gathered about people's own individual preferences. But this potentially exposes users to glitches in the algorithm, as well as to harmful or offensive content uploaded by others that might slip through the algorithmic filters. This all comes down to the work of content moderators, which is often a thankless and underappreciated task. On forums like Reddit, it relies on a large team of volunteer moderators who set the rules, tone, and content of each subforum. But, on big social media platforms like Facebook, it is done by low-paid workers, often in the Global South. This demonstrates the outsourcing of the ghost work discussed earlier that is essential to allow platforms to function.

Garfield Benjamin

India is one of the main sources of content moderation labour. It is impossible to say how many content moderators work globally, as the labour is purposefully shifted onto a whole range of outsourcing companies. However, one estimate stated that even ten years ago the number of content moderators – who it labels 'protectors of the Internet' – in India could easily be over 10,000, around 10 per cent of the number globally (Chaudhuri et al., 2014). Google alone had 10,000 total content moderators in 2017 (Levin, 2017), while one moderation company, SquadRun, based in the US and India but with platform workers worldwide, had 75,000 workers in the same year (Kar and Sarkhel, 2017). One study found 10 per cent more men than women in India, but women see common issues in achieving fair pay regardless of the country they are based in (Gray and Suri, 2019: 24, 113). The work is often seen as middle class, as it is tech-related, but it enjoys few of the benefits and security associated with those kinds of jobs and the pay, precarity, and working conditions are far from a good deal.

Irani (2015) showed the problems faced by content moderators in India. Never seen in the flashy images of Silicon Valley companies, these workers were essential to keeping porn, violence, and alcohol out of Google ads. But they were denied the benefits that were enjoyed by full employees based in California or other key offices in the Global North. Instead, these workers were made invisible and exploited for the benefit of the company. The image of Google as a space for free thinkers and great working conditions ignored the platform displacement onto these workers. They were kept out of view. But these roles, with their low-pay, long hours, and exploitative working conditions with no additional protections or benefits, are essential.

The cramped offices in India or the Philippines, where moderators are based, operate as call centres turned into digital sweat shops. These workers often have to sit in front of a computer for nine hours a day watching harmful content. Filmmakers Ciaran Cassidy and Aiden Chen produced a 2017 documentary called *The moderators* that shows the training these moderators go through. The workers are often given limited guidance, and inadequate support as they work. There is a significant psychological burden to spending all day, every day sifting through offensive and graphic content, made worse by the constant monitoring and high-pressure targets around the work (Ahmad and Krzywdzinski, 2022: 88). And yet, particularly as detached subcontractors rather than full employees, there is limited mental health support for this type of labour. It is not only about increased pay. What is needed is increased support and a voice within the process.

The entire global content moderation supply chain is highly unequal. There is a significant power asymmetry: the often US-based platforms (Google, Facebook, etc.) can use their oligopoly to define the terms for content moderation suppliers in India and elsewhere in the Global South (Ahmad and Krzywdzinski, 2022: 80). This occurs not only at the level of companies but also for specific teams. Roberts' study into content moderation found that moderation was controlled by teams in the Global North, who would often send certain types of content and complaints – mostly pornography – to teams in India (Roberts, 2019: 78, 118). The jobs of content moderators are considered low-skilled by the social media platforms, which helps keep them as a low-cost outsourced function. This, and the non-disclosure agreements that prevent workers from advertising which major company they are working for, means that those going into these jobs (many as recent graduates) struggle to use it to boost their reputation and career (Ahmad and Krzywdzinski, 2022: 86). By contrast, Indian computer programmers are often forced to relocate to countries like Germany in order to find work (Amrute, 2016). This siphoning off of more qualified labour further entrenches the devaluation of tech jobs located the Global South.

As Irani writes, 'automation doesn't replace labor, it displaces it' (Irani, 2015). The shiny image of automation as technological progress without human work conceals the realities of digital labour. The 'artificial' in artificial intelligence often means that it is 'fake AI' (Kaltheuner, 2021): outsourced and exploitative labour undertaken by marginalised workers often in the Global South. It is not just the labour that is immaterial. The workers themselves are treated as immaterial: available, exploitable, and disposable as the platform and management dictates.

Conclusion

Digital technologies have become essential to the way many people work today. The digital economy has become a dominating force in global capitalism. From the material manufacture of devices to the use of complex data and AI platforms to manage work in all sectors, technology impacts on what kinds of jobs people do and how they do them. This chapter has examined some of these types of work, who does them, and the issues they raise. It has discussed the labour that goes into designing and building the material and immaterial infrastructure that allow digital technologies to function. From the environmental damage of manufacturing and running digital systems, to the ghost workers who sort out data and fix the errors made by AI, there are huge numbers of low-paid workers in harmful conditions, often in the Global South and seeing little of the benefits of digital society. The chapter has also discussed the shift towards working on and through platforms. Whether it is the work of labelling data the platforms need or having every moment tracked for productivity, platform capitalism has amplified the expectations placed on workers. Human interaction has been replaced by metrics and constant surveillance in some sectors, often automated or managed through technology. This shifts responsibility onto platforms, and can be a way for companies to outsource, avoiding regulation and labour laws, including pay and other working conditions. The chapter also examined the collective labour required to resist platform capitalism and exploitative digital labour. This included tactics to get by day to day, as well as the work of critiquing unjust systems and building movements against them.

Finally, this chapter considered these different aspects through the case study of Google's content moderators who keep adverts and news feeds clear of scams, violence, and porn. The work of these people in places such as India and the Philippines is essential to fill in the gaps where technology fails, and yet they receive none of the benefits often associated with working for giant tech companies like Google. Across the different aspects of the issue, one thing remains consistent.

Digital technology is not so much replacing labour; it is shifting it to different types of work done by different people. And a lot of the design of these systems makes this work invisible. Digital labour creates new challenges for sociologists, for if work (and workers) are invisible, then it becomes harder to assess and highlight the inequalities these kinds of labour can produce.

STUDENT ACTIVITY

Choose a platform that you use on a regular basis. This could be social media, online learning, work, or a service. Using the list of key terms, and examples in this chapter as a guide, what different kinds of work and workers make the platform possible? Try mapping them out, connecting the flow of material and immaterial products as they make their way towards you. Where in the map does power sit? Who is benefiting from this digital system, and who is being exploited or harmed?

Practice Questions

1. To what extent has the platform economy created surveillance and insecurity at work?
2. What are the differences between digital work and digitalised work, and how are they seen in an online work platform?
3. Drawing on the case study as an example, what are the issues faced by content moderators?

Key Terms

Attention economy
one name for the shift within contemporary capitalism towards focusing on engagement. As platforms gain most of their income from advertising, keeping people scrolling, watching, liking, and sharing becomes the goal. It is often social, but it is highly media-based and usually managed by algorithms and data on what content keeps people watching.

Digital society
the changes in the way society is organised in the wake of widespread digital technology. There is some debate about whether this is a new form of society or just the same principles translated onto digital technologies. Either way, more and more parts of society, from work to public services to socialising, are being managed digitally, and this has implications for how sociologists understand social issues.

Digital work
the different forms of immaterial labour or knowledge work that go into making online platforms and systems. It can include designing and programming, developing interfaces, preparing data, and making content.

Digitalised work

the ways that any job can be affected by digital technologies, even though the work itself might not necessarily be digital. This includes using platforms to monitor workers' performance, manage people and resources to make them more efficient, and connect workers with clients. The gig economy is one example, that is, how Uber digitalises taxi driving.

Ghost work

the invisible labour that makes platforms and other digital systems work. It is linked to tasks like labelling data, moderating content and fixing errors in online platforms and related technologies. The work is often low paid, avoiding labour laws, and excludes workers from the benefits of working for a big tech company.

#Hashtag activism

the use of online platforms to organise and promote activism. Tools such as messaging apps and social media can be used to coordinate physical protests, document footage of police violence and other injustices, share information and resources, and raise awareness or recruit more people to a cause. It is often used by marginalised groups to engage wider audiences in issues of social justice.

Immaterial labour

a type of work that does not create material products. Instead, immaterial labour is about creating cultural products, intellectual property, and services. It has become a defining feature of late capitalism in the digital age, particularly in the Global North.

Infrastructure

the systems and structures that support certain activities. It can include physical infrastructure like network devices, energy, and cables, as well as the processes, protocols, and procedures that define how these structures operate. Infrastructure can therefore be a way of defining power over whole industries.

Invisible labour

work that is not able to be seen in outcomes. Whereas a physical product might show clear signs of how it was made, the work that went into it, a combination of global supply chains and immaterial labour makes lots of types of work invisible. This can cover over harsh working conditions, low pay, and other abuses.

Platform capitalism

the form of late capitalism run by digital platforms. It positions the platform as a place where activity happens and the medium through which people make that activity happen. It relies on communication and data, and often involves a shifting of work and shifting of responsibility, usually managed automatically by computers.

References

Ahmad, S., and Krzywdzinski, M. (2022) 'Moderating in obscurity: how Indian content moderators work in global content moderation value chains'. in M. Graham and F. Ferrari (eds), *Digital work in the planetary market*. Cambridge, MA: MIT Press, pp. 77–95.

Ahmed, S. (2017) *Living a feminist life*. Durham, NC: Duke University Press.

Amrute, S. (2016) *Encoding race, encoding class: Indian IT workers in Berlin*. Durham, NC: Duke University Press.

Bailey, M. (2021) *Misogynoir transformed*. New York: New York University Press.

Banerjee, B. (2021) 'Modern slavery is an enabling condition of global neoliberal capitalism: commentary on modern slavery in business'. *Business & Society*, 60(2): 415–419.

Bates, J., Gerakopoulou, E., and Checco, A. (2023) 'Addressing labour exploitation in the data science pipeline: views of precarious US-based crowdworkers on adversarial and co-operative interventions'. *Journal of Information, Communication and Ethics in Society*, 21(3): 342–357.

Benjamin, G. (2019) 'Playing at control: writing surveillance in/for gamified society', *Surveillance & Society*, 17(5): 699–713.

Benjamin, G. (2022) '#FuckTheAlgorithm: algorithmic imaginaries and political resistance'. *ACM FAccT Conference 2022*, 46–57.

Benjamin, R. (2019) *Race after technology: abolitionist tools for the New Jim Code*. Cambridge: Polity.

Carmi, E., Yates, S.J., Lockley, E., and Pawluczuk, A. (2020) 'Data citizenship: rethinking data literacy in the age of disinformation, misinformation, and mal-information'. *Internet Policy Review, 9*(2): 1–22.

Cassidy, C., and Chen, A. (2017) *The moderators*. FIELD_OF_VISION. https://fieldofvision.org/shorts/the-moderators.

CDDO (2023) 'Digital, data and technology Profession Capability Framework'. *gov.uk*. www.gov.uk/government/collections/digital-data-and-technology-profession-capability-framework.

Chaudhuri, P., Chatterjee, A., and Verma, V. (2014) 'Guardians of the Internet'. *Telegraph India*, www.telegraphindia.com/7-days/guardians-of-the-internet/cid/1669422

Coghlan, S., Miller, T., and Paterson, J. (2021) 'Good proctor or "Big Brother"? Ethics of online exam supervision technologies'. *Philosophy & Technology, 34*: 1581–1606.

Crain, M.G., Poster, W.R., and Cherry, M.A. (eds) (2016) *Invisible labor: hidden work in the contemporary world*. Berkeley, CA: University of California Press.

Crogan, P., and Kinsley, S. (2012) 'Paying attention: towards a critique of the attention economy'. *Culture Machine*, 13: 1–29.

D'Ignazio, C., and Klein, L. (2020) *Data feminism*. Cambridge, MA: MIT Press.

Davies, H., Goodley, S., Lawrence, F., Lewis, P., and O'Carroll, L. (2022) 'The Uber files'. *Guardian*. www.theguardian.com/news/series/uber-files

Duffy, B.E., and Schwartz, B. (2018) 'Digital "women's work?": Job recruitment ads and the feminization of social media employment'. *New media & society*, 20(8): 2972–2989.

Eubanks, V. (2018) *Automating inequality: how high-tech tools profile, police and punish the poor*. New York: St Martin's Press.

Goldhaber, M.H. (1997) 'The attention economy and the net'. *First Monday* 2(4, 7 April). https://doi.org/10.5210/fm.v2i4.519.

Gray, M.L., and Suri, S. (2019) *Ghost work: how to stop Silicon Valley from building a new global underclass*. Boston, MA, and New York: Houghton Mifflin Harcourt.

Guyan, K. (2022) *Queer data: using gender, sex and sexuality data for action*. London: Bloomsbury.

Hamraie, A., and Fritsch, K. (2019) 'Crip technoscience manifesto'. *Catalyst: feminism, theory, technoscience*, 5(1): 1–33.

Hicks, M. (2017) *Programmed inequality: how Britain discarded women technologists and lost its edge in computing*. Cambridge, MA: MIT Press.

Irani, L. (2015) 'Justice for "data janitors"'. *Public Books*. www.publicbooks.org/justice-for-data-janitors/

Jackson, S.J., Bailey, M., and Welles, B.F. (2020) *#Hashtagactivism: networks of race and gender justice*. Cambridge, MA: MIT Press.

Kaltheuner, F. (ed.) (2021) *Fake AI*. London: Meatspace Press.

Kar, S., and Sarkhel, A. (2017) 'Meet the Indian warriors who watch hours of beheadings, murders & gory content to clean the internet'. *Economic Times*. https://economictimes.indiatimes.com/internet/meet-the-indian-warriors-who-watch-hours-of-beheadings-murders-gory-content-to-clean-the-internet/articleshow/58901110.cms

Kassem, S. (2023) *Work and alienation in the platform economy: Amazon and the power of organization*. Bristol: Bristol University Press.

Kelly-Lyth, A. (2021) 'Challenging biased hiring algorithms'. *Oxford Journal of Legal Studies*, 41(4): 899–928.

Le Ludec, C., Cornet, M., and Casilli, A.A. (2023) 'The problem with annotation: human labour and outsourcing between France and Madagascar'. *Big Data & Society*, 10(2): 1–13.

Levin, S. (2017) 'Tech firms fail to stop abusive content – leaving the public to do the dirty work'. *Guardian*. www.theguardian.com/technology/2017/dec/05/youtube-offensive-videos-journalists-moderators.

Little, P.C., and Akese, G.A. (2019) 'Centering the Korle Lagoon: exploring blue political ecologies of e-waste in Ghana'. *Journal of Political Ecology*, 26(1): 448–465.

Lupton, D. (2014) *Digital sociology*. Abingdon: Routledge.

Ly, L. (2023) 'Spectral cities and rare earth mining in the North China Plain'. In P.R. Gilbert, C. Bourne, M. Haiven, and J. Montgomerie (eds.), *The entangled legacies of empire: race, finance and inequality*, Manchester: Manchester University Press, pp. 181–190.

McIlwain, C.D. (2019) *Black software: the Internet and racial justice, from the AfroNet to Black Lives Matter*. Oxford: Oxford University Press.

McQuillan, D. (2022) *Resisting AI: an anti-fascist approach to artificial intelligence*. Bristol: Bristol University Press.

Marres, N. (2017) *Digital sociology: the reinvention of social research*. Hoboken, NJ: John Wiley & Sons.

Noble, S. (2018) *Algorithms of oppression*. New York: New York University Press.

Otu, K.E. (2021) 'When the lagoons remember'. *Feminist Africa*, 2(2): 29–46.

Roberts, S. (2019) *Behind the screen: content moderation in the shadows of social media*. New Haven, CT: Yale University Press.

Russon, M.-A. (2021) 'Uber drivers are workers not self-employed, Supreme Court rules'. *BBC News*. www.bbc.co.uk/news/business-56123668.

Sadowski, J. (2022) 'Planetary Potemkin AI: the humans hidden inside mechanical minds'. In M. Graham and F. Ferrari (eds), *Digital work in the planetary market*. Cambridge, MA: MIT Press, pp. 229–240.

Skinner-Thompson, S. (2020) *Privacy at the margins*. Cambridge: Cambridge University Press.

Srnicek, N. (2017) *Platform capitalism*. Hoboken, NJ: John Wiley & Sons.

Spade, D. (2015) *Normal life: administrative violence, critical trans politics and the limits of law*. Durham, NC: Duke University Press.

Stephens, E. (2023) 'The mechanical Turk: a short history of "artificial artificial intelligence"'. *Cultural Studies*, 37(1): 65–87.

Stypinska, J. (2023) 'AI ageism: a critical roadmap for studying age discrimination and exclusion in digitalized societies'. *AI & Society*, 38: 665–677.

Treré, E. (2018) 'From digital activism to algorithmic resistance'. In G. Meikle (ed.), *The Routledge companion to media and activism*. Routledge Media and Cultural Studies. London and New York: Routledge, pp. 367–375.

chapter 13

Sex Work in the Digital Age

Helen M. Rand

Introduction

The internet has changed the organisation of sex work and therefore the working lives of sex workers. In Chapter 7, Santos discussed migrant sex work and survival sex, but in this chapter sex work and digital platforms are the focus. When considering changes in the organisation and regulation of sex work, it is imperative to listen to sex workers' lived experiences. Therefore, this chapter draws on empirical research with, or by, sex workers to understand these changes. Sex workers have a long and established history of collective action. At end of the discussion, there are links to advocacy organisations run by sex workers for sex workers, including a TED Talk by an activist.

The chapter considers the context in which sex work takes place and how other factors such as race, gender, class, sexuality, and disability intersect. Sex work, though engaged in by workers of all genders, can be framed as a 'feminised' form of labour. Prostitution has traditionally and continually been associated with what women do, and what (some) women are. For example, a survey conducted in 2015–2017 with 641 sex workers in the UK found that three-quarters were women (Sanders et al., 2018). Sex work is both gendered and stigmatised labour. Sex workers often operate in the shadow of criminalisation that targets prostitution and trafficking for sexual exploitation, thus producing discrimination, sometimes violence, and further social and economic uncertainty.

International research shows the violent and discriminatory repercussions for many sex workers globally. For instance, Vuolajärvi (2019) highlights the punitive consequences of legislation in Sweden, Norway, and Finland that aims to abolish 'prostitution' by criminalising the clients of sex workers. Social welfare policies sit alongside Sex Purchase Acts and promote exiting from sex work by enabling

DOI: 10.4324/9781003314769-17

nationals to access social services and therapeutic counselling. However, 70 to 80 per cent of those who sell sex in the Nordic region are migrant workers (Vuolajärvi, 2019). While nationals can access housing, healthcare, and social benefits, migrant sex workers are excluded from state support and often face detention, deportation, and eviction (see also Chapter 7, 'Migrant Sex Work and Survival Sex'). In 2017, in New York, repressive policing, specifically aimed at migrant populations led to the death of Yang Song, a massage worker. Tragically she died falling four storeys while trying to evade arrest during a police raid (Ho, 2021). Reports from India and from other Global South countries state sex workers are subject to 'raid and rescue' operations, forcibly removed from their place of work and detained without their consent in rehabilitation centres (Dasgupta, 2019), thus removing their ability to make an income and be full citizens (Ramachandran, 2017).

Stigma and discrimination are global experiences for sex workers, but how and in what ways it is experienced and navigated, is context-specific and intersects with racism, xenophobia, classism, and transphobia (Bowen and Bungay, 2016; Simpson, 2022). Intersectionality, a term discussed in Part 2 of this textbook, highlights how an individual's identities intersect with different axes of power and oppression to create privileges and discrimination. Intersectionality is a useful framework to analyse sex workers' experiences. It enables students to move beyond simplified arguments of oppression or empowerment and explore the nuances of peoples' lived experiences.

'Whore stigma' is a term coined by Pheterson (1993) to summarise the gendered hostile stereotyping and social exclusion experienced by sex workers, underpinned by sexual double standards. For example, sex workers' bank accounts are frozen without warning, they are fired from 'square work' (work outside of the sex industry), and are at risk of physical, sexual, and verbal harassment, and abuse. Yet, stigma is not experienced the same for all sex workers, because how whore stigma is experienced depends on the type of sex work, the legal context, and where the work takes place.

In many ways, online sex work in the United Kingdom has fewer physical, legal, and social risks; therefore online sex workers are more likely to be able to navigate whore stigma than sex workers working in criminalised public spaces, such as street sex workers. Indeed, the rise in popularity of subscription-based platforms like *OnlyFans* – where people can sell erotic photographs, video clips, and/or live-streaming sessions – suggests further mainstreaming of and ambivalence towards online, indirect sex work (Easterbrook-Smith, 2022).

The aims of this chapter are threefold: first, to understand the 'revolutionary' impact of the internet and associated technologies in the organisation of sex work. Second, to develop a knowledge of the benefits and potential drawbacks for workers when sex work is organised and mediated online, drawing on research by and/or with sex workers. Third, the chapter will evaluate the regulatory frameworks in the UK and the US and consider future opportunities and risks associated with legislation. A case study, based on the author's empirical research with sex workers in the UK, considers the themes of agency and consent concerning online sex work.

The Rise of Online Sex Work

In the last three decades, the sale of sexual services has increasingly been organised online (Bernstein, 2007; Jones, 2020; Sanders et al., 2018), like service industries more broadly – such as cleaning, taxi rides, and food delivery. Researchers noticed the decline in street-based sex markets, and indoor-managed premises, such as brothels and saunas, from around the late 1990s (Sanders et al., 2016). Due to legislative changes, policing, and the wide availability of the internet, increasing numbers of sex workers moved to online spaces to sell services and, more recently, also to produce and sell online content.

As with other forms of service work, platforms have increasingly become the working environment for many sex workers in the UK and beyond. 'Adult' platforms are digital, multimedia, interactive spaces that mediate sexual exchanges between sex workers and customers (Rand, 2019). Platform-managed sex work takes place online and offline. Indirect sex work can include webcam shows, phone calls, text exchanges, and other forms of communication mediated by the internet and associated technologies such as smartphones and web cameras. Webcamming is currently the most popular form of **synchronous online sex work**. Indirect sex work can also consist of **asynchronous online erotic content,** such as the sale of photographs and video reels produced by sex workers to sell, often on subscription platforms such as OnlyFans (Easterbrook-Smith, 2021). 'Adult' platforms are also online places to advertise and arrange direct in-person sex work, identified by Hardy and Barbagallo (2021) as a form of work that involves greater physical and health risks and risk of criminalisation than indirect sex work.

Despite sex work scholars arguing that sex work is part of the gig economy, it remains invisible in policy debates and discussions on platform labour, continuing to be a form of labour that is marginalised politically and socially (Easterbrook-Smith, 2021; Rand, 2019). Like other forms of gig work (see Chapter 5), the platform acts as a mediator between the worker and the customer, taking a percentage of the income of the worker. This fee ranges from 10 to 60 per cent of the worker's income (Rand, 2019). This form of labour organisation is intrinsically rooted in neoliberal logic, benefitting from the glorification of individualism and entrepreneurialism. This ethic is embedded in the technological architecture of the platforms. On the platforms, customers can browse the tessellation of small square thumbnails of individual sex workers' profiles, giving the appearance of endless supply and opportunities for sexual content and services. Workers compete for the attention of customers through entrepreneurial and innovative approaches to pricing, services, and digital content (Rand and Stegeman, 2023).

Opportunities and Challenges for Online Sex Workers

Sex work researchers argue that the digital revolution has created new work opportunities, diversified services, and increased access to sex markets. It appears online sex work is appealing to more workers than offline sex work, across class boundaries (Bernstein, 2007; Jones, 2020). This is in part due to better working

Helen M. Rand

conditions, autonomy over the work, and the pleasure people experience from selling sexual content and services. As this chapter's case study highlights, before digital platforms, mediated forms of sex work were mainly limited to erotic phone lines. Taking a Taylorist managerial approach (see Chapter 8 for a discussion of Taylorism and management styles), those working on erotic phone lines would often work shifts in call centres or their own homes. Monitored through the technology, workers would earn a set hourly wage, incentivised to work hard and consistently through bonuses based on the number of callers they received and the length of time the caller stayed on the line. **Direct sex work** is, and was, organised in various ways. In many cases, indoor-based sex workers would work in a brothel, sauna, or massage parlour. In these cases, sex workers were often working for a third party who had varying degrees of control over prices, hours, and fees (Sanders et al., 2016).

These forms of managerial practices contrast with selling sexual services through and on a platform. Online sex workers discuss the benefits of 'being their own boss' and the flexibility they have over working hours and income generation (Rand, 2019). In most cases, sex workers choose what services/shows they offer, determine price, and manage and liaise with clients directly. Research suggests this has increased sex workers' income and welfare by lowering transaction costs and decreasing the need to engage in risky business practices (Cowen and Colosi, 2020). Furthermore, online sex workers have control over content and how they appear online.

Jones (2020) argues that webcamming appeals to a greater number of people because it meets the capitalist obligation to make money, yet it is subversive as the work is pleasurable for many sex workers. Digital technology affords physical distance from the client, thus webcamming is generally safer and therefore more enjoyable. Historically, labour has been constructed as the binary opposite of pleasure. Yet, in Jones' study, some webcammers found pleasure in being paid to masturbate and climax to orgasm.

Performing online, interacting with clients via a telephone or webcam, or making a film can make people feel less inhibited than direct physical contact (Jones, 2020). As a result, online sex work can be a place for sexual and gender expression and freedom. Research in the United Kingdom found men as both workers and clients used online sex markets to express themselves sexually while maintaining an overt heterosexual identity outside of sex markets (Rand, 2022). Similarly, research in the Philippines with trans women or *transpinays*, found that online sex work did not only fulfil economic needs,[1] but was also an opportunity to meet life partners that would accept them as a woman (Gregorio, 2023). This was despite the criminalisation of webcamming and all forms of online sexual activity in the Philippines under the Cybercrime Prevention Act of 2012.

In some ways, however, platforms are the digital third party and the design of the platform instructs how services are sold (Easterbrook-Smith, 2022; Rand and Stegeman, 2023). There are several ways that adult platforms are organised. Some webcam platforms require workers to charge per minute for a show, in either private one-to-one sessions or in groups with several customers at once (based on a price decided by the sex worker). Other platforms require sex workers to put on a show for free and encourage customers to tip using tokens. In this business model, sex workers create a list and will perform certain acts for a set number of tokens (decided by the sex worker), encouraging customers to tip enough collectively so the act is performed (Jones, 2020). Subscription sites ask customers to pay a monthly fee. Online sex workers can make additional income by charging specific fees for additional content or live streams, often known as 'pay per view'. In this business model, communication between the worker and customer is usually through an instant messaging feature on the platform (Easterbrook-Smith, 2022). Similarly, like erotic phone companies, workers are incentivised to upload more content and to receive more (positive) reviews, as this positions them more advantageously on the homepage and/or in the search outcomes.

In all these instances, sex workers can set the price; however, there are market boundaries. Workers may set their prices based on what other sex workers charge. Due to the way platforms are designed, there is a visible oversupply of workers, and there are concerns in the literature that prices and standards could be pushed down (Van Doorn and Velthuis, 2018). Moreover, platforms limit pricing; for instance, OnlyFans set an upper limit on how much a worker could charge a customer for pay-per-view content, and how much a fan can tip in a single transaction (Easterbrook-Smith, 2022). AdultWork sets the price for text messages and does not charge customers for emails, but allows sex workers to choose the price for other services (Rand and Stegeman, 2023). In this way, the platform takes on the role of third-party management.

Due to the shift online, most sex workers are reliant on adult platforms to host and advertise their services, as other markets for commercial sex have declined (Caradonna, 2019). It has been noted, like other service industries in the gig economy, that one platform becomes the go-to place for customers, thus creating a monopoly. This is known as the **network effect,** as seen, for instance, with Uber and taxi rides. The network effect means there are just a handful of platforms to work on, resulting in sex workers having limited choices on where to work. This increases the control platforms have over the sector regarding workers' discretion on content, prices, and services. Research suggests that the reliance on a handful of platforms has led to a devaluation of digital sex work (Van Doorn and Velthuis, 2018), an increase in less enjoyable services (Hardy and Barbagallo, 2022), and the normalisation of more 'risky' practices (Caradonna, 2019).

In turn, platforms are reliant on financial institutions and payment processors to operate their business model (Easterbrook-Smith, 2022). 'Adult' sites are seen as high-risk investments, and several sites, including Pornhub, have faced banking discrimination, as do individual sex workers. Sex workers have reported that many online payment processing companies such as PayPal block and close sex worker accounts, only adding to sex workers' economic uncertainty and limiting their choices on where to work (Blunt et al., 2020). Thus, the organisation of online sex work results in sex workers being reliant on a handful of platforms to advertise their work and a handful of payment processing companies. Sex workers

Helen M. Rand

have historically been at the blunt end of often sudden policy changes that aim to eradicate the sale and purchase of sex. The introduction of anti-trafficking legislation in the United States, as discussed in the following section, has increased banking discrimination. Furthermore, most social media platforms have distanced themselves from sex work through the introduction of anti-sex work policies, and even sites such as OnlyFans, largely known for erotic content, ironically temporarily banned such content in August 2021. These practices have further excluded sex workers from the digital world.

The lived realities of online sex workers are complex and sometimes contradictory, showing that binary debates that suggest sex work is either empowering or exploitative are unworkable. Instead, there is tension for online sex workers who, on the one hand, are in control of their earnings, and resist capital exploitation by finding pleasure and excitement in their work, yet at the same time are limited by the structures of the platforms and the market demands. The flexibility of online sex work is important to many who do this work, but this is partly due to the increasingly precarious employment and labour market, and the retraction of state support in modern industrial societies that requires many to find work in the informal sector, often in the gig economy.

What is evident is that online sex work is a significant part of the gig economy, taken up predominantly by women who are already impacted by undervalued 'feminised' work. As Easterbrook-Smith (2022) argues, the precarity of online sex workers is twofold due to the inherent precarious nature of gig work (as discussed in Chapter 5, 'Precarious and Gig Work in the Global Economy', by McDonough and Pearson) and the whore stigma associated with sex work. As such, this form of stigmatised gendered work must be included in discussions on gig work, yet too often it remains invisible and outside of policy and academic debates (Rand, 2019).

Legislation

Globally, sex work is regulated through many different types of legislation. Broadly, this can be broken down into four regulatory frameworks, although there are specificities within each jurisdiction. The Global Network of Sex Work Projects website has a comprehensive breakdown of each country's approach to commercial sex, with case studies written by sex workers (see 'Useful Websites' for details). The majority of countries criminalise either the selling, purchasing, and/or organising of commercial sex. In this instance, sex workers are at risk of police harassment, imprisonment, and deportation. Recently, there has been a change in legislation in many Northern European countries where the purchasing of sex is criminalised, but sex workers are not. This form of regulation aims to end the demand for commercial sex through criminalisation. However, research using data from 33 countries found criminalisation in *all forms* – whether that be the criminalisation of sex workers and/or clients – impacts the well-being of sex workers, increasing their risk of sexual and physical violence and restricting access to services and justice (Platt et al., 2018). Other countries – for example, Germany – have legalised sex work. In these instances, sex workers are subject to regulation, often regarding their migration and/or health status. A fourth approach, seen in New Zealand, and some states in Australia, is to decriminalise sex work, meaning it is no longer processed through the criminal justice system but is regulated as a form of work. Thus, sex workers are protected by employment laws.

This section of the chapter focuses on US legislation, as **platform governance** in the US has a global impact due to the concentration of platforms originating in and operating from the country. Scholars of platform governance argue that, in many ways, the moral and cultural values of the US have created the internet (Gillespie, 2018; Poell et al., 2021). For instance, section 230 of the Communications Decency Act has protected the right to freedom of speech, but also allows platforms to moderate and control content motivated by the interests of US corporations (Tidenberg, 2021). It is within this context that laws regarding sex work in the US have had a global impact.

In 2018, the US government enacted the Fight Online Sex Trafficking Act and Stop Enabling Sex Traffickers Act. FOSTA-SESTA, as it is commonly known, amended the Communications Decency Act to hold platforms responsible for 'promoting or facilitating prostitution' or 'knowingly assisting, facilitating or supporting sex trafficking'. The law aims to stop trafficking for sexual exploitation in the belief that, if sex markets are eradicated, all forced and coerced sex will stop. It remains to be seen if it has had the desired impact and arguably a public health approach outside the criminal justice system may be more effective. FOSTA-SESTA has been widely criticised by sex workers in the US for being naive at best, and more likely to be motivated by sexual morality and anti-migration ideologies.

Many sex workers feel that FOSTA-SESTA has silenced sex workers online. Due to the vague language of the Act, it has been easier for platforms to ban sexual content and conflate all sex work with trafficking. Research in the US has shown that many platforms have failed to differentiate 'promoting prostitution' and 'supporting sex trafficking' with other content, such as sex work activism, sex work, and sex education (Tidenberg, 2021). Many platforms have banned and blocked individual sex worker accounts due to the legal and business risks of being shut down for 'promoting prostitution' (HackingHustling.org, 2023; see Useful Websites). Furthermore, platforms distance themselves from commercial sex, specifically full-service direct sex work, as seen with Only Fans, Tumblr, and Craigslist, and the closure of Backpage, a popular platform for advertising direct sex work.

Closing platforms, dissociation of other platforms, and the blocking of sex workers' online accounts impact sex workers' ability to participate in cultural, social, economic, and political life. This is evident in several ways. First, limiting choices on where and how to work does not eradicate sex markets, but rather marginalises the work into more dangerous and exploitative spaces. Second, it reduces opportunities for sex workers to screen clients. This has been reported as one of the key benefits of using platforms to sell sex (Sanders et al., 2016). Third, sex workers report that their activist accounts on social media platforms have been blocked and removed (HackingHustling.org, 2023; see Useful Websites), which reduces opportunities

Helen M. Rand

for sex workers to organise online and share information collectively, threatening their long history of self-advocacy and support (Easterbrook-Smith, 2022).

Both the EU and the UK seek to regulate platforms through legislation that responsibilises platforms for the content they host. The EU has recently passed the Digital Services Act (2022), responsibilising platforms to monitor and moderate 'illegal content', leaving national laws to define 'illegal content'. In the EU, there is not one legal framework regarding sex work, so the law is open to conflicting interpretations. In the UK context, the Online Safety Act (2023) has listed 'inciting prostitution for gain' as a priority offence. There are concerns from sex workers that further criminalisation will lead to online marginalisation. There is a risk that platforms will ban sex worker accounts, disassociating their business from sex work to meet the demands of the law.

Case Study

'Platformisation' of Sex Work in the UK

These accounts are based on nineteen in-depth interviews with online sex workers in the UK.[2] This research highlights how people (not only cis women) engage in online sex work to manage the economic uncertainty and individualised responsibility embedded in neoliberal economic and social policies. However, women remain at an economic and social disadvantage regarding pay and work opportunities, and therefore are the majority of those working informal, often low-paid, and 'gig' economy jobs (Phipps, 2020). Women in this study told their stories of entrepreneurialism and self-sufficiency to navigate uncertainty and avoid economic hardship.

At the time of her interview, Sarah was a single mother of a teenage daughter and had worked as a hairdresser for all of her adult life. She broke her right wrist, which meant she could no longer work as a hairdresser. Despite working in the same salon for over ten years, she was self-employed, so the owner of the salon was not obliged to pay her sick pay. She had a friend who made extra cash from erotic phone lines, so she gave it a go. The erotic phone line companies, which predate adult platforms, paid predetermined wages and expected workers to work specific shifts. This was at the time when platforms were gaining popularity in the sex industry in the UK. She said: 'I've been doing phone chat for about five years. I was on another site when I first started ... I was paid by the company. Then I heard about AdultWork, and you can set your own rates obviously on AdultWork, so decided to go on that as well.'

As Sarah notes, she was able to set her prices, choose the hours she worked, and offer more services. She worked across platforms, logging into different platforms to maximise her income. She started to make more money, primarily because she was selling escort services – direct sex work commands the most money – but also because the platform reached a larger audience. Although she still did some hairdressing, she has been able to live with greater economic security through online sex work. As she notes, 'I have quite a few regular customers now. So it is always steady.' Sarah's daughter doesn't know Sarah is a sex worker; nor does her wider family. But several friends do.

Katie was at another phase in her life to Sarah, having just left school with minimum qualifications a few years before the interview. She had worked in several jobs that would be considered typically 'women's work' – in care, retail, and administration. They paid minimum wage and she had felt unsatisfied with the hours she worked for the pay she received. As she states: 'I loved working in the care home. I stuck at that job even when the pay was really bad. But it wasn't making me happy.'

A friend was webcamming on a large US webcamming platform and Katie decided to try it. With a permanent address, Wi-Fi connection, and a web camera, it is fairly straightforward to sign up, create a profile, upload photos, and start streaming erotic content. Very quickly, Katie was making money from webcam shows across different platforms. Through chatting with other sex workers on online forums, Katie has developed her business as she has learned more about online sex work. She sells video reels, photos, and access to her social media accounts. She works long hours, and states she is always online, hustling for business: 'My phone does not stop. I get customers texting me all the time ... I used to enjoy going on Facebook, but I've got no time for it. My life has been taken over by work.'

Her statement reflects the 'presence bleed' noted by Gregg (2011), where the digital world has eroded boundaries between personal and professional identities. There is a 'consciousness of the always-present potential for engaging with work' (Gregg, 2011: 3).

Katie has considered the social stigma and states she may not do this work forever, but for now she is happy webcamming: 'At first I was worried about people's reactions but everyone knows now ... I have accepted it makes me happy and I don't actually feel like I am doing anything wrong.'

These brief accounts highlight the choices women make when engaging in sex work and how they rationalise whether the risks of social stigma outweigh the increased income based on alternative economic choices available to them.

Conclusion

The chapter has presented research that complicates the often-binary argument regarding sex work: empowerment or coercion; voluntary or forced. As the case study evidence shows, women make choices and use their agency to make economic decisions. Generally, women are still economically disadvantaged and, in this socioeconomic context, look for ways to make an income. For some, online sex work offers a pleasurable and exciting way to make money.

Platforms have offered new opportunities for many. They provide more physically safe forms of sex work and tools to screen clients. Yet, platforms also have an element of control over pricing, content, and payments, which challenges sex workers' autonomy over working practices. Yet, at the very same time, sex workers find ways to resist this control, finding opportunities through innovation and acts of solidarity (see Rand and Stegeman, 2023).

The chapter has also highlighted the economic uncertainty that is characteristic of gig work and how this is compounded within online sex work through criminalisation and the stigma associated with sex work. Whore stigma operates according to the positionality of the sex worker and the services offered; thus, it can be navigated and negotiated in varying degrees. Stigma is relational and intersects with various political and social identities. Furthermore, research into the impact of criminalising sex work, even when the intention is to protect sex workers, shows that criminalisation only increases physical, social, and economic risks for sex workers.

STUDENT ACTIVITY

Feminist scholar Chandra Mohanty's (2003) seminal work *Feminism without borders* raises the concept of oppositional agency. She asks us to think beyond binary power relations of oppressed/oppressor and instead acknowledge the 'idea of multiple, fluid structures of domination' (Mohanty, 2003: 53) that intersect and influence women's daily lives. The concept of oppositional agency allows us to understand women's choices within broader social, economic, and political forces. In this way, women's status as the oppressed gender is not frozen, but rather women resist subjugation through dynamic, oppositional agency. As sex worker Graceyswer (2020) states in their blog, 'It's important to make the distinction between "I" had no choice" and "I had limited choices" … My limited choices may have led me to this decision, but it doesn't give anyone the right to mistreat me whilst I am here.'

Based on the case study, and the wider research presented in the chapter, discuss the risks and opportunities available to online sex workers. What is the context? Consider the lack of state support available to Sarah and the low wages for Katie. How do gender, race, and class intersect with their choices? What are the social risks associated with online sex work? What have Katie and Sarah done to manage the risks? How are their approaches different? What opportunities does online sex work offer?

Additionally, how, if at all, might you regulate online sex work? Justify your answers and consider the potential side effects of legislation, drawing on the information provided by sex workers through the Network of Sex Work Projects website.

Practice Questions

1. How, and in what ways, has the internet changed the organisation of sex work?
2. What risks are associated with sex work, and how has the internet increased and/or decreased risks for sex workers?
3. 'Sex work is exploitative.' Critically discuss in relation to online sex work.

Key Terms

Asynchronous/synchronous online erotic content
refers to how the clients and the workers are communicating. When the exchange is **synchronous,** both the customer(s) and the worker are online at the same time, simultaneously exchanging text or talk, in real time. **Asynchronous** communication implies there is a time lack, such as with emails.

Direct/indirect sex work
can be a useful distinction to make when considering the physical work and risks involved for sex workers. Many sex workers may engage in both, but direct, in-person sex work has greater physical, health, and legal risks (Hardy and Barbagallo, 2021).

Network effect
what happens once a platform has a significant market presence – it becomes the 'go-to' platform for customers often creating a monopoly. Workers have little choice but to work on the platform.

Platform governance
a concept used in two ways – on a macro level, it relates to how platforms are regulated in relation to content regulation, data protection regulation, and competition laws, and on a micro level, it captures how platforms govern their online spaces through platform policies and technological architectures and affordances.

Platformisation
a concept adopted by Van Doorn and Velthuis (2018) to measure the significance of digital platforms in shaping the economic, cultural, legal, and social infrastructures of sex markets.

Raid and rescue
a term coined to describe operations, often in developing countries, where the state, sometimes accompanied by non-governmental organisations (NGOs) raid brothels and other places of (sex) work to 'rescue' sex workers from 'exploitation', resulting in forced detention in rehabilitation homes.

Sexual double standards
these conceptualise the historical and persistent expectation that women are less socially, culturally, and economically 'valuable' if they have sex outside of monogamous, heterosexual marriages. Men, however, are respected and honoured as sexually accomplished if they have more than one sexual relationship, adding to their masculine status.

Square work
a term coined by sex work scholar Bowen (2015) to describe work outside of the sex industry, thus recognising the multiple positions and identities of sex workers.

Helen M. Rand

Whore stigma

a term that expresses the hostile stereotyping, social exclusion, and potential loss of status that sex workers can experience. Pheterson (1993) argues this is a form of social control to police female sexuality that confronts normative expectations of femininity.

Notes

1 It should be noted that the global sex industry provides work for many transgender people due to the difficulties and discrimination faced in obtaining an income from 'straight' work.
2 All the names used here are pseudonyms and the biographies of the sex workers have been scrambled to protect their anonymity.

References

Bernstein, E. (2007) *Temporarily yours: intimacy, authenticity, and the commerce of sex*. Chicago: University of Chicago Press.

Blunt, D., Coombes, E., Mullin, S., and Wolf, A. (2020) 'Posting into the void'. Accessed 24 August 2023 from

https://hackinghustling.org/wp-content/uploads/2020/09/Posting-Into-the-Void.pdf

Bowen, R. (2015) 'Squaring up: experiences of transition from off-street sex work to square work and duality – concurrent involvement in both – in Vancouver, BC'. *Canadian Review of Sociology, 52*(4): 429–449.

Bowen, R., and Bungay, V. (2016) 'Taint: an examination of the lived experiences of stigma and its lingering effects for eight sex industry experts'. *Culture, Health and Sexuality*, *18*(2): 184–197. https://doi.org/10.1080/13691058.2015.1072875

Caradonna, A., 2019. 'From brothels to independence: the neoliberalisation of (sex) work'. In C. Thisbos and J. Quirk (eds), *Future of work, beyond trafficking and slavery: opendemocracy*, 44–47. Accessed 24 August 2023 from www.cracy.net/en/beyond-trafficking-and-slavery/from-brothels-to-independence-neoliberalisation-of-sex-work/

Cowen, N., and Colosi, R. (2020) 'Sex work and online platforms: what should regulation do?' *Journal of Entrepreneurship and Public Policy, 10*(2): 284–303. https://doi.org/10.1108/JEPP-03-2019-0009

Dasgupta, S. (2019) 'Of raids and returns: sex work movement, police oppression, and the politics of the ordinary in Sonagachi, India'. *Anti-Trafficking Review, 12*: 127–139.

Easterbrook-Smith, G., 2022. 'OnlyFans as gig-economy work: a nexus of precarity and stigma'. *Porn Studies*, *10*(3): 252–267. https://doi.org/10.1080/23268743.2022.2096682.

Gillespie, T., 2018. *Custodians of the internet: platforms, content moderation, and the hidden decisions that shape social media.* London: Yale University Press.

Graceyswer (2020) 'Consent and choice in survival sex work'. *wordpress.com*, 4 August. Accessed 10 May 2023 from https://streethooker.wordpress.com/2020/08/04/consent-and-choice-in-survival-sex-work/

Gregg, M. (2011) *Work's intimacy.* Cambridge: Polity.

Gregorio, V.L. (2023) 'Reaffirming womanhood: young transwomen and online sex work in the Philippines'. In G.B. Radics and P. Ciocchini (eds), *Criminal legalities and minorities in the Global South.* London: Palgrave Macmillan. https://doi.org/10.1007/978-3-031-17918-1_13

Hardy, K., and Barbagallo, C. (2021) 'Hustling the platform: capitalist experiments and resistance in the digital sex industry'. *South Atlantic Quarterly,* 120(3): 533–551. https://doi.org/10.1215/00382876-9154898

Ho, R. (2021) 'Migrant massage workers do not need to be rescued'. *The Nation,* April 2. Accessed 22 August 2023 from www.thenation.com/article/activism/red-canary-song-wu-interview/

Jones, A. (2020) *Camming: money, power, and pleasure in the sex work industry.* New York: New York University Press.

Mohanty, C. (2003) *Feminism without borders.* New York: Duke University Press.

Pheterson, G. (1993) 'The whore stigma: female dishonor and male unworthiness'. *Social Text, 37*: 39–64.

Phipps, A. (2020) *Me, not you: the trouble with mainstream feminism.* Manchester: Manchester University Press.

Platt, L., Grenfell, P., Meiksin, R., Elmes, J., Sherman, S.G., Sanders, T., Mwangi, P., and Crago, A-L. (2018) 'Associations between sex work laws and sex workers' health: a systematic review and meta-analysis of quantitative and qualitative studies'. *PLoS Medicine, 15*(12). https://doi.org/10.1371/journal.pmed.1002680

Poell, T., Nieborg, D., and Duffy, B. (2021) *Platforms and cultural production.* Cambridge: Polity.

Ramachandran, V. (2017) 'Critical reflections on raid and rescue operations in New Delhi'. *Opendemocracy.* Accessed 29 September 2022 from www.opendemocracy.net/en/beyond-trafficking-and-slavery/critical-reflections-on-raid-and-rescue-operations-in-new-delhi/

Rand, H.M. (2019) 'Challenging the invisibility of sex work in digital labour politics'. *Feminist Review, 123*(1): 40–55. https://doi.org/10.1177/0141778919879749

Rand, H.M (2022) '"As straight as they come": expressions of masculinities within digital sex markets'. *Sexualities.* https://doi.org/10.1177/13634607221085484

Rand, H.M., and Stegeman, H.M. (2023) 'Navigating and resisting platform affordances: online sex work as digital labour'. *Gender, Work and Organization.* https://doi.org/10.1111/gwao.13047

Sanders, T., Connelly, L., and Jarvis King, L. (2016) 'On our own terms: the working conditions of internet-based sex workers in the UK'. *Sociological Research Online, 21*(4): 133–146. https://doi.org/10.5153/sro.4152

Sanders, T., Scoular, J., Campbell, R., Pitcher, J., and Cunningham, S. (2018) *Internet sex work: beyond the gaze*. London: Palgrave Macmillan. https://doi. org/10.1007/978-3-319-65630-4_3

Simpson, J. (2022) 'Whorephobia in higher education: a reflexive account of researching cis women's experiences of stripping while at university'. *Higher Education*, 84: 17–31. https://doi.org/10.1007/s10734-021-00751-2

Tidenberg, K. (2021) 'Sex, power and platform governance'. *Porn Studies*, 8(4): 383–193. https://doi.org/10.1080/23268743.2021.1974312

Van Doorn, N., and Velthuis, O., 2018) 'A good hustle: the moral economy of market competition in adult webcam modeling'. *Journal of Cultural Economy*, 11(3): 177–192. https://doi.org/10.1080/17530350.2018.1446183

Vuolajärvi, N. (2019) 'Governing in the name of caring – the Nordic model of prostitution and its punitive consequences for migrants who sell sex'. *Sexuality Research and Social Policy*, 16(2): 151–165. https://doi.org/10.1007/s13178-018-0338–9

Useful Websites

https://hackinghustling.org/
A collective of sex workers, survivors, and accomplices working at
the intersection of tech and social justice to interrupt violence facilitated
by technology

www.opendemocracy.net/en/beyond-trafficking-and-slavery/
Independent international media platform that aims to encourage
democratic debate. See section 'Beyond Trafficking and Slavery'

www.nswp.org/
Global Network of Sex Work Projects

www.ted.com/talks/juno_mac_the_laws_that_sex_workers_really_want
Juno Mac, sex worker activist, discusses the laws sex workers really want.

chapter 14

Blogging and Online Work

Jane Parry and Brian J. Hracs

Introduction

Personalised online writing has been a part of the internet since 1994, and the term 'weblog' was coined in 1997 (Parry and Hracs, 2020). Since then, access to digitised publishing has become more readily available and blogging has proliferated. Today blogging is embedded in many occupations and forms of work, and there are well over 500 million blogs worldwide producing over 2 million posts per day (Parry and Hracs, 2020). Although the styles and aims of blogs continue to evolve, they are commonly understood as regularly updated websites featuring text, images, and video content produced by individuals in an informal style. While blogging can generate money directly, through subscriptions, advertising, or pay for commissioned content, it is often also fundamental to the paid work of bloggers in subtler and less direct ways. Indeed, blogging may be a pathway into paid work, or be part of a job or role. For example, Jack Monroe's cookery writing and lobbying career was launched through their Cooking on a Bootstrap blog, the fashion writer Alicia Fashionista has used her Alicia Fashionista blog to platform her work, and the musician Amanda Palmer blogs to promote her creative content.

Previous research has documented how work-related blogging extends beyond digitised writing to include time-intensive website design and maintenance, marketing, and audience interaction (Parry and Hracs, 2020), labour that might not be evident to the outside observer. Furthermore, the **'aesthetic labour'** provided by a blog's visible author is often fundamental to a blog's success (Brydges and Sjöholm, 2019). Building on Hochschild's (1983) work on emotional labour, and how service workers, including flight attendants and retail clerks, manage their feelings and emotions while interacting with customers, aesthetic labour includes a worker's deportment, style, accent, voice, and attractiveness (Williams and Connell, 2010).

DOI: 10.4324/9781003314769-18

While many workers must 'look good' and 'sound right' based on the expectations of their employers, self-employed bloggers are required to become entrepreneurs of the self, taking responsibility for managing their own bodies, emotions, image, schedules, and priorities to create a covetable self (Williams and Connell, 2010). For example, even after exhausting performances on stage, or long days in the studio, Amanda Palmer produced blogs late at night or in the early morning before going to bed. Often apologising for the delay or shortness of the post, stating 'this'll be brief because I'm totally destroyed', she sacrificed her own mental and physical well-being to update, thank, and engage with her audience. For fashion style bloggers, who frequently publish 'outfit of the day' posts that include images and commentary, aesthetic labour entails an ongoing commitment to body maintenance through diet and exercise (Brydges and Sjöholm, 2019).

These combined labours, which produce the consumable product of the blog, are, for the most part, coordinated by individual bloggers as part of a self-directed enterprise. The work may have a complicated or non-existent relationship to recompensation in creating value for blogs. Bloggers are often seeking to reconfigure rather than follow pre-existing work rules to establish a market niche and build their blog following. As such, studying bloggers helps us understand emerging professions and work more broadly. Indeed, their work involves creative, and often exhausting, labour that extends beyond traditional nine-to-five working hours to include evenings, weekends, and holidays. The **extensification of work** (Pratt and Jarvis, 2006) is particularly acute when bloggers work across time zones (as is easily done in a workplace without physical boundaries) and are under pressure to be responsive to an international audience.

Bloggers' work pushes the boundaries between **the public and the private spheres**, with the distinctions between paid and unpaid work, homes, and workplaces often being blurred (see Chapter 1, Parry's 'Introduction'). In one sense, blogging could be taken as an example of the increasing flexibility of work in modern societies. In a global economy, the spatially dispersed and seemingly privatised (in its being, largely, non-institutional) work of blogging has enabled bloggers to develop professional and support collectives through virtual channels rather than more traditional forms of physical interaction. This provides a strong counter to the individualisation and isolation that is said to accompany digital work (Webster and Randle, 2016). It also offers evidence that, rather than dissipating, social solidarities are being reassembled virtually around emerging occupations and outside of traditional organisational structures, such as through blog comments and on alternative social media platforms. This chapter explores how collectivities – that is, meaningful and productive social connections between otherwise disparate bloggers – have developed in a changing world of work and how they have been used to help bloggers counter precarity and effect mobility in emerging digitised occupations. In so doing, it provides evidence of how collectivity is being reconfigured around new occupations, which is a counter to the individualistic way that career theory often assumes is the response to an increased lumpiness of organisational trajectories (Arthur and Rousseau, 1996; Hall, 2002).

The chapter is illustrated with examples and a case study from research on work-related bloggers which involved an in-depth qualitative analysis of ten blogs and 1,304 blogposts (Parry and Hracs, 2020). The sample of blogs outlined in Table 14.1 was diverse in nature, ranging from a blog over a decade long to one that was completed over the course of a year, blogs that changed format over the period of analysis, and blogs that included long reflective pieces, interaction with imagery, reportage, or humorous pieces. The bloggers were mainly UK-based, but the sample also included Australian, Canadian, South African, and American bloggers, who (as digitised workers) frequently performed across global labour markets.

Table 14.1 Sample of Blogs

Blog name	Blog genre	Field of paid work	Location	Timeline	Notable features
A Girl Called Jack	Political	Food writer	UK	2012–2015	Became 'Cooking on a Bootstrap'; very successful, generated bestselling books
Amanda Palmer. Net	Music	Musician	US	2009–present	A leading example of fan engagement and crowdfunding
Alicia Fashionista	Fashion style	Fashion writer	Canada	2009–present	Sustained blogging over time
The Thesis Whisperer	Academia	Higher education	Australia	2010–present	Moved into collaborative blogging; global readership
Stuff About Unis	Academia	Higher education	UK	2014–present	Focus on mid-career experience
PhD in A Hundred Steps	Academia	Higher education	South Africa	2013–present	Focus on early-career experience
Notes from Another Land	Expat	Finance writer	Australia / Ireland / UK	2013–present	Focus on entrepreneurial perspective
Diary of a London Call Girl	Entertainment	Sex worker	UK	2003–2005	Blogged anonymously to do exposés; very successful, generated bestselling books
Fleet Street Fox	Political	Journalist	UK	2011–present	Blogged anonymously to do exposés; very successful, generated a bestselling book
The Woolamaloo Gazette	Culture	Book store/ Retail	UK	2003–present	Gained notoriety as 'The Waterstones Blogger'

Source: authors' research.

Jane Parry and Brian J. Hracs

While the focus here is on blogs, these cannot be separated from the interconnected context of vlogs and social media platforms which bloggers use simultaneously to perform their work and emphasise different aspects of their professional identity. Blogging may yet turn out to be a transient occupational practice, as technology and communication patterns evolve and raise new possibilities, but it seems likely that digital storytelling will be sustained as the appetite for insight into workers' daily lives is increasing, particularly in an ever-changing world of work. Henceforth, analysts of work and organisation can draw insight from following how workplace relationships are reimagined, and made meaningful, in these self-directed virtual workspaces. Before positioning blogs as a form of digitised work, the chapter considers how this online writing helps bloggers negotiate a changing world of work, the new occupational resources that are afforded through **digitised solidarities**, and how the work is enabling bloggers to counter labour market precarity. The case study of 'The Thesis Whisperer' is offered to illustrate the overlooked way that making digitised connections and building reputation through blogging has provided occupational mobility in an uncertain world of work.

Blogging as Digitised Work

Digitised working has proliferated over the past decade, disrupting spatial relationships between work and how it is physically organised, an association that has been further challenged by **pandemic working** (see Parry's Chapter 1, 'Introduction', and Felstead and Blakely's Chapter 21, 'Changing Places of Work'). The term 'digital nomad' has been used for over 20 years to denote mobile remote workers whose working practices are dependent on ICT (information and communication technology) (Makimoto and Manners, 1997; Richter and Richter, 2020). More recently, work theorists' attention has turned to the different kinds of resources or capital that are amassed and exchanged through digitised work (Duffy, 2016). The idea of nomadic digital working is particularly relevant to travel bloggers, who visit and write about different locations, accommodations, and experiences (Willment, 2020). Spatially, blogging can also be placeless or linked to specific places and contexts. For example, mummy bloggers – a blog genre involving women who write about family and motherhood – focus on the home and present the domestic sphere as a workplace of interest to audiences. Yet, others blog from within their workplaces, both in sponsored formats (writing a company blog that engages with topical issues) or in unauthorised capacities (such as through a comedy or exposé blog on a particular organisation).

Digitised work offers new possibilities for how work can be organised around space, time, and in terms of its daily practices, aspects which bloggers have made use of in presenting their stories. Technology, including bespoke digital publishing platforms and blogging apps, allows bloggers to create and share content around the clock, connecting with audiences located all over the world who instantly receive updates on their mobile devices. As mostly autonomous workers, bloggers can develop their own working practices around their other responsibilities, such as family or a full-time job. The concept of the **gift economy** (Cheal, 2017; Mauss,

1990) is relevant to understanding how individualised bloggers upskill, investing in unpaid and exchanged work, such as sharing website development tips, in the knowledge that this will accrue its own benefits, be they psychic, financial, or reputational. By becoming part of broader blogging communities that connect across multiple platforms, they can share knowledge that will enhance the administration of their blog and enable them to respond quickly to the fast-moving technological expectations of their audience. This cooperative practice provides a counter to the marketisation of neoliberal economies, and it is a creative system of social interconnection that has been facilitated by digital platforms.

This kind of knowledge exchange may also enable bloggers to avoid the **technostress** that it has been suggested accompanies work that relies heavily upon technologies (Ayyargari et al., 2011) and it might thus be regarded as a part of work well-being. Digital work has been associated with challenges around disconnecting from work (Richter, 2020), especially as work continues to extend beyond the traditional working day, and this might be accentuated for bloggers who feel under pressure to be endlessly responsive to their audience's desire for new content if they are to maintain their place in the blogging market. For example, Brydges and Sjöholm (2019) highlight the challenge of 'always working' faced by personal style bloggers.

Negotiating a Changing World of Work

Work-related bloggers are a diverse occupational community, not only with respect to the range of blog genres that they cover, from food to photography, but also in terms of their individual characteristics, including age, gender, race, education, location, and class. Importantly, bloggers are driven by a range of motivations, which are shifting over time (Parry and Hracs, 2020). A useful parallel can be drawn with art curators of physical exhibitions, since bloggers are fundamentally digitised curators, managing their audience's relationship with the words and images that are presented to them. This comparison enables a deeper understanding of what sustains bloggers in undertaking their work, as well as how bloggers position themselves in relation to their occupational communities. Research on curators in the fashion, food, and music industries has drawn attention to their range of work motivations. These go beyond economic factors, such as profit and growth, and include intrinsic enjoyment of the work, enhancement of brand and reputation, shaping tastes and practices, exerting influence, and building connections and communities (Jansson and Hracs, 2018; Joosse and Hracs, 2015). Brydges and Hracs's (2019) research with female entrepreneurs in the fashion industry also highlighted a number of motivations that provided a counter to the more masculinist profit-driven conceptualisations of entrepreneurialism, including a desire to increase work–life balance, to develop alternative ways of working, and to pursue more sustainable work.

A similarly diverse range of motivations was observed in examining work-related bloggers (Parry and Hracs, 2020), including career development, reputation-building, coping with broader economic insecurity, and resisting traditional work expectations. By contrast, few work-related bloggers were blogging with economic gain as their primary incentive. The non-organisational structure of blogging entrepreneurialism offered greater flexibility for working lives to be organised in more meaningful ways, an aspect that can be particularly appealing to women around the period of family formation. However, bloggers may not conceptualise their blogging work as their main job, and it may be unpaid, despite the considerable efforts which they invest in it and the tangible product it generates.

The literature has noted that creative careers occupy a complicated position within labour markets, offering job satisfaction and autonomy, qualities offset against the precarity of the work (Banks, 2019; Brydges and Hracs, 2019; Duffy, 2016). This set of tensions may provide the impetus for the development of new forms of collective resistance (Sandoval, 2016). For work-related bloggers, blogging often operated in a way that complemented their creative work. For example, Amanda Palmer blogged widely around her tours, regarding this labour as essential in connecting with her audience, but it was also a coping mechanism to provide stability amid a punishing schedule. Most work-related blogging, however, is not self-sustaining or high profile, with bloggers having greater commonality with the occupational insecurity of other groups in the labour market where the certainties of work have become unstable (Arnold and Bongiovi, 2013). Blogging, in this context, can provide an aspect of work that bloggers have control over. They can feel a sense of accomplishment and enjoyment while earning appreciation and respect from other bloggers and their audience. These aspects can be quantified in terms of views, impressions, and comments, providing evidence of the value of their work beyond pay.

Digitised Solidarities as an Occupational Resource

While blogging might be imagined as a solitary pursuit, qualitative research on work-related blogging over a sustained period has uncovered the importance of digitised solidarities, that is, the meaningful connections that are mobilised online. These online relationships enable bloggers to develop shared understandings and support, and to create new sources of knowledge around career pathways in an emergent field (Parry and Hracs, 2020). In a relatively new occupation like blogging, the mechanisms for career progression are less established, or even non-existent. For example, a mid-career academic who blogged on Stuff About Unis observed that need-to-know information about academic pathways was not accessible in any single, accessible location. Instead, it had to be accumulated separately by individuals as they moved into academia, often through informal conversations, a situation which is inefficient, open to misunderstanding, and potentially perpetuates organisational privilege. His blog was intentionally written to develop an accessible information resource that would help early career academics negotiate this occupational minefield. He applied the same logic to his own career, with blog posts frequently consolidating his organisational knowledge and discussing how it could be used to affect mobility across the higher education labour market. Comments on blog or social media posts built discussion and connections around the work issues that bloggers raised in their posts, and provided evidence of the meaningful occupational solidarities that populated their everyday lives.

Another way that digitised solidarities can be utilised as an occupational resource is through collaboration and network-building. These networks entail both the relationships that bloggers build with their audience and connections with their fellow bloggers, who are effectively bloggers' occupational community. These relationships are important in building reputation and developing an effective support structure around work that is organised on an individualised basis as opposed to the natural collectivity of organisational life. Amanda Palmer discussed socialising with fellow bloggers and using this opportunity to exchange ideas on new blogging working practices that might enhance their occupational prospects, such as using Kickstarter or Crowdfunder to stimulate funding.

In contrast to the solitary work of writing, blogging outputs can tap into collective aspects of work. Ashton and Patel (2018) have noted the importance of cross-promotion within vlogging communities, with the recognition, or signalling, of occupational expertise developed in relation to other vloggers. This practice is replicated in some work-related blogging communities (Parry and Hracs, 2020). Rather than positioning allied bloggers as competition, shared and complementary expertise was emphasised and valorised as an asset. For example, fashion bloggers might reference and promote interactions with other fashion bloggers, and make a feature of these relationships, posting about blogger meet-ups as an opportunity to showcase their styles. In this way, online solidarities can lead to physical interactions and other traditional forms of solidarities. Cooperative working styles can thus be utilised by bloggers to negotiate a new self-determined set of working practice that contrast with more oppositional styles of business operation. The tactic of cross-promotion has mutual benefits around developing reputation, audience, and recognition of a field, as well as offering intrinsic rewards around the deepening of social relationships in workplaces where physical colleagues are lacking.

Interactive practice between bloggers offers value in helping bloggers to counter misgivings or modesty around self-promotion, since their blogs become embedded within supportive niche blogging communities, through which mutual marketisation occurs, a phenomenon which could be interpreted as a reimagining of the traditionally organisationally based **psychological contract** (Rousseau, 1995) by entrepreneurial communities. Yet, mutuality can be a double-edged sword, since co-promotion adds another labour onto bloggers' portfolio of work, as well as putting pressure on bloggers to identify and network with suitable virtual communities, an area where exclusion can also occur. Where successful, however, networking can provide valued occupational resources, such as PhD bloggers accessing peers with shared interests, whom it would otherwise be difficult to connect with, being at the start of their careers, with greater economic constraints on conference participation. In one sense, blogging offered an alternative to the time-constrained conference networking that academics are expected to become experts in, but which might be less accessible to parents and disabled academics, as well as to neurodiverse scholars. It provides a platform for interaction with content on a more supportive basis than that of traditional academic dynamics, and at a pace and level of engagement that bloggers can control. Hence, the virtual connections of bloggers may have provided a particular strength during COVID-19 restrictions that put physical conferences and interactions with academics from outside of individuals' institutions on hold. The increasing popularity of blogging conferences has also enabled bloggers to reappropriate physical spaces, and illustrates the interplay between virtual, temporary, lasting, and physical spaces of blogging connection.

A different set of digitised connections was forged with bloggers' audiences, which were fundamental to the sustainability of work-related blogs. Musician Amanda Palmer demonstrated a transactional model around this, monetising her readers' connection to the blog by offering them the opportunity to invest in different levels of 'patronage', in exchange for accumulating levels of access to creative content. Notably, this was not a unidirectional relationship: blogging had complicated roles in bloggers' lives, with Palmer documenting the psychic support that she drew from her invested audience, comparing it to a 'family' in its importance to her motivation and well-being. Other bloggers were positioned rather differently to their audiences, blogging anonymously to whistle-blow on their professions, such as Fleet Street Fox, who blogged about journalism during the Leveson inquiry into UK press practices following a period of alleged phone hacking. This more subversive kind of blogging did not enable connections to be made with fellow bloggers, and these blogs were consciously crafted to maximise audience, and sometimes to achieve mobility into a desired labour market position from which bloggers could then operate non-anonymously and with an established reputation.

Countering Precarity

In a labour market where employment has become increasingly flexible and insecure (Arnold and Bongiovi, 2013), blogging can offer strategies for pursuing or creating more stable work (Parry and Hracs, 2020). It can offer both a tool and a self-contained identity in the search for occupational continuity, with digitised connections a key part of these resources. Notably, digitised connections (that is, bloggers' virtual relationships with other bloggers) were not necessarily an explicit part of blogs, being only visible to audiences where bloggers chose to disclose them. For example, the Waterstones Blogger, author of 'The Woolamaloo Gazette', was dismissed from his post as a bookseller in 2005 for parodying his workplace in his satirical and culturally orientated blog (Schoneboom, 2011). The reader was largely unaware of the Waterstone Blogger's digitised connections from these posts, or of how they affected his occupational trajectory. However, amid the precarity of his dismissal, he reflected upon the importance of the support that he had received from his fellow bloggers and audience, which included well-known writers – some indication of his growing occupational positioning as a writer. These digitised solidarities enabled him to cope with an unprecedented situation and court case that threatened his career and gave him the confidence to develop a critical response to his employer's encroachment upon his private sphere activities. Blogging, then, and the new ways in which it enables collectivity and belonging to be negotiated, can be compared to Marx and Engels' concept of **class consciousness** (1968), which has been more traditionally associated with industrial working experiences and an understanding of shared socioeconomic interests. However, these collective experiences are not limited to a specific industrial context and can provide an important protection against the isolation of atomised virtual work (Webster and Randle, 2016).

Evidence of resistance to perceived inequities can be a common feature of work-related blogs. For example, Belle de Jour, a now-successful writer, who blogged under this pseudonym, documented her 14 months' experience as a sex worker to support her PhD work as a research scientist, illustrating some of the complex role combinations that bloggers were managing. The blog was an explicit attempt to debunk some of the popular myths about sex work. She presented her decision to fund her study through sex work as entirely rational, since the occupation needed no training or investment, could be compartmentalised, and did not distract from her studies in the way the long hours of a low-paid job would. Blogging put her in touch with other sex work bloggers, creating digitised solidarities that provided the kind of support and information that she had lacked previously as an escort working alone. This kind of alternative strategising around workplace relations, to provide new kinds of knowledge and support, provides some evidence of how the givens of neoliberal work culture can be imaginatively countered by bloggers. Comparably, Amanda Palmer repeatedly acknowledged that one of the resources she drew from her blog was that it enabled her to 'vent' her work-life frustrations and simultaneously access support from her community anywhere in the world, and at any time. Both bloggers were drawing upon **digitised solidarities** in a context where the way in which their paid work was structured had made physical occupational connections more sparse in their daily lives.

Other bloggers were traversing relatively new occupations without a traditional workplace or workplace relations. Here blogging offered a means to establish and reimagine workplace relationships. For example, the style blogger Alicia Fashionista, who noted that she missed having co-workers, was recreating a virtual workplace for herself; she dressed for work and depicted this on her blog, making use of organisations such as Futurpreneur to substitute for a mentor and colleagues. This supported her in building confidence around her occupational capabilities. Work-related bloggers often operated in precarious environments, where their labour provided a counter-response and opportunity to effect autonomy (Parry and Hracs, 2020).

Jane Parry and Brian J. Hracs

Case Study

Blogging Academic Life

'The Thesis Whisperer' is a well-established blog that has been running since 2010, having acquired over 100,000 followers and 11 million hits in this time. It was created by the Australian academic Inger Mewburn. 'The Thesis Whisperer' aims to share content demystifying the PhD process and academic careers, with a support function for early career researchers in an international labour market, something which Mewburn found to be lacking in traditional higher education structures. She has reflected explicitly on the blog about the lack of spaces for working together on shared goals within higher education and compared the digitised labour of academics on individualised computers to the work of a small business, with academics forging a pattern of individualised working that was established during the PhD and valorised for its productivity. The blog evolved over time, from starting out on her university's learning management system, Blackboard, where it was set up as a closed blog called 'Research News Blog', with a small readership. When a student jokingly referred to her as 'The Thesis Whisperer', the name stuck, and soon after she took the blog to the more traditional blogging space of Wordpress. Mewburn has developed successful spin-off MOOCs and books around the blog and is active across multiple social media platforms promoting it.

For a large part of its history, 'The Thesis Whisperer' was innovatively run on a community collaboration model. Mewburn was reflective of the role that digitised collaboration played in the blog's long-standing success, a strategy that was to some degree pragmatic, since at times the demands of an academic career constrained her ability to post as much as her audience demanded. She was able to mobilise the connections that she had made with other academics through blogging, appointing them as guest bloggers who offered new insight and a diverse voice on issues. Reciprocally, this work gave guest bloggers access to 'The Thesis Whisperer's' large and committed audience.

Mewburn contemplated that 'The Thesis Whisperer' has become more central to her academic reputation than any individual institutional position that she held. So, too, she observed that networking through her blog was significantly more efficient than traditional academic networking, which tends to take place via in-person conferences: 'I would recommend a blog to any practising academic as a way to grow their network.' She also referenced the numerous prestigious presentations that she had been asked to give around the blog and the traction that it had generated: 'I would have been writing papers 'til I was 60 years old and not come to the attention of the right people to help me with my career.' Her academic trajectory was covered in real time in the blog as she moved from early career researcher (ECR) to professor, and her CV presented the blog as a central part of her academic capital and connectedness in research communities. Such was the intellectual capital of her blog that she had it formalised in her contract when she moved jobs, and she reflected on the systematic process that she built into her week(ends) to ensure that her blogging work was prioritised as a key part of her academic work.

Although comments on posts were an important feature of the blog for a long time, providing a visible manifestation of the digital communities that coalesced around 'The Thesis Whisperer', in 2022 Mewburn took the decision to switch these off. She spoke of the heavy labour of moderating, another invisible aspect of blogging work, which was necessary to ensure that the comments reflected the supportive environment that was central to the blog's ethos. However, due to 'The Thesis Whisperer's' success, it had become unsustainable for her to manage this moderation work alone, and at the time of writing she was considering how the blog archive might be reconfigured in a lasting and valuable way.

Conclusion

Online or digitised work can take a diverse range of forms and continues to evolve and provide new challenges to work theorists' assumptions about the features of work. The focus here on work-related bloggers highlights the role that digitised solidarities play in negotiating the labour market as well as in occupational mobility for this emerging occupational group. Brand development and professional recognition are important in building and maintaining an audience base for bloggers working in creative and knowledge-based industries, whether through personalised material that fans strongly connect with or anonymised revelatory writing that attracts a mass audience. Digitised relationships are also forged through collectives and informal networks, reflecting the range of motivations and practices around blogging, and correspondingly the different relationships that bloggers negotiate between work and solidarities. The knowledge provided through connectivity is valuable in countering isolation and in sharing scarce occupational information, as well as in helping bloggers make better sense of their work and positioning within emerging occupational structures. Digitised solidarities provide occupational capital that can be particularly valuable in negotiating precarious working conditions.

Digitised solidarities are less immediately accessible than the connections of physical workplaces, and arguably their pursuit constitutes another invisible labour for bloggers, but they form no less valuable a workforce resource for that. Looking at the dynamics of blogging provides insight into digitised relationships in new occupations and the value that they accumulate over time. This learning can also be applied to the growing field of hybrid working, constituting imaginative responses to formulating consequential networks across dispersed and emerging workspaces. In terms of contributing to knowledge about the intrinsic motivations of work, this focus on social connections emphasises the continued importance of meaningful relationships in digitised or remote workplaces and provides counterevidence to the assumption that physical organisation is essential in the formulation and sustainability of consequential occupational connections.

Blogging also provides insight into the changing world of work and organisation, since it is combined with both traditional and emerging forms of paid work, at the same time as it comprises multiple labours beyond the most evident writing work performed by a blogger. It can be regarded, then, as a microcosm of the interplay between paid and unpaid work that underpins industrial economies, which continues to hold force in more information-based or knowledge economies (see Taylor's analysis of unpaid work in Chapter 15, 'Unpaid Work'). Blogging can attach itself to different labour market relationships and can shift in format from leisure to informal employment, self-employment, and integration with employment for a single blogger. As occupational expectations are revised in a transformed world of work, blogging illustrates how paid and unpaid work are combined in complex ways around individual labour market experiences (Pettinger et al., 2005), and offers bloggers the space to resist the givens of neoliberal work culture, particularly at a time when work structures are making physical occupational connections more remote.

STUDENT ACTIVITY

After reading the case study, reflect on these questions:

1. What is an example of the gift economy in this account of 'The Thesis Whisperer'?
2. What kinds of transferrable skills are being developed from running this kind of blog?
3. Looking at 'The Thesis Whisperer' in the case study, read three posts from the author (you can use the search facility to follow up on areas of interest to you). What kinds of inequalities in higher education did these make you think about?

Practice Questions

1. Discuss the ways in which bloggers form and benefit from collectives or digitised solidarities.
2. Reflect on a blog or social media account that you read and follow. Assess the level of labour involved, including the range of tasks that the author performs and the nature and volume of posts and audience comments/interaction/moderation.
3. Drawing upon examples from the chapter and your own experience with blogs and social media accounts, explain the ways in which bloggers perform and experience aesthetic labour.
4. To what extent do you consider blogging to be a precarious form of labour?

Key Terms

Aesthetic labour
the work that is invested in presenting the body in a particular way that aligns with occupational expectations around what customers or audiences demand – for

example, retail assistants being stylish or receptionists being smartly put together. This might include bodily maintenance around hair, nails, physique, clothing, and voice (all of which are likely gendered); the time this labour entails seldom forms part of employees' contracted time.

Class consciousness
a recognition and understanding that others, typically workers, share socioeconomic circumstances and interests; commonly used in Marxist theory with reference to the working class.

Digitised solidarities
meaningful connections that are developed online – in the case of bloggers, either with fellow bloggers, or other virtual co-workers, or with audiences and readers.

Extensification of work
the expansion of work to a range of spaces and times, outside of the traditional nine-to-five, site-based expectation.

Gift economy
a culture or system in which valued goods or services are exchanged for non-economic gain.

Pandemic working
changes in everyday working practices that were experienced during the COVID-19 pandemic and its associated lockdowns. These included: extended working from home rather than in offices; keyworking, often wearing heavy personal protective equipment (PPE); or being furloughed from work while industries temporarily shut down their operations.

Psychological contract
the implicit mutually agreed understandings and obligations between employees and employers about what each will provide and gain from the employment relationship. For example, it might be expected that organisations will provide secure work, agreed compensation, and good working conditions in exchange for employees achieving particular job- or role-related outcomes within a timeframe.

Public and private spheres
an important sociological distinction, between the public sphere of institutions and paid work (such as employing organisations and political activity) and the private sphere of households and unpaid work (where family and relationships are more typically based). This distinction is very often discussed in terms of gender in industrial societies.

Technostress
a feeling of being overwhelmed by the demands posed by new technology, to the point of it being detrimental to well-being.

Jane Parry and Brian J. Hracs

References

Arnold, D., and Bongiovi, J.R. (2013) 'Precarious, informalising and flexible work: transforming concepts and understandings' *American Behavioral Scientist*, 57(3): 289–308.

Arthur, M.B., and Rousseau, D.M. (eds) (1996) *The boundaryless career: new employment principles for a new organisational era*. New York: Oxford University Press.

Ashton, D., and Patel, K. (2018) 'Vlogging careers: everyday expertise, collaboration and authenticity'. In S. Taylor and S. Luckman (eds), *The new normal of working lives: critical studies in contemporary work and employment*. London: Palgrave Macmillan, pp. 147–169.

Ayyagari, R., Grover, V., and Purvis, R. (2011) 'Technostress: technological antecedents and implications'. *Management Information Systems Quarterly*, 35(4): 831–858.

Banks, M. (2019) 'Precarity, biography, and event: work and time in the cultural industries'. *Sociological Research Online*, 24(4): 541–556.

Brydges, T., and Hracs, B. (2019) 'What motivates millennials? How intersectionality shapes the working lives of female entrepreneurs in Canada's fashion industry'. *Gender, Place and Culture*, 26(4): 510–532.

Brydges, T., and Sjöholm, J. (2019). 'Becoming a personal style blogger: changing configurations and spatialities of aesthetic labour in the fashion industry'. *International Journal of Cultural Studies*, 22(1): 119–139.

Cheal, D. (2017) *The gift economy*. London: Routledge.

Duffy, B.E. (2016) 'The romance of work: gender and aspirational labour in the digital culture industries'. *International Journal of Cultural Studies*, 19(4): 441–457.

Hall, B. (2002) *Careers in and out of organizations*, Thousand Oaks, CA: Sage.

Hochschild, A. (1983) *The managed heart: communication of human feeling*. Berkeley, CA: University of California Press.

Jansson, J., and Hracs, B. (2018) 'Conceptualising curation in the age of abundance: the case of recorded music'. *Economy and Space*, 50(8): 1602–1625.

Joosse, J., and Hracs, B. (2015) 'Curating the quest for "good food": the practice, spatial dynamics and influent of food-related curation in Sweden'. *Geoforum*, 64 (August): 205–216.

Makimoto, R., and Manners, D. (1997) *Digital nomad*. New York: Wiley.

Marx, K., and Engels, F. (1968) *The Communist manifesto: selected works in one volume*. London: Lawrence and Wishart.

Mauss, M. (1990) *The gift: the form and reason for exchange in archaic societies*. London: Routledge.

Mewburn, I. (2017) *How to be an academic: The Thesis Whisperer reveals all*. Sydney: NewSouth Publishing.

Parry, J., and Hracs, B. (2020) 'From leisure to labour: towards a typology of the motivations, structures and experiences of work-related blogging'. *New Technology, Work and Employment*, 35(3): 314–335.

Pratt, A.C., and Jarvis, H. (2006) 'Bringing it all back home: the extensification and "overflowing" of work –the case of San Francisco's new media households'. *Geoforum*, 37(3): 331–339.

Pettinger, L., Parry, J., Taylor, R., and Glucksmann, M. (2005) *A new sociology of work?* Oxford: Blackwell.

Richter, A. (2020) 'Locked-down digital work'. *International Journal of Information Management*, 55: 102157.

Richter, S., and Richter, A., (2020) 'Digital nomads'. *Business and Information Systems Engineering*, 61(1): 77–81.

Rousseau, D.M. (1995) *Psychological contracts in organizations: understanding written and unwritten agreements*. London: Sage.

Sandoval, M. (2016) 'Fighting precarity with cooperation? Worker cooperatives in the cultural sector'. *New Formations*, 88: 51–68.

Schoneboom, A. (2011) 'Sleeping giants? Fired workbloggers and labour organisation'. *New Technology, Work and Employment*, 26(1): 17–28.

Webster, J., and Randle, K. (2016) 'Positioning virtual workers within space, time and social dynamics'. In J. Webster and K. Randle (eds), *Virtual workers and the global labour market*. London: Macmillan, pp. 3–34.

Williams, C.L., and Connell, C. (2010) '"Looking good and sounding right": Aesthetic labor and social inequality in the retail industry'. *Work and Occupations*, 37(3): 349–377.

Willment, N. (2020) 'The travel blogger as digital nomad: (re-)imagining workplace performances of digital nomadism within travel blogging work'. *Information Technology & Tourism*, 22: 391–416.

chapter 15

Unpaid Work

Rebecca Taylor

Introduction

Unpaid work is an embedded feature of the global economy. It takes multiple forms, from **internships** to **volunteering**, and can be found in the private, public, and non-profit sectors, in community spaces, in the Global North and South, and on digital platforms that connect workers internationally. It is embedded in a range of occupations and fields, from the creative industries to social care, and from technology to law. Unpaid work encompasses roles as diverse as a figurehead of a large aid organisation or an intern in a small media company. There is nothing intrinsic to a task that means it is not paid. Unpaid work is defined and shaped by the context and the social relations in which it is located (Taylor, 2016).

The multiplicity of forms that unpaid work takes creates some challenges for defining and measuring it, and, as a result, for providing a view of its broad parameters. Questions like 'How many people work unpaid?' and 'How does that differ by country?' are difficult to answer. However, studies of specific forms and contexts help to illuminate what unpaid work is, and this chapter begins by examining four distinct forms: **voluntary work, internships, platform work**, and **open source labour**. Other chapters also include examples of unpaid labour (see Chapter 14, Parry and Hracs' 'Blogging and Online Work'). The focus here is on unpaid work that takes place outside the family and the private sphere. The four distinct forms provide insight into the ways unpaid labour is shaped by divisions of class, race, and gender, and highlight some of the global inequalities that underpin it. The case study, drawn from research on open source software developers' careers, features the experiences of Nikhil, a software developer from Sri Lanka juggling unpaid open source development with the pressures of a job in a commercial global technology company and being a parent to young children.

Looking at the forms that unpaid work takes also highlights the different ways it might be theorised and understood. The second half of the chapter seeks to make sense of unpaid work by looking at various theoretical frameworks that are

DOI: 10.4324/9781003314769-19

used to explain why people work unpaid and how unpaid work is embedded in global capitalism. Rather than viewing unpaid work as a choice or a predisposition, these conceptual framings – **gift exchange**, immaterial labour, and symbolic labour – anchor unpaid work in social structures and practices. The final section investigates a broader theoretical question that helps make sense of unpaid work. It asks *how* people do this work if they are not being paid, highlighting how different forms of labour (paid or unpaid, inside or outside the home) are interconnected. For individuals and households, different modes of work must be juggled and managed. Unpaid work is possible only if it is supported by other types of work and other resources. The case study of Nikhil illustrates this point. The conclusion recaps the key points raised by the chapter around the forms of unpaid work and highlights further questions that might be asked about unpaid work.

Forms of Unpaid Work: Volunteering

Volunteering or voluntary work is unpaid work that usually takes place in non-profit (charitable and non-governmental) and public sector organisations in the Global North and South. The work varies in duration and regularity, from full-time long-term positions to short, part-time placements. It can be highly skilled, sometimes requiring professional expertise or rigorous training, such as those working on helplines for abuse survivors. It may command considerable status and power, such as civic leadership roles on charitable boards (Daniels, 1988). A large swathe of volunteering involves care in some form, and that work can be as diverse as befriending older people or supporting refugees. It can also be low-skilled manual work, such as driving, cleaning, or gardening. Krinsky and Simonet's (2017) ethnographic study of the maintenance of New York City parks highlights the various strata of low-paid and unpaid workers operated by non-profit Parks' Foundations and state employment programmes. At a global level, **Volunteer tourism** involves tourists from the Global North travelling to the Global South to undertake social development projects, frequently paying substantial sums of money to do so (Vrasti, 2013).

While formal volunteer roles are usually found in non-profit and public sector organisations (and occasionally the commercial sector), volunteering also takes place informally in the context of local neighbourhood relationships and community networks. Shopping for a neighbour with mobility issues, moderating or editing an online forum, even organising a demonstration or protest, all involve informal voluntary work. Parry's (2003) study of deindustrialised communities in the Welsh valleys following the closure of coal mines, documented various types of informal work, much of it in community support, undertaken by women (Parry, 2003). More recently, the COVID-19 pandemic mobilised a range of informal support networks at a local level. A Danish study documents the role played by local social media platforms in helping volunteers to coordinate support to isolated neighbours who were struggling during lockdown (Carlsen et al., 2021).

Since definitions and cultural understandings of voluntary work vary, national and pan-national surveys, such as the United Nations' State of the World's

Volunteerism report (UN volunteers 2021), find it challenging to compare trends. At the country level, however, there is evidence that socio-demographic factors such as class, education, and income are significant in shaping who volunteers. Higher rates of volunteering compared with the rest of the population are generally found among those who are educated and with higher socioeconomic status (Musick and Wilson, 2008). Socio-demographic factors also shape the activities that volunteers engage in, with women concentrated in education or health and disability roles and formal and informal care, and men involved in sport, leisure, and transporting. The United Nations Report (United Nations Volunteers, 2021) found women in the Global South more likely to be engaged in informal and social service-focused roles than men.

Forms of Unpaid Work: Internships

Internships are, in essence, work placements undertaken by young people, often graduates, at the start of their career journey and can last anything from a week to a year, and sometimes longer. Not all internships are unpaid, although Perlin reports data from the US suggesting at least half of all internships were. A few come with a generous salary, albeit short-term. Unpaid interns might be paid expenses (their travel and food costs), and some receive a nominal wage or small stipend (Perlin, 2012). They can be found in commercial, public, and non-profit organisations and in many professional fields and sectors. In some cases they have become part of a normalised transition into employment, particularly in occupations like the **cultural and creative industries** (art, media, film, etc.), which are characterised by high levels of insecurity, low pay, and what the sector calls 'working for free' (Hesmondhalgh and Baker, 2013). Unpaid roles range from internships in media companies, to 'runner' positions on film sets (Grugulis and Stoyanova, 2012). Unpaid internships are also the norm are in sectors like public policy and global health and are found in high-profile organisations such as the United Nations, the World Health Organization, and the US Department of State.

As with volunteering, the challenges of measurement (definitions and coverage in national surveys vary) prevent global comparison around interning practices. However, the studies that do exist reveal some broad trends and characteristics. Internships are increasing, particularly in low- and middle-income countries (Stewart et al., 2021), and the predominantly middle-class profile of interns mirrors that of volunteers. This is unsurprising given that internships tend to be focused in middle-class professional domains and only those with financial support can afford to undertake unpaid work. For example, World Health Organization (WHO) data show that 80 per cent of their unpaid interns are from high-income countries (McBride et al., 2018). Studies of interns' experiences are revealing. Frenette's (2013) ethnographic study of interns in the music industry provides insight into the daily routines capturing some of the mundane admin tasks they were required to do, including, but not restricted, to 'the Starbucks run' and fixing photocopier jams. While internships are assumed to lead to paid employment, this is often not the case (Perlin, 2012; Stewart et al., 2021). Many of the interns in Frenette's study undertook several years of unpaid work in a cycle of internship roles before they found a paid role, and many left the sector before they found paid work (Frenette, 2013).

Forms of Unpaid Work: Platform Work

Unpaid work on platforms is less visible than more clearly defined forms of unpaid work such as voluntary work or internships. Platforms distribute work, jobs or 'gigs', in both local geographical contexts (i.e. delivering food to customers) or remotely, providing a site for customers to solicit workers to undertake digital tasks such as entering data or designing a website. As such they encompass a range of forms of work from low-paid micro tasks to lucrative consultancy work in professional services. Much of this work is paid, albeit often very poorly, and on an insecure contractual basis, such as a task or piece rate (Fairwork, 2023). However, unpaid work is a hidden but endemic feature of platform labour.

Research has documented a range of mechanisms through which platform workers are not always paid for some or all of the work they do, or the time that they spend working (Pulignano et al., 2021). These include workers not being paid for travel and waiting time between paid tasks and compulsory unpaid breaks; having to invest time resolving disputes (for example, where their work has not been deemed to have met the required standard); finding that technical glitches on the platform have prevented payment for their work; investing unpaid time updating/maintaining their profile to ensure work was allocated to them; preparing bids for work that was awarded elsewhere sometimes using their proposal; and having payment penalties imposed for poor reviews (even where these were not the fault of the worker). In some cases, these mechanisms of enforced unpaid work are contractual and explicit such as non-payment of breaks; in others, there is a systemic appropriation of wages that constitutes a form of **wage theft** by platforms and their clients, such as the non-payment for work following spurious disputes or unresolved technical glitches (Howson et al., 2023).

Pulignano and colleagues' (2021) European study of local and remote platforms highlighted how mechanisms for non- or underpayment were in some cases part of the algorithmic management of platform work. For example, one food delivery platform allocated work 'based on workers' availability, speed and order acceptance/rejection' (Pulignano et al., 2021: 4). Workers have to wait around for orders to come in so they can accept immediately and ensure they are prioritised for further allocation. Unpaid work and wage theft not only exploited precarious workers but tended to replicate global inequalities. In their study of 14 platforms across 74 countries, Howson et al. (2023) found that amounts of unpaid work were much higher for workers in the Global South, suggesting a strategy of value extraction of their labour by the Global North.

Forms of Unpaid Work: Open Source Labour

The final example of unpaid work outlined in this chapter is open source labour, the work of software engineers building open source products like Linux and

Firefox, many of which are central to the digital infrastructure that supports the web. Unlike commercial forms of software which protect their source code, open software shares its code in publicly accessible repositories using Creative Commons licences that enable them to be widely distributed and freely used. Developers and software engineers access those repositories, contributing to building, modifying, bug fixing, and innovating tools in a shared space, but do not receive direct payment for that work (Berry, 2008). The work is not located in organisations but takes place in online project-based communities – globally distributed, self-organised groups (Crowston et al., 2007). Many developers do open source work in their spare time; often they are employed or freelance developers working in the commercial technology sector in their day job. Like the other forms of unpaid labour explored in this chapter, there are blurred and shifting boundaries between what is paid and what is not. For example, commercial companies that are using open source products might be supporting and contributing to them via the work of their in-house developer teams (Ciesielski and Westenholtz, 2016).

It is challenging to measure the unpaid work of open source developers. GitHub, the repository for code, reports 100 million users worldwide, a substantial proportion of whom will be contributing to open source projects. Software developers, like other technology workers, have tended to be white, male, middle-class computer science graduates but, as open source software is free to use, barriers to entry are low and many are self-taught. Recent years have seen an influx of contributions to open source projects by developers in the Global South with active communities in India, Brazil, and China (Wachs et al., 2022). More women have entered the industry supported by a range of initiatives to promote 'women in code', although a survey of available data sources suggests that women still only constitute 5 to 10 per cent of open source developer populations (Trinkenreich et al., 2022).

Examining these four forms of unpaid work demonstrates the variety of contexts in which it takes place, (occupations, sectors, locations), and its diversity. It is clear that unpaid work cannot be understood in simple terms that reduce it to 'care' work, or 'training', although it can be those things. While some forms of unpaid work might be a choice shaped by class or geographical privilege, such as volunteering, other forms involve some degree of exploitation of workers who might have little autonomy. Either way, it is clear that unpaid work can play an important part in individuals' careers and working lives. The next section looks at how different scholarly debates have made sense of unpaid work and introduces some theoretical tools used to understand the different contexts and social structures in which it is embedded.

Making Sense of Unpaid Work

Understanding why people work unpaid has occupied scholars in a range of disciplines for decades. The answer depends a lot on which form of unpaid labour is in focus. There are also disciplinary differences in the tools which are applied.

Studies of volunteering, for example, are often positioned within policy debates and primarily concerned with promoting volunteering as a form of '**pro-social**' **behaviour** – behaviour that has a social benefit. These tend to draw on individualised understandings of motive, but miss the social and structural contours of unpaid work (Shachar et al., 2019) However, there are a variety of theoretical tools from sociology, anthropology, and political economy that have sought to make sense of how that work is structured by social practices and capitalist markets. This section outlines ideas of gift exchange, immaterial labour, and symbolic labour that provide different conceptual approaches to understanding unpaid work. The final part of the section then examines how unpaid work is possible for individual and households, how it is organised and managed alongside other forms of work, and is supported by other resources.

Gift Exchange, Immaterial Labour, and Symbolic Capital

The notion of gift exchange is drawn from classical anthropological studies by Mauss (1925/1990) and others that conceptualised gift-giving rituals in primitive societies as a complex set of practices that served to maintain social order. The giving and receiving of gifts is guided by cultural expectations and social hierarchies that define who gives, what and when they give, and what is expected in return. This notion of gift exchange provides a way to understand volunteering (the act of giving time, or a service) as structured by expectations of social recognition and reciprocal reward. Gift exchange has also been mobilised by 'hacker anthropologists' writing about what Barbrook (1998) called the 'hi-tech gift economy'. The freebies and inducements that are gifted by technology companies set up expectations and obligations that consumers and workers will gift labour, or content, or data in return creating markets for digital capitalism (Elder-Vass, 2016). Velcova's (2016) ethnographic study of Blender – an open digital media company – and its sharing practices, highlighted the gifts, in the form of free films, software tutorials, and open software tools, given to workers created indebtedness to the company. This ensured that workers were willing to reciprocate by doing more work for free, contributing to software, reporting bugs, and requesting new features in online forums. Velcova's point is that relations were asymmetrical – the company used gifts to extract value and profit from the unpaid labour of workers.

The importance of unpaid work to the cultural and creative industries was described earlier, in the section on internships. Scholars writing about these industries have sought to understand the precariousness of creative work by drawing on the notion of immaterial labour proposed by Italian Marxist writers at the end of the 20th century (see Chapter 12, 'Digitalised Work', by Benjamin). These writers theorised the changing nature of capitalist production, from the traditional manufacturing of material products to the dispersed collective labour of cultural content creation that happens in homes, coffee shops, and on trains (Gill and Pratt, 2008). This immaterial labour is often unpaid, involving activities such as creative projects and hobbies that are not recognised as work. Terranova's (2000) eminent article on free labour written at the turn of the new century drew on the notion of immaterial labour to examine unpaid work in the new digital economy of software and games development, 'building websites, modifying software packages, reading and participating in mailing lists and building virtual spaces' (2000: 33). She argued that this was not a new form of freedom for workers, but an extension of capitalist business practices into the digital domain and generated substantial profit for capitalism.

Another approach that sociologists have taken to understanding forms of unpaid work is through notions of social and **symbolic capital**. These draw on Bourdieu's (1984, 1990) theoretical ideas, particularly his framework outlining forms of capital, to understand how unpaid labour paradoxically provides a mechanism for acquiring resources and power. 'Capital' refers to wealth in the form of assets or money, but Bourdieu (1984) extends the idea to the social, the connections and ('old boys') networks that enable middle- and upper-class people to get the right kind of jobs. Unpaid work such as volunteering or an internship can be a key mechanisms through which individuals build social capital (Taylor, 2005). Gandini's (2016) study of platform freelancing in creative and knowledge work examines how social capital takes the distinct form of reputation metrics (star ratings, etc.) created by algorithmic management of the platform. That 'reputation' requires unpaid work from the freelancer to manage and curate their profile and ensure that they can generate new paid work.

Bourdieu's (1990) notion of symbolic capital is important in understanding unpaid work. Symbolic capital is a form of capital that adds value to the apparently disinterested (not for economic gain) activities of those with privilege – collecting art, charitable work, academic study, moral endeavours, self-actualisation, and philanthropy (Bourdieu, 1990). These examples show how the acquiring and displaying of symbolic capital often requires unpaid labour. For example, the volunteer tourism mentioned in the previous section reveals how symbolic capital also lends value to unpaid work. The white middle-class volunteers hoping to 'make a difference' and develop better versions of themselves are undertaking unpaid work that gives them symbolic capital, valued by Global North labour markets. Vrasti (2013) notes that volunteer tourism's effectiveness should be judged by its ability to support global capitalism rather than any benefits to Global South communities.

These conceptual tools (gift exchange, immaterial labour, and social and symbolic capital) shed light on how unpaid work of various forms is embedded in social practice and structured by capitalist relations and labour markets.

How is Unpaid Work Possible?

In making sense of unpaid work, a final question to ask is one that explicitly draws attention to the economic underpinning of that labour. How is it possible that someone can work unpaid when economic survival is fundamental to well-being?

What is the income or resources that support that unpaid work (employment, a working spouse, well off parents, a student loan, a pension, income from property)? For example, the young person doing a full-time unpaid internship in a New York record company might be living rent free at home with wealthy parents who provide an allowance (Frenette, 2013). Refugees' legal status might restrict them from paid employment, and unpaid voluntary work in refugee support centres and humanitarian organisations provides a way for them to work and gain experience (Ward, 2022). To understand these mechanisms requires examining the division of labour at the individual and household level, and the distribution of economic resources. Glucksmann (1995, 2009) draws attention to the interdependencies between different modes of work – paid and unpaid, public and domestic, formal and informal – and how these operate at the macro and micro levels. Studies draw on her framing of the division of labour to understand how unpaid labour and other forms of work outside standard paid employment are managed and organised in working lives.

Research on workers in two UK non-profit organisations mapped their daily and weekly work, often in multiple paid and unpaid jobs, and revealed how this was managed at the household level (Taylor, 2004, 2005). Elizabeth, for example, worked in a figurehead role for large national charity, speaking at events, talking to government policy-makers, and representing the organisation to the press. This unpaid work took two or three days a week, and the rest of her week was spent managing the family's farm and being parent to four children. The household division of labour was structured along traditional gender and class lines. The property and her husband's job in banking provided income and she was not expected to take paid work. In contrast, Jose, a Latin American refugee, undertook multiple paid and unpaid roles. His paid work as an administrator for a non-profit community organisation supported his various unpaid activities which included informal support and advocacy for refugees and migrants and promoting musicians (Taylor, 2004). The different arrangements of paid and unpaid work in Jose and Elizabeth's working week were shaped by their social class position and gender.

The importance of mapping how work is organised is also revealed in an account of Danish visual artists by Alacovska and Bille (2019). Their study explored the diverse spectrum of work practices that the artists juggled as part of the everyday management of their precarious creative livelihoods. Alcovska and Bille (2019) drew on Glucksmann's ideas to describe complex arrangements of household labour, including formal unpaid work (internships), informal cash-in-hand work such as uncontracted work for galleries, and non-monetised barter exchanges swapping artwork for dental treatment, counselling, or hairdressing. They show how these were underpinned by the economic support of partners, family, and state assistance. The multiplicity of artistic labour in this study made clear the need to transcend a focus on formal contractual paid employment when understanding working lives and how unpaid work fits into these lives.

Case Study

Open Source Labour

Nikhil was a software developer from Sri Lanka, and lived with his young family in Scandinavia. He learned about open source software at school, discovering that Ubuntu, an open source operating system, 'would send CDs to your house': 'I was a kid and I was excited, and I just ordered 10 or 15 of them and they just came, and started giving out to my friends; and we already had a small Linux group at our school.' By the time Nikhil graduated with a computer science degree, he had acquired considerable experience developing software through a combination of freelance web development work and unpaid contributions to open source projects. He was active in the local and online open source community and met a friend and mentor who helped him develop his skills and offered him a job in his open source start-up when he graduated.

The start-up, which was 'fun' but badly paid, did not survive, and Nikhil moved on to an established local software company that was more secure. He continued to contribute to various open source projects, working long hours, evenings and week-ends. During the next few years, as the political situation in Sri Lanka deteriorated, Nikhil, now married with young children, found the daily violence and insecurity in-creasingly stressful. When he was headhunted by a commercial technology company that had an office in Scandinavia, he jumped at the chance to leave. The company were looking for software engineers, but particularly those with open source experi-ence, and had used GitHub to identify and recruit open source developers like Nikhil.

Nikhil was enjoying this new life with his family in Scandinavia and appreciated the work culture that discouraged long hours. Part of his week was spent on sup-porting the development of open source within the company, although he felt pro-gress was slow. With two small children, he was struggling to find time to commit to unpaid work on the open source projects that he used to support: 'I can't put that much time aside (for OS) as before when I am working because, family ... yeah, life.' He envisaged having more time to contribute to these communities as his children got older. 'I am getting more and more free time right now and [X] is starting play-school in May, so some time.' Nikhil's case provides a typical account of engagement with unpaid open source work in developer careers. A peak happens at early career stage, then declines somewhat as the demands of full-time employment and family and caring responsibilities reduce flexibility and time.

Conclusion

This chapter has provided a broad account of unpaid work, capturing some of its diverse forms and various theories that scholars have used to try and understand why and how people do it. Examining volunteering, internships, platform work, and open-source labour highlighted the different contexts in which unpaid work is embedded. Formal, institutional volunteering and internship roles contrasted with digital platforms and less formal project-based communities that structure open-source labour.

Issues with the definition, and therefore measurement, of all forms of unpaid work meant the extent of this works and characteristics of workers was not always clear. However, volunteering, internships. and open source labour, were more likely to be conducted by middle-class people with a good level of education in the Global North. Unsurprisingly perhaps, the more exploitative forms appeared disproportionately to affect low-income workers and those in the Global South. There are many other forms of unpaid work that were not discussed, and it is worth thinking and reading more about these, from blogging (see Chapter 14, 'Blogging and Online Work', by Parry and Hracs), to welfare and offender rehabilitation programmes or domestic labour in the home.

The second section outlined some of the tools that scholars have used to understand why people do unpaid work and how it underpins global capitalism. The concepts of gift exchange, immaterial labour, and social and symbolic capital each provided important insights. Gifts giving and receiving rituals revealed the way unpaid work, whether volunteering or digital content creation, was part of a set of practices and expectations. Companies created a reciprocal debt to mobilise commitment and free labour from workers and consumers. Immaterial labour captured the unpaid or low-paid crowdsourcing of knowledge and cultural content to create commercial value. Social and symbolic capital were important rewards and resources operating in the self-realisation and resumé-building goals of volunteer tourism.

Finally, the chapter looked at how unpaid work is undertaken, how different forms of labour are organised, and the financial underpinning of unpaid work for individuals and households. Studies drawing on Glucksmann's framework have revealed the embeddedness of unpaid work and its complex relationship with paid work for many workers. The conceptual tools have uncovered something of the intersecting inequalities that shape unpaid work and define who does unpaid work and how and why they do it. Overall, the chapter has opened up the world of unpaid work and showed the many ways in which it is an embedded element of working lives inextricably intertwined with other forms of labour.

STUDENT ACTIVITY

Identifying Unpaid Work

Think about yourself, or one of your friends or family, and the types of unpaid work they do. It might be a form explored in this chapter (volunteering, an internship, platform work, or open source labour), or others that haven't been covered, such as blogging, or moderating an online chatroom, or organising a fundraiser event. There are many.

Sketch a 200–300-word case study for this person, like that of Nikhil earlier (you might need to ask them for some details about it). Describe their career to date, noting down how it started, what is involved in their unpaid work, how much time they spend doing it, and its regularity. Referring to Glucksmann's ideas, describe how it is financially supported and managed in relation to family, caring responsibilities, studies, and other forms of work such as paid employment.

Rebecca Taylor

Practice Questions

1. Explain why it is difficult to define and measure unpaid work.
2. What are the main differences between an internship and a volunteer role?
3. Taking open source labour as an example, explain how gift exchanges provide a way to understand the relationships within which unpaid work takes place.

Key Terms

Cultural and creative industries
industrial sector focused on the production of cultural products, performances, and artefacts, and encompassing fields such as visual and performing arts, literature, music, film, television, design, fashion, gaming, architecture, advertising, and more.

Gift exchange
drawing on anthropological theories, this refers to the social and symbolic dimensions of gift-giving in traditional and contemporary societies. Gift exchange is not merely an act of altruism or generosity, but a complex social phenomenon involving reciprocity, obligation, and social cohesion.

Internships
structured work experience placements of varying lengths provided by organisations or companies, typically to students or recent graduates, presented as a training and learning opportunity for individuals to gain practical skills and real-world experience related to their field of study or career interests.

Open source labour
the work of improving, or maintaining, open source projects in a collaborative effort. Such projects make their source code freely available, allowing anyone to use, modify, or distribute it, enabling a cooperative and community-driven approach to software development.

Platform work
a type of employment facilitated through digital platforms. Workers use these platforms to find or freelance work, short-term jobs or tasks, such as ride-hailing, food delivery, or other on-demand services; other platforms act as an agency and hub for distrusting freelance digital work such as design or website building.

Pro-social behaviour
actions such as sharing, helping, volunteering, and cooperating, intended to benefit individuals, a community, or society as a whole.

Symbolic capital
a form of reward that comes from activities or practices that are apparently not for economic gain, such as collecting art, charitable work, academic study, self-actualisation, and philanthropy. These activities involve the creation of symbolic value for individuals and signal their possession of economic, social, and cultural capital.

Unpaid work
comes in many forms and a variety of contexts, and involves work activities undertaken without pay.

Volunteer tourism
involves individuals travelling to a destination to volunteer in social, environmental, or community-based projects and activities aimed at making a positive impact.

Volunteering/voluntary work
unpaid work of varying duration and hours undertaken on a voluntary basis; can be found in non-profit or public sector organisations or more informal locations such as in community spaces (including online).

Wage theft
the illegal practice where employers withhold their workers' wages. It can take various forms – such as underpayment of wages, unpaid overtime, denial of benefits, illegal deductions, or misclassification of employees as independent contractors – to avoid paying compensation and labour protection.

References

Alacovska, A., and Bille, T. (2021) 'A heterodox re-reading of creative work: the diverse economies of Danish visual artists'. *Work, Employment and Society*, 35(6): 1053–1072.

Barbrook, R. (1998) 'The hi-tech gift economy'. *First Monday*, 3(12).

Berry, D.M. (2008) *Copy, rip, burn: the politics of copyleft and open source*. London: Pluto Press.

Bourdieu, P. (trans. Richard Nice) (1984) *Distinction: a social critique of the judgement of taste*. London: Routledge and Kegan Paul.

Bourdieu, P. (trans. Richard Nice) (1990) *The logic of practice*. Stanford: Stanford University Press.

Carlsen, H.B., Toubøl, J., and Brincker, B. (2021) 'On solidarity and volunteering during the COVID-19 crisis in Denmark: the impact of social networks and social media groups on the distribution of support'. *European Societies*, 23 (supp. 1): 122–140.

Ciesielski, M., and Westenholz, A. (2016) 'Dilemmas within commercial involvement in open source software'. *Journal of Organizational Change Management*, 29(3): 344–360.

Crowston, K., Howison, J., Masango, C., and Yeliz Eseryel, U. (2007) 'The role of face-to-face meetings in technology-supported self-organizing distributed teams'. *IEEE Transactions on Professional Communication*, 50(3): 185.

Daniels, A.K. (1988) *Invisible careers: women civic leaders from the volunteer world*. Chicago and London: University of Chicago Press.

Elder-Vass, D. (2016) *Profit and gift in the digital economy*. Cambridge: Cambridge University Press.

Fairwork (2023) *Work in the planetary labour market: Fairwork Cloudwork Ratings 2023*. Oxford: Oxford Internet Institute.

Frenette, A. (2013) 'Making the intern economy: role and career challenges of the music industry intern' *Work and Occupations* 40(4): 364–397.

Gandini, A. (2016) 'Digital work: self-branding and social capital in the freelance knowledge economy'. *Marketing Theory*, 16(1): 123–141.

Gill, R., and Pratt, A. (2008) 'In the social factory? Immaterial labour, precariousness and cultural work'. *Theory, Culture & Society*, 25(7–8): 1–30.

Glucksmann, M. (1995) 'Why work? Gender and the total social organisation of labour'. *Gender, Work and Organisations*, 2(2): 63–75.

Glucksmann, M.A. (2009) 'Formations, connections and divisions of labour'. *Sociology*, 43(5): 878–895.

Grugulis, I., and Stoyanova, D. (2012) 'Social capital and networks in film and TV: jobs for the boys?' *Organization studies*, 33(10): 1311–1331.

Hesmondhalgh, D., and Baker, S. (2013) *Creative labour: media work in three cultural industries*. Basingstoke: Routledge.

Howson, K., Johnston, H., Cole, M., Ferrari, F., Ustek-Spilda, F., and Graham, M. (2023) 'Unpaid labour and territorial extraction in digital value networks'. *Global Networks*, 23(4): 732–754.

Krinsky, J., and Simonet, M. (2017) *Who cleans the park? Public work and urban governance in New York City*. Chicago: University of Chicago Press.

Mauss, M. (1990/1925) *The gift: the form and reason for exchange in archaic societies*. London and New York: Routledge.

McBride, B., Mitra, S., Kondo, V., Elmi, H., and Kamal, M. (2018) 'Unpaid labour, #MeToo, and young women in global health'. *The Lancet*, 391(10136): 2192–2193.

Musick, M., and Wilson, J. (2008) *Volunteers: a social profile*. Bloomington: Indiana University Press.

Parry, J. (2003) 'The changing meaning of work: restructuring in the former coalmining communities of the South Wales Valleys'. *Work, Employment & Society*, 17(2): 227–246.

Perlin, R. (2012) *Intern nation: how to earn nothing and learn little in the brave new economy*. London: Verso.

Pulignano, V., Piasna, A., Domecka, M., Muszyński, K., and Vermeerbergen, L. (2021) *Does it pay to work?* Belgium: ETUI (European Trade Union Institute).

Shachar, I.Y., von Essen, J., and Hustinx, L. (2019) 'Opening up the "black box" of "volunteering": on hybridization and purification in volunteering research and promotion'. *Administrative Theory & Praxis*, 41(3): 245–265.

Stewart, A., Owens, R., O'Higgins, N., and Hewitt, A. (eds) (2021) *Internships, employability and the search for decent work experience*. Cheltenham and Geneva: Edward Elgar Publishing/ILO.

Taylor, R. (2016) 'Volunteering and unpaid work'. In S. Edgell, H. Gottfried, and E. Granter (eds), *The SAGE handbook of the sociology of work and employment*. London: Sage, pp. 485–502.

Taylor, R.F. (2004). 'Extending conceptual boundaries: work, voluntary work and employment'. *Work, Employment & Society*, 18(1): 29–49.

Taylor, R.F. (2005) 'Rethinking voluntary work'. *The Sociological Review*, 53(2): 119–135.

Terranova, T. (2000) 'Free labor: Producing culture for the digital economy', *Social Text*, *18*(2): 33–58.

Trinkenreich, B., Wiese, I., Sarma, A., Gerosa, M., and Steimacher, I. (2022) 'Women's participation in open source software: a survey of the literature'. *ACM Transactions on Software Engineering and Methodology, 31*(4): 1–37.

United Nations Volunteers (2021) *2022 state of the world's volunteerism report: building equal and inclusive Societies*. Bonn: United Nations.

Velkova, J. (2016) 'Open cultural production and the online gift economy: the case of Blender'. *First Monday, 21*(10).

Vrasti, W. (2013) *Volunteer tourism in the global south: giving back in neoliberal times*. London and New York: Routledge.

Wachs, J., Nitecki, M., Schueller, W., and Polleres, A. (2022) 'The geography of open source software: evidence from github'. *Technological Forecasting and Social Change*, 176: 121478.

Ward, P. (2022) 'The worth of their work: the (in)visible value of refugee volunteers in the transnational humanitarian aid sector'. *Work, Employment and Society*, 36(5): 928–944.

part 5

Workforce Marginalisation

chapter 16

Xenophobia and the Migrant Labour Force

Amy Duvenage

Introduction

People migrate, from one region or country to the next, for a range of different reasons. Some people move to find better employment opportunities; others, greater economic security. These are **migrant workers** – those who move from one region to another for full-time employment, temporary or seasonal work. Other people migrate to escape hardships including natural disasters, persecution,or war. These are **refugees** or undocumented migrants. People also move to be with family or friends. Some migrate for a fresh start in a new place. Migratory flows create **diasporas** or diasporic communities. The term 'diaspora' refers to the spread of people from their birthplace or homeland. The circumstances of leaving one's homeland are just as important as the experience of arriving and settling in a new place (see Brah, 2003). But not all migrants, whether documented or undocumented, feel welcome in their new country or region. To understand why, the impact of rapid globalisation in the late 20th and early 21st centuries must be considered. An interrogation of the past further reveals why some migrant labour forces experience low wages, poor working conditions, and lack of security. The past will also help to contextualise contemporary tensions around (un)belonging in some regions such as South Africa. Broadly speaking, rapid **globalisation** and advances in information technology in the late 20th and early 21st centuries made migration and mobility much easier than ever before. Globalisation refers to the free flow of ideas, people, technology, trade, information, and capital around the world, and the profound cultural, economic, political, technological, and social changes that happened as a result of globalisation. Information technology (computer systems and devices) made it easier for people to communicate and share lifestyle information across borders while advances in air travel made it easier for people to migrate and move from one region to the next. Because it became easier to migrate, societies grew increasingly diverse as did the global labour force. Advances in information technology also changed how nations and corporations organise, trade, and exchange across borders. These advances opened up new and emerging markets in developing nations. Developing nations are those that seek to be more economically and politically advanced on the global stage. The world has always been characterised by uneven development and inequality, and as history shows oppression is not a new phenomenon. But the gap between developed and developing regions is one factor that drives contemporary international and internal migration, as some migrants travel to countries with better economic and security prospects while others are forced to flee their homelands to save their lives. Some are even made stateless.

This chapter focuses on two factors that contribute to the power gap between developed and developing regions: **colonialism** and the globalisation of neoliberalism. The terms **Global North** and **Global South** are used to better conceptualise the inequalities experienced by those who inhabit developed and/or developing regions. Global North and Global South are spatial, not geographic, terms that signify two distinct but entangled worlds in which the North enjoys cultural, economic, and political dominance over the South (Blagg and Anthony, 2019). Inhabitants of the Global North are more privileged and more powerful than those of the South. It is important to note that inhabitants of the South can live in the geographic North and that inhabitants of the North can live in the geographic South. The divide between the Global North and Global South is not only a result of globalisation, but a colonial legacy intensified by the forces of **capitalism, patriarchy,** and **neo-imperialism**. Growing income inequality between the Global North and Global South is one factor that drives migration. Regarding the Global North/Global South divide, it is important to understand that the globalisation of neoliberalism and neoliberal philosophies changed the world in unprecedented ways. Neoliberalism refers to an ideology or political approach that favours free market competition, deregulation, free-market capitalism, and privatisation.

Advocates of neoliberalism claimed that it would reduce global inequality insofar as opening borders would enhance freedom of movement and free trade would generate fairer resource distribution and cheaper production costs (Castles, 2013). But neoliberalism did not reduce global inequality (Castles, 2013). Neoliberal policies changed the shape of capitalism by allowing large global corporations access into developing countries to seek out raw materials, emerging markets, and cheaper labour as well as to invest capital in resource-rich developing countries in Africa, Asia, and South America (see Sivanandan, 2008). The globalisation of neoliberalism is relevant to migration and migrant workers because it institutionalised a socioeconomic and political opposition between developed and developing nations that (a) allowed the Global North to grow rich off the Global South and (b) collapsed the potential for any power balance (Amin, 1997). Because the contemporary capitalist system has failed to engage with regions on the periphery in Africa, Asia, and South America in inclusive and fair ways, those on the global margins continue struggle to compete in the global market (Amin, 1997).

As the gap between the Global North and Global South widens and the nation-state's capacity effectively to manage global migratory flows diminishes (evidenced by the current global refugee crisis and subsequent geopolitical tensions regarding issues of national security, sovereignty, and hospitality (see Bhabha and Stierst-ofer, 2015), internal and international migration expands but grows increasingly precarious. This chapter examines migrant workers, discusses identity politics, considering notions of 'insiders' and 'outsiders', and examines tensions around (un)belonging. The chapter also explores the inequalities experienced by some migrant labour forces such as low wages, poor working conditions, and lack of security. Using the concept of **xenophobia** and drawing on a South African case study, this chapter pays close attention to rural–migrant experiences of exclusion. Xenophobia refers to the fear or hatred of strangers, often migrants. The case study explores how rural migrants travel to urban centres to find work and anal-yses the different forms of xenophobia produced, shared, and consumed in social organisations and institutions. This chapter explains why some migrant workers become victimised and used as 'scapegoats' in society, blamed for social problems, such as crime and other social issues.

Inequalities in the Global Migrant Labour Force: Low Wages, Poor Working Conditions and Lack of Security

Immigration plays an increasingly important role in world economies, and as workers veer towards better employment opportunities labour forces continue to diversify culturally and ethnically in almost all parts of the world (Castells, 2010). Recently, there has been a rise in precarious working conditions, such as gig econ-omies (see also Chapter 5, 'Precarious and Gig Work in the Global Economy', by McDonough and Pearson). Working conditions have shifted dramatically since the global COVID-19 pandemic. Labour, and working, conditions may be more flexible now than ever before, but job security and long-term employment oppor-tunities continue to decline dramatically. Threats to human security in the Global South make SouthNorth (international) migration particularly high. The United Nations (UN) define threats to human security as those that challenge human 'sur-vival, livelihood and dignity' (2012: 1). Think, for example, of war, persecution, or environmental crises. Within this context, the road to legal documentation for migrant workers is long and hard. Border controls and immigration policies in the Global North are tougher and more stringent than they have been in the past. Even though the State has the power to decide who gets to enter and who does not, undocumented migrants continue to cross borders into the Global North in high numbers every year. Consider the countless numbers of refugees who risk their lives crossing the English Channel to the UK each year. Thirty-one refugees died crossing the Channel in 2021, despite making emergency calls for help. In-cidents like these are growing more and more common in the geographic North. And they raise certain questions. How should society respond to the migrant refu-gee condition? What is at the heart of survival: hospitality or sovereignty (Bhabha and Stierstofer, 2015)?

The State tends to use three main strategies to exclude non-nationals: legal citizenship status and migration documentation for non-nationals; processes of arrest, detention, and threat of deportation; and limited access to support services and constitutional rights or protection (Landau, 2011). Many countries, including Australia, Canada, and the United Kingdom, rely on points-based immigration systems (PBS) to manage immigration. These systems differentiate between highly skilled, low -skilled and unskilled labour granting highly skilled workers legal entry to work and settlement and low-skilled workers temporary and precarious migration contracts. Points-based systems shape and control the labour force generating greater insecurity in some industries more than others and institutionalising inequality rather than creating security or stability (Anderson, 2010). It is important to note, however, that temporariness is not always an outside-in phenomenon; some migrants, especially documented ones, do have agency and make choices to stay or go based on career, family, or health demands as well as living conditions and opportunities among others (Anderson, 2010; Castles, 2013).

Precarity relates not just to working conditions but also social relations (Anderson, 2010). Because migration systems, like points-based systems (PBS), are underpinned by intersecting inequalities such as class, gender, race, nationality, and human capital, they can generate differential processes of othering insofar as points-based systems determine 'desirable' and 'undesirable' migrant workers (Brah, 1996; Castles 2013: 130). Notions of 'desirability' and 'undesirability' create polarisations within the labour force but also among the general public. 'Undesirable' migrants, typically unskilled or low-skilled migrants but especially undocumented ones (asylum seekers and refugees), tend to be seen as a problem. Undocumented migrants frequently emerge as a social problem in political and social discourse. In some cases, the undocumented become scapegoats for wider social ills. Some even become social pariahs.

Documented migrant workers are not exempt from differential processes of othering. To other is to exclude individuals or social groups who do not fit the desired social norm, or to treat someone as distinctly and inherently different from yourself. Documented migrant workers, like the undocumented, can be accused of stealing jobs or putting pressure on social services such as housing and healthcare. Scapegoating discourses that blame immigrants for wider social ills typically appear in the popular press. Anti-immigrant sentiment tends also to emerge in populist politics as members of the host nation and/or political leaders, clinging to homogenous versions of national life in the name of the people, advance discourses of us versus them.

Because 'undesirable' migrant workers tend to display markers of difference, such as an inability to speak the language of the host nation, they are more likely to be on the receiving side of exploitation and discrimination at work. Consider the treatment of migrant workers in the lead-up to the 2022 Fifa World Cup in Qatar: migrant workers from Bangladesh, Pakistan, and Nepal were put to work in dangerous conditions; many were recorded as injured or killed in work-related incidents, prompting international criticism and human rights scrutiny (see Al Thani, 2022; Millward, 2017, for example). Overwhelmingly, migrants in the Global North tend to be seen as a problem external to the North itself, a kind of outside-in phenomenon, and not a colonial legacy (see Hall, 1978) or a product of the forces of global neoliberal capitalism. Perceived as a threat to national security and stability (and in some cases national life), undocumented migrants are more vulnerable to exploitation in the labour market than migrants with legal documentation (Castles and Delgado Wise, 2008).

Workers who do not immigrate but remain in the Global South are not left untouched by the forces of neoliberal globalisation. Neoliberal changes to the global economy have had a significant impact on people and work in the Global South. As regions in Asia, Africa, and South America are drawn further into the neoliberal agenda so internal migratory flows also change. Internal migration or rural–urban migration is driven by the same factors that drive international migration. One of the biggest drivers is work. Like migrants who move abroad, people migrate from rural to urban spaces to find better employment and income opportunities. **Rural–urban** (or internal) **migrants** are workers who move from rural areas to urban areas for full-time employment, temporary or seasonal work. Other factors, such as political and climate insecurity, drive rural–urban migration. Changes in technology can also cause rural–urban migration. Technological advances in agricultural, for example, tend to diminish agricultural job opportunities which can lead to rural–urban migration (Castles, 2013).

Life in the city may be better for some rural–urban migrants, but not all; for many, life does not improve as stable work and safe affordable living conditions remain hard to secure (Castles, 2013). Rural–urban migration also reduces urban employment opportunities which worsens job competition for those already living and working in cities (Castles, 2013). That said, unemployment is not the only factor driving rural–urban migration. The encroachment of global corporations into developing regions in Africa, Asia, and South America has displaced entire populations, creating a global underclass of refugees and asylum seekers (Sivanandan, 2008). The undocumented are widely considered to be the new global 'aliens' with regards to international and internal migration. As anxieties about job and resource scarcity become more intense, the desire to distinguish between citizens and non-citizens grows stronger.

Insiders and Outsiders: Identity Politics and Tensions around (Un)Belonging

Because the local has become increasingly global, people tend to cling to **identity politics** specifically nativist notions of nationalism (see Mbembe, 2019). Identity politics is when people build political alliances with others who share similar characteristics, such as gender, ethnicity, or religious affiliation. In the West, identity politics developed through the cultural and political revolutions of the 1960s and 1970s. Movements such as the feminist and the US civil rights campaign offer two examples. People continue to form alliances with those they perceive to be inherently like them. People live their identities psychologically and socially insofar as they draw on the identity narratives available to them and use these to construct and shape their lives; the ideas individuals have about themselves and others determine how they react and respond socially and psychologically (Appiah, 2018).

Regarding migration and migrant workers, identity politics can generate discourses of 'us/insiders' versus 'them/outsiders' – especially if people within the host nation feel that immigrants threaten their fundamental rights. **Nativism** or nativist politics emerge within this context. Nativism emphasises the value of the 'native', or established inhabitant, over that of the immigrant. Nativism focuses on protecting 'native', or established inhabitants, against the 'threat' of immigrants. Under nativism, the immigrant emerges as the stranger or othered figure. Nativism has a lot to do with feeling vulnerable in an insecure and rapidly changing world. People tend to cling to nativist notions of nationalism when they feel like their fundamental rights are under threat. In this context, the immigrant performs a significant function: he/she/they embody established inhabitants' anxieties about what is often chaos caused by wider global phenomena such as inflation, recession, or political instability. Constructed as other, the immigrant becomes the site on which the collective (group) derives its sense of belonging (Ahmed, 2000; Tamale, 2020).

Autochthony is important in this context and to this chapter. 'Autochthony' means 'from the soil' in classical Greek and *autochthon* refers to an indigenous inhabitant of a region (Geschiere, 2011). Autochthonous claims are not unlike nativist politics, but are usually deployed by those seeking to stake a claim over a particular region. Conflict can arise where there are two or more competing claims. Consider the Israeli–Palestinian conflict. Israel and Palestine both maintain historic claims to the same land. Autochthonous claims are problematic in that they are often based on mythical origin stories, making it hard to differentiate between who belongs and who does not (Geschiere, 2011). Autochthonous responses to rises in migration come about for a range of reasons and do not necessarily have to have anything to do with origin stories – mythical or not. Rapid democratisation and Western-led decentralisation policies are two possible reasons why people stake 'indigenous' claims to a country's resources and wealth (Geschiere, 2011). Lack of access to resources, employment, and wealth may also generate autochthonous claims.

Migrants fulfil the role of stranger or outsider-within against typically external forces (Landau, 2011; Nyamnjoh, 2006). The migrant comes to inhabit the social position of scapegoat in this context and is blamed for wider, often chaotic, economic and sociopolitical changes such as dispossession, inflation, and unemployment. Exclusionary practices, some radical and some less radical, are deployed against 'foreigners' by a range of actors, including the nation-state, state institutions, global corporations, and the public. The forces of globalisation have revived the politics of identity to the extent that even documented migrant workers struggle for legitimacy in their host nations (Landau, 2011; Nyamnjoh, 2006). To rid the nation-state of the threat within, some host citizens turn to aggressive identity politics and forms of violent and non-violent intolerance rooted in **xenophobia** (Landau, 2011; Nyamnjoh, 2006). Xenophobia refers to the fear or hatred of strangers, often migrants. Migrants tend to be scapegoated, or blamed, for social ills such as crime, inflation, housing shortages, rising unemployment rates, and even disease.

Contemporary illustrations of xenophobic scapegoating are not hard to find. Human Rights Watch (2020) reports that, since the outbreak of the COVID-19 pandemic, Asian people and people of Asian descent were targeted with xenophobia, discrimination, and racist violence in regions across the world. The divisions triggered by former US president Donald Trump's controversial wall along the US–Mexico border and Britain's referendum on European Union (EU) membership in 2016 generated similar discourses of xenophobia. Examples like these illustrate what happens when people build literal and figurative borders between the familiar/'us' and the unfamiliar/'them'. That said, it is not always easy to know who belongs and who does not ('us' versus 'them'). The speed and unpredictability at which the world changes can make autochthonous claims ambiguous and further complicates the discourse of (un)belonging to the nation-state. Typically, anti-immigrant sentiment is taken as a sign of chaos within the nation-state. And it can be. But some critics suggest that xenophobia may be a sign of citizens politically engaged in matters of the nation (Landau, 2011; Nyamnjoh, 2006). This argument has been applied to South Africa. The following case study draws on examples from South Africa to illustrate how and why some migrant workers, including rural–urban ones, become victimised and used as scapegoats in society.

Case Study

Xenophobia and Migrant Labour in South Africa

On 11 May 2008, a series of xenophobic attacks broke out in Alexandra, Johannesburg, South Africa. The violence spread to other parts of the country and lasted two weeks. Over 60 people died, and thousands were harmed and seriously injured. People were dragged from their homes, attacked in the streets, and tens of thousands of people were displaced. Although some South Africans were targeted, most victims of xenophobic violence were Black African migrants. Black African migrants are commonly referred to as *Makwerekwere* in South Africa. *Makwerekwere* is a derogatory and dehumanising term for foreigner that, as Francis Nyamnjoh (2006) argues, extends the logic of *apartheid* by a refusal to recognise the dignity of those who appear different. Apartheid unfolded in May 1948, when the National Party (NP), driven by a resurgence of Afrikaner nationalist unity, won with a narrow majority (Welsh, 2009). Afrikaners are a South African ethnic group descended mainly from Dutch 17th-century settlers. Under apartheid, South Africans were categorised into four so called 'racial' groups – Black, Coloured,[1] Indian, and white – and forced to live under racialised and discriminatory separate development policies. Following the growth of Black resistance and the anti-apartheid struggle (see Lodge, 1983), apartheid ended in 1994 and South Africa became a constitutional democracy. To date, the country has one of the most progressive constitutions in the world, but for millions precarity remains a feature of South African life. Precarious living and working conditions are symptomatic of deep structural inequality in the country. Because difference continues to shape socioeconomic and political relations post-apartheid, African immigrants looking to work and/or settle in South Africa are not unaffected by the country's colonial and apartheid past.

Gavaza Maluleke (2018), in her study of South–South migration, says that markers of difference, such as accent, ethnicity, language, darker skin colour, and religion, were used to distinguish between 'desirable' and 'undesirable' African migrants in the context of xenophobic violence in South Africa. Here, the body functions as a sign of difference (Maluleke, 2018). Racialised stereotypes about dark skin colour made some people more likely to be targeted than others. Differential processes of othering also make some migrants more socially acceptable than others. Because belonging is not fixed but shifting, documented and undocumented migrants have little choice but to 'constantly shift their subjectivities' to stay safe from harm – whether that be violent or non-violent (Maluleke, 2018: 281). Within this context, Loren Landau (2011) has suggested that xenophobia in South Africa may be a sign of active citizenship – South Africans actively engaged in controlling, policing, and shaping the physical and political spaces of the nation-state, spaces traditionally controlled by the state itself. Why would some South African citizens use violence against documented or undocumented migrants? South Africa's colonial and apartheid past holds some answers.

Migrant labour has been fundamental to the building of modern industrial South Africa (see Delius et al., 2014). The country is especially indebted to the mine labour system made up of internal South African migrant workers and South–South migrant labourers from neighbouring countries including Eswatini and Lesotho. Colonialism and apartheid shaped the racialised and gendered character of South Africa's migrant labour system. Apartheid was a system of *racial capitalism* inasmuch as it was a white supremacist regime (see Robinson, 1983). Under apartheid, South Africa's labour force consisted mainly of two types of workers: Black and white. White workers had more citizenship rights than Black workers, who had little, if any, rights. Apartheid's migrant labour force was also differentiated by gender: Black men typically worked on white-owned farms, factories, and mines, whereas Black women were predominantly employed as domestic workers in white urban households. Without full citizenship rights, neither could settle permanently in South Africa's cities.

Because apartheid was a racially segregated spatial system of control, it created ethnic divisions between Black workers. Under policies of separate development and independent governance, the apartheid government divided the Black South African population into 'ethnic homelands' or territories (see Welsh, 2009). These ethnic divisions were illogical and haphazard. The aim was to prevent Black South Africans from settling permanently in cities but mostly to maintain white supremacy by sowing seeds of division among the Black majority. Denied their political rights and forced to live on 'independently' governed territories, apartheid involuntarily turned Black South Africans into rural–urban migrants with little choice but to live in temporary urban accommodation, typically urban hostels, under the draconian and racist administrative system – or stay in temporary accommodation in 'ethnic home-lands' controlled by ethnic groups they were not a part of (Naicker, 2016).

Black rural–urban migrants did find ways to survive, even thrive, in precarious living and working conditions (see Epprecht, 2013, for example) but, unlike white workers, were paid poorly by white bosses who used repressive tactics to prevent Black workers from mobilising collectively against capitalism and the apartheid state. The presence of Black African migrants desperate to work in South Africa, a more economically developed region, further problematised the exploitation and subordination of the country's internal migrant labour population; moreover, be-cause the 'devaluation of black humanity' persists post-apartheid (Nyamnjoh, 2006: 125), contemporary rural–urban Black migrant mine workers are more recent victims of discrimination and xenophobic violence in the country.

Many male migrant workers still live in cramped same-sex hostels because of a migrant labour system not yet fully democratised post-apartheid, while those who choose not to live in urban hostels are not paid enough to rent a house in the city, so resort to building shacks on the outskirts of the mining districts without access to running water and electricity (Naicker, 2016). The 2012 'Marikana massacre', in South Africa's North West Province, offers a salient illustration of discrimination in the workplace and the inequalities experienced by some migrant labour forces, such as low wages, poor working conditions, and lack of security, post-apartheid. On 16 August 2012, members of the South African Police Service (SAPS) shot and killed 34 striking mineworkers at Lonmin plc (now Sibanye-Stillwater) Marikana in South Africa. Ten people were killed in circumstances relating to the strike during the three-day period of strike action. Lonmin plc was a British-owned company at the time of the strike. The massacre took place in the middle of the **wildcat strike**. Striking miners had been demanding a pay rise and better working conditions after years of industry precarity. The massacre attracted international attention, as well as attention from organisations such as Amnesty International. Former South Africa President Jacob Zuma announced that he would appoint a Commission of Inquiry into Marikana, and the report was published in 2015.

Many of the murdered miners were rural–urban South African migrants from Pondoland in the Eastern Cape Province (Cook, 2018). The amaMpondo are isiX-hosa speaking people. AmaMpondo workers made up a third of the Lonmin mine workers at the time of the wildcat strike. These amaMpondo miners lived on land controlled by local 'ethnic authorities', an apartheid hangover, such as the Bafokeng, a Setswana-speaking community, but the amaMpondo were not welcomed by their hosts (Cook, 2018). The Bafokeng, for example, were not willing to supply their guests with basic services such as water networks or waste removal (Cook, 2018). The amaMpondo rural–urban migrant miners faced frequent discrimination at local community schools, shops, clinics, and other state institutions; acts of prejudice and discrimination illustrate resource division and resource sharing continue to be ethni-cally divided post-apartheid (Cook, 2018).

Significantly, members of the Bafokeng delegation who met with striking miners after the massacre were reported to have suggested that the amaMpondo migrant workers had, in part, provoked the tragedy that unfolded on 16 August, the sugges-tion being that the miners were 'knowingly "wild" and "uncivilized" Xhosas' (Cook, 2018: 214). Within this context, Camalita Naicker suggests that the experiences of some social groups in South Africa, especially poor and working-class Black people, illustrate that those on the urban peripheries of post-apartheid South Africa, whether local or migrant, continue to be made to feel like outsiders unable buy into 'elite civil society' (2016: 53). In some cases, as seen in Marikana, victimisation has devastating consequences.

Conclusion

This chapter has examined documented and undocumented workers. Drawing on a range of examples, it has discussed identity politics, considering notions of 'insiders' and 'outsiders', and examined tensions around (un)belonging. Looking to the past to make sense of the present, the inequalities experienced by some migrant labour forces, such as low wages, poor working conditions, and lack of security, have been explored. Colonialism and the globalisation of neoliberal capitalism have been central to the discussion. Using the concept of xenophobia and drawing on a South African case study, the challenges faced by international and internal (rural–urban) migrants have also been considered. Colonial and apartheid legacies have been a part of the discussion. It is important to note that the South African case study discussed in this chapter provides an overview of what were complex cultural, discursive, ideological, sociohistorical, and political exchanges.[2] Finally, this chapter also explained why some migrants become victimised and scapegoated for wider social ills.

STUDENT ACTIVITY

Drawing on this chapter, create a visual representation of the factors that drive international and internal migration in the contemporary world, as well as those that underpin anti-immigrant sentiment and exclusionary discourses. Your representation should include key concepts introduced in this chapter (see 'Key Terms'). It should also include a case study on xenophobia of your own choosing.

Practice Questions

1. Identify the factors that drive international and internal migration especially economic migration.
2. Why is the road to legal documentation long and hard for most migrant workers?
3. Outline the reasons why documented and undocumented migrants can be scapegoated for wider social ills.
4. As the local grows increasingly global, why might established inhabitants of a country or region cling to nativist politics?
5. Drawing on the South African case study in this chapter, explain how xenophobia is produced, shared, and consumed in social organisations, institutions, and among citizens.

Amy Duvenage

Key Terms

Apartheid
system of racial segregation and white minority rule in South Africa (1948–94).

Autochthony
inhabiting a place or region from earliest known times. Means 'from the soil' in classical Greek (Geschiere, 2011).

Capitalism
an economic and political system organised around the need to expand for profit and where private owners control trade and industry rather than the State.

Colonialism
to take control, physically, of another country by conquering land and people.

Diaspora
the spread of people from their birthplace or homeland.

Global North and Global South
spatial, not geographic, terms signifying two distinct but entangled worlds in which the North enjoys cultural, economic, and political dominance over the South (Blagg and Anthony, 2019).

Globalisation
the free flow of people, trade, information, and capital around the world.

Identity politics
when people build political alliances with others who share similar characteristics, such as gender, ethnicity, or religious affiliation.

Migrant workers
those who move from one region to another for full-time employment, temporary or seasonal work.

Nativism
a politics that emphasises the value of the 'native' (or established inhabitant) over that of the immigrant.

Neo-imperialism
modern practices of imperialism, such as one country's political and/or economic dominance over another independent country with or without settlement.

Patriarchy
in a Western context, refers to a society or system of authority where men dominate and hold power; based the belief that men are inherently superior to women.

Racial capitalism
the racialised development, expansion, and organisation of capitalist society through racialised labour exploitation; associated with the theory-work of Cedric J. Robinson (1983).

Refugee

a person who is forced to their country, to migrate, to escape hardships including natural disasters, persecution, or war.

Rural–urban migrants

also 'internal migrants'; workers who move from rural areas to urban areas for full-time employment, temporary or seasonal work.

Wildcat strike

a strike carried out by union mineworkers without the union leaders' authorisation.

Xenophobia

the fear or hatred of strangers, often migrants.

Notes

1 Richard van der Ross (2015) explains that the Coloured people are an anthropological group of people unique to South Africa who live across South Africa but mainly in the Western Cape province. See Richard van der Ross's *In our own skins: a political history of the coloured people* (2015).
2 For more on xenophobia in South Africa, see Matsinhe (2011) and Neocosmos (2010); see Epprecht (2013) for a detailed examination of migrant labour and the mine industry in South Africa; and see Lodge (1983) for a discussion of Black politics in 20th-century South Africa.

References

Ahmed, S. (2000) *Strange encounters: embodied others in post-coloniality*. London and New York: Routledge.

Al Thani, M. (2022) 'Channelling soft power: the Qatar 2022 World Cup, migrant workers, and International Image'. *International Journal of the History of Sport*, 38(17): 1729–1752. https://doi.org/10.1080/09523367.2021.1988932

Amin, S. (1997) *Capitalism in the age of globalization: the management of contemporary society*. Reprinted Cape Town: IPSR, 2000.

Anderson, B. (2010) 'Migration, immigration controls and the fashioning of precarious workers'. *Work, Employment and Society*, 24 (2), pp. 300–317. https://doi.org/10.1177/0950017010362141

Appiah, K.A. (2018) *The lies that bind: rethinking identity – creed, country, class, culture*. Great Britain: Profile Books.

Bhabha, H.K., and Stierstofer, K. (2015) 'Homi K. Bhabha in interview with Klaus Stierstorfer on "Diaspora and Home"'. In F. Kläger and S. Stierstorfer (eds), *Diasporic constructions of home and belonging*. Berlin/Boston: De Gruyter, 11–20.

Blagg, H., and Anthony, T. (2019) *Decolonising criminology: imagining justice in a postcolonial world*. London: Palgrave Macmillan.

Brah, A. (1996) *Cartographies of diaspora: contesting identities*. London and New York: Routledge, reprinted 2003.

Castells, M. (2010) *The Rise of the Network Society*, 2nd edition. Chichester: Wiley-Blackwell.

Castles S., and Delgado Wise, R. (eds) (2008) *Migration and development: perspectives from the south*. Geneva: International Organization for Migration.

Castles, S. (2013) 'The forces driving global migration'. *Journal of Intercultural Studies*, 34(2): 122–140. Doi: 10.1080/07256868.2013.781916

Cook, S. (2018) 'Corporate kings and South Africa's traditional-industrial complex'. in J.L. Comaroff and J. Comaroff, (eds), *The politics of custom*. Chicago and London: University of Chicago Press, pp. 211–230.

Delius, P., Phillips, L., and Rankin-Smith, F. (eds) (2014) *A long way home: migrant worker worlds 1800–2014*. Johannesburg: Wits University Press.

Epprecht, M. (2013) *Hungochani: the history of a dissident sexuality in southern Africa*. Canada: McGill-Queens University Press.

Geschiere, P. (2011) 'Autochthony, citizenship, and exclusion – paradoxes in the politics of belonging in Africa and Europe'. *Indiana Journal of Global Legal Studies*, 18(1): 321–339. https://doi.org/10.2979/indjglolegstu.18.1.321

Hall, S. (1978) 'Race and "moral panics" in postwar Britain'. In P. Gilroy and R. Wilson Gilmore (eds), *Selected writings on ace and Difference*. Durham, NC: Duke University Press, reprinted 2021, pp. 56–70.

Human Rights Watch News (2020) 'Covid-19 fueling anti-Asian racism and xenophobia worldwide'. *Human Rights Watch*, 12 May. Accessed 8 November 2020 from www.hrw.org/news/2020/05/12/covid-19-fueling-anti-asian-racism-and-xenophobia-worldwide.

Landau, L.B. (2011) *Exorcising the demons within: xenophobia, violence and statecraft in contemporary South Africa*. Tokyo and New York: United Nations University Press.

Lodge, T. (1983) *Black politics in South Africa since 1945*. London and New York: Longman.

Maluleke, G. (2018) 'Women and negotiated forms of belonging in post-apartheid South Africa'. *Critical African Studies*, 10(3): 272–286. https://doi.org/10.1080/21681392.2019.1613901

Matsinhe, D.M. (2011) 'Africa's fear of itself: the ideology of "makwerekwere" in South Africa'. *Third World Quarterly*, 32(2): 295–313. https://doi.org/10.1080/01436597.2011.560470

Mbembe, A. (2019) *Necropolitics*. Durham: Duke University Press.

Millward, P. (2017) 'World Cup 2022 and Qatar's construction projects: relational power in networks and relational responsibilities to migrant workers'. *Current Sociology*, 65(5): 756–776. https://doi.org/10.1177/0011392116645382

Naicker, C. (2016) 'The languages of xenophobia in post-apartheid South Africa: reviewing migrancy, foreignness, and solidarity'. *Agenda*, 30(2): 46–60. https://doi.org/10.1080/10130950.2016.1215647

Neocosmos, M. (2010) *From 'foreign natives' to 'native foreigners': explaining xenophobia in post-apartheid South Africa – citizenship and nationalism, identity and politics*. Senegal: Codesria.

Nyamnjoh, F. (2006) *Insiders & outsiders: citizenship and xenophobia in contemporary South Africa*. London and New York: Zed Books.

Robinson, C. (1983) *Black Marxism: the making of the Black radical tradition*. Chapel Hill, NC: University of North Carolina Press, reprinted 2000.

Sivanandan A. (2008) *Catching history on a wing*. London: Pluto Press.

Tamale, S. (2020) *Decolonization and feminism*. Ottawa: Daraja Press.

United Nations Trust Fund for Human Security (2012) 'What is human security?' *United Nations*. Accessed 12 December 2021 from www.un.org/humansecurity/wp-content/uploads/2018/04/What-is-Human-Security.pdf

Van der Ross, R. (2015) *In our own skins: a political history of the coloured people*. Johannesburg and Cape Town: Jonathan Ball Publishers.

Welsh, D. (2009) *The rise and fall of apartheid*. Johannesburg and Cape Town: Jonathan Ball Publishers.

Amy Duvenage

chapter 17

Inequalities of a Global Workforce
The Shipping Industry

Helen Devereux

Introduction

In the last 50 years or so, developments associated with economic globalisation have resulted in workers in some industries becoming increasingly mobile globally (Peck et al., 2005), with workers leading a somewhat transnational existence. This existence beyond the boundary of a single nation, however, is not new to the international shipping workforce. And, while comparisons could be made between workers in the seafaring workforce and those who are employed in the offshore oil and gas installation industry, or even the aviation industry, the truly global nature of the shipping industry means that much of what are known to be issues regarding mobile global workforces – such as worker exploitation, poor employment conditions, and worker inequalities – are particularly pronounced. Consequently, the international shipping industry is a particularly interesting workforce on which to focus attention. Thus, this chapter is about global workers, and it uses workers in the international shipping industry as its prime example.

In this chapter, the inequalities experienced by the workforce in the international shipping industry are explored, an industry which is responsible for transporting approximately 80 per cent of global trade (UNCTAD, 2018). The workforce is comprised of an estimated 1.65 million individuals (ICS, 2022). These workers are referred to as seafarers and work on board various types of seagoing vessels, including cruise ships, ferries, tankers, container ships, and offshore supply vessels. There are seafarers of all nationalities, with the largest seafaring labour supply nations being China, the Philippines, Indonesia, the Russian Federation,

DOI: 10.4324/9781003314769-22

and Ukraine (ICS, 2021). These five nations represent approximately 44 per cent of the global seafaring workforce (ICS, 2021). Ships have a strong on-board occupational hierarchy and those higher in the hierarchy are known as officers. Officers hold professional licences, which are awarded by governments around the world. While the requirements to obtain these licences vary between nations, they are considered to be of an equivalent standard regardless of which government awards them. 'Ratings' is a term that refers to a group of seafarers who are lower in the on-board hierarchy. These are skilled seafarers who carry out support work for officers on board.

It is estimated that two-thirds of internationally trading ships have multinational crews onboard with workers of three or more nationalities (Lane et al., 2002). The use of multinational crews is a deliberate crewing strategy in which shipowners try to inhibit the ability of workers to organise and collectively bargain, an issue which is discussed later in this chapter. First, however, in order to understand the inequalities faced by seafarers, there are some pieces of context about the shipping industry that need to be understood. Thus, the chapter begins by considering the structure of the international shipping industry. In doing so, the issues regarding the ownership of ships, how (and where) ships are registered, and how this relates to those who work on board them are explored. Scrutiny is also given to how a globalised industry, in which workers work in areas beyond national jurisdictions, is regulated, the difficulties of such regulation, and the various ways in which this enables the exploitation of the workforce. Second, the employment terms and conditions experienced by the seafaring labour force are considered. In particular, some of the readily apparent inequalities within a global workforce, such as tour of duty duration, as well as more discreet inequalities, such as food on board, are considered. Finally, the chapter focuses on actions taken to challenge these inequalities and improve the lives of those who work at sea, including a reflection on industrial relations in the industry and the ways in which trade unions have tried to combat inequalities. In particular, the work of the International Transport Workers' Federation is considered.

Structure of the Industry

In this section the structure of the international shipping industry is considered, along with the ways this may contribute to many of the inequalities experienced by those who work at sea. First, it is necessary to consider the work of the International Maritime Organization (IMO), a specialised agency of the United Nations. The IMO was formally established in 1948 and met for the first time in 1959 (IMO, 2023). Its purpose is 'to provide machinery for cooperation among Governments in the field of governmental regulation and practices relating to technical matters of all kinds affecting shipping engaged in international trade; to encourage and facilitate the general adoption of the highest practicable standards in manners concerning maritime safety, efficiency of navigation and prevention and control of marine pollution from ships' (IMO, 2023). In other words, the purpose of the

Helen Devereux

IMO is to create a level playing field so that regulations that relate to shipping are universally implemented. This should, in theory, make shipping safer, more secure, and better for the environment, as shipowners all abide by the same rigorous standards across the globe. This is particularly important given the changes to the practice of 'flagging' in the shipping industry.

Historically, shipping companies tended to be family-run, with each ship associated with a particular 'home' port (Farthing and Brownrigg, 1997). These ships would be registered or 'flagged' to the national ship registry in the country in which the shipping company was located, with the shipping company needing to demonstrate a significant connection with the national flag it wished to register under. The country under whose registration a ship operates is known as the **flag state**, and flag states are obliged to implement and enforce international regulations for all ships flying their flag (EMISA, 2021).

Today, many ships are registered under open registers. Open registers – also referred to as '**flags of convenience**' – permit ships to be registered in a country without the owner having any connection with the country. Flag states are supposed to be the main regulatory body, and each flag state should utilise legislation, inspection, and certification to implement and enforce its own regime. It is widely accepted, however, that many flag states – particularly 'open registers' – lack the infrastructure (and will) to ensure compliance (DeSombre, 2006). The consequence is that there are substantial variations in the level of regulatory regime by different flag states and consequently the level playing field desired by the IMO remains a long way off.

This impacts on the seafaring workforce in a number of ways. First, for many seafarers who work on board 'flag of convenience' ships, low wages are the norm (ITF, 2023a). Workers on board these vessels are also more likely to experience poor on-board living conditions (ITF 2023a). For example, on board some ships workers may not have the ability to control the temperature in their own cabin and endure sleeping in an environment that is too hot or cold (Sampson et al., 2016). Other issues with poor living conditions include lack of natural light, insufficient washing facilities, and noisy environment (Sampson et al., 2018). Roberts (2003: 7) explored the work-related mortality of British seafarer employed onboard 'flag of convenience' ships and concluded: 'British seafarers who work for flags of convenience registries appear to be at increased risk of mortality through maritime disasters, as well as through occupational accidents and suicide. Many of the occupational accidents, such as asphyxiation in cargo holds, were caused by hazardous working practices.'

For shipowners, however, by flagging their ships to 'flags of convenience' they are able to take advantage of minimal regulation, cheap registration fees, low taxes, and the freedom to employ cheap labour from anywhere in the world (ITF, 2023a). For an industry in which crewing costs account for approximately 60 per cent of operating expenditure (Greiner, 2017) it is not hard to see why shipowners seek to utilise cheap labour. Nevertheless, various incidents have led some governments to decide that flag states were no longer enough to prevent substandard ships for entering national waters and posing a threat to safety and the environment. Thus, **Port State Control** (PSC) was introduced. The IMO states that

> PSC is the inspection of foreign ships in national ports to verify that the condition of the ship and its equipment comply with the requirements of international regulations and that the ship is manned and operated in compliance with these instruments and ensure maritime safety and security and prevent pollution. The role of PSC is intended to be a 'second line of defence'.
>
> (IMO, 2019)

PSC plays an important role in regulating the international shipping industry and protecting those who work in it. It does so by inspecting ships and detaining those which are found to be operating in ways which are not in compliance with various international conventions.

As an example, in March 2022, five foreign-flagged ships were detained in UK ports. One of these was the Liberian flagged 'Stellar Alazani', which was seen to have nine deficiencies, including non-payment of wages to the seafarers onboard and expired workers' employment contracts, which are known in the industry as seafarers' employment agreements (Maritime and Coastguard Agency, 2022). Thus, in situations where flag states are not ensuring compliance with regulations, PSC can be an effective way of ensuring enforcement. It should be noted, however, that, just like flag states, not all PSCs ensure regulatory compliance. For example, it is commonly understood that just 14 of the 22 countries on the West and Central African coasts undertake inspections on ships calling at their ports (Dryad Global, 2022). Thus, it is clear to see why, given the global nature of the shipping industry, implementing and enforcing regulations can be especially challenging (Walters and Bailey, 2013).

Employment Terms and Conditions

The employment terms and conditions experienced by those working at sea vary greatly. Some seafarers are employed as officers and work in the roles higher in the on-board hierarchy. These seafarers are also predominantly employed on **permanent employment** contracts with annual salaries. Consequently, they receive pay when they are at home on leave and these workers tend to have predetermined periods of leave. For example, a junior British officer working on board a deep-sea chemical tanker could have an employment contract which stipulates that, for each three months worked on board, two months of paid leave would be received.

In contrast, other seafarers are employed as 'ratings', which are positions lower in the on-board hierarchy. The vast majority of these seafarers experience **precarious employment,** as they are employed on temporary contracts, which are commonly referred to as 'single voyage' contracts. These contracts last for the period of time that the seafarer is on board and these workers are paid only while on board. Some of these may be paid a 'day rate', which they negotiate prior to joining the ship, and may be paid 'overtime' for additional hours worked onboard.

Once they leave the ship, they are unemployed and must seek another contract. The duration of their leave will be determined by when the seafarer secures their next employment.

On board a single ship it is not unusual to find some workers who are permanently employed and others who are employed precariously (see Chapter 5, 'Precarious and Gig Work in the Global Economy', by McDonough and Pearson). It may even be the case that workers employed on the same vessel in the same role experience vastly different employment terms and conditions. Previous research regarding the presence of precariously and permanently employed workers on board the same ship indicates that the presence of precariously employed workers serves to remind those who are permanently employed that they are easily replaceable (Devereux and Wadsworth, 2020). This was something which was acutely apparent in the COVID-19 pandemic, when seafarers from the cruise sector became unemployed and sought employment in the offshore support sector (Devereux and Wadsworth, 2022). There is limited literature indicating what tensions the presence of both permanently and precariously employed seafarers employed on the same ship poses. However, as with the use of multinational crews, the presence of both precariously and permanently employed workers makes it difficult for seafarers to organise and collectively bargain. Research from other industries also indicates that the presence of both permanently and precariously employed workers in the workplace can result in a divided workforce in which resentment is exacerbated, and additionally that social relationships tend not to form between those employed differently (see, for example, Wethal, 2017).

Many of the workers on board will have different tour-of-duty durations and some will work on board for much longer than others. For example, while a British junior officer may work for three months on board it would not be unusual for a Russian junior officer to be on board for six months. Moreover, the salary received by each individual can differ substantially. It could be the case that a junior officer from Western Europe is paid more than the Asian captain of the same ship. The vastly different employment terms and conditions experienced by seafarers are clear indicators of the widespread inequalities in the industry. While some of the conditions, such as salary and tour-of-duty duration are clear to see, others are more discreet, such as the on-board food budget. Given that seafarers generally have no access to food other than what is provided to them, it is perhaps unsurprising that the quality of food on board and the choice of food provided is of great importance to those who work at sea. It is the norm for shipping companies to implement a food budget which determines the provisions which can be ordered by the on-board cook. This is often calculated on the basis of a maximum number of United States dollars to be spent per day, per person on board. Food budgets vary greatly for different shipping companies (Baum-Talmor, 2020). Interestingly, the food budget can also vary within a shipping company depending on the type of ship. For example, within one shipping company workers on board container ships had much lower food budgets than those who worked on offshore support vessels. Consequently, while the workers on board the container ship had severely limited desserts during a tour of duty, it was not unusual for workers on the offshore support vessel to be consuming luxury-branded ice creams and other varieties of desserts on a daily basis.

In a similar vein, seafarers' access to the internet while onboard can vary greatly, despite the fact that the most commonly used strategy by seafarers to combat loneliness on board is utilising the internet to contact friends and family (Sampson and Ellis, 2019). While some shipping companies provide unlimited free internet access to all workers, others charge for access (Sampson et al., 2018). Thus, those seafarers from less economically developed countries, who earn lower salaries, may struggle to afford to use the internet on board, particularly when prices tend to be set based on the 'norm' for more economically developed countries. For example, seafarers from Southeast Asia who are employed on the current ILO minimum monthly basic wage of USD658 (ITF, 2023b) can rarely afford the internet on board.

Clearly, workers in the seafaring industry are acutely aware of the inequalities present among the workforce, observing them close-up every day. Seafarers who face the greatest inequalities have little choice but to accept less than ideal employment, due to economic pressures (Devereux and Wadsworth, 2020). This may particularly be the case if they come from a country in which seafarers experience negative listing, whereby workers are placed on a list for the purpose of making adverse recruitment decisions regarding those workers. This can happen for any number of reasons, but it could occur for some seafarers if they decline an employment contract.

It is perhaps unsurprising that the inequalities experienced faced by the seafaring workforce have been seen to impact on occupational health, safety, and well-being outcomes (Devereux and Wadsworth, 2020). For example, seafarers employed on temporary contracts may accept new employment even if they have not experienced a sufficient leave period at home to recover from their previous tour of duty. The consequence of this is that some seafarers may arrive at a new vessel in a fatigued state, which can increase the risk of accidents (Devereux and Wadsworth, 2020). The need to accept employment and return to sea prior to a suitable period of time at home also adversely impacts on the well-being of seafarers' family members. A study by Thomas et al. (2003) highlights how a seafarer's time at home may be at a 'premium', in the sense that it is much longed for but in short supply, and spouses experience worry regarding the uncertainty of when the seafarer will have to leave home and return to sea.

Challenging Inequalities

In this section the various ways in which the inequalities experienced by the seafaring workforce have been challenged. First, as with many industries, trade unions have played an important role in the safeguarding of workers. However, the globalisation of the seafaring industry, and the fact that ships often have seafarers from a range of different countries on board, has meant that national trade unions have needed to coordinate action across nationalities and between other transport workers' unions. Through this approach, there has been some considerable success – for example, the recent work of the International Transport Workers' Federation (ITF) – in securing a minimum basic wage for seafarers working on board vessels covered by an ITF agreement.

The achievement of the ITF to agree a basic wage is particularly impressive, given that reaching a cohesive consensus from workers with vastly different expectations is notoriously difficult. Lillie's (2004) work on the global **collective bargaining** on 'flag of convenience' shipping details the numerous hurdles which the ITF had to overcome. The basic minimum wage provides an international safety net for the protection of seafarers, which is particularly valuable for those from less economically developed countries (ITF, 2023b).

Second, there have been various ways in which workers with relatively more power have sought to protect others and mitigate some of the issues caused by inequalities. For example, work exploring the work scheduling and work location control of precariously and permanently employed seafarers found that some captains refused requests to extend the duration of precariously employed seafarers' tour of duty (Devereux and Wadsworth, 2020). While permanently employed seafarers, who would be paid while at home, prioritised leaving the ship on time, precariously employed seafarers – who would receive no pay while at home – prioritised any opportunity to remain on board. Thus, these captains refused requests by precariously employed seafarers to extend their tour of duty, as they felt these seafarers needed to go home and rest.

Case Study

The Mass Redundancy of P&O Ferries Workers

In March 2022, P&O Ferries made redundant 786 UK seafarers who were employed on board eight ferries. The seafarers were employed on permanent contracts and typically worked a rotation of two weeks on board followed by two weeks leave and received an annual salary. At the time P&O Ferries operated four routes: Dover (UK) to Calais (France), Hull (UK) to Rotterdam (Netherlands), Liverpool (UK) to Dublin (Republic of Ireland), and Cairnryan (UK) to Larne (UK). The eight affected ferries were flagged in Cyprus, Bermuda, and the Bahamas. P&O Ferries is owned by DP World, which has its headquarters in Dubai.

Peter Hebblethwaite, the CEO of P&O Ferries, told a Commons hearing that the firm were moving to a 'new operating model' (Hebblethwaite, 2022). The new model meant that international seafarers were replacing UK seafarers. It is reported that the replacement seafarers receive an hourly rate of £5.15, much less than the £9.18 required in the UK at the time.

Prior to the mass redundancies in 2022, P&O Ferries failed to consult their employees or union representatives. They should also have notified their ships' flag states (Cyprus, Bermuda, and the Bahamas) between 30 and 45 days in advance rather than on the day. In response to the events, the RMT union said the issue was 'fast turning into one of the most shameful acts in the history of British industrial relations' (RMT, 2022).

Despite the ferries operating out of UK ports and the widespread outrage at the treatment of the workers from the general public, there was little the UK government could do in terms of preventing the job losses. Other than referring P&O Ferries to the Insolvency Service (which the UK Government did, but after investigation decided not to commence criminal proceedings), the only avenue open was that of PSC. Simply put, as the ships were in ports in the UK, the government were able to revoke PSC rights to board and inspect foreign flagged ships. Thus, operating under the PSC regime, the UK Maritime Coastguard Agency (MCA) surveyors inspected several of the ferries operated by P&O Ferries and detained three vessels due to a number of deficiencies. These ferries were allowed to sail following rectification of the issues identified and further visits from MCA surveyors.

While there is limited information regarding the new workforce onboard P&O Ferries, it is known that seafarers have been sought from various locations, including India, Poland, Romania, and Montenegro. The new employment contract has these seafarers working for durations of 17 weeks on board with no shore leave – a situation very different from the previous rotation of one week on board followed by one week leave. These workers will undoubtably be cheaper to P&O Ferries in the sense that their wages will be lower than those workers sacked, but more importantly this new highly multinational workforce is likely to be more fragmented and harder to organise collectively. Given their various nationalities, it is unlikely that these new workers will be represented by the same trade union and it is likely that the various trade unions representing the workers will have competing priorities. Furthermore, collective agreement is going to be even harder to come by, given that these new workers are precariously employed via crewing agencies. Thus, it appears that these workers will have limited ability to be able to resist the unfavourable working conditions imposed on them, and it is expected that many of them will change employers if they are able to.

In response to the P&O Ferries incident, the UK Government passed the Seafarers' Wages Bill in March 2023. The Bill states that seafarers engaged on vessels that visit UK ports 120 times or more per year are paid a rate equivalent to the UK National Minimum Wage. Other than rate of pay, the Bill offers no other forms of employment protection. Furthermore, on some routes shipping companies could avoid needing to comply due to slight adjustments in a vessel's schedule by avoiding 120 UK port visits (Nautilus, 2022). Thus, while it is too early to understand the impact of the Bill fully, current indicators suggest that, unless the Bill is amended to include a cap on the length of a tour of duty of seafarers operating in short sea trades, little progress in safeguarding the seafaring workforce has been made.

Conclusion

In this chapter, the inequalities faced by the labour force in one industry, the international shipping industry, have been considered. These inequalities include numerous issues relating to workers' quality of life on board, such as on-board living

Helen Devereux

conditions, access to the internet, and the quality of the food provided. It is clear from the chapter that many of the inequalities among seafaring workforces arise from strategies which are purposely deployed by those who control the seafaring labour force. These include the use of precarious employment contracts and the widespread use of multinational crewing, whereby workers of multiple nationalities work on board the same ship, which serves to inhibit the ability of the workers to organise and collectively bargain. The work of the ITF, however, gives hope that the seafaring workforce can be protected and can experience fair and decent work. It is clear from incidents such as the mass redundancy of the P&O Ferries workforce, however, that much more needs to be done. While PSC can in some circumstances be utilised to protect workers – such as the detention of the Stellar Alazani – this is only the case when ships visit ports in which an effective PSC regime is in place. For those ships flagged to 'flags of convenience' which sail predominantly in areas where PSC does not conduct inspections, the workers on board remain especially vulnerable.

STUDENT ACTIVITY

Unfortunately, P&O Ferries are not the first (or last) employer to make a large group of workers redundant, only to quickly replace these workers with new employees. Have a look at other employers and workplaces around the world to find other examples of where this (or similar) has happened. Think about the various experiences of workers in different industries who have experienced this scenario. How similar/dissimilar was the employment of the workers? How were the workers protected? Did the workers have a collective voice? What role did the relevant trade union play? Were there public outcries? What could be put in place to better protect workers in the future?

   Produce a mind map which briefly outlines these key points. Try to use arrows and lines to show how your thoughts are linked together.

Practice Questions

1. 'A lack of regulation is not a problem for the international seafaring work-force, rather it is the lack of enforcement of regulation that is the problem.' To what extent do you agree with this statement? Provide a balanced response, considering the various sides of this argument.
2. 'The ways in which some workers in the international seafaring workforce are poorly treated by employers is similar to workers in other industries.' To what extent do you agree with this statement? Provide a balanced response – make sure to consider the various sides of this argument.
3. 'Those who control the seafaring labour force purposely utilise strategies which perpetuate inequalities, and this is not dissimilar to workers in other industries.' To what extent do you agree with this statement? Provide a balanced response that considers the various sides of this argument.

Key Terms

Collective bargaining
'the official process by which trade unions negotiate with employers, on behalf of their members' (Trades Union Congress, 2023).

Flag state
'the term "flag State" originated in the past when ships were using flags as a symbol of the nation or tribe to which they belong. Today, a flag State is a country under whose registration a ship operates. However, for a country to be a flag State, it must have the necessary financial and technical maritime infrastructure and adhere to all the norms and regulations established by the IMO). Flag States are obliged to implement and enforce international maritime regulations for all ships flying their flag' (EMISA, 2023).

Flags of convenience
'also known as open register. A flag of convenience ship is one that flies the flag of a country other than the country of ownership. In a competitive shipping market, FOCs lower fees and minimise regulation, as ship owners look for the cheapest way to run their vessels' (ITF, 2023a).

Permanent employment
employment which is of unlimited duration with no pre-determined end date.

Port State Control
'the inspection of foreign ships in national ports to verify that the condition of the ship and its equipment comply with the requirements of international regulations and that the ship is crewed and operated in compliance with these rules. Many of IMO's most important technical conventions contain provisions for ships to be inspected when they visit foreign ports to ensure that they meet IMO requirements' (IMO, 2023).

Precarious employment
'precarious employment is multifaceted but can be described as employment which is usually defined by uncertainty as to the duration of employment, multiple possible employers or a disguised or ambiguous employment relationship, a lack of access to social protection and benefits usually associated with employment, low pay, and substantial legal and practical obstacles to joining a trade union and bargaining collectively' (ILO, 2011: 5).

References

Baum-Talmor, P. (2020). 'The importance of food on board cargo ships – a multidisciplinary approach'. *International Seafarers Welfare and Assistance Network*. www.seafarerswelfare.org/news/2020/talking-point-the-importance-of-food-on-board-cargo-ships-a-multidisciplinary-approach

DeSombre, Elizabeth R. (2006) *Flagging standards: globalization and environmental, safety, and labor regulations at sea*. Cambridge, MA: MIT Press.

Devereux, H., and Wadsworth, E. (2020) 'Work scheduling and work location control in precarious and "permanent" employment'. *Economic and Labour Relations Review*, 32(2): 230–246.

Devereux, H., and Wadsworth, E. (2022) 'Forgotten keyworkers: the experiences of British seafarers during the COVID-19 pandemic'. *Economic and Labour Relations Review*, 33(2).

Dryad Global (2022) 'Only 14 West Central African countries conduct port checks on ships'. *Dryad Global.* https://channel16.dryadglobal.com/only-14-west-central-africa-countries-conduct-port-checks-on-ships

EMISA (2021) 'The role of flag states'. *EMISA.* https://emisa.eu/the-role-of-flag-states/

Farthing, B., and Brownrigg, M. (1997) *International Shipping*, 3rd edition. Business of Shipping Series. London and Hong Kong: LLP.

Greiner, R. (2017) 'Ship operating costs are set to increase'. www.moore-greece.gr/MediaLibsAndFiles/media/greeceweb.moorestephens.com/Documents/1-Richard-Greiner.pdf

Hebblethwaite, P (2022) 'Letter to UK Transport Minister'. www.tradewindsnews.com/cruise-and-ferry/p-o-ferries-boss-will-not-reinstate-crews-but-supports-increase-in-minimum-wage/2-1-1192619

ICS (2021) 'Shipping and world trade: Global supply and demand for seafarers'. www.ics-shipping.org/shipping-fact/shipping-and-world-trade-global-supply-and-demand-for-seafarers/#:~:text=China%2C%20the%20Philippines%2C%20Indonesia%2C,the%20Russian%20Federation%20and%20Ukraine

International Labour Organization (ILO) (2011) 'Policies and regulations to combat precarious Employment'. www.ilo.org/wcmsp5/groups/public/—ed_dialogue/—actrav/documents/meetingdocument/wcms_164286.pdf

IMO (2019) 'Port state control'. www.imo.org/en/OurWork/IIIS/Pages/Port%20State%20Control.aspx

IMO (2023) 'Brief history of IMO'. www.imo.org/en/About/HistoryOfIMO/Pages/Default.aspx

ITF (2023a) 'Flag of convenience'. www.itfglobal.org/en/sector/seafarers/flags-of-convenience

ITF (2023b) 'Wages'. www.itfseafarers.org/en/your-rights/wages

Lane, A.D., Obando-Rojas, B., and Wu, B. (2002) 'Crewing the international merchant fleet'. In T. Lane (ed.), *Crewing the international merchant fleet*. Redhill, London: Lloyd's Register-Fairplay.

Lillie, N. (2004) 'Global collective bargaining on flag of convenience shipping'. *British Journal of Industrial Relations*, 42(1): 47–67.

Maritime and Coastguard Agency (2022) 'Foreign flagged ships detained in the UK during March 2022 under Paris MOU'. *Gov.uk*, 14 March. www.gov.uk/government/news/foreign-flagged-ships-detained-in-the-uk-during-march-2022-under-paris-mou#:~:text=The%20Maritime%20and%20Coastguard%20Agency,State%20Control%20(PSC)%20inspection.&text=During%20March%2C%20there%20were%20five,vessel%20in%20a%20UK%20port

Nautilus (2022) 'MPs express concerns as Seafarers' Wages Bill moves through Parliament'. www.nautilusint.org/en/news-insight/news/mps-express-concerns-as-seafarers-wages-bill-moves-through-parliament/

Peck, J., Theodore, N., and Ward, K. (2005) 'Constructing markets for temporary labour: employment liberalization and the internationalization of the staffing industry'. *Global Networks*, 5(1): 3–26.

RMT (2022) 'P&O sackings'. www.rmt.org.uk/news/pando-sackings/

Roberts, S.E. (2003) 'Work-related mortality among British seafarers employed in flags of convenience shipping, 1976–95'. *International Maritime Health*, 54(1–4): 7–25.

Sampson, H., and Ellis, N. (2019) 'Seafarers' mental health and wellbeing'. Cardiff: Cardiff University. https://iosh.com/media/6306/seafarers-mental-health-wellbeing-full-report.pdf

Sampson, H., Ellis, N., Acejo, I., Turgo, N., and Tang, L. (2018) 'The working and living conditions of seafarers on cargo ships in the period 2011–2016'. Cardiff: Seafarers International Research Centre (SIRC).

Thomas, M., Sampson, H., and Zhao, M. (2003) 'Finding a balance: companies, seafarers and family life'. *Maritime Policy & Management*, 30(1): 59–76.

Trades Union Congress (2023) 'Guide to collective bargaining'. *TUC*. www.tuc.org.uk/workplace-guidance/organising-and-bargaining/collective-bargaining#:~:text=Collective%20bargaining%20is%20the%20official,on%20the%20scope%20of%20negotiations

UNCTAD (2018) 'Review of maritime transport 2018'. *UNCTAD*. https://unctad.org/webflyer/review-maritime-transport-2018#:~:text=Maritime%20transport%20is%20the%20backbone,upswing%20in%20the%20world%20economy

Walters, D., and Bailey, N. (2013) *Lives in peril: profit or safety in the global maritime industry?* Basingstoke: Springer.

Wethal, U. (2017) 'Workplace regimes in Sino-Mozambican construction projects: resentment and tension in a divided workplace'. *Journal of Contemporary African Studies*, 35(3): 383–403.

chapter 18

Global Relations and Workers at the Border

María E. López

Introduction: Global Workers at the Border

Every year, millions of people make the difficult decision to leave their homes and travel to another country for safety (refugees and asylum seekers) or to better their lives (economic migrants). At some point, those people will have to cross a border. Border crossings can be fraught with danger. People can be held at borders for long periods of time while their papers are checked, and decisions made on whether they can enter the country or not. All around the globe there are also **border corridors** – these are routes created by a large flux of people who travel a specific route to enter another country. For some people, being 'at the border' or living on a border corridor is perilous – they have left their homes but not yet reached their destination – and people at the border are particularly vulnerable. Some will arrive at a border with very little (in terms of money and assets) and are desperate to find work and ways of making a living for food and accommodation.

In many parts of the world, borders and border corridors are spaces where people work. In 1965, for example, the Border Industrialisation Program (BIP) was set up at the US–Mexico border, with the aim of creating tariff-free and duty-free goods, used for exporting. The Program helped create lots of factories, known as **maquiladoras,** where cheap goods are produced and workers are paid very low wages. Today, there are 'over 3,000 factories' that provide employment for over one million local people and import more than '$51 billion in supplies into Mexico' (Howard, 2004: 333). Most of these factories are set up with foreign capital in Mexican border cities, such as Tijuana, Mexicali, Ciudad Juárez, Reynosa, and Nogales.

Since the 1990s, many maquiladoras in Mexico have been criticised for substandard working conditions and excessively long work weeks (up to 75 hours, without overtime compensation), as well as for contributing to environmental pollution.

DOI: 10.4324/9781003314769-23

Institutional neglect to the factory workers was obvious during the COVID-19 pandemic, where in 2020 business lobbyists related to the maquiladoras pressured the Mexican president to relax the lockdown so that the country did not drop in productivity. In a letter, the National Council of the Maquiladora and Export Manufacturing Industry (INDEX) expressed to President López Obrador its deep worry at the forced closure of its companies. At the beginning of the health crisis, only 64 of the 180 maquiladora companies in the Chihuahua region suspended their activities, leaving 180,000 of the 300,000 workers without pay (Padilla Delgado, 2022). Many workers were obliged to falsify resignation letters or return to work, despite proper health and safety measures put in place. Workers who were willing to work still lost up to half of their salaries during pandemic closures, as well as food vouchers or punctuality and productivity bonuses (López, 2020).

In May 2021, at the peak of the pandemic, President López Obrador announced a plan to ease restrictions and return to a 'new normality' (López Díaz, 2020). The plan allowed for the resumption of certain non-essential business activities, including within the maquiladoras. On the one hand, the Mexican government recommended complying with social distancing, hygiene regulations, and voluntary isolation. On the other hand, the government set reactivating the economy as a priority, leaving factory workers facing an important dilemma: isolating themselves at home without being paid, or going to work at the risk of losing their lives. Most maquiladora workers could not afford to isolate themselves without being paid, so they returned to the maquiladoras.

Border corridors in the newly industrialised economies in Latin America and Asia are attractive to foreign investment. There is a constant flow of **migrant labour supply** – people who are desperate for work and willing to sell their labour 'on the cheap'. In such situations, border corridors become global hotspots, exploited by transnational corporations who rely on this **cheap labour** in outsourcing their low-cost production (Gereffi, 2005). Global markets make use of border corridors – the so-called competitive strategies in globalised production centres depend on the smooth flow of large-scale labour migration.

This chapter examines how work 'at the border' is driven by the market-oriented economic approach, neoliberalism, which drives cheap production. Free markets, and the multinational organisations that operate within them, are often celebrated as bringing prosperity to people's lives, and organisations will always present themselves as supporters of equality and freedom for all. But, as this chapter shows, the reality for workers 'at the border' is that neoliberalism creates spaces where poor working environments are manifest. Borders and border corridors are spaces where 'citizens' have few or no rights and people are exploited for their cheap labour. The free market and the organisations that operate within it care little about people's access to education, their legal rights, or access to medical and healthcare services. On the contrary, workers 'at the border' are chosen precisely because they can feed the economic model without disruption or hindrance to production.

This chapter addresses how **neoliberal ideology** both exacerbates the dynamics of violence against vulnerable social groups in conflict border corridors and limits access to resources, including an appropriate salary and security provision, for

María E. López

the working, migrant, and poor populations. It begins with a brief discussion on bordering, capitalism, and neoliberalism. Next, it addresses how neoliberalism in particular manifests itself in the specific context of the **US–Mexico border**, compounded by US political and economic interests. It then explains how this ideology deprives workers in manufacturing factories (maquiladoras) of living salaries and other rights at work. Finally, the chapter explains how this situation impacts the well-being of poor and working women, limiting their chances of breaking the cycle of inequality and marginality from which they often flee, and ends with a case study of women who, looking for work, 'die' (or 'disappear') at the border.

Bordering and Neoliberalism

In their book *Bordering* (2019), Yuval-Davis et al. say that bordering not only refers to the processes linked to the movement of people between and within territories, but also to practices of control and containment in border crossings (Yuval-Davis et al., 2019). Often, we think about a country's border as one that encircles its territory, but in fact borders are much more fluid. For example, there are 'US border checks taking place in Canadian airports and British ones in Eurostar terminals in continental Europe' (Yuval-Davis et al., 2019: 1). Borders are effectively spread all around the globe. At present, border processes and practices between rich and poor countries occur, in a way which benefits capitalism. In a neoliberal system, borders operate to support the means of global production and operation of profit.

Sociological research on the origins and functions of borders shows that the appearances and meanings of territorial borders have varied throughout history. In premodern times, borders separated territories for defensive and commercial reasons (Popescu, 2012). Modern borders developed when territorial law started to delimit the sovereignty of spatial territories, resulting from colonialism, invasions, and wars, many of which continue to this day (consider, for example, the expansion of NATO territory, or the Russian invasion of Ukraine in 2022, and the ongoing and consequential war over territory). However, most modern borders are sustained by cultural, social, and economic activities, which determine who belongs and who does not (Yuval-Davies et al., 2019: 7).

Modern borders are intrinsically linked to **imperialism** and imperialist projects that favour the interests of rich and powerful countries at the expense of less wealthy countries (Walia, 2014). Wealthier nations not only pick and choose who they want to enter, but draw on migrants as a form of cheap labour supply, reaping the benefits of productivity in the pursuit of becoming wealthier nations. The epitome of capitalist ideology is perhaps the 'American Dream', the idea that anyone can achieve anything if they work hard. But, in economies where jobs are scarce or do not pay, people look overseas to improve their life chances. Set against this background, markets fluctuate around the globe, and the neoliberal ideology destroys local economies without creating alternative systems, driving thousands of people from areas of low or no economic growth to areas and countries with developed economies. They arrive in borders often with no safe guarantee of crossing over. At a time of increased global mobility and widespread diversification, border practices become intensified, controlling who does and does not belong. Different control mechanisms seep into everyday life, impacting not only the rights of people who move across territorial lines but also those who reside within state border regions. In doing so, bordering delineates the boundaries of belonging and creates multiple layers of 'us' and 'them'.

Many government-states support the interests of global business that speculate with natural resources, such as mining, fishing, and commercial agriculture, as well as the cultivation and smuggling of illegal substances, such as opium/poppies, firearms, and people (Paley, 2014: 16). Entire populations become targets for criminal gangs, which act as corporate lobbies in search of financial gain. Here, the government-state actively represses political dissidents and competitors and protects armed groups hired by criminal organisations and businesspeople to drive entire populations from their homes (Paley, 2014: 16). Left unattended, these groups use their bodies and their physical capacities to obtain protection and ensure their subsistence. Through their journey across Mexico, for example, migrants use the term *cuerpomátic* to refer to the use of the body (human flesh) as a credit card to 'buy' security, protection for companions, or a more comfortable train journey (Martínez, 2018: 89).

This idea legitimises the identification of undocumented immigrants and cheap labour workers as common enemies to be beaten up, vilified, and objectified. The Mexico government facilitates their mistreatment by minimising the suffering of these groups and neglecting them. The neoliberal and violent system is particularly harsh with poor and undocumented working women. This is because cheap female labour wrests women control of their bodies from women, obscures their identities, minimises their problems, and makes their political status invisible (Alemán, 2022), as this chapter explores using the scenario of the US–Mexico border.

Capitalism and Legitimising Cheap Labour at the Border

At the US–Mexico border, the authorities use vulnerable individuals as cheap labour. They present this as legitimate, by seemingly helping people in need of work and fulfilling a labour shortage for factory production. This simplistic narrative tries to minimise and silence the problems and needs of these groups, revealing structural and long-term problems in the region derived mainly, but not solely, from government agreements with the US.

Neoliberalism exacerbates the dynamics of violence and social exclusion against workers in this area. Neoliberalism and its political arm, capitalism, merge at the Mexican border in a form of government that acts in strict compliance with the mercantile logic imposed by rich countries on 'those considered Third World' (Valencia, 2010: 34). Mexican academic Valencia (2010) refers to '**gore capitalism**' as a specific form of government that turns the nation-state into a nation-market, legitimising the use of human capital for lucrative purposes. Moreover, gore capitalism subordinates the safety and well-being of vulnerable groups (factory workers and undocumented migrants included) to the logics of the global market (Valencia, 2010: 32).

María E. López

The market logic in this border corridor follows the agreements reached in the North American Free Trade Agreement (NAFTA), which was signed in 1994 by Canada, Mexico, and the US. The NAFTA trade bloc was meant to remove or reduce the barriers to trade and investment among the three members, aiming to encourage the respective economies to achieve a greater degree of integration and competitiveness in the face of international competition, with China at the forefront. Moreover, this agreement sought to stimulate new business opportunities and initiatives and achieve the efficient reallocation of production factors. The treaty aimed to ensure that trade liberalisation exclusively benefited companies that produced in the members' territories, preventing third parties from introducing their products. Mexico, the US, and Canada were intended to become more competitive in regulating and trading supply chain production, manufacturing, electronics, and consumer products in the global market.

Most economic analyses indicate that, while NAFTA was beneficial to the US economy and the average US citizen, it severely reduced economic growth in both the short and long term in Mexico. This is because the agreement legitimised the use of workers and residents, but also people in transit, as cheap labour in the manufacturing factories, set up with foreign capital in Mexico.

When former President Donald Trump took office in January 2017, he tried to replace NAFTA with the US–Mexico–Canada Agreement (USMCA). During renegotiations of the treaty, the (then) Mexican President Enrique Peña Nieto challenged President Trump's claim to continue building the 'wall' that separated Mexico and the US. For Mexico the wall was a US internal matter, while for Trump it was a necessary measure to control and contain undocumented migrants. Trump continued to prioritise the securitisation and militarisation of the US–Mexico border with the construction of this wall, which turned Mexico into a major waiting room for thousands of asylum seekers, who were separated from their families and deprived of their fundamental rights. Many people got stuck in border cities waiting to get their passes to cross. While waiting, they started working in the factories to provide for themselves.

In December 2020, the US, Mexico, and Canada finally signed a USMCA 'Protocol of Amendment' (NAFTA 2.0), which is in place today. The USMCA includes major changes to the trading, supply chain production, and manufacturing of vehicles; new policies on labour and environmental standards and intellectual property protection; and some provisions on digital commerce. Regarding labour rights, the USMCA lowers the threshold at which unfair labour practice complaints can be filed and improves the procedures for investigating those complaints and resolving formal disputes (Corvaglia, 2021). This agreement preserves policies of control and containment of people in transit at the border, impacting issues such as employment, the environment, and economic growth in Mexico.

This explains how undocumented migrants are subject to a neoliberal ideology that racialises communities and legitimises the control and use of bodies in all spheres of life, including work. Extortion, disappearances, and deaths of the poorest and undocumented are rarely reported, investigated, or punished (Human Rights Watch, 2021). In this way, individuals are neglected through legal-administrative devices that leave most cases unpunished. A governance with no gender perspective in the border exposes female poor, female workers, and female migrants to high levels of a type of violence and marginalisation. For example, the lack of institutional support and networks at the US–Mexico border forces many women in transit, and others, to join a precarious labour market in which their lives are in danger. Such is the case with hundreds of Central American migrant women who are forced to join the sex industry (see Chapter 7, 'Migrant Sex Work and Survival Sex', by Santos). Their value in this business depends on their age: the younger the women, the higher their value (Martínez, 2018: 107). When they stop providing benefits to the club or brothel owners, these women are extorted and disappeared, with impunity for the perpetrators.

Gender Exploitation at the US–Mexico Border

Women do some of the lowest paid and least rewarding jobs in the factories. They report enduring humiliating policies and practices that make them feel disposable in a corrosive system. From the start, the maquiladora industry attracts a multitude of 'peasant families' in search of jobs that would allow them to send money back home. Single women also come in large numbers, hoping that the industry would allow them to create a new lifestyle away from the circles of violence and precariousness in which they may have lived (Williams, 2005). They unknowingly arrived at a ground zero of labour exploitation protected by the Mexican government-state. Moreover, many women doing maquila work also carry the weight of being heads of household with children to care for, as most males are unemployed or underemployed. However, most employees are single women, between 17 and 25 years old, without children, with at least six years of formal education and availability for morning and night shifts. Working in sectors like clothing and electronics production, to get the job, they must fit strict selection criteria, passing one or more manual dexterity tests and a pregnancy test (Fernández Kelly, 2007). Woman workers in the factories must carry out manual activities that require precision, as well as patience and submission to the authority at the factory. In this regard, some employers favour young single women without work experience and with very few economic resources, as they are more willing to accept low salaries and strict factory rules. This happens because women workers offer the necessary flexibility required to adapt to a fiercely competitive market.

The main industrial sectors of the maquiladoras at the US–Mexico border are electronics and clothing. The electronics sector is a relatively stable sector with very strict delivery dates and selective employment practices. Most employees are single women, between 17 and 25 years old, without children, with at least six years of formal education and availability for morning and night shifts. To get the job, they must pass one or more manual dexterity tests and a pregnancy test (Fernández Kelly, 2007).

The garment sector, on the other hand, is more precarious due to intense competition, combined with relatively low capital investment per plant. Consequently, female workers have a weaker position in the local garment labour market than those hired in electronics. The average age of female workers in this sector is 26

María E. López

years old (compared to 20 for female workers in the electrical/electronics industry); many are single mothers, with this job often being the only means of support for their children (Fernández Kelly, 2007).

At present, women workers in the factories work 48 hours per week in a day shift, 42 hours in a night shift, and 45 hours in a day-and-night combined shift (Mexico Manufacturing News and Blog, 2018). Despite working long hours performing strenuous and risky work, the average salary for an assembler in a Mexico manufacturing operation is $2.60 an hour, equalling an average daily salary of $20. Even low salaries are subject to productivity levels (Mexico Manufacturing News and Blog, 2018).

Williams's (2005) research found that female workers were obligated to submit to routine urine tests and monitoring of their menstrual cycles and sexual activity, enabling the factories to avoid employing pregnant women. With the implicit consent of the authorities, the stress generated to maintain the high level of productivity required causes headaches, digestive problems, joint pain, and other symptoms of exhaustion among female employees. Job insecurity in factories forces women to endure long working hours without permission to drink water or rest. Workers have restricted access to social security and other benefits. In addition, only 3 per cent of female employees work over the age of 50. Most lose their jobs at the age of 45 – the age when the company detects a drop in productivity among employees (Vega, 2019). Many denounce being fired 'for uselessness' when suffering from one of the most common joint ailments among this group: 'trigger finger'. This is an inflammation in the tendon of the thumb that makes movement difficult and reduces the strength of the hand (Arriola, 2007). These employees must leave their posts once they are no longer useful to the system.

Institutional neglect of the maquiladora women workers is a continuation of the logics and processes impacting the lives of other vulnerable groups in the border. The Mexican government's main aim of being competitive in the global market shows how the neoliberal ideology operates within the framework of a powerful production system that reduces women's access to security, health systems, and good living standards.

Case Study

Disappearing Workers at the US–Mexico Border

The US–Mexico border corridor is one of the most dangerous spots in the world, where thousands of people endure the systematic violation of their rights (Black and Viales Mora, 2021). For thousands of migrants and people in transit, this border represents an illusory and remote space related to the idea of access to better-paid work and a free life, when in reality it is a securitised space governed by mechanisms of exploitation, surveillance, and control. Moreover, many people at the US–Mexico border have died or 'disappeared'.

Thousands of people travel to find work in the US, to provide a better life for themselves and their families, yet get stuck at the US–Mexico border waiting for their papers to be stamped. Most of them come from Central America, Haiti, and Cuba, with women, unaccompanied children, and LGBTIQ+ people being the most vulnerable to the various dangers in the area (Cortés, 2018). Women and children can be targeted by criminals and criminal gangs, subjected to sexual abuse and rape. Members of LGB-TIQ+ communities are subjected to forms of hatred and have no authority to report to.

In this context, Celia, a 30-year-old Cuban woman, is travelling from Cuba to the US where she has family but finds herself stuck at the US–Mexico border while her papers are being checked. Celia has little money and is offered cash for sex, but refuses. She is continually sexually harassed by men who control the border and must find a way of working at the border to survive. A few weeks later, Celia is reported missing. Celia is one of almost 3,000 undocumented migrants to have been reported dead or disappeared at the US–Mexico border between 2014 and 2020 (IOM, 2022). The killings and disappearances of people in transit, like Celia, happen due to causes related to the lack of shelter, food, and water in impenetrable terrain, such as the Sonoran Desert in the northwest of Mexico, and mighty rivers, such as the Rio Grande (known in Mexico as the Río Bravo). There are also accidents related to freight trains (in which migrants have hidden), falls off the wall that separates Mexico and the US, and the criminal activity of organisations. Migrants also face armed groups linked to organised crime that compete for control of the border area, as well as face immigration guards that try to take advantage of the migrants. Moreover, alleged human rights violations committed by state forces are reported in the context of institutional abandonment of the most disadvantaged – some seeking asylum report being kidnapped and then left kilometres away from where their court hearings are taking place (Human Rights Watch, 2020). There are also other precarious and violent men, some of whom allegedly work for the State. Life is extremely complex for residents, who are on permanent alert to various types of violence everywhere at all times, including in their (transient) workplaces.

The institutional abandonment of people at the US–Mexico border is arguably the result of successive US governments and their imperialist approach towards Latin America. For example, during his presidential campaign, former US President Donald Trump promised to deport up to three million undocumented Latin American immigrants, most of them Mexican, with criminal records, to their countries of origin. Trump adhered to the imperialist and xenophobic discourse of his predecessors (see Chapter 16, 'Xenophobia and the Migrant Labour Force', by Duvenage). Furthermore, during the nearly eight years of President Barack Obama's administration, more than three million undocumented immigrants were deported to their countries of origin, regardless of their new living conditions or who they left behind in the US (Harrington, 2017).

Trump presented the US–Mexico border as a focus for criminals and terrorists and a gateway for illegal people and substances (Salama, 2017). During his 2020 presidential campaign, he floated the idea of continuing the wall from Tijuana to Arizona and New Mexico, without paying attention to upholding international human rights treaties. US President Joe Biden (who assumed office in 2021) did not relax the immigration control policy on the US–Mexico border, forcing Mexico to maintain an armed military and police machinery under the Ministry of National Defence (SEDENA). In 2022, the militarisation of the border had an irreparable humanitarian cost for people in transit, including insecurity, corruption, and loss of rights (Basok and Rojas Wiesner, 2018; Human Rights Watch, 2021).

María E. López

Conclusion

This chapter examined workers at the border and in border corridors, and showed how, through neoliberalism, global markets require forms of cheap global labour, encouraging and creating maquiladora factories. It showed that these are places of exploitation for workers, where people receive low pay, with poor working conditions, and where there is a systematic abuse of human rights.

The chapter revealed how rich countries benefit from the growing flow of migrant and vulnerable populations in complex settings, such as border corridors, with precarious labour arrangements that exacerbate dynamics of violence, death, and marginalisation. Capitalism requires an intensive and highly productive labour model, but this impacts on the well-being of individuals, limiting the security provision and human rights protection in conflict-heavy border corridors. Neoliberalism favours a system of production that treats workers, many of whom are migrants or people in transit, as a uniform gendered and racialised mass, and whose bodies are treated as cheap labour.

Based on the conceptual framework of neoliberalism, this chapter used the US–Mexico border as a case study. This example shows how, in this space, the neoliberal ideology converges with other issues specific to this border area, such as the crisis of violence and security provision related to organised crime, the migratory crisis, poverty, and corruption within the framework of a **chauvinist ideology** that minimises the role of women in society and the problems that affect them. Finally, the chapter reviewed some of the mechanisms by which women workers in the assembly factories (maquiladoras) are exploited, sexually harassed, and subjected to cycles of violence from which they try to flee.

STUDENT ACTIVITY

This chapter explores how neoliberalism encourages the use of cheap labour at the border, drawing on workers from largely vulnerable groups, including poor and undocumented migrants.

Using information from this chapter and your own internet research, report on the following:

1. The inequalities and violations of human rights in the US–Mexico border corridor.
2. The forms of institutional violence against poor and marginal groups (through impunity and profit-seeking).
3. How women working in border corridors are sexually harassed or violently attacked. Explain how this happens and why.

Practice Questions

1. Which factors drive cheap labour in border corridors, especially economic factors?

2. Why is the process to achieve legal status so restricted for poor migrants?
3. Explain why factory workers, particularly women, are mistreated as cheap labour.
4. Focusing on the US–Mexico border case study, explain how misogyny, classism, and xenophobia operate in the labour environment through politics and policies of control and containment.

Key Terms

Border corridors
borders are spaces policed by nation states and surround the territory of those nations; once geographical boundaries, they can now be found in many places where people attempt to cross over. Border corridors run towards border routes and can be precarious and volatile environments.

Chauvinist ideology
a set of ideas based on unreasonable assumptions that one's own group is more virtuous and superior to others.

Cheap labour
offered by someone who is working hard for relatively little salary and under poor conditions.

Gore capitalism
conceived by the Mexican philosopher Sayak Valencia (2010), the notion of 'gore capitalism' offers an analysis of violence as the new commodity of today's hyper-consumerist stage of capitalism at the US–Mexico border.

Imperialism
extending a country's power or influence via colonisation or military means. Neo-imperialism represents domination through new and more modern approaches, such as economic power and cultural influence.

Maquiladoras
refers to maquiladora factories, established with foreign funding, involving the export of manufactured products to the company's country of origin; these factories benefit from duty-free and tariff-free imports of raw materials, machinery, and equipment, to be used in the manufacturing process.

Migrant labour supply
employment sourced from foreign workers; migrant labourers are usually cheap, often because they are vulnerable, desperate for work, and in need of a source of income.

Neoliberal Ideology
a set of ideas that believes in global market-oriented competition of private companies and a reduction of state intervention, such as trade restrictions, as well as a belief in the deregulation of labour and financial markets.

US–Mexico border
the border between Mexico and the US, extending from the Pacific Ocean in the west to the Gulf of Mexico in the east and crossing a variety of terrains, ranging from urban areas to deserts.

References

Alemán, M. (2022) Maquiladoras, human rights, and the impact of globalization on the US-Mexico border. *Foreign Affairs Review*, 16 June. Accessed 11 March 2023 from https://jhufar.com/2022/06/16/maquiladoras-human-rights-and-the-impact-of-globalization-on-the-us-mexico-border/

Arriola, E.R. (2007). Sociocultural consequences of free trade: accountability for murder in the maquiladoras: linking corporate indifference to gender violence at the US-Mexico border'. *Seattle Journal for Social Justice* 5 (Spring): 603.

Basok, T., and Rojas Wiesner, M. (2018). 'Precarious legality: regularizing Central American migrants in Mexico.' *Ethnic and Racial Studies*, 41(7): 1274–1293.

Black, J., and Viales Mora, E. (2021) '"If not for pure necessity." Deaths and disappearances on migration journeys in North and Central America'. Accessed 11 March 2023 from https://missingmigrants.iom.int/sites/g/files/tmzbdl601/files/publication/file/MMP%20LAC%20data%20briefing%20ES.pdf

Cortés, A. (2018) 'Violencia de género y frontera: migrantes centroamericanas en México hacia los EEUU'. *European Review of Latin American and Caribbean Studies*, 105: 39–60.

Corvaglia, M.A. (2021) 'Labour rights protection and its enforcement under the USMCA: insights from a comparative legal analysis'. *World Trade Review*, 20(5): 648–667. Accessed 11 March 2023 from https://doi.org/10.1017/S1474745621000239

Fernández Kelly, P. (2007) 'The "Maquila" women'. *North American Congress on Latin America (NACLA)*, 25 September. Accessed 11 March 2023 from https://nacla.org/article/%27maquila%27-women

Gereffi, G. (2005) 'The global economy: organization, governance and development'. In N.J. Smelser and R. Swedberg (eds), *The handbook of economic sociology*. Princeton, NJ: Princeton University Press, pp. 160–182.

Giroux, H.A. (2014) 'Neoliberalism and the machinery of disposability'. *Truthout*, 8 April. Accessed 11 March 2023 from https://truthout.org/articles/neoliberalism-and-the-machinery-of-disposability/

Harrington, R. (2017) 'Obama deported 3 million immigrants during his presidency – here's how Trump's new immigration order compares'. *Business Insider,* 22 February. Accessed 11 March 2023 from www.businessinsider.nl/whats-the-difference-between-trump-obama-immigration-orders-2017-2/

Howard, R. (2004) *Understanding the global economy*. Santa Barbara, CA: Peace Education Books.

Human Rights Watch (2020) 'Mexico events 2019'. *Human Rights Watch*. Accessed 11 March 2023 from www.hrw.org/es/world-report/2020/country-chapters/336494

Human Rights Watch (2021) 'Mexico events 2020'. Accessed 11 March 2023 from www.hrw.org/world-report/2021/country-chapters/mexico

International Organization for Migration (2022) 'Missing Migrants Project'. Accessed 11 March 2023 from https://missingmigrants.iom.int/

López, M.A. (2020) 'Empleados acusan que los obligan a trabajar pese a muertes por COVID en maquiladoras de Chihuahua'. *Animal Político*, 18 May.

López Díaz, M. (2020) 'The lives of Mexico's maquiladora workers are being put at risk by lax COVID-19 rules and the demands of international trade'. *LSE Latin America and Caribbean Blog*, 25 May. Accessed 11 March 2023 from https://blogs.lse.ac.uk/latamcaribbean/2020/05/25/the-lives-of-mexicos-maquiladora-workers-are-being-put-at-risk-by-lax-covid-19-rules-and-the-demands-of-international-trade/

Martínez, O. (2018) *Los migrantes que no importan*. La Rioja: Pepitas de Calabaza.

Mbembe, A. (2003) 'Necropolitics'. *Public Culture*, 15(1): 11–40.

Mbembe, A., and Corcoran, S. (2019) *Necropolitics*. London: Duke University Press.

Mexico Manufacturing News and Blog (2018) 'A workweek in Mexico: shifts, costs and labor in maquiladoras'. *Co-production International*, 12 November. Accessed 11 March 2023 from www.co-production.net/mexico-manufacturing-news/workweek-in-mexico.html

Mize, R.L. (2008) 'Interrogating race, class, gender and capitalism along the US–Mexico border: neoliberal nativism and maquila modes of production'. *Race, Gender & Class*, 15(1–2): 134–155.

Padilla Delgado, H.A. (2022) 'Ciudad Juárez y los desafíos de la gobernanza: ciudad, frontera, pandemia y flujos migratorios 2019–2021'. *Revista Cuestión Urbana*, 6(11, June).

Paley, D.P. (2014) *Drug war capitalism*. Oakland, CA: AK Press.

Popescu, G. (2012) *Bordering and ordering the twenty-first century: understanding borders*. Lanham, MD: Rowman & Littlefield Publishers.

Roy, A. (2014) *Capitalism: a ghost story*. Chicago, IL: Haymarket Books.

Salama, V. (2017) 'Trump to Mexico: take care of "bad hombres" or US might'. *Associated Press*, 2 February. Accessed 11 March 2023 from https://apnews.com/article/0b3f5db59b2e4aa78cdbbf008f27fb49

Valencia, S. (2010) *Capitalismo gore*. Barcelona: Melusina.

Vega, A. (2019) 'Maquiladoras trabajan largas jornadas, padecen malestares físicos y falta de prestaciones'. *Animal Político*, 4 June. Accessed 11 March 2023 from www.animalpolitico.com/2019/06/maquiladoras-trabajan-largas-jornadas-padecen-malestares-fisicos-y-falta-de-prestaciones/

Walia, H. (2014) *Undoing border imperialism*. Oakland: AK Press.

Williams, N. (2005) 'Pre-hire pregnancy screening in Mexico's maquiladoras: is it discrimination?' *Duke Journal of Gender Law & Policy*, 12: 131–151. Accessed 11 March 2023 from https://scholarship.law.duke.edu/djglp/vol12/iss1/6

Yuval-Davis, N., Wemyss, G., and Cassidy, K. (2019) *Bordering*. Hoboken, NJ: John Wiley & Sons.

part 6

The Future of Work

chapter 19

Climate Change and Work

Melahat Sahin-Dikmen

Introduction

Climate change has entered public discourse in a way that could not have been imagined only a few years ago, with millions of young people and activists around the world taking to the streets to call for action. Much of the popular attention falls on its environmental consequences, such as rising temperatures, biodiversity loss, and extreme weather events. The effects of climate change on sectors such as agriculture are unsurprising, but the fact is that climate change has implications for work and organisations in all sectors of the economy. These consequences have only recently begun to be appreciated and, so far, have received little attention within the sociology of work (Davidson, 2022).

Climate change and work are inextricably connected because economic activities are the primary source of greenhouse gas emissions driving the climate emergency. Work, in all its forms, is at the heart of this crisis because tackling climate change depends on changing how goods and services are produced and the economy is organised, a shift often described as the transition to a green or sustainable society. The overarching question raised for the sociology of work is how the world of work is changing as we adapt to a changing climate and what the transition to a green economy means for working lives.

This chapter draws on evidence from across the social sciences and policy research to trace the main contours of the transformation under way and seeks to illuminate the socially embedded nature of this complex and globally uneven process. The chapter begins by underscoring the scientific evidence connecting work activities and climate change. It then briefly outlines the United Nation's (UN) climate change and sustainability vision, because this global framework informs mainstream policies and plans for greening the world of work. This approach is

DOI: 10.4324/9781003314769-25

then contrasted with critical sociological perspectives to emphasise the role of social, economic, and political structures and relations in the emergence and tackling of the climate crisis. Subsequent sections map out the main ways in which work is changing in response to climate change, focusing on four areas: the disappearance of work in fossil fuel industries due to the transition to renewable energy, implications for work skills and processes, working and employment conditions in green jobs, and the embedding of sustainability in occupational cultures.

The chapter illustrates how the social relations and inequalities characterising work in global capitalism play out in the transition to a green economy and how different institutions and organisations shape this process. It is argued that the dominant green economy policies prioritise emission reductions through technology adoption without addressing the social aspects of work. In contrast to the overwhelmingly positive narrative surrounding green jobs, the transition to a sustainable world of work is far from smooth (Lipsig-Mumme and McBride, 2015). Building on Clarke et al. (2020; 2024), green technology initiatives are shown to co-exist with poor working and employment conditions and disparities by race and gender in terms of vulnerability to climate change impacts and access to green jobs. The depth and breadth of sustainable work initiatives, such as alterations to work skills and processes, are limited by the continuing prioritisation of economic gains. At the same time, the transformation of work is a contested process; trade unions, labour organisations, and occupational institutions seek to influence policy to address the effects on working lives and challenge the neglect of the social dimension of the transition.

Connecting Climate Change and Work

Climate change describes long-term changes in temperature, precipitation, and weather patterns. Scientific evidence gathered by the International Panel on Climate Change (IPCC) shows that, since the Industrial Revolution, these changes have been driven by increases in greenhouse gas emissions in the atmosphere, particularly carbon dioxide (CO_2): 'Human activities, principally through emissions of greenhouse gases, have unequivocally caused global warming, with global surface temperature reaching 1.1°C above 1850–1900 in 2011–2012' (IPCC, 2023: 4).

Work and related activities rely on energy from fossil fuels such as coal, gas, and oil. Sites of work are, therefore, the primary source of greenhouse gas emissions, with all sectors of the economy contributing; over 73.2 per cent of emissions are due to energy use in industry, buildings, and transport, followed by 18.4 per cent from agriculture, forestry, and land use, 5.2 per cent from direct industry processes such as cement production, and 3.2 percent from waste (Ritchie et al., 2020). Since the 1950s, extraction of fossil fuels has increased exponentially. The consequences include rising sea levels, as much of the extra heat is absorbed by oceans, and an increase in extreme weather events such as floods, wildfires, and heatwaves. The dramatic intensification of disruption to ecosystems and biodiversity, destruction of forests, and air, soil, and water pollution poses severe risks to human societies (IPCC, 2023).

Melahat Sahin-Dikmen

These changes affect workers directly – for instance, by making work unsafe through extreme heat, by rendering conditions of work hazardous, or by destroying livelihoods, for example, in agriculture. The effects also stem from climate policies. Emission reduction and sustainable economy policies are led by the United Nations through a framework that informs action at all levels, from global to organisational.

Greening Work to Tackle Climate Change – Global Policy Response

The global strategy for reducing greenhouse gas emissions is guided by the **United Nations Framework Convention on Climate Change**. The Parties to the Convention, meaning the countries that ratified it, meet annually to ensure the implementation of the targets agreed. These gatherings are known as the Conference of the Parties, or COP for short. The Paris Agreement, a key milestone in intergovernmental negotiations and ratified by 196 countries at COP 21 in 2015, commits to keeping global warming below 2°C above pre-industrial levels, with the ambition to keep it to 1.5°C. The United Nations set the goal of reaching **net zero emissions** by 2050 (UNFCCC, 2023). The transition to a green economy is central to achieving this goal; the efforts to that end are guided by the United Nations Sustainable Development Goals. The term 'sustainability' was defined in the **Brundtland Report** as 'meeting the needs of the present without compromising the ability of future generations to meet their needs' (Mulligan, 2018: 15). The United Nations advocates a three-dimensional concept encompassing environmental, economic, and social sustainability. To reduce emissions, both mitigation and adaptation measures are recommended. Climate mitigation aims to prevent or reduce greenhouse gas emissions, for example, by adopting clean energy sources such as solar, hydro, wind, and bioenergy. Climate adaptation measures aim to minimise the effects of climate change, for example, investing in disaster management services and adapting industries to reduce reliance on fossil fuels. Further steps to build a **circular economy** are proposed to reduce the exploitation of finite natural resources and minimise waste (UN, 2023).

These strategies imply a restructuring of the economy and changes in all sectors, from manufacturing to farming, transport to tourism, with significant implications for work. The depth and breadth of the transformation will vary by country, sector, and occupation, but the overall landscape of the world of work is set to change dramatically. To give just a few examples, the transition to electric vehicles in the automobile industry means that the expertise needed now includes electrical, mechanical, and software engineering. Auto maintenance and service workers need to be retrained. Building the car charging infrastructure and producing, storing, and recycling batteries for electric vehicles are new areas of work calling for engineering and chemistry expertise. The increased demand for metals such as lithium for battery production impacts work in mining countries and global supply chains (IEA, 2023). In agriculture, protecting biodiversity, conserving water, and adopting crops resilient to rising heat mean alterations to farming practices, while **vertical farming** is emerging as a new area of work. Building a circular economy involves embedding waste minimisation in all stages of production, from design to end-use, in all industries from fashion to construction, which calls for a reconfiguration of the production process and new types of expertise (Ellen MacArthur Foundation, 2023).

Although implementation varies hugely, the path set out in the United Nations Sustainable Development Goals has become the mainstream narrative of the transition to a green economy. This vision then cascades down, as it is taken up by governments, local authorities, occupational and industry bodies, and business organisations. For example, all signatories of the Paris Agreement have set emission reduction targets. Governments set out plans to build a low-carbon economy at the national level. Policies are developed to address sustainability in specific industries, such as agriculture and building construction. Driven by regulation, sustainability measures are also adopted in the workplace, often articulated in **corporate social responsibility** policies of particularly large, international companies. However, these ideas' global reach does not mean they are without criticism. Evidence also suggests that the strategies proposed may not be adequate for the task.

Sociological Approaches to Climate Change and the Green Transition

In the approach led by the United Nations, technological innovation is given a central role, and governments are expected to ensure the implementation of mitigation and adaptation measures through policies and regulations. This vision has a lot in common with the idea of ecological modernisation, a perspective developed initially by Mol and Spaargaren (2020), who argued that environmental concerns are compatible with the objective of economic growth. In other words, capitalism does not pose a significant barrier to building a sustainable economy (2020: 36). In contrast to this framing of climate change as a primarily environmental and regulatory issue, critical sociological perspectives place climate change within the historical context of conflictual and unequal social, economic, and political relations. Dunlap and Brulle (2015) draw attention to the root causes of climate change and argue that there is a fundamental conflict at the heart of the relationship between humans and nature; the current mode of human existence is based on exploiting natural resources without constraint. From a Marxist perspective, Gould et al. (2008: 7) describe the capitalist economic model as a 'treadmill of production' designed to enhance profits and productivity. This, in turn, depends on more and more intense exploitation of both nature and labour, creating an endless cycle of resource extraction and environmental degradation. Critiques also argue that the more radical transition strategies that are needed to tackle the structural causes of climate change – policies such as degrowth, reduction in working hours, or the reconfiguration of the economy to include women's unpaid work at home – are excluded from a vision oriented to reforming and greening capitalism (Foster et al., 2010; Littig, 2018).

These critiques are supported by growing evidence of the failure to achieve the transformation necessary. Regarding environmental sustainability objectives,

Melahat Sahin-Dikmen

there is increasing concern that the targets for limiting temperature rises will not be met. The goal of net zero emissions is to be achieved by *balancing* the greenhouse gases released and removed from the atmosphere. Long-term climate adaptation measures are part of the plan, but technologies such as carbon capture, carbon offsetting schemes such as tree planting, and market-based measures such as **carbon emissions trading** are also heavily promoted. As emission reductions fail to materialise, the strategies promoted by the United Nations have been criticised for obscuring the urgency with which emissions must stop (Dyke et al., 2021). Another example is that large, multinational energy producers have comprehensive corporate social responsibility policies claiming commitment to reducing emissions but continue to extract fossil fuels and rely on offsetting emissions. Such practices are often criticised for **greenwashing** or dangerous domination of the climate adaptation agenda by business interests, prioritising profit over social and environmental sustainability (Rhodes, 2022; Wright and Nyberg, 2017). Evidence also suggests that the motives of growth and profit clash with environmental and social sustainability objectives. The rush to mine lithium, for example, the metal that powers the renewable energy transition, bears all the hallmarks of the exploitation of nature and labour for rapid economic gain at high environmental and social costs (Dunlap and Riquito, 2023; Kara, 2023).

Work is addressed in Sustainable Development Goal 8 (SDG8), which calls for the promotion of 'sustained, inclusive and sustainable economic growth, full and productive employment and decent work for all' (UN, 2023). The commitment to maintaining the continuity of the economic system and the priorities of 'growth' and 'productive employment' are also revealed in this definition. In this approach, economic sustainability is primarily taken for granted, and it is implied that companies must be financially viable and business-profitable. Environmental sustainability at work refers to technologies, methods, and systems designed to reduce emissions and reliance on fossil fuels – for example, installing solar panels for energy, using recycled or more sustainable raw materials, using low-energy light bulbs in offices, setting up recycling stations to reduce waste, or supporting low-carbon travel such as cycling for employees. Social sustainability at work is captured in the idea of 'decent work', a concept developed by the International Labour Organization (ILO), an agency of the United Nations. Decent work refers to jobs that pay fair wages, adhere to health and safety standards, provide secure and inclusive work, social protections, access to training and development, and recognise the right to unionisation (ILO, 2018). This is, therefore, an effort to ensure that green economy policies also improve working and employment conditions.

Analysis shows that the technology-focused and reform-oriented approach to tackling climate change also underpins efforts to green work processes and activities. While the sustainable economy narrative promises a future of green and 'decent' work that reconciles the conflict between economic, environmental, and social sustainability, in practice, the broader social structures that give rise to inequalities, poor working and employment conditions, and lack of worker representation remain unaddressed.

Climate Change and Work in 'Brown' Industries

A much-debated implication of climate policies is that phasing out fossil fuels will lead to industrial restructuring with significant consequences for work. The case of **brown jobs** is a stark example of the uneven effects of climate change on workers; some jobs will be lost while new jobs are created. By closing high-carbon and -greenhouse-gas-emitting and -polluting industries such as coal, gas, and oil extraction, job losses are expected in brown jobs, that is, jobs in mining, coal-fired power plants, and in the supply chains of energy production and transportation. The impact will vary between and within countries and will be experienced more profoundly at the regional level, as these industries are geographically concentrated. For example, in the UK, employment in offshore oil platforms is situated in Scotland. It is easy to assume that these workers can simply take up the new opportunities created, but the new, green jobs are unlikely to be in the same region or even country. Historical cases such as the closure of coal mines in many parts of the world show that the impact on workers and their communities can be devastating and long-lasting. For workers, this often means losing well-paid, secure, and unionised jobs, devaluing expertise, and undermining occupational identities (Parry, 2003; Strambo et al., 2019).

At the global level, labour organisations tried to influence the global climate action framework to consider the impact on workers. These efforts have included the principle of **just transition** in the United Nations' climate adaptation guidelines. A just transition calls for the benefits and burdens of the transition to be shared fairly between workers and employers. For example, business organisations, industry bodies, and governments are called upon to implement measures for workers losing their jobs, to enable training and access to new jobs as well as regional regeneration initiatives (Morena et al., 2020). In practice, the extent to which workers have a voice is determined by the existing institutions of industrial relations. In most countries, the arrangements are such that trade unions are excluded from policy-making and decisions in the workplace. Worker representation is also critical for shaping the phase-out policies – despite the calls to speed up the renewable energy transition (Dyke et al., 2021), the complete closure of fossil fuel industries is, currently, a long-term project for many countries, with no opportunity for employees to have a say on company strategies.

Finally, it is also unclear how workers up or down the production chain operating in the informal economy or self-employed capacity will be protected as whole industries disappear or are fundamentally transformed. An example is auto-maintenance workers, who are directly impacted by the shift to electric vehicles but do not receive much attention from policy-makers, highlighting, once again, the importance of representation structures so that those affected by climate policies are able to shape policies affecting their working lives.

A New Kind of Work – Jobs and Skills in the Green Economy

A predominantly positive policy narrative surrounds the question of what green transition means for work. It is projected that, across the world, millions of new jobs will be created (Godinho, 2022; ILO, 2018; World Economic Forum, 2023). The policy emphasis on job creation and paid work reveals that economic output and growth continue to be prized. However, the number of jobs, estimated or actual, does not tell us much about the nature, quality, or conditions of work. Evidence on work in the green economy is sparse, and, to complicate matters further, there is no consensus on the definition of green jobs. Consequently, research on green jobs raises more questions than it answers.

The United Nations Sustainable Development Goals define green jobs as 'decent jobs that contribute to preserve and restore the environment', whether in traditional industries such as construction or emerging green industries (ILO, 2018). This definition has two elements: the purpose or the output of the job and the conditions of work and employment. Regarding output, jobs that positively impact the environment would be considered green, such as renewable energy, waste management, and nature conservation. The first question is how to classify jobs whose output is green, but the production process is not (Stevis, 2013). For example, producing electric vehicles would be considered a green job, but manufacturing the batteries and recharging the cars could rely on fossil fuel energy. Further along the supply chain, mining lithium for electric vehicle batteries involves using chemicals that pollute land and water. Lithium extraction is also a water-hungry process and competes with local communities over scarce reservoirs of water. The claim that electric vehicle manufacturing is a green job is undermined when the entire supply and production chain is considered.

Second, as all sectors of the economy begin to adapt, the distinction between green jobs and jobs that are not green is becoming blurred. In many industries, climate adaptation is driven by legislation and implies alterations to materials and methods of production and the acquisition of new knowledge and skills. For instance, as outlined in the case study that follows, all building design and construction occupations must upgrade their education and training and review work processes to embed sustainability. A recent study by Valero et al. (2021) suggests that all jobs are included in measuring the green economy, classified into three categories according to changes in skill requirements. These are: (i) jobs that require entirely new and green skills (e.g. wind turbine engineers); (ii) pre-existing occupations whose skill and task profile have changed through climate adaptation (e.g. architects); and (iii) jobs that support the green economy indirectly but whose requirements have not changed that much (e.g. materials scientists). They present evidence that jobs in the UK and Europe in the first two categories require higher education and skills, with variations between countries and sectors. A similar pattern is found in the US (Consoli et al., 2016). This attention to skills is not a coincidence; the green economy narrative is accompanied by an equally positive anticipation of high-skilled jobs (World Economic Forum, 2023). Yet, defining and measuring green skills is far from easy. A challenge with statistical evidence on high-skilled jobs in the green economy is that it is impossible to unpick how requirements and work processes in any one occupation might alter. It is also difficult to establish what is meant by 'high skills', whether these are indeed 'new' skills or pre-existing high skills applied in a new, green industry.

In-depth analysis of skill changes in green and greening industries and occupations paints a more complex picture. These illustrate that green skill development takes place in the context of social relations and institutional structures. What kinds of green skills are developed depends on how work processes are organised in the workplace and across occupational divisions and what skills are valued and demanded in the labour market. Bozkurt and Stowell (2016) find that, in the UK, there is little evidence of skills being developed in the recycling industry, despite waste management being lauded as the cornerstone of a green economy. They show that resource recovery (i.e. sorting and identifying waste) does not require higher education or skills, but it is a job high in demand, as it creates outputs valued in the market. By contrast, there is little demand for repair skills as repaired goods are not valued in our consumption-oriented economy. Evidence from a recent study bears out their concerns; waste management is beset by continuing skills and labour shortages (CIWM, 2023). In the construction industry, Clarke et al. (2020) found that, in most European Union countries, the approach to green skills training for building workers is narrow because it caters to a task-based and fragmented Taylorist labour process typical of the industry (see Chapter 8, 'Managing People and Democratisation of Organisation', by Green and McNeill, for further discussion of Taylorism). Bozkurt and Stowell (2016) also argue that the same approach is adopted for green skills in countries where investment in skills development has historically been weak. These examples, therefore, also underline the importance of not taking for granted the claims of 'high-skilled' work in the green economy and call for an in-depth analysis of the approach to skill development and its outcomes.

Working and Employment Conditions in Green Jobs

The policy ambition is that green jobs, by definition, are also decent jobs (see also Parry's discussion in Chapter 1, 'Introduction'). As already defined, decent work refers to ILO labour standards and addresses working and employment conditions. The goal of ensuring 'decent work' in the green economy speaks to the poor and insecure working and employment conditions across much of the world, particularly in the Global South, and it is hugely significant as an attempt to establish minimum labour standards. However, evidence suggests that greening work can be synonymous with adopting technology to modernise work processes and systems ecologically; for example, using digital technology to monitor and reduce energy use or using recycled water in production. There is no guarantee that 'greening' strategies will involve efforts to provide 'decent' work. Adopting decent work standards can be voluntary, and monitoring their implementation is weak or non-existent. Further, existing inequalities such as gender and race can be reproduced in green jobs.

For instance, in waste management and recycling in Europe and the US, migrant workers are employed on temporary contracts for low wages, working long hours (Gregson et al., 2016; Pellow et al., 2000; Weghmann, 2017). In many countries in the Global South where waste from European countries is sent for processing,

Melahat Sahin-Dikmen

recycling is a largely informal economy where workers have no access to employment rights and protections or training (Fevrier, 2022). Cobalt, lithium, and cadmium for EV batteries are mined, for example, in Zimbabwe and Congo, in hazardous conditions, often involving child labour, women, and immigrants (Kara, 2023). In building construction, Clarke et al. (2024) show that, despite the industry being subject to significant climate adaptation policies, poor work and employment conditions, health and safety breaches, exploitation of migrant workers and the exclusion of women continue to be prevalent across the Global North and the Global South. Some high-profile cases covered in the media are also telling. For instance, electric vehicle production is a highly prized green industry, but some manufacturers (e.g. Tesla) are notoriously anti-union, just as Ford was over a century ago. Gender representation in the green economy also seems to be far from equal. A recent study by Christie-Miller and Luke (2021) examined employment in UK net zero industries. These are jobs associated with the production of renewable energy and energy-efficient products. They found that the workforce is 82 per cent male, with a 17 per cent gender pay gap (see Chapter 3, 'The Gender Pay Gap', by Velija and McDonough). Similarly, Valero et al. (2021) found that, in the UK, jobs in the newly emerging green sectors are more likely to be held by men from a white ethnic background.

A much less researched consequence of climate change relates to occupational health and safety, increasingly brought to attention by trade unions (ETUC, 2020). Many people have now experienced days when it is just too hot to work. Extremely high temperatures previously associated with countries in the Global South are now also recorded in the northern hemisphere, and yet most employees have no choice but to continue to labour, which is rarely problematised as a social issue. High temperatures lead to heat stress for all, but particularly for workers in agriculture, building construction, tourism, street cleaning, and postal services, in hot and humid factories not equipped with cooling systems, and in sectors where working from home is not an option. These are also the sectors where racial and ethnic minorities and immigrants are employed. The effects are stronger for older workers and other vulnerable groups, such as pregnant women. Some adaptation strategies, such as shifting working hours to an earlier or later time, affect work organisation. They can also exacerbate gender divisions by making it difficult for women to continue working in these industries (ETUC, 2020; ILO, 2019). Similarly, risks associated with new materials used to enhance sustainability, such as building insulation products, are unknown (Cater, 2022). Occupational health and safety legislation seems to have not caught up with the green economy. Weghmann (2020) shows that the European circular economy strategy does not address health and safety in waste management, a problem exacerbated by the extent of informal employment in the sector (Scheinberg et al., 2016). Finally, an increase in extreme weather events such as floods and wildfires means that the risk for disaster management workers is higher and includes extended exposure to excessive heat, hazardous fumes, and the psychological impact of working in challenging and stressful conditions. Yet, little, if anything, is known about the experiences of these workers.

Changing Occupational Narratives

Evidence suggests that, in addition to the impact of climate policies on jobs, work skills, and processes, the rising awareness of the climate crisis also exerts a diffused yet strong influence, reshaping occupational narratives and identities. For instance, Meilvang (2019) shows that engineers in Denmark are beginning to redefine their role as managing rainwater as a resource rather than a potential risk factor in cities. As discussed in the case study below, architects now describe achieving sustainability in the built environment as a primary goal of the profession. Indeed, all building construction professionals, such as engineers, surveyors, and planners, now embed sustainability objectives in their work. Other occupations are also reappraising their role to respond to the consequences of the climate crisis. For example, social workers support disadvantaged communities more vulnerable to climate change's impact (Appleby et al., 2017), and the nursing profession is concerned with the health implications of climate change (Kalogirou et al., 2020). In these cases, it seems that the imperative of rebalancing our relationship with nature is beginning to be embedded in occupational narratives and cultures.

Case Study

Climate Adaptation and Work in Architecture in the UK

One of the occupations already affected by climate change is architecture. This case study focuses on how work in architecture is changing. It illustrates several points raised in the chapter about skills and expertise, work organisation, and changing occupational cultures.

Greening building design and construction is of major significance to tackling climate change, as buildings are responsible for nearly 40 per cent of greenhouse gas emissions in the UK. The government aims to reach a net zero carbon economy by 2050 and has implemented specific policies to reduce building emissions. The Future Homes Standards require that, from 2025, all new homes produce 75 to 80 per cent fewer emissions, rely on renewable energy sources, and no longer connect to the gas network. Every home has to have an Energy Performance Certificate that indicates the energy efficiency standard achieved. Targets have also been set to improve existing buildings.

The new building regulations have direct consequences for work in architecture. First, architects must update their training to develop sustainable design and construction expertise. Architectural education has been reviewed for new entrants to the profession to include knowledge and understanding of environmental and social sustainability. On the ecological side, this covers knowledge of climate science, climate policy, legislation, circular economy principles, waste management and biodiversity. Social sustainability is addressed through inclusive design considering, for example, community relations and transport needs in large housing and urban developments or the impact of building materials on occupants' health. New areas of expertise are emerging, with some architects specialising in the green renovation of existing buildings or innovative environmental technologies, methods, and materials. Second, the

　　　　　　　　　　　　　　　　　　　Melahat Sahin-Dikmen

organisation of the design process is changing so that sustainability requirements are established in full detail and built into the work plan right from the beginning. This differs from a traditional approach whereby decisions regarding, for example, waste management could be made later, even after construction begins. Advanced planning also means interacting with other occupations, such as engineers and building contractors, early in the process and working more closely to ensure sustainable design plans are implemented as intended. Third, architects have proactively embraced the transition to a green built environment and committed to changing the culture of the occupation to prioritise environmental sustainability alongside the traditional objectives of design originality and financial viability.

There are, however, disparities by practice size and by sector. For architects in small practices and specialising in small residential projects such as house extensions and loft conversions, the transition to green design involves more modest changes in work tasks and processes, partly reflecting the scale of the work and partly the budgets available. By contrast, architects working in the commercial sector or on large and well-known buildings draw on more extensive and specialist expertise to reach higher sustainability standards. The meaning of green architecture, therefore, varies in terms of the standards of the building produced and the work involved. Finally, architects also disagree on what sustainability means and how to achieve it. Some call for more radical measures – for example, refusing to build high-carbon projects such as motorways and airports or refusing to design in authoritarian countries with poor labour standards.

Conclusion

It is impossible to disentangle the effects of climate change on work from the structures and relations within which both are firmly embedded. The transition to a green and sustainable world of work is shaped by policies whose aim is to reform the capitalist economic and social model. It is clear that much of the effort goes to 'greening' work in the environmental sense; work and production are being ecologically modernised. The reconfiguration of work tasks, processes, and skills is shaped by the current organisation of work, employment patterns, and labour market structures. While the dominant policy calls for 'decent' work, in reality, many characteristics of fossil fuel capitalism – such as informal employment, poor and unsafe working conditions, lack of diversity and inclusion, and limited worker representation – are reproduced in the green economy, in both the Global North and the Global South.

There is thus an urgent need for in-depth, critical analyses of the extent and the nature of the transformation under way to look beyond the policy proclamations of a bright, green future world of work. A significant gap in our understanding is the views and experiences of workers in the green transition, be it in lines of work set to disappear (e.g. oil extraction), those affected by adaptation policies (e.g. building or automobile workers), in the newly emerging green sectors (e.g. waste management), or those subject to more hazardous conditions due to climate change (e.g. the fire service). This is essential for understanding the impact on everyday working lives, for giving voice to all the different views of green and sustainable work, and for ensuring that the outcomes of the transition are fair and equitable.

STUDENT ACTIVITY

Investigating Working and Employment Conditions in the Green Economy

Choose one of waste management, building design and construction, and electric car production as an industry. Research how climate adaptation policies are impacting work, addressing the following questions:

- Outline the requirements of climate adaptation regulations.
- What kinds of changes are being implemented by organisations in the workplace?
- What are the implications for work and workers? Consider changes in knowledge, skills, and work processes.
- Do the jobs in the industry meet decent job standards as defined by the International Labour Organization?

Practice Questions

1. Explain the relationship between work activities and climate change.
2. Critically evaluate the concept of sustainability promoted by the United Nations Sustainable Development Goals.
3. What is a green job? How is work in the green economy different?
4. Why are green jobs described as 'high-skilled' jobs? Are they?
5. According to the International Labour Organization, what is a 'decent job'? Are green jobs decent jobs?

Key Terms

Brown jobs
jobs in greenhouse-gas-emitting and -polluting industries such as coal, gas, and oil extraction, mining, and coal-fired power plants.

Carbon emissions trading
an approach that involves using a market to buy and sell credits that allow individuals, companies, investors, or countries to emit a limited amount of carbon dioxide. Additional credits can be purchased to emit more; those emitting less than their allowance can sell their credits.

Circular economy
a model of production and consumption that involves reusing, recycling, repairing, refurbishing, sharing, and leasing, to use natural resources more efficiently and minimise waste.

Melahat Sahin-Dikmen

Corporate social responsibility
the idea that businesses are responsible to society and the environment and should not be driven by profits.

Greenwashing
using communication strategies or adopting practices to influence public perceptions of a company's green credentials. Greenwashing strategies create an image that obscures environmentally unsound or determinedly harmful activities.

Just transition
originating in the American labour movement, the International Labour Organization uses this term to describe a set of principles to guide the transition to an environmentally sustainable economy, the aim being to ensure that the transition is fair and inclusive, leaves no one behind, and is managed through social dialogue among all stakeholders.

Net zero emissions
when the amount of carbon added to the atmosphere is no more than the amount removed.

Vertical farming
growing crops on vertical, stacked-up tower-like structures in controlled environments, using less land, water, and energy to produce more food all year round.

Organisations

Brundtland Report
the 'Report of the World Commission on Environment and Development: Our Common Future' was published in 1987. It is a milestone for explicitly connecting the world's economic, social, and environmental challenges.

United Nations Framework Convention on Climate Change
an international environmental treaty signed in 1992 by 198 countries, to combat human-induced climate change.

United Nations Sustainable Development Goals
in 2015, the 17 goals were adopted to protect the planet, eliminate poverty, and balance economic, social, and environmental sustainability.

References

Appleby, K., Bell, K., and Boetto, H. (2017) 'Climate change adaptation: community action, disadvantaged groups and practice implications for social work'. *Australian Social Work*, 70(1): 78–91.

Bozkurt, O., and Stowell, A. (2016) 'Skills in the green economy: recycling promises in the UK e-waste management sector'. *New Technology, Work and Organisation*, 31(2): 146–160.

Cater, L. (2022) 'Europe's renovation wave risks exposing workers to asbestos'. *Politico* (2 June). Accessed 12 May 2023 from www.politico.eu/article/europe-renovation-wave-risk-exposing-workers-asbestos/

Chartered Institution of Wastes Management (CWIM) (2023) 'Essential skills for a greener tomorrow'. *Circular Online*. Accessed: 19 July 2023 from www.circularonline.co.uk/wp-content/uploads/2023/03/Beyond-Waste-Essential-Skills-for-a-Greener-Tomorrow.pdf

Christie-Miller, T., and Luke, A. (2021) 'Qualifying the race to net zero: how to solve the net zero skills challenge'. *Onward*. Accessed 12 March 2023 from www.ukonward.com/reports/net-zero-labour-market-challenge-report/

Clarke, L., Sahin-Dikmen, M., and Werna, E. (2024) 'Climate change, inequality and work in the construction industry', in C. Forson, G. Healy, M. Ozturk, and A. Tatli (eds), *Research Handbook on Inequalities at Work*. Cheltenham: Edward Elgar Publishing. www.e-elgar.com/shop/gbp/research-handbook-on-inequalities-and-work-9781800886599.html

Clarke, L., Sahin-Dikmen, M., and Winch, C. (2020) 'Overcoming diverse approaches to vocational education and training to combat climate change: the case of low energy construction in Europe'. *Oxford Review of Education*, 46(5): 619–636.

Consoli, D. Marin, G.M., Marzucchi, A., and Vona, F. (2016) 'Do green jobs differ from non-green jobs regarding skills and human capital?' *Research Policy*, 45(5): 1046–1060.

Davidson, D.J. (2022) 'Climate change sociology: past contributions and future research needs'. *Plos Climate 1*(7), https://doi.org/10.1371/journal.pclm.0000055

Dunlap, A., and Riquito, A. (2023) 'Social warfare for lithium extraction? Open-pit lithium mining, counterinsurgency tactics and enforcing green extractivism in northern Portugal'. *Energy Research and Social Science*, 95: 102912, https://doi.org/10.1016/j.erss.2022.102912

Dunlap, R.E., and Brulle, R.J. (2015) *Climate change and society: sociological perspectives*. Oxford: Oxford University Press.

Dyke, J., Watson, R., and Knorr, W. (2021) Climate scientists: the concept of net zero is a dangerous trap'. *The Conversation*. Accessed 24 January 2023 from https://theconversation.com/climate-scientists-concept-of-net-zero-is-a-dangerous-trap-157368

Ellen MacArthur Foundation (2023) https://ellenmacarthurfoundation.org/ Accessed 22 December 2022.

ETUC (2020) 'Adaptation to climate change and the world of work: A guide for trade unions'. *ETUC*. Accessed 10 November 2022 from www.etuc.org/en/publication/adaptation-climate-change-and-world-work-guide-trade-unions

Fevrier, K. (2022), 'Informal waste recycling economies in the global South and the chimera of green capitalism.' *Antipode*, 54: 1585–1606. https://doi-org.uow.idm.oclc.org/10.1111/anti.12841

Foster, J.B., York, R., and Clark, B. (2010). *The ecological rift: capitalism's war on the earth*. New York: Monthly Review Press.

Godinho, C. (2022) 'What do we know about the employment impacts of climate policies? A review of ex-post literature'. *WIREs Climate Change*, 13(6): e794. https://doi.org/10.1002/wcc.794

Gould, K.A., Pellow, D.N., and Schnaiberg, A. (2008) *Treadmill of production: injustice and unsustainability in the global economy*, London and New York: Routledge.

Gregson, N., Crang, M., Boticello, J., Calestani, M., and Krzywoszynska, A. (2016) 'Doing the "dirty work" of the green economy: resource recovery and migrant labour in the EU'. *European Urban and Regional Studies*, 23(4): 541–555.

International Energy Agency (IEA) (2023) *Global EV outlook 2023 – catching up with climate ambitions*. Accessed: 13 June 2023 from www.iea.org/reports/global-ev-outlook-2023

International Labour Organization (ILO) (2018) *Greening with jobs – world employment and social outlook*. ILO. Accessed 9 January 2023 from www.ilo.org/global/research/global-reports/weso/greening-with-jobs/lang--en/index.htm

International Labour Organization (ILO) (2019) *Working on a warmer planet: the impact of heat stress on labour productivity and decent work*. ILO. Accessed 14 January 2023 from www.ilo.org/global/publications/books/WCMS_711919/lang--en/index.htm

International Panel on Climate Change (IPCC) (2023) *AR6 synthesis report: climate change 2023*. Accessed 1 June 2023 from www.ipcc.ch/report/ar6/syr/

Kalogirou, M.R., Olson, J., and Davidson, S. (2020) 'Nursing's metaparadigm, climate change and planetary health'. *Nursing Inquiry*, 27(3): e12356. https://doi.org/10.1111/nin.12356

Kara, S. (2023) *Cobalt red: how the blood of Congo powers our lives*. New York: St Martin's Griffin.

Lipsig-Mumme, C., and McBride, S. (eds) (2015) *Work in a warming world*. Montreal and Kingston, ON: McGill-Queen's University Press.

Littig, B. (2018) 'Good work? Sustainable work and sustainable development: a critical gender perspective from the Global North'. *Globalisations*, 15(4): 565–579.

Meilvang, M.L. (2021) 'From rain as risk to rain as resource: professional and organisational changes in urban rainwater management'. *Current Sociology*, 69(7): 1–17.

Mol, A.P., and Spaargaren, G. (eds) (2000) 'Ecological modernisation theory in debate: a review'. *Environmental Politics*, 9(1): 17–49.

Morena, E., Krause, D., and Stevis, D. (2020) *Just transitions – social Justice in the shift towards a low-carbon world*. London: Pluto Press.

Mulligan, M. (2018) *An introduction to sustainability: environmental, social and personal perspectives*. London and New York: Routledge-Earthscan.

Parry, J. (2003) 'The changing meaning of work: restructuring in the former coal mining communities of the South Wales Valleys'. *Work, Employment and Society*, 17(2): 227–246.

Pellow, D.N., Schnaiberg, A., and Weinberg, A. (2000) 'Putting the ecological modernisation thesis to the test: the promises and performance of urban recycling'. *Environmental Politics*, 9(4): 109–137.

Rhodes, C. (2022) *Woke capitalism: how corporate morality is sabotaging democracy*. Bristol: Bristol University Press.

Ritchie, H., Roser, M., and Rosado, P. (2020) 'CO_2 and greenhouse gas emissions'. *Our World in Data*. Accessed 8 April 2023 from https://ourworldindata.org/co2-and-greenhouse-gas-emissions

Scheinberg, A., Nesić, J., and Savain, R. (2016) 'From collision to collaboration – integrating informal recyclers and re-use operators in Europe: a review'. *Waste Management & Research*, 34(9): 820–839.

Stevis, D. (2013) 'Green jobs? Good jobs? Just jobs? USA labour unions confronting climate change', in N. Rathzel and D. Uzzell (eds), *Trade unions in the green economy – working for the environment*. London and New York: Routledge.

Strambo, C., Aung, M.T., and Atteridge, A. (2019) 'Navigating coal mining closure and societal change: learning from past cases of mining decline'. *Stockholm Environment Institute*. Accessed 3 November 2022 from www.sei.org/publications/navigating-coal-mining-closure-and-societal-change/

United Nations (UN) (2023) THE 17 GOALS | Sustainable Development. Accessed 26 June 2023 from https://sdgs.un.org/goals

United Nations Framework Convention on Climate Change (UNFCCC) (2023) 'Cop 28: what was achieved and what happens next?' Accessed 26 June 2023 from https://unfccc.int/

Valero, A., Li J., Muller S., Riom, C. Nguyen-Tien, B., and Draca, M. (2021) *Are 'green' jobs good jobs? How lessons from the experience to-date can inform labour market transitions of the future*. London: Grantham Research Institute on Climate Change and the Environment/Centre for Economic Performance, London School of Economics and Political Science. https://cep.lse.ac.uk/pubs/download/special/cepsp39.pdf

Weghmann, V. (2017) *Waste management in Europe: Good jobs in the circular economy? European Circular economy Stakeholder Platform*. Accessed 28 May 2023 from https://circulareconomy.europa.eu/platform/en/knowledge/waste-management-europe-good-jobs-circular-economy

Weghmann, V. (2020) *Safe jobs in the circular economy: health and safety in waste and wastewater management. EPSU*. Accessed 4 April 2023 from www.epsu.org/article/safe-jobs-circular-economy-new-epsu-report,

World Economic Forum (2023) *The future of jobs report* 2023. *World Economic Forum*. Accessed 15 May 2023 from www.weforum.org/reports/the-future-of-jobs-report-2023/

Wright, C., and Nyberg, D. (2017) 'An inconvenient truth: how organisations translate climate change into business as usual'. *Academy of Management Journal*, 60(5): 1633–1661.

chapter 20

Changing Work
Universal Basic Income

Brian McDonough and
Jessie Bustillos Morales

Introduction

Imagine living in a society where a regular income is given to every citizen, regardless of whether they are in employment or not, and this income was sufficient to lead a full and healthy life. This might sound like a radical idea, or utopian, but is exactly the kind of world that is discussed and examined in this chapter – an idea that has been labelled (among other labels) a **universal basic income** (also known as UBI). This idea is very controversial: for some scholars, a universal basic income is a way forward, a way of achieving a more egalitarian world in which the lives of every citizen are looked after and cared for by the safety and economic security of the State; and, for other scholars and critics, a universal basic income is an extension of the 'nanny state', an absurd idea, which is both unrealistic and unaffordable – it may stifle economic growth, crashing the economy and bankrupting the State. In recent years, universal basic income has been gathering significant attention and is currently a 'hot topic' being discussed all over the globe. This popularity is not simply based on talk and debate, but also policy and practice, with countries around the world conducting 'basic income' pilots and experiments.

What is a universal basic income? It is 'a regular cash income paid to all on an individual basis, without means test or work requirement' (McDonough and Bustillos Morales, 2020: 3). The basic income is 'universal' because it is paid to all in a community or society. Whether or not individuals are rich or poor, and regardless of whether they receive income from work or other sources, a universal basic income is paid to everyone by virtue of being a member or citizen of that community or society. It is for this reason that a universal basic income has also

DOI: 10.4324/9781003314769-26

been referred to as a 'citizen's wage' or 'citizen's income' – 'an unconditional, automatic and non-withdrawable payment to each individual as a right of citizenship' (Torry, 2016). In various books and articles, a 'universal basic income' or 'basic income' has also been referred to as an 'existence income', 'universal dividend', 'universal grant', or 'guaranteed universal subsidy', as well as a range of similar terms in a variety of languages. Universal basic income may appear to be an exotic topic, a utopian idea, or ambitious set of policy ideas academics and politicians alike enjoy debating. But in recent years governments around the world have started putting this idea into practice by experimenting with it. Universal basic income is a real practice that is an important and yet controversial topic all over the world.

Universal basic income is not a new idea, but one established at least 200 years ago. In 1797, the (English-born) American activist (and Founding Father) Thomas Paine advocated a citizen's dividend to all US citizens as compensation for 'loss of his or her natural inheritance, by the introduction of the system of landed property' (Paine, 1797). More than 150 years later, Paine's sentiments were echoed by another revolutionary of his time, Martin Luther King. During the US civil rights movement of the 1960s, King (1967) suggested that a guaranteed minimum income was the most effective way of abolishing poverty in the US, arguing for an end to social inequality, and social justice for all. Less than ten years later, one US state created a policy which has resonance with the idea of a universal basic income, or citizen's income. In 1976, the state of Alaska created the Alaska Permanent Fund, a dividend paid to Alaskan residents using oil revenues, one of the state's most abundant and rich resources. The fund may not exactly be what Thomas Paine or Martin Luther King had in mind (in that it is a very limited amount), and has become a topic of discussion and scrutiny for Alaskan residents, but, until recently, it has been one model that has resonance with the notion of a permanent and universal basic income (with residents receiving US $2,000 per annum in some years by virtue of living in Alaska).

Over the last few decades, the idea of a universal basic income has become increasingly popular, and more and more governments and NGOs (non-government organisations) all over the world have begun piloting and experimenting with the notion. The popularity of universal basic income in recent years is not due to chance, but comes in response to a changing economic climate – one that has been based upon neoliberal economics, ideas, and values. With a 'cost of living crisis' squeezing the Global North in the mid-2020s, the appetite for a basic income has never been stronger. This chapter explores how a universal basic income can change people's relationship with work. It also examines the example of basic income in Madhya Pradesh, India, presented in the next case study.

Changing People's Relationship Towards Work

A universal basic income can change people's relationship towards paid employment and other types of work in several ways. First, it can help disrupt unequal labour power relations and increase the **bargaining power** of workers. This becomes more important in current societies where the rise of insecurity and uncertainty has grown proportionally with the rise of unequal accumulations of wealth globally (Piketty, 2022). The position of workers is becoming more precarious across different countries and different types of industries (Standing, 2021). It is becoming increasingly more difficult to secure forms of employment that guarantee basic rights and benefits for workers and a salary with which an individual can have access to decent housing, services, leisure, health, and other activities. A universal basic income can compensate those whose precarious employment arrangements are thwarted by neoliberal economics (Stern, 2016).

In *Reclaiming work: beyond a wage-based society*, Gorz (1999) argues for an end to work that is peculiar to capitalist society. When we say to a certain woman that she 'doesn't work' when she is raising her children, but she 'does work' if she is a paid nanny or nursery school worker, we are strengthening the divisions around work in our society. In capitalist society, work is seen as paid employment and not the 'real work' people do in everyday life, even when they are not formally employed: caring and cleaning for others; raising the next generation; voluntary, community, and other non-paid work (see Taylor's discussion in Chapter 15, 'Unpaid Work'). Gorz's (1999) critique of work rests on how Marx (1818–1883) viewed the mode of production of societies influencing social meanings in all aspects of society: from culture and education, to the world of work, everything is designed to serve the purposes of the particular mode of production. In the case of capitalism, work is reduced to the exchange of labour for a wage, workers are reduced to wage earners, and work can only be supplied to the economic institutions which have gained recognition in a neoliberal economy. Consequently, any situation which does not resemble these structures is not viewed as real work by capitalist societies.

A better understanding of real work incorporates the wide scope of human activity, rather than being limited to those things we do during paid employment. Gorz (1999) argues that we should try to produce a system that provides a decent livelihood for all, a basic income, sufficient for a decent level of subsistence. Only a basic income can recompense the voluntary, community, caring, and non-market activities that the foundations of society depend upon. Gorz says we should recognise that 'neither the right to an income, nor full citizenship, nor everyone's sense of identity and self-fulfilment can any longer be centred on and depend on occupying a job' (1999: 54). The introduction of a universal basic income could widen the interpretations around work that we currently hold as a society. Universal basic income could contribute to the creation of more comprehensive and egalitarian social arrangements where work is not solely validated when a person is working for a wage, but instead recognises that most people in society partake in important work that sustains the way we live.

Global markets drive employment patterns, characterised by an erosion of workers' rights, with the disempowering of trade unions, the rise of insecure work due to technological advancements, zero-hour contracts, and the widening gap between the rich and the poor (Pitts et al., 2017; Standing, 2021). The rise of job insecurity has been disguised by a significant rise in self-employment, which in most cases precludes basic employment rights, such as the right to a minimum wage, sick pay, pension contributions, and parental leave. These issues arise from neoliberal imperatives which, by their very nature, create adverse side effects for workers and across society: uncertainty, insecurity, poverty, and social inequalities. A welfare provision like universal basic income has emerged as a response to these side effects. It can reduce uncertainty, because it is a regular, and therefore constant, resource available for use. It can also provide a **basic security,** because it is a sustained income which takes families above the poverty line and is provided continuously. This financial provision is akin to Child Benefit in the UK, in the sense that it provides large swathes of a nation with a very basic security provision. Having a stable and constant income provides a stability and assurance which allows individuals and families the time and resources to plan their future, giving them the means with which to provide self-improvement, escaping poverty and acquiring a better quality of life.

Universal Basic Income, Work, and Welfare Provision

One of the problems with current means-tested benefits in developed nations is the way in which they are perceived by the public. People often oppose the idea of 'handouts' from the State, because of populdist ideologies that narrate how taxes are given to those who seem too 'lazy' or 'idle' to work. A universal basic income, however, is paid to everyone, so there is no envy or strong opposition to those who receive it, when it is a provision for all (McDonough and Bustillos Morales, 2020). Many critics ask: If a basic income aims to eradicate poverty, then why not target the poorest in society? One reason is that benefits targeted at the poor often require those eligible to take steps which they may fail to take, whether out of 'ignorance, shyness, or shame' (Van Parijs and Vanderborght, 2017: 17). In Britain, for example, some estimate that UK households are missing out on £19 billion a year in unclaimed welfare benefits (Butler, 2023).

Current welfare systems in developed nations usually require countless hours filling out forms with personal information and involve continuously collecting data to support evidence that recipients are 'honest' in their claims. Aside from the high costs to implement this, there are the costs involved in investigating those who have tried to dupe the system by making false claims for welfare. Governments often outsource work to private companies to carry out the administrative functions of the welfare system. In the UK, for example, companies such as Serco (a leading outsourcing business for professional services), G4S (a leading supplier of security solutions and other services), Pertemps, and Seetec are paid millions of pounds in order to enforce welfare rules and regimes in Britain. The implementation of a universal basic income could eliminate the need for corporate outsourcing, which drains the welfare budget and diverts the money that should be helping all members of society. It is for some of these reasons that governments are continuing to experiment with universal basic income.

In July 2022, the Welsh government invested £20 million to set up a basic income pilot study, in which 500 care leavers were given £1,600 tax-free cash every month for a period of two years (Gov. Wales, 2022). The scheme is one of the largest basic income trials to have been implemented in the United Kingdom and Europe and, while the results and impact of the pilot are still being evaluated, it is expected this basic income will help these vulnerable young people overcome adversities in their transition to adulthood. In 2027, in Finland, a two-year basic income trial, called *perustulokeilu*, involved giving €560 to around 2,000 people aged between 25 and 58. The study was said to have improved well-being of the group overall, having a positive impact on the lives of the people of the study, though some reports were more critical, saying that the trial had left people 'happier but jobless' (Nagesh, 2019). Joblessness is unlikely and, while some critics believe that a basic income could encourage a reliance on the welfare state and reluctance to want to work (Goldin, 2018), much of this is based on media speculation.

In contrast, other scholars who have studied basic income in recent years claim that the policy minimises **economic shocks**, like the hike in fuel and energy prices during the cost-of-living crisis (such as the UK in 2023), as well as providing a stable position from which individuals can look for work, invest in education, or plan new forms of entrepreneurialism. Basic income is particularly beneficial for riding the ups and downs of a neoliberal economy, where changing occupations is commonplace, and the need for a short-term financial safety net is crucial to keeping families secure and out of poverty. From this perspective, a basic income policy could support the economic development of individuals, where moving from job to job is less risky. A universal basic income would have mitigated the financial costs to families during the COVID-19 pandemic, where swathes of nations were in lockdown (in 2020) and unable to work. This has resonance with the UK furlough scheme, where government grants covered up to 80 per cent of employees' wages. Countries could be more resilient to future pandemics with a basic income in place.

In Standing's (2017) book *Basic income: and how we can make it happen*, the economist explains that a universal basic income would be an effective way of overcoming 'poverty traps' and reducing 'precarity traps' (Standing, 2017: 76–77). **Poverty traps** (also known as the 'unemployment trap') occur when an increase in someone's income through employment is offset by a consequent loss of state benefits and set of costs involved in employment activity (travel or childcare costs, for instance). Torry (2016) gives the example of a British carpenter who was pleased to be promoted to foreman and then wished he had not been. His wages had risen, but the effects of additional Income Tax and National Insurance contributions, and the loss of Family Income Supplement (as the means-tested benefit was then called in the UK) resulted in the man being no better off financially.

In contrast to means-tested benefits, a universal basic income provides a source of cash that is not means-tested and is paid to every citizen regardless of whether a person is in paid employment. A universal basic income can overcome **precarity traps,** too, which happens when delays in paying means-tested benefits act as a 'disincentive to take short-term casual jobs' (Standing, 2017: 77). An example is the rollout of Universal Credit in the UK in 2018, which took up to six weeks for recipients to receive payment. The delays created long periods of debt and poverty and discouraged people from applying for casual, short-term, low-paying jobs they may otherwise have been interested in.

A universal basic income is not just aimed at alleviating poverty, but can also be seen as a progressive policy for overcoming the necessity to means-test, degrade, and devalue citizens who are unemployed. One of the best examples of how current welfare systems fail is depicted in the film *I, Daniel Blake* (2017). A 59-year-old joiner called Daniel Blake is depicted as a victim of the British system of work and welfare, in which he is sent from 'pillar to post' to claim state benefits when he loses his long-term job. Having suffered a heart attack, Blake is instructed by doctors to rest. But, because he is able to walk 50 metres an to raise either arm to his top shirt pocket, the welfare state considers him 'fit for work' and sends him on a number of CV-writing workshops and classes in order to find work. The film depicts the British welfare regime as a cruel system that stigmatises unemployment and vilifies people for not having a job, and Blake, the protagonist, eventually dies.

Case Study

Universal Basic Income in Madhya Pradesh (India)

We can examine the impact of implementing this model In one of the world's largest-ever basic income experiments, carried out in rural areas of Madhya Pradesh, India. In 2009–2010, UNICEF funded a basic income experiment, supported by a local organisation called SEWA (Self-Employed Women's Association). The experiment evaluated the impact that unconditional transfers, or basic income grants, would have on communities consisting of about 6,000 men, women, and children (Davala et al., 2017). For 18 months, recipients would receive a cash sum which could be spent however they wished, regardless of whether they worked in paid employment. The recipients' situation before, during, and after receiving the grants was evaluated by three rounds of statistical surveys and case studies, comparing all the changes during the period with a control group that did not receive the grants. There were two pilots. The first was called MPUCT (Madhya Pradesh Unconditional Cash Transfer), which involved eight villages in which everybody received monthly grants. Twelve villages were used as control villages. The second pilot was called TVUCT (Tribal Village Unconditional Cash Transfer). This involved providing grants to everybody in one tribal village, with one other tribal village as a comparison (Davala et al., 2017). The trials aimed to identify the effects of a basic income on individual and family behaviour and attitudes. In the selected villages, every man, woman, and child was provided with a modest unconditional grant each month. Initially, in the larger project, every adult received 200 rupees a month and every child got 100 rupees. After a year, these amounts were raised to 300 and 150 rupees a month respectively. In the second pilot (tribal village), the amounts were 300 and 150 rupees for the entire year. This meant that an average family earned the equivalent of $24 (£19) per month. The amount given was calculated based on working out what was a quarter of the income of median-income families, at just above the current poverty line.

   The basic income trials in the villages of Madhya Pradesh provided several findings. In terms of work, the basic income did not dissuade family members from

Brian McDonough and Jessie Bustillos Morales

partaking in work activities or pursuing careers. On the contrary, the income allowed more investment in things that would improve or enhance the prospects of better-paid work, such as purchasing bicycles and motorbikes, enabling family members to get to and from work more easily. Another investment in the future of work was education. In preparation for better careers and future jobs, families used the basic income to send their children to school, enabling them to have the skills required for their futures. One woman, who was a wage labourer from the SEWA village of Jagmalpipliya, explained how the basic income helped to send her children to school:

> My husband passed away two months ago due to a kidney failure, and because of that our condition has become very bad. My only source of income is casual labour, which also is not available regularly. Our main expenditure is on food. I buy food items for only five to ten days because I have very little money. My eldest son is 20 years old. He and I are the only two people who go to work in my family. My three other sons go to school. They get lunch in the school, and they recently got money for their uniform. After my husband's demise, my son Nerendra and I increased our hours of labour, but one of my sons is mentally challenged, so he is not able to do much labour. Employers easily exploit him. Three of my boys are studying and we have to bear the expenditure for their education. This money has helped us a lot. If it were not for it, we would have had to send our children for labour work. But because of this money we are able to send them to school.
>
> (cited in Davala et al., 2017: 135)

The basic income enabled some families to change the circumstances in which they lived. But this was not the same for everyone in the Madhya Pradesh experiment. Some recipients were resigned to taking their children out of school despite the implementation of the basic income (Davala et al., 2017). In many nations around the world, schooling comes at significant cost, and the onus is often on bringing in a wage for the family (even working children), not on education.

The basic income experiments of Madhya Pradesh helped tackle inequalities with regard to health and nutrition, too. Food deficiency fell, diets were more nutritious, and there was a shift from the reliance of ration shops to the market and own production of food. In particular, child nutrition improved, tested by the weight-for-age measures (Davala et al., 2017). Improvements in nutrition affected capabilities, enabling children to attend school more regularly, boosting economic growth, and enabling adults to be more productive in the world of work. Importantly, these social factors, when sustained, worked accumulatively to enhance the well-being of individuals, families, and whole communities, which has a knock-on effect for providing future societal gains.

Overall, the basic income experiments in Madhya Pradesh yielded several positive results, including better nutrition, lower debt, greater job opportunities, higher rates of school attendance for children, and better healthcare. The impact on women was particularly empowering, as an income being given directly to women provided them with more independence, not relying on their husbands (or needing a husband) in order to survive.

Costs, Benefits, and Other Issues with Universal Basic Income

With a means-tested scheme, there are considerably more human and administrative costs than with a universal basic income. Furthermore, the means test itself is problematic. Van Parijs and Vanderborght (2017: 18) say that decisions to include or exclude can 'leave a lot of room for arbitrariness and clientism'. Unlike other welfare schemes, there is no stigma attached to receiving a basic income when it is the right of *every* citizen. But it is not only the dignity of people which is afforded by a universal basic income. Such a scheme also enhances the effectiveness of poverty alleviation. There are other reasons why a universal basic income is better than welfare policies targeted at the poor. In a neoliberal economy, where work is often characterised by insecurity and precariousness (McDonough, 2017), a universal basic income not only frees people from a lack of money, but also provides more flexibility for individuals to take on work they require'; 'If they are unsure about how much they will earn when they start working, about whether they will be able to cope, or about how quickly they might lose the work and then have to face more or less complex administrative procedures in order to re-establish their entitlement to benefits, the idea of giving up means-tested transfers holds less appeal' (Van Parijs and Vanderborght, 2017: 18–19). With current welfare policies, it can take months and a great deal of form-filling and administrative work to sign up someone to the right benefits based on their specific circumstances. The prospect of signing off and losing benefits is a disincentive to work. By contrast, with a universal basic income, people can take on jobs with less fear.

Some people who are sceptical of basic income policies believe that poorer people will squander their money on bad habits, known as **'private bads'** (Standing, 2017: 79). There is an underlying discourse which depicts poorer people in society as untrustworthy and irresponsible; giving people 'free cash' could result in money being wasted on alcohol and drugs. However, many basic income pilots show quite the opposite – that additional income is put to positive use. Between 2007 and 2009, the Namibian Tax Consortium (NAMTAX) provided residents living in the Otjivero-Omitara region of Namibia below the age of 60 with a grant of NAD100 per person per month. Namibia's Basic Income Grant (BIG), according to the organisers, increased economic activity (Basic Income Grant Coalition, 2019), and helped people to kick-start their own businesses in construction (such as bricklaying), fashion design (such as dressmaking), and food (such as breadmaking). Some reports suggested a reduction in child malnutrition and dramatic improvement in school attendance (see McDonough and Bustillos Morales, 2020: 67). Standing (2017) argues that the evidence from examples of basic income for the most part shows that recipients of basic income or cash transfer programmes spend their money on **'private goods'**. Standing (2017) argues that, contrary to popular prejudice, studies show that basic income is more likely to be spent on food for children, family healthcare, and education. Standing (2017) further expands this argument by saying that receipt of a universal basic income can reduce spending on drugs, alcohol, and tobacco. Because a universal basic income can reduce poverty and radically alter a hopeless situation, it can also change the mindset of families and entire communities. A shift in the way people understand their situation can reduce the need to alleviate a difficult and hopeless situation by turning to alcohol and drug misuse.

A universal basic income can be viewed as **emancipatory**. It is a means of enhancing, or in some cases reclaiming, personal freedom or basic rights, such as not being forced to work or tied for years to a job one dislikes. Some argue that a universal basic income has the potential to be particularly emancipatory for women and those who normally receive lower priority in social policy-making, including those with disabilities or older people (Davala et al., 2015). The case study of Madhya Pradesh (see earlier) revealed that women need not be financially dependent on their husbands, with a regular income provided. However, some authors are critical as to whether a universal basic income will give women (particularly in the Global North) more freedom or encourage them back to traditional domestic duties and care responsibilities in the home (Higgs, 2018; McDonough and Bustillos Morales, 2020). While a universal basic income could favour women, by compensating them for the otherwise unpaid work of childcare and domestic responsibilities, it also means that women might be discouraged from re-entering the workplace. Pateman (2004: 99) says that the private and public sexual division of labour 'continues to be structured so that men monopolise full-time, higher paying, and more prestigious paid employment, and wives do a disproportionate share of unpaid work in the home' (see Chapter 1, where the 'breadwinner model' is discussed).

While there are pros and cons to a universal basic income, much of these issues depend on the context, such as *where* it is being implemented (country), *by whom* (political party), and in *what ways* it will be implemented (e.g. how much income citizens will receive).

Conclusion

This chapter discussed the idea of a universal basic income. It discussed several examples, such as the experiments in India, Finland, and Wales. For many, a universal basic income is a way of achieving a more egalitarian society, in which citizens have their economic security provided for by the State. Some might believe a universal basic income is unrealistic and unaffordable, but in the Global North, with advanced welfare states, most individuals already contribute large amounts in taxes, which provide forms of welfare. A universal basic income requires rethinking about current welfare policies, with the prospect of abolishing means-tested benefits, in favour of a basic income, or citizen's income, for all.

The discussion in this chapter is not merely for theoretical debate, but is also based upon solid policy and practice, since there are many countries around the world conducting 'basic income' pilots and experiments right now. In terms of people's relationship towards work, this chapter explained that a basic income can ameliorate precarious and exploitative conditions of work and employment, which are becoming more prevalent within neoliberal society. Above all, a universal basic income can act as a safety net, providing a fallback for when the market fails to provide a secure job or regular income.

STUDENT ACTIVITY

Read this chapter's case study and answer the following questions:

- Explain how women in *Madhya Pradesh* may have been particularly advantaged from receiving a regular basic income.
- In what ways did the basic income in *Madhya Pradesh* provide opportunities for families to escape poverty?

Practice Questions

- In what ways might a universal basic income prepare families for economic shocks (such as job redundancies or future pandemics)?
- In what ways might a universal basic income help address precarious work?
- What evidence is there to suggest that a basic income will be spent on 'private goods' rather than 'private bads'?

Key Terms

Bargaining power
ability of people (e.g. workers) to bargain and negotiate over better pay or working terms and conditions. Arguably, a universal basic income can increase the bargaining power of workers, as they will not be desperate to work in any job if they already have a constant and regular source of income.

Basic security
the security of food provision and place to live for oneself and one's family. A universal basic income can provide basic security because it is a sustained income which takes families above the poverty line and is provided continuously. Having a stable, constant income provides assurance, which allows individuals and families the time and resources to plan their future (providing a better quality of life).

Economic shock
refers to an unpredictable event, usually resulting in loss of income, or less worth of income in real terms (such as during periods of high inflation). An economic shock might involve a job loss, such as being made redundant. A universal basic income can help individuals and families manage such financial shocks.

Emancipatory
a universal basic income can arguably be viewed as emancipatory. It is a means of enhancing, or in some cases reclaiming, personal freedom or basic rights, such as not being forced to work or tied for years to a job one dislikes.

Poverty traps
also known as the 'unemployment trap', occurs when an increase in someone's income through employment is offset by a consequent loss of state benefits and set of costs involved in employment activity (such as travel costs or childcare costs).

Brian McDonough and Jessie Bustillos Morales

Precarity traps

When delays in paying means-tested benefits act as a 'disincentive to take short-term casual jobs' (Standing, 2017: 77). A universal basic income would overcome precarity traps, as there is no restriction on working to receive the entitlement.

Private bads

sceptics of basic income policies believe that poorer people will squander their money on bad habits, known as 'private bads' such as alcohol and drugs (Standing, 2017: 790 – a belief based around an underlying discourse that depicts poorer people in society as untrustworthy and irresponsible.

Private goods

many basic income studies show that cash from basic income trials is not wasted (on alcohol, drugs, or other 'private bads'); however, studies show that basic income is more likely to be spent on food for children, family healthcare, and education (see Standing, 2017).

Universal basic income

also referred to as a 'citizen's wage' or 'citizen's income', this is 'a regular cash income paid to all on an individual basis, without means test or work requirement' (McDonough and Bustillos Morales, 2020: 3).

References

Basic Income Grant Coalition (2019) 'BIG Coalition Namibia'. Available at www.bignam.org

Butler, P. (2023) 'UK households missing out on £19bn a year in unclaimed welfare benefits'. *Guardian*, 30 April. Available at https://amp.theguardian.com/society/2023/apr/30/uk-households-missing-out-on-19bn-a-year-in-unclaimed-welfare-benefits

Davala, S., Jhabvala, R., Mehta, S.K., and Standing, G. (2017) *Basic income: a transformative policy for India*. London: Bloomsbury.

Goldin, I. (2018) 'Five reasons why a basic income is a bad idea'. *Financial Times*, 11 February. Available at www.ft.com/content/100137b4-0cdf-11e8-bacb-2958fde95e5e

Gorz, André (1999) *Reclaiming work: beyond a wage-based society,* trans, C. Turner. Cambridge: Polity Press.

Higgs, R. (2018) 'Is basic income a solution to persistent inequalities faced by women?' *The Conversation*, 7 March. Available at http://theconversation.com/is-a-basic-income-the-solution-to-persistent-inequalities-faced-by-women-92939

King, Martin Luther (1967) *Where do we go from here: chaos or community?* Boston, MA: Beacon Press.

Loach, K. (dir.) (2016) *I, Daniel Blake*. UK: Sixteen Films.

McDonough, B (2017) 'Precarious work and unemployment in Europe'. In S. Isaacs (ed.), *European social problems*. London: Routledge.

McDonough, B., and Bustillos Morales, J.A. (2020) *Universal basic income*. London: Routledge.

Nagesh, A. (2019) 'Finland basic income trial left people "happier but jobless"'. Retrieved from www.bbc.co.uk/news/world-europe-47169549

Paine, T. (1797/ 2015) *Agrarian justice*. South Carolina: Create Space Independent Publishing Platform.

Pateman, C. (2004) 'Democratizing citizenship: some advantages of a basic income'. *Politics and Society*, *32*(1): 89–105.

Piketty, T. (2022) *A brief history of equality*. Cambridge, MA: Harvard University Press.

Pitts, F.H., Lombardozzi, L., and Warner, N. (2017) 'Speenhamland, automation and the basic income: a warning from history?' *Renewal: A Journal of Labour Politics* 25(3): 145–155.

Standing, G. (2017) *Basic income: and how we can make it happen*. London: Penguin.

Standing, G. (2021) *The precariat: a new dangerous class – special COVID-19 edition*. London: Bloomsbury.

Stern, A. (2016) *Raising the floor: how a universal basic income can renew our economy and rebuild the American dream*. New York: PBG Publishing.

Torry, M. (2016) *Citizen's basic income: a Christian social policy*. London: Darton, Longman and Todd.

Van Parijs, P., and Vanderborght, Y. (2017) *Basic income: a radical proposal for a free society and a sane economy*. Cambridge, MA: Harvard University Press.

Gov.Wales (2022) 'Wales pilots Basic Income scheme'. *Gov.Wales,* 28 June. Retrieved from www.gov.wales/wales-pilots-basic-income-scheme

chapter 21

Changing Places of Work

Alan Felstead and Helen Blakely

Introduction

All social activities take place in locations of one sort or another. This applies to non-work activities – such as attending a football match, going to the gym, or organising a birthday party – as well as working in a bar, shop, or office. However, not all paid work, particularly office work, needs to be carried out on the premises of the employer. Advances in digital technology have made it easier for office workers to make almost any place their place of work.

Over 40 years ago, futurologists were predicting that by the start of the new millennium the majority of work would be carried out in 'electronic cottages' and that there would be a 'new emphasis on the home as the centre of society' (Toffler, 1980: 210). However, in 2000 only around 2.3 per cent of people worked at home – the revolution had failed to materialise (Felstead et al., 2005: Table 3.3). Instead, attention shifted to the idea that work would become spatially fluid, such that 'for a substantial proportion of workers, work in 20 years' time will be more about movement than staying put' (Moynagh and Worsley, 2005: 101). The study of mobility therefore became fashionable, with attention focusing on the idea of the 'digital nomad' – individuals able to work in a wide variety of places (e.g. 2000).

As a consequence, researchers became fascinated by work carried out while on the move and in places outside of the conventional workplace or the home. These transitional places of work included the car, the train, and the plane, as well as stop-over points used while travelling. Examples of these 'third places' included motorway service stations, hotel lobbies, and airport lounges from where work can be carried out (Burchell et al., 2021; Felstead et al., 2005; Hislop and Axtell, 2007). Mobile phones, laptops, email, the internet, and wireless connections enabled more and more work, office work in particular, to be carried out wherever

DOI: 10.4324/9781003314769-27

workers happen to be and whatever the time. Both working at home and mobile working were growing, but at a much slower pace than anticipated. Managers who were used to seeing their staff were resistant to off-site working, and technology – such as video conferencing – was not well developed and widely used.

The response to coronavirus taken by governments across the world changed all that. One of the principal means of halting the spread of the virus was the request, sometimes the insistence, that work was carried out at home if possible. This turned on its head the long-held understanding that work and home are separate spheres of life. Instead, the pandemic forced work back into the home on a massive scale. Many employees were new to this way of working and many employers had to manage a disparate workforce for the first time.

This chapter reviews what impact this shift had on the lives of millions of employees, the organisations which employ them, and the societies in which they live. It also looks to a future in which more work is carried out remotely – at home, in the local café or library, or while moving from place to place. The case study focuses on some of the technologies used to make homeworkers visible and the issues these raise for privacy.

Impact on Employees

It is important to situate the explosion of interest in the location of work into an historical context since, like coronavirus, working at home has evolved and varied over time. For example, many of today's homeworkers – office workers who were ordered to work at home to prevent the spread of coronavirus during the pandemic – are very different from the homeworkers of 40 years ago who sewed garments for local factories, assembled goods for sale or packed items for distribution (Allen and Wolkowitz, 1987; Felstead and Jewson, 2000; Phizacklea and Wolkowitz, 1995). The modern-day homeworker is relatively well paid and highly educated, while the one which preceded tended to be poorly paid and subject to exploitation.

These different forms of **homeworking** have grown at staggeringly different rates. The historic form of homeworking has been a constant, but relatively small, part of the economy – never going away, but never rapidly growing either. Modern-day homeworking, on the other hand, has been steadily growing for decades with the pandemic triggering an explosion in its prevalence. Across Europe as a whole, 37 per cent of the working population reported working at home in April 2020 because of the pandemic (Eurofound, 2020). In the US around a third (35 per cent) of the workforce in April 2020 were asked to ditch the daily commute and work at home instead, and in the UK the figure was 43 per cent (Brynjolfsson et al., 2020; Felstead, 2022). While these figures are not directly comparable, since they use different measures of working at home, they all indicate a dramatic increase in homeworking. Many high-profile companies closed their offices and ordered their staff to work at home. The numbers involved have subsequently fallen, but remain high by historical standards. According to official labour market statistics, the proportion of workers working exclusively at home was 14 per cent in May 2022, compared with 5 per cent in 2019. In addition, a further 24 per cent reported working some of the time at home and some of the time elsewhere, or what is referred to as **hybrid working** (Felstead and Reuschke, 2021; ONS, 2022b).

Working at home has often been promoted and sought by employees as a means of raising their well-being and readjusting their work–life balance (Kelliher and de Menezes, 2019). However, some employees find that bringing work into the home makes it more difficult to draw these boundaries, especially for those who have children or other dependants. For these individuals, working at home can be both challenging and rewarding. The experience of those who work at home is shaped, on the one hand, by spatial proximity to the domestic life of the household and, on the other, by geographical distance from co-workers located elsewhere in the organisation. These dual characteristics pose distinctive dilemmas, challenges, and opportunities for maintaining work–life balance (see Chapter 10, 'Work–Life Balance', by Xu and Kelliher). These issues are not faced by workers whose working lives and home lives take place in spatially distinct and separate environments – they can leave the office or factory and go home. This is not an option for those working at home, whose journey to and from work is a matter of steps, if that, given that they work and live in the same space. This, of course, was especially problematic during the pandemic, when many had to work at home regardless of their domestic circumstances (Chung, 2018; Chung et al., 2022). After the pandemic, these conflicts have lessened, as employees are no longer required to limit their physical movement by working at home.

Nevertheless, for those who continue to work and live in the same space, conflicts may arise. After all, it is difficult to achieve a 'good functioning of work and home, with a minimum of role conflict' when the worlds of work and home are intentionally blurred (Clark, 2000: 751). Homeworkers tend to report working longer hours – often unpaid – and put more physical and/or mental effort into their work than their office-bound counterparts (Felstead and Henseke, 2017). These two aspects are conceptualised as **extensive** and **intensive work effort**. The former refers to the time spent at work, behind the desk, on the computer, and/or on the phone. The number of hours spent working can be counted by the day, week, month, or year. Intensive work effort, on the other hand, refers to the intensity of effort expended during those working hours (Green, 2001).

Working off-site, and particularly at home, can increase both forms of work effort. For example, evidence suggests that the switch to working at home lengthens the working day, with commuting time becoming working time. Furthermore, homeworkers tend to be connected to work for longer, are more likely to be in email communication outside of office hours, and are more willing to attend video-conference calls early in the morning, in the evening, or over the weekend (Barrero et al., 2020; ONS, 2021; Thulin, 2019).

Homeworking can also increase work intensity. For example, provided the home is relatively quiet, those working at home can avoid office-based interruptions and therefore concentrate harder on work tasks. Zoom meetings scheduled end-on-end with little, if any, break in between calls can also intensify work effort.

When asked to evaluate what effect working at home as opposed to the office had on their experience of work, survey respondents report that working at home is more intense. As homeworkers, they are three times more likely to report doing more work, operating under greater pressure, and working at a faster pace (Taylor et al., 2021). Furthermore, the pressures of work tend to spill over into non-work life, with homeworkers reporting difficulties in being able to 'switch off' or unwind when 'off work' (Felstead, 2022: 75–98).

Circumstances where employees feel that they need to be available all the time to answer emails, calls, or simply deal with rising workloads, is known as the 'availability creep' (Pocock, 2021). This 'always on' culture is not a new phenomenon. However, it is one which has been accelerated by the shift to homeworking and the difficulties of drawing and maintaining temporal boundaries around work. This has intensified interest in initiatives designed to give employees the 'right to disconnect'. National governments across Europe have begun to take action. To varying degrees, there is a legal right to disconnect in France, Belgium, Spain, and Italy (Varges-Llave et al., 2020: 41). Sparked by the pandemic, legislative intervention is also under discussion in the European Parliament and in many individual member states.

Another one of the downsides often reported by employees who work off-site is the fear that they become 'out of sight and out of mind'. They are therefore passed over for promotion and have fewer opportunities to develop their skills and experience. Newcomers in particular may suffer most from the increased geographical dispersion of workers, since it makes their induction into a community of practitioners more difficult (Jewson, 2008). Physical proximity with co-workers facilitates serendipitous contacts and promotes non-verbal communication through body language, eye contact, and touching rituals such as the handshake. It also allows unintentional, on-the-job learning to take place and increases face time with line managers and colleagues. Pre-pandemic research, for example, shows that the most effective learning is that which takes place in physical proximity to others (e.g. Engeström, 2001; Eraut et al., 1998). Similarly, trust between team members has been found to 'gradually dissipate over time without collocated, face-to-face social interactions' (Nandhakumar and Baskerville, 2006: 371).

Working at home may also have heightened the tendency for workers to work while ill. While out of sight, workers have fewer ways of demonstrating their commitment to the organisation. They cannot make themselves visible by arriving early in the office and leaving late or by symbolically leaving personal possessions – coats, jackets, and bags – on the desk when in the office (but elsewhere in the building). However, they can more easily work at home when ill, since they no longer have to commute. This tendency was evident before the pandemic, when homeworking was relatively low. A pre-pandemic study of call centre operators showed that those who worked at home took fewer sick days than their office-based counterparts. When questioned, operators put this down to the fact that, even when ill, they would continue to work at home, whereas they would take sick leave if they had to come into the office to work (Bloom et al., 2015: 191–192).

Impact on Employers

A key feature of traditional factories, offices, and warehouses is the allocation of large numbers of workers to particular premises and then to particular locations within them, such as a desk, a bench, or a department. The physical presence of employees on-site also enhances the potential for them to participate – intentionally and/or serendipitously – in relation with their peers and others in acts of learning, social bonding, and building organisational camaraderie. For centuries, employers have designed workplaces with the intention of making employees both 'visible' and 'present'. Visibility refers to the ability of managers, supervisors, and work colleagues to observe employees at work.

These developments are usually discussed in the sociological literature in relation to factory workers. However, as with the assembly line, managerial control was also built into the fabric of the office and the allocation of workers to desks. Like the factory, then, the office also constitutes a personal place of work. This might take the form of a walled cell (cellular office) or a desk in an open-plan office. Either way, each worker has their own tiny plot or cube of space dedicated to their use. Some workers can symbolically personalise their designated cubes of space to differentiate themselves from less privileged members of the workforce and project their own identities into the world of employment. The cubes of space occupied by office workers are never, of course, their personal property. Nevertheless, employees often develop a strong sense of personal identification with 'their' office space. As a result, they often furnish their working environment with pictures, plants, photographs, souvenirs, and other memorabilia. Staff not 'in the office' are, by definition, not 'at work' and are not eligible for payment. Equally, staff who 'put in the hours' in the designated location are deemed worthy of reward and promotion. Like factory workers, office workers signal that they are working by being present and visible to their managers and/ or colleagues.

However, by occupying the sites that they have been allocated, office workers are open to managerial regulation, control, and disciplinary gaze (Felstead et al., 2005: 97–135). In contrast, allowing employees the opportunity to work in places outside of the employers' premises – such as the home – upends the traditional management approach of making employees visible and physically present. A primary concern of employers is that, when out of sight, employees' levels of work effort will fall: they will work shorter hours, will not work as hard, and employee productivity will fall.

Yet, as reported earlier, off-site working does not appear to reduce work effort, and productivity is, if anything, boosted when employees work at home. Employers' fears, therefore, seem ill-founded. One of the most rigorous studies to test these fears focused on the booking department of a leading Chinese travel agency based in Shanghai (Bloom et al., 2015). The nine-month experiment was a randomised control trial of call centre workers who were put into two groups: those working at home (the treatment group); and those remaining in the office (the control group). The treatment group was required to work four days a week at home and one day a week in the office – in fact, operating as hybrid workers. To ensure comparability, they worked the same schedule and under the same team leader as their office-bound counterparts. Both groups also used the same computer terminals, communications equipment, and software.

The experiment produced striking results. The working at home group outperformed office bound workers by 13 per cent. This came about by increasing the hours spent logged onto the system during shifts and increasing the number of calls taken per minute. Both are examples of intensive work effort; that is, reducing the 'porosity' of the working day by reducing the gaps between tasks during which the body or mind rests. This was explained by two main factors: the greater convenience of being at home (e.g. the ease of making a tea or coffee, or using the toilet), and the relative quietness of the home environment.

A series of studies carried out during the pandemic have confirmed that homeworking may not dent productivity, but may in fact boost it. Moreover, they also suggest that the selection effects may serve to boost productivity when employees have a free choice in deciding whether to work at home or not rather than everyone being told to do so. Those with the lowest self-reported levels of productivity in the study reported the strongest desire to return to the office. On the other hand, those with the highest productivity levels were keen to continue to work at home even when social restrictions are fully lifted. This sorting effect means that increased levels of homeworking in the future may boost rather than reduce productivity levels (Felstead and Reuschke, 2021: Table 5). However, managers and workers continue to disagree about its effect on productivity. For example, recent evidence suggests that managers are significantly more likely than workers to say that productivity is lower when work is carried out at home. Nevertheless, more than 40 per cent of both groups say that relocating work away from the office makes little difference (Barrero et al., 2022).

One should remember that, even before the pandemic, offices were changing. The most significant of these changes was the growth of open-plan office design in the 1960s and 1970s (Duffy, 1992). This facilitated greater visibility by managers of their staff and made employees more visible to their colleagues. However, stripping down office walls did not eliminate the idea of personal space; that is, a chair, desk, and personal computer allocated to an individual worker for their own use.

A further shift came in the 1990s with the sharing of space and equipment. Occupancy surveys showed that space and equipment set aside for single person use – referred to as **personal offices** – were rarely fully occupied. Workers were away from their desks when visiting clients, consulting colleagues, attending meetings, looking up information, on holiday, and off sick. Some surveys even suggested that workstations and offices might go unoccupied for as much as two-thirds of a typical working week. When weekends and holidays were factored in, the cost of unused space rose even further (Nathan and Doyle, 2002). Attention therefore turned to more efficient use of office space and equipment. Hence, the growing use of hot desks – workstations not 'owned' by any one individual, but available to all on a first-come, first-served basis – and the use of office equipment, such as printers, to which everyone had access. This has been referred to as the '**collective**

　　　　　　　　　　　　　　　　　　　Alan Felstead and Helen Blakely

office', since space is no longer allocated on an individual basis, but is shared with others (Felstead et al., 2005).

A sustained change in the location of work – through **remote** and hybrid **working** arrangements – will mean that *more* employees spend *more* time away from the office, thereby further reducing the need for office space. Employers are therefore seeking smaller and more dispersed offices. This will enable employers to better cater for the needs of a workforce which visits the office more infrequently, as well as providing them with an opportunity to lower their estate costs.

Impact on Society

Early advocates of homeworking emphasised its environmental benefits by coining the term 'telecommuting'. This referred to using technology to work at or near home, thereby minimising the need to travel to and from a place of work (Nilles, 1991). However, apart from during occasional fuel shortages – such as the tanker driver dispute of 2000 in the UK, when petrol supplies were in short supply for several weeks – greater use of homeworking as way of minimising travel was not really considered a viable policy option. The situation has changed markedly since then.

Heightened awareness of the environmental damage caused by the burning of fossil fuels (with the UK government declaring a climate emergency in 2019), and the enforced use of homeworking during the pandemic, has led to many organisations considering how they can minimise their carbon footprint. The UK is legally committed by the Climate Change Act 2008 to reduce carbon emissions by 80 per cent relative to their 1990 levels by 2050.

One of the biggest and most noticeable effects of locking society down on several occasions in 2020–2021, and therefore limiting mobility, was the drop in traffic. Roads became quieter and roadside pollution levels fell. But the scale of the environmental impact is debatable. For example, the decline in nitrogen dioxide was lower than the decline in traffic levels would suggest. This is because the number of heavily emitting vehicles on roads, such as diesel-powered freight trucks, fell only slightly compared to commuter traffic. Also, although fewer people were going to the office, many were using cars for local journeys – possibly due to anxieties about social distancing – when previously they would have used less polluting buses or trains. In addition, using the home as a place to work meant that the heating was on for longer. To make matters worse, homes tend to be heated using gas-burning boilers, which are more polluting than electric heating systems commonly used in offices (Shi and Bloss, 2021). The situation has become even more complicated post-pandemic, as offices have reopened, often with low occupancy rates, but an undiminished carbon footprint. The lights and heating remain on in large office blocks despite many desks remaining empty. All of this suggests that remote and hybrid working has positive and negative impacts on the environment; the actual scale of the environmental benefits remain uncertain and subject to debate.

Nevertheless, the desire to reduce carbon emissions is one of the factors behind the interest of governments in promoting more remote working in the future. The Welsh Government has stated that its long-term ambition is 'to see around 30%

of Welsh workers working from home or near to home', even in the absence of the need for social distancing. This forms part of its five-year programme for government (Welsh Government, 2021). According to ONS estimates, this figure was reached in January–March 2022, when over 30 per cent of those working and living in Wales reported working mainly at, from, or in the same grounds and buildings of the home (i.e. adopting a wide definition of homeworking) (ONS, 2022a). The Irish Government has made a similar commitment, but it has set a lower target of 20 per cent. However, this target only applies to the public sector (Government of Ireland, 2021). Other governments – such as the Japanese, Portuguese, and Finnish – signalled their desire to promote homeworking among their own staff long before the pandemic began (Messenger et al., 2017: 45–46). These policies have been prompted by the possible environmental benefits of homeworking, but also by the desire to give workers more flexibility about where they work (Lodovici, 2021).

Other policy debates have shifted as the dominant character of homeworking has changed over time from sewing machinists working at home to office workers connected electronically to others. Concerns about protecting employees (particularly women and ethnic minorities) against low pay, unfair treatment, and poor working conditions have been displaced by other issues. Today, debates on the right to work at home from day one and the right to disconnect have taken centre stage as the appetite to work at home has risen, and the boundaries between home and work have become increasingly blurred.

The steep rise in homeworking and its prolonged use during the pandemic will have a long-lasting impact on the spaces of work and the societies in which we live. As hybrid working has taken root, employers are reducing the office space they need. Before the pandemic, office occupancy levels in cities such as London, New York, and Sydney were running at around 60 per cent (Zetti, 2022). After the pandemic they were running at half that level, and have failed to recover to pre-pandemic levels. Employers are starting to act by getting rid of expensive, open-plan large offices located in major cities. As a result, city centres are becoming quieter and the suburbs busier, with a differential impact on house prices and patterns of economic activity which have traditionally catered for office workers who commuted into work (De Fraja et al., 2021).

Case Study

Monitoring Work at Home

Teleperformance is one of the largest call centre companies in the world. It was established in 1978 and headquartered in Paris, France. It employs around over 400,000 people and operates in 91 countries. The company provides services for a range of clients, including Apple, Amazon, Uber, and a number of UK government departments.

As was the case with most companies, during the pandemic the majority of the Teleperformance workforce shifted to working at home. This made the work of

Alan Felstead and Helen Blakely

employees invisible to management. In response, Teleperformance introduced technology to monitor work done at home. It was one of many companies eager to make work visible to managers.

Press coverage described how Teleperformance rolled out artificial intelligence powered webcams into the homes of their workers to scan workspaces for violations of work rules (Walker, 2021). The technology can periodically take photographs of employees at their desks to monitor their behaviour, and can detect any unauthorised activity and alert supervisors in real time. These breaches could include using a mobile phone, leaving a desk, or eating at a desk.

In response, workers around the world expressed concern about the intrusive surveillance and their right to privacy. One Columbian worker was reported as saying: 'The contract allows constant monitoring of what we are doing, but also our family … I think it's really bad. We don't work in an office. I work in my bedroom. I don't want to have a camera in my bedroom' (Solon, 2021).

The press coverage drew attention to the extension of workplace surveillance during the pandemic and its implications for workers. This case is one example of a wider, pandemic-related trend: as workers have moved to working at home, some employers are introducing surveillance technology to increase their oversight and control over the home workforce.

In 2020, as millions of us began to work at home global demand among employers for employee surveillance software rose enormously (increasing by 108 per cent in April and 70 per cent in May 2020, compared to 2019) (Ball, 2021). Many companies sell employee surveillance software, and the use of these types of technology is becoming normalised. This includes screening communication and social media, monitoring desktops, and webcams. These tools can be used to read instant messages and emails, record application usage, view calendars and reminders, monitor internet activity, log keystrokes, track mouse movements, and take screenshots of screens.

Not only are workers required to provide a separated workspace free from background noise and distractions, and cover costs including internet and electricity, but they are also asked to consent to remote monitoring of their homes. These surveillance technologies can be intrusive and can have a significant, detrimental impact on workers. Surveillance at home can uncover sensitive information about workers and undermine their right to privacy (for example, in terms of a worker's sexuality or disability). More broadly, workers can also lose autonomy and dignity when monitoring technologies are used to manage each aspect of each task. Electronic monitoring that closely tracks workers can have a detrimental effect on health and well-being. For example, intensive forms of productivity monitoring can discourage workers from taking the breaks to which they are legally entitled (Bernhardt et al., 2021).

Conclusion

The coronavirus pandemic raised fundamental questions about where we work and why. Many have subsequently suggested that it represents a pivotal moment from which there is no turning back. The location of work received enormous attention as governments around the world placed unprecedented restrictions on what their citizens could and could not do, and where they were allowed to go during the pandemic.

The removal of social distancing rules and the opening up of economies has resulted in greater mobility and a movement away from working exclusively at home. Even so, some form of homeworking has remained in place for many, but it has mutated in two ways. The first is a situation where some work is carried out at home and some is done on the employers' premises – known as hybrid working. The second is remote working, where work is completely detached from any particular place and can be carried out anywhere – at home, in a local café, library, or while moving from place to place – and at any time.

This chapter has briefly reviewed the issues that changes in the location of work may have for employees, employers, and society. This includes the lengthening of the working day, the intensification of work, the spill-over of work into family life, the difficulties of learning on-the-job, the fear that individuals may be passed over for promotion when out of sight, and concerns relating to intrusive forms of worker surveillance and monitoring (see Case Study). For employers who have traditionally relied on making workers visible and requiring their presence, off-site working is challenging, with the fear that employees may become less productive. For society, too, there are challenges and opportunities. Less travel may help to reduce carbon emissions, but businesses catering for city-centre office-based workers may struggle to survive in a world where commuting levels fail to bounce back to pre-pandemic levels. If more work is carried out at locations outside of the office in the future, this will have implications for city and town planning, as there appears little prospect of turning the clock back completely to pre-pandemic ways of working.

STUDENT ACTIVITY

Do some qualitative research by finding out if any of your friends and family worked at home during the pandemic. Ask them a series of questions related to the evidence presented in this chapter.

- What did they like and dislike about the experience?
- Where did they work at home – in a separate room, on the kitchen table, or the sofa? How and why was this space chosen?
- Did they work longer hours? Was it easier or more difficult for them to concentrate on their work, and why?
- How did they cope with living and working in the same space?
- Did they experience conflicts with other members in the household?
- How were they managed? What changes did they notice? Was monitoring technology used?
- Did their experience of working at home during the pandemic influence where they work today? If so, how and why?

Alan Felstead and Helen Blakely

Practice Questions

1. How and why has the location of work changed over the last few years?
2. Can you give examples to illustrate the differences between remote working, hybrid working, and homeworking?
3. What issues does the changing location of work raise for employees, employers, and society at large?

Key Terms

Collective offices
'characterized by an absence of personal space. Staff do not have permanent workstations for their sole use. Instead, they use facilities that are collectively provided and shared with other workers. Workstations are occupied on a temporary basis by whoever requires them' (Felstead et al., 2005: 63).

Extensive work effort
'the *time* spent at work' (Green, 2001: 56, original emphasis). This is relatively easy to measure with data on the amount of time spent on the job counted by employers, workers, and/or survey researchers.

Homeworking
where 'the two worlds of home and work are carried out in the same spatial boundaries'. Consequently, 'the home simultaneously becomes a place where paid work is done, and a place where domestic relationships are played out and unpaid domestic labour is undertaken' (Felstead, 2022: 30).

Hybrid working
a 'blend of home-based and office-based working, which may be fixed or fluid in terms of the proportion of time spent in either location' (Parry et al., 2022: 7).

Intensive work effort
'the rate of physical/or mental input to work tasks performed during the working day' (Green, 2001: 56). This concept is more difficult to measure, since it depends on the nature of the tasks undertaken and it can vary from worker to worker. For example, measuring the level of physical input workers put into their jobs is difficult, and measuring the level of mental input is harder still. Given this, reliance on managers' reports or the views of work measurement experts is dubious. Much research on work effort, therefore, is based on workers' responses to surveys. After all, workers themselves are best placed to know how intensively they work, even if their reports are subject to an element of social desirability bias.

Personal office
'a personal location in a place of work. It might take the form of a walled cell (cellular office) or ... a desk within an "open plan" floor plate.' Either way, workers are 'allocated their own cube of space, dedicated to their use [whereas] ...

in collective offices there is an absence of personal or individual space' (Felstead et al., 2005: 3–6).

Remote working
'where work, which could also be performed at the employer's premises, is carried out away from those premises on a regular basis' (Government of Ireland, 2021: 6).

References

Allen, S., and Wolkowitz, C. (1987) *Homeworking: myths and realities*. London: Macmillan.

Ball, K. (2021) *Electronic monitoring and surveillance in the workplace: literature review and policy recommendations*. Luxembourg: Publications Office of the European Union.

Barrero, J.M., Bloom, N., Buckman, S., and Davies, S.J. (2022) *Survey of working arrangements and attitudes, November 2022 updates*, Mexico City: WFH Research.

Bernhardt, A., Kresge L., and Suleiman, R. (2021) *Data and algorithms at work: the case for worker technology rights*. University of California, Berkeley: Center for Labor Research and Education.

Bloom, N., Liang, J., Roberts, J., and Ying, Z.J. (2015) 'Does working from home work? Evidence from a Chinese experiment'. *Quarterly Journal of Economics*, *130*(1): 165–218.

Brynjolfsson, E., Horton, J., Ozimek, A., Rock, D., Sharma, G., and TuYe, H.-Y. (2020) 'Covid-19 and remote work: an early look at US data'. *NBER Working Paper Series, Working Paper 27344*, Cambridge, MA: National Bureau of Economic Research.

Burchell, B., Reuschke, D., and Zhang, M. (2021) 'Spatial and temporal segmenting of urban workplaces: the gendering of multi-locational working'. *Urban Studies*, *58*(11): 2207–2232.

Chung, H. (2018) 'Gender, flexibility stigma and the perceived negative consequences of flexible working in the UK'. *Social Indicators Research*, *151*(2): 521–545.

Chung, H., Jaga, A., and Lambert, S. (2022) 'Possibilities for change and new frontiers: introduction to the Work and Family Researchers Network special issue on advancing equality at work and home'. *Community, Work and Family*, *25*(1): 1–12.

Clark, S.C. (2000) 'Work/family border theory: a new theory of work/family balance'. *Human Relations*, *53*(6): 747–770.

De Fraja, G., Matheson, J., and Rockey, J. (2021) 'Zoomshock: the geography and local labour market consequences of working from home'. *Covid Economics*, *64*: 1–41.

Duffy, F. (1992) *The changing workplace*. London: Phaidon Press.

Engeström, Y. (2001) 'Expansive learning at work: toward an activity theoretical reconceptualization'. *Journal of Education and Work*, *14*(1): 133–156.

Eraut, M., Alderton, J., Cole, G., and Senker, P. (1998) 'Learning from other people at work'. in F. Coffield (ed.), *Learning at work*. Bristol: Policy Press.

Eurofound (2020) *Living, working and COVID-19*. Luxembourg: Publications of the European Union.

Felstead, A. (2022) *Remote working: a research overview*. London: Routledge.

Felstead, A., and Henseke, G., (2017) 'Assessing the growth of remote working and its consequences for effort, well-being and work–life balance'. *New Technology, Work and Employment*, 32(3): 195–212.

Felstead, A., and Jewson, N. (2000) *In work, at home: towards an understanding of homeworking*. London: Routledge.

Felstead, A., and Reuschke, D. (2021) 'A flash in the pan or a permanent change? The growth of homeworking during the pandemic and its effect on employee productivity in the UK'. *Information Technology and People*. https://doi.org/10.1108/ITP-11–2020–0758

Felstead, A., Jewson, N., and Walters, S. (2005) *Changing places of work*. London: Palgrave.

Government of Ireland (2021) *Making remote work: National Remote Work Strategy*. Dublin: Department of Enterprise, Trade and Industry.

Green, F. (2001) '"It's been a hard day's night": the concentration and intensification of work in late twentieth-century Britain'. *British Journal of Industrial Relations*, 39(1): 53–80.

Hislop, D., and Axtell, C. (2007) 'The neglect of spatial mobility in contemporary studies of work: the case of telework', *New Technology, Work and Employment*, 22(1): 34–51.

Jewson, N. (2008) 'Communities of practice in their place: some implications of changes in the spatial location of work'. in J. Hughes, N. Jewson, and L. Unwin (eds), *Communities of practice: critical perspectives*. London: Routledge.

Kelliher, C., and de Menezes, L.M. (2019) *Flexible working in organisations: a research overview*. London: Routledge.

Lodovici, M.S. (2021) *The impact of teleworking and digital work on workers and society*. Luxembourg: European Parliament.

Messenger, J., Vargas-Llave, O., Gschwind, L., Boehmer, S., Vermeylen, G., and Wilkens, M. (2017) *Working anytime, anywhere: the effects on the world of work*. Geneva: International Labour Office.

Moynagh, M., and Worsely, R. (2005) *Working in the twenty-first century*. King's Lynn: The Tomorrow Project.

Nandhakumar, J., and Baskerville, R. (2006) 'Durability of online teamworking: patterns of trust'. *Information Technology and People*, 19(4): 371–389.

Nathan, M., and Doyle, J. (2002) *The state of the office: the politics and geography of working space*. London: Industrial Society.

Nilles, J.M. (1991) 'Telecommuting and urban sprawl: mitigator or inciter?' *Transportation*, 18(4): 411–432.

ONS (2021) *Homeworking hours, rewards and opportunities in the UK: 2011 to 2020*, Newport: Office for National Statistics.

ONS (2022a) *Homeworking in the UK – regional patterns: 2019 to 2022*, Newport: Office for National Statistics.

ONS (2022b) *Is hybrid working here to stay?* Newport: Office for National Statistics.

Parry, J., Young, Z., Bevan, S., Veliziotis, M., Baruch, Y., Beigi, M., Bajorek, Z., Richards, S., and Tochia, C. (2022) *Work after lockdown: no going back: what we have learned from working from home through the COVID-19 pandemic.* Southampton: University of Southampton.

Phizacklea, A., and Wolkowitz, C. (1995) *Homeworking women: gender, ethnicity and class at work.* London: Sage.

Pocock, B. (2021) 'As boundaries between work and home vanish, employees need a "right to disconnect"'. *The Conservation*, 29 April.

Shi, Z., and Bloss, W. (2021) 'First lockdown's effect on air pollution was overstated, our study reveals'. *The Conversation*, 13 January.

Solon, O. (2021) 'Big Tech call center workers face pressure to accept home surveillance'. *NBC News*, 8 August. Accessed 9 February 2023 from www.nbcnews.com/tech/tech-news/big-tech-call-center-workers-face-pressure-accept-home-surveillance-n1276227

Taylor, P., Scholarios, D., and Howcroft, D. (2021) *Covid-19 and Working from Home Survey: preliminary findings.* Glasgow: University of Strathclyde.

Thulin, E., Vilhelmson, B., and Johansson, M. (2019) 'New telework, time pressure, and time use control in everyday life'. *Sustainability*, *11*(11): 3067–3084.

Toffler, A. (1980) *The third wave.* New York: William Morrow.

Urry, J. (2000) *Sociology Beyond societies: mobilities for the twenty-first century.* London: Routledge.

Vargas-Llave, O., Weber, T., and Avogaro, M. (2020) *Right to disconnect in the 27 EU member states.* Dublin: European Foundation for the Improvement of Living and Working Conditions.

Walker, P. (2021) 'Call centre used by UK firms accused of intrusively monitoring home workers'. *Guardian*, 8 August. Available at theguardian.com/world/2021/aug/08/call-centre-uk-firms-accused-intrusively-monitoring-home-workers-teleperformance#:~:text=Unions%20say%20Teleperformance%2C%20which%20also,targeted%20several%20staff%20who%20objected

Welsh Government (2021) *Programme for government.* Cardiff: Welsh Government.

Zetti, M. (2022) 'Office buildings are still less than 50% occupied. Who should worry?' *Forbes*, 29 November. Accessed 9 February 2023 from www.forbes.com/sites/markzettl/2022/11/29/office-buildings-are-still-less-than-50-occupied-who-should-worry/

chapter 22

Conclusion
New Ways of Working

Jane Parry and Brian McDonough

Introduction

It could not have been anticipated just how timely a new perspective on work and organisations would be when this book was initiated, but given the way that COVID-19 has disrupted the organisation of work, and the rapid proliferation of AI (artificial intelligence), there have been far-flung consequences for both practitioners and theorists of work. The book has incorporated a wealth of exciting case-study evidence from researchers looking at a diverse range of countries and experiences of work, with the intention of prompting readers to start delving further into this rich seam of sociology. Yet, amid this complex and ongoing transformation, sociological concepts and theories continue to offer vital functionality in making sense of these reconfigurations: there is never a more apt time to be using 'the sociological imagination' to study work (Wright Mills, 1959). The Economic and Social Research Council, the UK's main funder of sociology research, picked up on the urgency of responding to these fluctuating times, in launching its Transforming Working Lives programme in 2022, which has been able to focus on emerging issues like how young people are negotiating a reconfigured labour market, unheard employee voices, and flexible working vulnerabilities in small and medium-sized enterprises (SMEs). Meanwhile, Horizon Europe, the European Union's funding programme (worth €95.5 billion of investment between 2021 and 2027), set out its second pillar as 'global challenges and European industrial competitiveness', which includes multiple ways in which knowledge about work will prove fundamental to their research priorities.

Emerging Trends in the Sociology of Work

A very significant trend, touched upon by many of the book's contributors, is the rapid growth of atypical work or non-standard employment (Taylor, 2017), and with it a decline in occupational security, often for the most vulnerable groups in societies. For many, work has become less predictable, and this has long-lasting consequences, not just for workers' standards of living, but upon lifetime expectations about progression, with implications for family and later life security. Amid this, there has been campaigning around the human right to decent work, one aspect of which is security (Kalleberg, 2016; UN, 2023). Indeed, many of the UN's Sustainable Development Goals (SDGs) are inseparable from a foundation of fairly-rewarded paid work across the world: no poverty (SDG1), zero hunger (SDG2), good health and well-being (SDG3), gender equality (SDG5), decent work and economic growth (SDG8), industry, innovation and infrastructure (SDG9), reduced inequalities (SDG10), and sustainable cities and communities (SDG11).

Back in the sphere of more traditional employment, there have been dramatic changes in terms of how work is organised. Early in 2020 the term 'hybrid working' was rarely used to analyse work; now it is an embedded part of many businesses' strategies and stimulating a rich new seam of sociological analysis. As discussed in Chapters 1 and 21, as formerly office-based work has moved from remote work to increased engagement with hybrid ways of organising employment, so too flexible work has become increasingly used as a way of retaining staff, particularly on an informal basis (Parry et al., 2024, forthcoming). Indeed, with the UK's Employment Relations (Flexible Working) Act coming into force in April 2024, statutory flexible working is likely to become more accessible to a broader range of employees.

At the same time that (for some) work has become less about physical presence, debate has shifted again towards emotional labour (Hochschild, 1983) – for example, in the way that colleagues cared for one another during the pandemic – and this became a central part of keeping organisations functioning. For others, work remains very much about bodies and presence, and particularly in the service industry aesthetic labour has become a key part of work role expectations and success (Williams and Connell, 2010).

While attention concerning the organisation of work has focused mainly upon the **formal economy**, these discussions can divert attention from the hidden, but huge, economic contribution of the organisationally 'messier' **informal economy**. This can range from hidden work with blurred boundaries around legality, such as moonlighting or cash-in-hand work, to work that is concealed because it is stigmatised, such as sex work, discussed in Chapters 7 and 13. Modern-day slavery, which it is estimated affects 50 million people across the globe (Walkfree, 2023), appears to break a key conceptual link between work and payment, but often presents very much like paid labour, being 'hidden in plain sight'. For example, in the global shipping industry (discussed in Chapter 17), crews can comprise a combination of those on paid contracts working alongside those in debt bondage, or who have not been paid at all and who are essentially trapped on board waiting for the means to leave. So too there is huge global variation in modern-day slavery, with Walkfree's 2023 Global Slavery Index estimating that this ranges from 8,000 people in Finland to 2,696,000 in North Korea.

The analysis of work has become increasingly concerned with how people's intersecting inequalities shape their experience of work in meaningful ways. Work theorists have used intersectionality (Acker, 2006; Özbilgin et al., 2011) to draw attention to how it is not only single differences, but combinations of differences, that affect people's opportunities and working biographies, and that looking at these will help sociologists understand working lives better. So, for example, work theorists might look at how visible differences such as gender, ethnicity, and age affect work (as in Chapters 3, 4, and 6), but semi- or invisible factors can also be important, including disabilities, sexuality, and class, as well as more hidden aspects of experience, such as household circumstances and well-being. Take, for example, how a Black female single parent in her twenties might face distinctive labour market challenges to a white, married, middle-class, visually impaired man. Overlaid across this are the multiple geographical differences that affect work, most notably between Global North experiences of formalised work compared to many Global South experiences where informal work predominates. Recent changes in how work is organised, including the growth in atypical work, have raised distinctive new sets of inequalities, presenting novel analytical challenges around divergent experiences of autonomy, belonging, meaningfulness, and relationships in work. Certain roles, such as knowledge work, have been able to sustain these more easily than others, suggesting new kinds of polarisations around work quality that are interconnected with socioeconomic factors.

While there is not a chapter devoted specifically to class in this book, it continues to underpin many of the inequalities and experiences of work that we discuss, intersecting with other inequalities. Partly, as occupations have restructured, class identity has become more complex, with the traditional Goldthorpe/Nuffield classification scheme (Goldthorpe, 1980) criticised for its reliance upon traditional employment categories, and not adequately covering gender or the economically inactive, such as students, retirees, the unemployed, and parents caring for children full-time. In one response to this, Savage et al. (2013) sought to capture a more meaningful range of socioeconomic differences in their Great British Class Survey, which collected data on a range of economic (savings, property, and household income), social (measured in terms of people's connectedness to those in a range of jobs), and cultural capitals (ranging from 'highbrow' culture, such as architecture and classical music, to 'emergent culture', such as videogames and going to concerts) to construct a more diverse range of seven class groupings on a sliding scale of income, which aligned with particular types of work. For example, dentists and CEOs could be considered 'elite', while cleaners and the unemployed were classified as in the 'precariat' group. This new scheme was more representative of changing occupations, illustrated the vast range of income across the class spectrum, and drew attention to life-course influences in class positioning. The researchers found that the boundaries between extreme wealth and poverty were entrenched and difficult to penetrate – in other words, social class mobility is limited within the UK, despite changes in occupations and work. Class, then, the way that these socioeconomic inequalities are structured, remains an important analytical tool for sociologists, although it manifests differently in different country contexts.

The digitalisation of work has been a common theme in the book (see the chapters in Part 4), with far-reaching consequences, from the wholesale reshaping of occupations to the transformation of how individual jobs are performed. So, too, technology has increasingly shaped the organisation of work, most notably in terms of the algorithmic control of work and the inequalities which that can create (Noble, 2018), particularly around the platform working that has become a growing component of atypical work (Srnicek, 2017). It is likely that the full implications of how artificial intelligence is transforming the working landscape are only just beginning to be seen.

While unpaid work has always been an inescapable part of understanding how paid work is organised and sustained across households, industries, and societies (Glucksmann, 2009), here we have drawn attention to how this continues to be as relevant as ever to understanding new formations for work. The boundaries between the paid and unpaid work performed in new digitalised professions are slippery, as the authors showed in Part 4, for example, around blogging and open-source platform development.

As so much work has become a more individualised, often spatially dislocated experience, with organisational transformations separating workers from one another, so too workers have found new ways to express their resistance to management and employment conditions. Coming out of the pandemic, the UK has seen revived trade union activity in the early 2020s, with a sustained period of industrial resistance, with professional and blue-collar workers united in their opposition to diminished working conditions and income security. Hospital consultants have joined junior doctors and nurses in withholding their labour across the NHS, along with university lecturers and transport workers, in a cross-class opposition to declining occupational certainty that has seen their income drop substantially during a cost-of-living crisis. It has not gone unnoticed that many of the strikers are the same workers who were valued as 'keyworkers' during the pandemic. So, alongside the digitalisation of work, online resistance is a also growing trend (Kassem, 2023; Taylor and Parry, 2015).

In other parts of the globe, people are also taking to the streets to demand change, where pay does not meet the cost of living. The Chilean protests between 2019 and 2022 involved several mass demonstrations with thousands of people. These were sparked by an increase in the metro fare – the main underground transport system of the capital city, Santiago. A fare evasion campaign initiated by secondary school students led to spontaneous occupations by the public of train stations (see Woods, 2023). While the protests were a response to the cost-of-living increases, it is wages that often determine what is affordable. In France, a notable social protest movement fighting against the cost-of-living crisis and work inequalities is the *mouvement des gilets jaunes*, the 'yellow jacket protests'. Since 2018, this social movement has called for lower fuel taxes, an increase on wealth tax for the rich, and an increase in the minimum wage. Back in the UK, the significance of resistance in work sociology has been so heightened that the bi-annual Work, Employment, and Society (WES) conference was themed around it in 2023, where hundreds of sociologists of work convened to consider issues such as the resistance of marginalised workers, identity resistance work, and digital resistance. Future research in the sociology of work and organisation relies not only on contemporary scholars, like the authors of this textbook or sociology of work conference attendees, but also on the readers of this book. The turbulent and uncertain future of work requires new sociologists. Without doubt, future researchers will face new challenges and barriers to investigating workplaces and work issues, requiring new **methodologies** in exploring work.

Researching the Future of Work: New Horizons

Work is rapidly changing, and future sociologists (including many readers of this textbook) will have to adapt their research styles, techniques, and approaches to investigate new phenomena in the sociology of work. For example, researchers during the COVID-19 pandemic had to move towards online methods, since being face to face was at that time unethical and impractical given that many workplace buildings had become empty of employees. Sociologists not only need to research hard-to-reach places on a local or national level, but also must consider how work organisations, processes, and labour is spread out across the globe. For example, the production of Apple's iPhone allows people to work in many countries spread across the Global South and Global North, resulting in a practical difficulty for the researcher to be in several places at once (see Benjamin's discussion in Chapter 12, 'Digitalised Work'). Technologies are forever altering ways of working, but they also change the approaches of researchers. Thirty years ago, research interviews would be conducted with cassette tapes and Dictaphone devices, but today's researchers use smartphones and recording apps, as well as audio transcription (AI) software.

Throughout the various chapters of this textbook, authors have presented examples and contemporary case studies drawing on their own research investigations. Some of the research has drawn on **primary data** collection, where the authors have researched the topics first-hand. For example, McDonough and Pearson (Chapter 5) investigated precarious workers by interviewing 25 people who shared their experiences of being either self-employed (such as taxi drivers), working on fixed-term contracts (such as actors and professional dancers), or freelancing (such as business consultants). The interviews (an hour long and electronically recorded) were qualitative, in that they centred on the quality of data (richness and depth), focusing on mapping out the experiences of precarious work. Parry's introductory Chapter 1 drew upon a **longitudinal** qualitative dataset, in which a combination of 43 leaders, managers, and workers were interviewed in three organisations multiple times over the course of eighteen months in order to capture change during the pandemic, generating some 73 qualitative transcripts, case-study, and photographic evidence with which to analyse work.

Other researchers have used **secondary data**: research data produced by other scholars or organisations (sometimes produced for other purposes). Secondary data analysis involves looking at data in a new way to produce different insights. Benjamin's investigations on digitalised work across the globe (Chapter 12) and Lòpez's research on workers at US–Mexico border (Chapter 18) both draw on secondary data. Researching issues that take place in difficult-to-reach places, or in multiple locations around the world, makes primary data collection very difficult (impossible in some cases), and hence researchers look for alternative techniques to study the phenomenon. Some forms of secondary data include statistics gathered by government agencies, such as Velija and McDonough's investigation of the gender pay gap (Chapter 3), which looked at figures reported by organisations to government bodies.

Secondary data is often discussed in terms of conducting more complex statistical analysis on numerical datasets, but, as researchers have been required to archive their data from funded projects, the UK data archive now contains a wealth of well-documented qualitative datasets that are available for secondary analysis. **Cohort studies** have provided a valuable secondary data source for capturing changes in work over time. For example, the 1958 National Child Development Study has collected information from 17,415 babies born within the same week and has followed these individuals, collecting information at regular intervals, capturing data that now covers the majority of their working lives (Brookfield et al., 2018; Power and Elliott, 2006). This longitudinal dataset has provided an invaluable resource for researchers studying workplace change over this period and has generated over 5,000 publications. However we choose to gather data, we must always consider the best way to conduct our **data analysis**: ways in which to make sense of our data, and provide evidence to support our arguments or claims.

In the social sciences, there are a plethora of primary data collection methods that can be utilised in conducting sociological research, including surveys, interviews, focus groups, participant observation, participatory action research (PAR), and documentary research. New methods (the tools we use to conduct research) and methodologies (the theories we use to carry out research) emerge as the world of work is continually changing (Amsbary and Powell, 2018). The COVID-19 pandemic, for instance, accelerated the use of online research methods, such as virtual interviewing through platforms, which allowed data to be collected without the need for bodily presence (for useful readings on online interviewing, see James and Busher, 2009; also see Salmons, 2014). The proliferation of working online has also increased the need for virtual research methods (see Hine, 2012). Understanding how an employee interacts with a manager's requests made on a Microsoft Teams or Zoom call might involve getting online alongside them (although there are practical and ethical limitations, which should always be considered in research design – see ethics section that follows). Getting hold of the right people for research purposes is the purpose of a **sampling strategy** – a method of attaining the best representation of the people you wish to investigate. Sampling is important to employ for practical reasons – we are unlikely to be able to interview or survey every single person we might want to because we do not usually have access to, or resources for, including everyone relevant to our study.

Jane Parry and Brian McDonough

Quantitative methods, such as the use of surveys, seek to quantify data and understand the relationships between different variables (for a good discussion on survey design, see De Vaus, 2014). For example, attitudinal surveys can be used to make sense of the opinions of employees across large-scale organisations. Universities can use attitudinal surveys as a way of understanding the thoughts of staff within the organisation, which might be important in developing policy. The National Student Survey (NSS) is used to analyse students' experiences of their course at the end of a three-year degree programme, which is valuable in making improvements. From teaching and assessment to learning resources and equipment, the NSS can provide a measurement of what students think about their course, with scores compared across different years and across different universities. Survey data can also be misused if not interpreted properly. For example, courses can enter the NSS with as few as just ten students completing the survey, which is statistically very weak. Much larger samples provide a better understanding of issues affecting experience.

Qualitative methods, such as interviews and focus groups, can help researchers understand the motives and intentions of research participants. For example, not only is speaking with frontline workers important for understanding their experiences but observing them can also be valuable. Built on a methodological tradition from the discipline of anthropology, many sociologists of work employ ethnographic methods to gather data and investigate sociology of work topics. 'Ethnography' literally translates from Greek as 'writing about a people' (*ethnos* = 'people, folk' and *grapho* = 'I write'). Ethnographers often 'hang out' with people in order to make sense of their experiences first-hand, such as Calvey's (2018) use of covert ethnography for understanding the world of bouncers (doormen) in the city of Manchester, UK.

In recent years there has been increased use of what are called multimodal (multi-sensorial) or sensorial research methods (see Pink, 2015, 2021). Thinking about the researcher's body as its very own way of gathering data, sociologists of work have turned closer attention to how different senses (sight, sound, smell, taste, and touch) are a better method for understanding workers' experiences, such as McDonough's (2017) use of haptics in flying aeroplanes alongside commercial pilots. A relatively new qualitative method is **netnography** (Kozinets, 2019), an adaptation of ethnography to digital environments; for example, following social interactions on social media or platform message boards. Parry and Hracs collected virtual secondary data for the research that they discuss in Chapter 14. They followed 10 work-related bloggers over a number of years and filtered their posts to obtain a sample of those that explicitly concerned bloggers' work, giving a dataset of 1,304 posts, on which they then performed **content analysis** (Drisko and Maschi, 2016).

Research Ethics

Most researchers will have to follow a strict ethical code of conduct before embarking on research and will usually require their research to be considered by an ethics committee in their institution before they can collect any data. Key ethical principles include avoiding harm in the way that research is conducted, establishing informed consent, avoiding deception, and protecting participants' confidentiality/anonymity (McDonough, 2021). By their very presence in a workplace, or in simply meeting with a worker, sociologists can change employee perceptions, alter work relationships, or at the very least distract people from work activities that may get them into trouble with their employer. It is for these reasons that there are several internationally recognised sociological associations and 'governing' bodies that set out information and support for studying work organisations. For example, the American Sociological Association (ASA) provides a strict code of ethics for researchers wishing to conduct sociological research. This includes such aspects as: professional integrity and competence; professional and scientific responsibility; respect for people's rights, dignity, and diversity; social responsibility; and human rights. Associations like the ASA provide guidance on the principles and standards that researchers should strive towards when researching the world of work.

Ethical codes of conduct are important in doing research. There is an expectation that sociologists are 'honest, fair, and respectful of others in their professional activities' (ASA Code of Ethics, 2018: 5). It is unethical for researchers to make false promises to research participants – above all else, it is simply dishonest, and will have detrimental impacts upon research for future generations of researchers. Another recognised body, the British Sociological Association (BSA), advise that researchers need to be good at 'recognising the boundaries of their professional competence' (BSA, 2017: 4). Participating in the work experiences of research participants may well be valuable but teaching a classroom full of children with no teaching qualifications or child protection certification (such as a Disclosure and Barring Service in the UK), or driving an Uber taxi without a private hire licence, is not only unethical but may also be against the law. Even when we are not breaking the law, we may well be breaking ethical codes of conduct, which may result in disciplinary or other academic integrity actions.

Students studying the sociology of work and organisation will wish to investigate varied topics and should adhere to the highest standards of professional conduct. Unlike fiction writers, it is not the job of a sociologist to make up stories or put a 'spin' on real events, as some journalists do (McDonough, 2021), but to understand them and to build knowledge in this way (Bauman and May, 2019). While values such as honesty and transparency are important for doing sociological research, sociologists may have to make compromises on what to report and what not to report when disseminating research findings so as to protect their participants. An organisation with management practices involving 'bullying' and 'intimidation' may terminate the whistle-blower's employment if they were found to be involved in your research. It is for this reason that pseudonyms (fake names) are used to maintain confidentiality and the practice of making both individuals and organisations anonymous is commonplace in sociological research.

It is important to consider how taking part in research can affect participants, and to mitigate against any harm or discomfort for them as a result of that experience. Hammersley and Atkinson (2019: 268) reflect that, 'at the very least, being researched can sometimes create anxiety or worsen it, and where people are already in stressful

Jane Parry and Brian McDonough

situations research can be judged to be unethical on these grounds alone'. For example, a study on a sensitive issue like sexual harassment at work or rape would require thoughtful design and data collection, with consideration given to how support will be provided should participants become distressed, and care taken to disguise participants' identity in any written outputs. It is for these reasons that students beginning a research project should carefully consider the codes of conduct displayed in bodies such as the ASA or BSA as well as their own institutional ethics process, and discuss their research thoroughly with their supervisor. A recent challenge for research ethics is the increased use of **'big data'**, data that has not been generated for research purposes but which might offer strong value in exploring social trends, being reappropriated as research data. This raises issues around consent and confidentiality, particularly so when it involves health-related data (Howe and Elenberg, 2020).

Some Resources for Sociologists of Work

In this fast-changing field, it can be valuable to study some of the materials that are being collected about work, as well as written *on* it. The academic journal that leads the field, *Work, Employment, and Society,* has an excellent and very readable series, 'On the Frontline', in which an academic researcher teams up with a worker to provide a unique analysis: the worker's first-hand account is complemented by a sociological account of their work. Some of their recent spotlights have included the work of a funeral director, a professional footballer, and a supermarket 'keyworker' during the restrictions of the pandemic. Podcasts such as *Thinking Allowed* often have some excellent discussions on work. Some films to get you applying your sociological thinking to these issues include: Ken Loach's *I, Daniel Blake* for precarious work, workforce marginalisation, and inequalities; Nigel Cole's *Made in Dagenham*, around sexual discrimination and the labour process; and Loach's *Bread and Roses* on migrant workers and union resistance. Journalist Polly Toynbee also provides unique and very rich accounts of her time working undercover in a range of precarious jobs in *Hard work: life in low-pay Britain* (2003): telesales, factory work, hospital porter, and school 'dinner lady'. Barack Obama's Netflix series, *Working: what we do all day*, picks up many of the issues explored in this book in a US context, including inequalities, decent work, and atypical work.

The world of work is ever-changing, and never as rapidly as it is right now. It is vital to take a global perspective on these transformations, applying the learning provided in one context to the unique circumstances of another. Consider one key driver of change – demographic ageing – which is occurring at varied pace across the world. This is a key issue for sociologists of work to apply in their analyses, since paid work has tended to be associated with the period of life around 16 to 65, so we need to be able to anticipate and plan around changes in this age group. **Population pyramids** are one useful way of visualising demographic differences and the implications of these for societies, as the age structure of a population changes over time, which will have a fundamental impact on how we work. Global population growth has been impacted by factors such as access to contraception and improved healthcare, with the ageing of the world's population occurring at the same time as reduced infant mortality, with patterns related to countries' stage in economic development. This has presented different challenges across the globe, with (for example) China managing its rapidly growing population with its now-repealed one-child policy (1979–2015).

For all societies, population structure matters in terms of age dependency ratios; that is, the proportion of the working-age population in relation to dependants (children and older people), as this will have implications for the demands placed upon workers and for the country's prosperity. The world's richer countries (mainly, but not exclusively, located in the Global North) have been through a demographic shift (moving from high birth and death rates to low birth and death rates) more rapidly than those in the Global South, who have felt the benefits of scientific advancement more slowly. Thus, for example, while in 2021 Japan had a median age of 48.4 in 2021, Niger's was significantly lower, at 14.5 (Ritchie et al., 2023; UN, 2022) The effect of this is that, in certain countries, which are concentrated disproportionately in sub-Saharan Africa, the working-age population not only has a shorter life expectancy, but there are greater economic pressures upon this group to support its dependants. There will be also dramatic societal changes as younger working populations age, and here we can apply the learning from industrialised countries' experiences of managing and retaining older workers to support this demographic transition (see Chapter 6, 'Age Discrimination in the Workplace', by Paraskevopoulou).

When considering the impacts of changes in the working-age population, we should also consider that in the Global South the informal labour market employs the majority of the workforce and the impacts which this might have upon long-term security and working conditions (Williams, 2023). Overlaid across this is the way that entrepreneurship has been able to drive innovation and job creation in challenging economic conditions (Global Entrepreneurship Monitor, 2023), and in particular can provide a sustainable route out of poverty for households in the Global South, which can offer a constructive approach to tackling inequalities for women (Akhmadi and Tsakalerou, 2023).There will inevitably be gaps in any book that attempts to cover the vast and ever-changing world of work. What we hope to have done here is introduce you to some of the myriad areas where you can apply your sociological thinking to better understand some of the challenges and transformations being seen around the world, and to bring this to life with the case-study evidence from our authors' research.

Key Terms

Big data
large datasets, often generated by social media or consumer behaviour. The volume of such data is too vast to be handled by traditional processing software and often uses machine learning. The dataset is usually changing and is often drawn from multiple sources.

Jane Parry and Brian McDonough

Cohort studies

a form of longitudinal research that follows the same group of individuals over time, by taking repeated observations – for example, in the forms of surveys or interviews. Cohort members will have a characteristic of interest in common, such as their age.

Content analysis

an approach to analysing documents and artefacts, by systematically classifying their meanings and themes and using these to identify patterns and theories.

Data analysis

an approach to making sense of data gathered, such as that from interviews or surveys. Researchers have many different types of data analysis to choose from, including methods of quantitative data analysis (such as conducting univariate, bivariate, or multivariate analysis) in analysing survey data, or methods of qualitative data analysis (such as thematic, narrative, grounded theory or discourse analysis) in making sense of interview, focus group, or visual data.

Formal economy

the institutions and organisations in which participation and employment is monitored and measured; for example, positions where people are paid a wage and work is taxable.

Informal economy

the organisations and activities that have a productive market value, but which are unmonitored and untaxed by governments, such as working cash-in-hand.

Longitudinal research

studies which usually take place over a time period, taking repeated observations to make sense of changing events in people's lives and in organisations.

Methodologies

the theories 'behind the methods', providing a set of ideas about why certain methods are better or more suitable than others.

Netnography

a methodology for approaching certain types of qualitative data, applying ethnographic techniques to digital environments.

Population pyramid

a visual and dynamic representation of how populations are structured around age and sex, usually organised around country-level information. As populations grow, a pyramid shape can be observed, which changes over time, highlighting demographic transitions – useful in predicting future trends; see www.populationpyramid.net.

Primary data

research data, such as interview transcripts or survey responses, gathered first-hand by the researchers themselves.

Qualitative methods

an approach to collecting data which centres on gathering rich in-depth data, focusing on quality more than quantity. Open-ended interviews and focus groups are just two examples of typical qualitative methods.

Quantitative methods

approaches to gathering data using quantifying procedures, such as the use of questionnaires, statistics, and other numerical data; useful for understanding patterns of behaviour and for establishing relationships (correlations) between different variables.

Research ethics

a set of moral principles or standards used in social research to determine and help govern what is, or is not, acceptable. Researchers will often abide by an ethical code of conduct in doing sociological research.

Sampling strategies

for practical reasons researchers cannot study every person, in every organization everywhere, so they usually develop a strategy for selecting a subset (sample) of the wider research population to investigate.

Secondary data

research carried out by someone else, prior to the researcher's use of the dataset, such as secondary statistics or reports.

References

Acker, J. (2006) 'Inequality regimes: gender, class and race in organizations'. *Gender and Society*, 20: 441–464.

Akhmadi, S., and Tsakalerou, M. (2023) 'Exploring gender imbalances in innovation and entrepreneurship: evidence from a global south country'. *International Journal of Gender and Entrepreneurship*, 15(3):275–292.

Amsbary, J.H., and Powell, B. (2018) *Interviewing in a changing world: situations and contexts*. Abingdon: Routledge.

ASA (2018) American Sociological Association home page. Asanet.org

Bauman, Z., and May, T. (2019) *Thinking sociologically*. London: Wiley-Blackwell.

Brookfield, K., Parry, J., and Bolton, V. (2018) 'Getting the measure of prosocial behaviours: a comparison of participation and volunteering data in the National Child Development Study and linked Social Participation and Identity Study'. *Non-Profit and Voluntary Sector Quarterly*, 47(5): 1081–1101.

BSA (2017) British Sociological Association home page. Britsoc.co.uk

Calvey, D. (2018) 'The everyday world of bouncers: a rehabilitated role for covert ethnography'. *Qualitative Research*, 19(3): 247–262.

De Vaus, D. (2014) *Surveys in social research*. London: Routledge.

Drisko, J.W., and Maschi, T. (2016) *Content analysis*. Oxford: Oxford University Press.

Global Entrepreneurship Monitor (2023) *GEM 2022/2023 Global Report: Adapting to a 'New Normal.'* Available at https://gemconsortium.org/report/20222023-global-entrepreneurship-monitor-global-report-adapting-to-a-new-normal-2

Glucksmann, M.A. (2009) 'Formations, connections and divisions of labour'. *Sociology*, 43(5): 878–895.

Goldthorpe, J.H. (1980) 'Intellectuals and the working class in modern Britain'. In D. Rose (ed.), *Social stratification and economic change*. London: Routledge.

Hammersley, M., and Atkinson, P. (2019) *Ethnography: principles in practice*. London: Routledge.

Hine, C. (2012) *Virtual research methods*, London: Sage.

Hochschild, A. (1983) *The managed heart: communication of human feeling*. Berkeley, CA: University of California Press.

Howe, E.G., and Elenberg, F. (2020) 'Ethical challenges posed by big data'. *Innovations in Clinical Neuroscience*, 17(10–12): 24–30.

James, N., and Busher, H. (2009) *Online interviewing*. London: Sage.

Kalleberg, A.L. (2016) 'Good jobs, bad jobs'. In S. Edgell, H. Gottfried, and E. Granter (eds), *The SAGE handbook of the sociology of work and employment*. London: Sage.

Kassem, S. (2023) 'The power of Amazon workers and platform workers'. In *Work and alienation in the platform economy*. Bristol: Bristol University Press.

Kozinets, R.V. (2019) *Netnography: the essential guide to qualitative social media research*. London: Sage.

McDonough, B. (2017) 'The hands have it: tactile participation and maximum grip in the aviation sector'. *Qualitative Research*, 19(2): 199–214.

McDonough, B (2021) *Flying aeroplanes and other sociological tales: an introduction to sociology and research methods*. London: Routledge.

Noble, S. (2018) *Algorithms of oppression*. New York: NYU Press.

Özbilgin, M.F., Beauregard, T.A., Tatli, A., and Bell, M.P. (2011) 'Work–life diversity and intersectionality: a critical review and research agenda'. *International Journal of Management Reviews*, 13: 177–198.

Parry, J., Bradbury, B., and Veliziotis, M. (2024, forthcoming) *Organisational case studies on flexible working: variations in practice*. London: Acas.

Pink, S. (2015) *Doing sensory ethnography* London: Sage.

Pink, S. (2021) *Doing visual ethnography*. London: Sage.

Power, C., and Elliott, J. (2006) 'Cohort profile: 1958 British birth cohort (National Child Development Study)'. *International Journal of Epidemiology*, 35: 34–41.

Ritchie, H., Rodés-Guirao, L., Mathieu, E., Gerber, M., Ortiz-Ospina, E., Hasell, J., and Roser, M. (2023) 'Population growth'. *OurWorldInData.org*. Available at https://ourworldindata.org/population-growth

Salmons, J. (2014) *Qualitative online interviews*. New York: Sage.

Savage, M., Devine, F., Cunningham, N., Taylor, M., Li, Y., Hjekbrekke, L., Le Roux, B., Friedman, S., and Miles, A. (2013) 'A new model of social class? Findings from the BBC's Great British Class Survey Experiment'. *Sociology*, 47(2): 219–250.

Srnicek, N. (2017) *Platform capitalism*. Hokoken, NJ: John Wiley and Sons.

Taylor, M. (2017) *Good work: the Taylor review of modern working practices*. www. gov.uk/government/publications/good-work-the-taylor-review-of-modern-working-practices

Taylor, R., and Parry, J. (2015) 'As CEO exits, Reddit finds to its cost that even unpaid workers can go on strike'. *The Conversation*. Available at https:// theconversation.com/as-ceo-exits-reddit-finds-to-its-cost-that-even-unpaid-workers-can-go-on-strike-44530

Toynbee, P. (2003) *Hard work: life in low-pay Britain*. London: Bloomsbury.

United Nations (2022) 'World population prospects'. Available at https://population. un.org/wpp/

United Nations (2023) 'The 17 Goals'. Available at https://sdgs.un.org/goals

Walkfree (2023) 'Global Slavery Index'. *Walkfree*. Available at www.walkfree.org/ global-slavery-index/

Williams, C.C. (2023) *A modern guide to the informal economy*. Cheltenham: Edward Elgar Publishing.

Williams, C.L., and Connell, C. (2010) '"Looking good and sounding right": Aesthetic labor and social inequality in the retail industry'. *Work and Occupations*, 37(3): 349–377.

Woods, M. (2023) *On the Chilean social explosion*. London: Routledge.

Wright Mills, C. (1959) *The sociological imagination*. New York: Oxford University Press.

Index of key terms referenced in the chapters

Index